Christian Democracy in Venezuela

Christian Democracy in Venezuela

Donald L. Herman

The University of North Carolina Press Chapel Hill

© 1980 The University of North Carolina Press

All rights reserved

Manufactured in the United States of America

ISBN 0-8078-1425-3

Library of Congress Catalog Card Number 79-24582

Library of Congress Cataloging in Publication Data

Herman, Donald L
   Christian Democracy in Venezuela.

   Bibliography: p.
   Includes index.
   1. Partido Socialcristiano. 2. Venezuela—
Politics and government. I. Title.
JL3898.s6H47   329.9′87   79-24582
ISBN 0-8078-1425-3

TO MY FAMILY,
   Bluma, Debbie, Randy, Jeff,
      and
         Snoopy

Contents

Tables, Maps, and Charts

CHARTS

Preface

THE CHRISTIAN DEMOCRATIC victories in Chile (1964) and Venezuela (1968) aroused my interest in the Latin American Christian Democratic movement. Many of my colleagues began to study and write about the administration of Eduardo Frei in Chile, but for some reason very few, if any, North American and European academicians were investigating the Venezuelan Christian Democrats. When the opportunity arose, academic interest and the law of supply and demand led me to Venezuela.

My family and I spent a year in the country. Through this experience and return trips, I was able to compile many interviews and a good quantity of primary and some secondary material. Although the focus of my study was on the Christian Democrats, I interviewed people from other political parties so that I could better understand the political context in which the Christian Democrats operated.

Three people were very helpful in this endeavor. My wife, Bluma, is a native of Mexico. Her many hours on the telephone, particularly persuading overprotective secretaries of my need to see their *jefes*, were invaluable. Two Christian Democratic leaders, Valmore Acevedo and Dagoberto González, were very generous with their time and in making much of their personal material available for my use. They made the Venezuelan expression *a la orden* a reality.

I would also like to thank Professor John D. Martz of Pennsylvania State University, who read an early draft of this study. His suggestions proved most valuable.

Allendale, Michigan
January 1979

Donald L. Herman

Introduction

A PERUSAL OF the literature on Latin American affairs indicates that scholars—particularly those from the United States—give most of their attention to violence, revolution, and analyses of particular groups, countries, and inter-American affairs. In recent years, however, the number of books dealing with Latin American political parties has increased substantially. Those dealing with Mexico's Institutional Revolutionary Party (PRI) and National Action Party (PAN), the Communist parties of particular countries, and the Aprista party of Peru are noteworthy. There are two excellent treatments of Venezuelan political parties and one which deals with the Christian Democratic Parties in Latin America.[1] But no one has written a full-length account of the Christian Democratic party in Venezuela. It is my fervent hope that this study does something substantial to fill the void.

The Christian Democratic movement may be down in some countries, but it certainly is not out. A military dictatorship rules Chile, but the Christian Democrats, as the major political party, continue to act as a significant force. In Guatemala the military leaders denied the presidency to the Christian Democratic nominee in a disputed election. In Venezuela the Christian Democrats regained power in March 1979, following their December election victory. In the spring of 1980, the democratically elected government of Ecuador had a Christian Democratic vice-president, and two of the three civilians in El Salvador's five-man governing junta were Christian Democrats.

This study is divided into two major sections. The first deals with the Christian Democratic party—its evolution, history, ideological development, and internal structure. The second deals with the policies and performance of the Christian Democratic government of former President Rafael Caldera.

In the course of this study, which extended over several years, I was able to test some of my hypotheses about the Christian Democratic movement and anticipate some of the developments during this period. Foremost among these was the Christian Democrats' effective-

---

1. See John D. Martz, *Acción Democrática*, and Robert J. Alexander, *The Communist Party of Venezuela*. In a pioneering effort, Edward J. Williams, in *Latin American Christian Democratic Parties*, was the first scholar to write comprehensively about that subject.

ness in shaping the political environment in Venezuela after the period of dictatorship had passed. Also interesting was the development of a new generation within the party which clashed with the founders over such major ideological questions as nationalization of industry and land reform. The evolution of this party from the predictatorial period to the present is a major theme of this book.

However, I did not anticipate the importance of the book's other major theme: the evolution of the relationship between the Christian Democratic party and the other major party of the country, Acción Democrática. That relationship was affected by several developments: changes within the respective parties, the need to deal with crisis management, and recognition of the importance of political democracy to the growth and development of the parties.

These two major themes are interwoven throughout the book. They appear in the first three chapters, which deal with the early student movement and the foundation of the Christian Democratic party, the period of revolution and dictatorship, and the experiences in exile and prison culminating in the overthrow of the dictatorship. The fourth chapter brings the evolution of the Christian Democratic party into the present; ideological questions and internal power relationships are examined in detail. The three chapters on the Caldera government demonstrate the importance of the two themes, particularly the Christian Democratic–Acción Democrática relationship, and examine how that government dealt with political reality and efforts to realize its electoral promises. The government's foreign policy, however, was primarily determined by other factors.

The concluding chapter draws the two major sections together through an evaluation of the Caldera government's performance in the light of party policies and ideology. An analysis of the 1973 election is presented, along with an assessment of the Christian Democratic party as the principal opposition to the Acción Democrática government. This is followed by an analysis of the 1978 election, some observations concerning the present political system, and thoughts on the future of the Christian Democratic party in Venezuelan politics.

PART I

The Christian Democratic Party

CHAPTER 1

Background

S T U D E N T S   O F   Venezuelan history have pointed out that major changes have occurred every twenty-five to forty years with great regularity. In earlier years, such changes took place in an environment of violence and civil war dominated by flamboyant and colorful leaders. Recently, however, the catalyst has changed: the charismatic leader has been replaced by the political party.

The roots of these developments extend far into Venezuela's past. According to an anthropological study of Latin America, the seeds of violent change in nineteenth-century Venezuela had been sown during the colonial period.[1] The area was not attractive to the Spanish conquerors because of the lack of good soil for agriculture, a shortage of cheap Indian labor, and a scarcity of precious metals. The Spanish therefore turned to cattle raising in the *llanos* of the Orinoco River, an area comprising vast plains approximately six hundred miles from east to west. However, the area was very inhospitable, with a high incidence of disease and meager soil for agriculture. As a result, there flourished a predatory society in which banditry nearly became a social necessity if one was to survive.

Given such an environment, it was not surprising that formal religious and political institutions were very weak. Among other things, the church leaders were interested in landed wealth to increase their prestige and influence. Venezuela did not have much to offer, and to this day the Roman Catholic church is not as influential there as in other Latin American countries. With little to administer, the colonial government was weak. The Spanish crown did not make a serious effort to strengthen its institutions.

So we can understand some of the causes of this quasi-political anarchy in the nineteenth century. Only in rare cases was it possible to establish a strong government for a limited period of time. The country lacked resources; key segments of the population would not support the government; the armed forces were not organized. Interestingly, the wealthy class was also divided in its attitude toward government authority. Those with wealth based on land (cattle and plantations) opposed a strong government—they did not want any challenges to their power and prestige. But another group, whose wealth was based on cash transactions, wanted a strong government to secure their financial manipulations.

For the most part, the major military leaders who held power during the nineteenth century, José Antonio Páez (1830-63) and Antonio Guzmán Blanco (1870-88), based their power on the *llaneros*. For example, the fact that General Páez controlled enormous cattle estates assured the loyalty of his troops. Nevertheless, he was forced to balance the *llaneros* against the land-based wealthy to secure his position. Without the resources on which to base power, the rule of the nineteenth century *caudillo* (chief) was tenuous. This situation was to persist until the discovery and exploitation of petroleum in the twentieth century—a phenomenon which led to the rise of a new money-based capitalist group and altered class relations.

In the early part of the twentieth century, leaders who came from the Andean states of Venezuela took the reins. The principal figures from 1899 to 1935 were Cipriano Castro and Juan Vicente Gómez, with the latter holding power for most of this period. From 1935 to the present, the importance of the *caudillo* has declined. It is true that key figures have played important roles: Rómulo Betancourt, Marcos Pérez Jiménez, Rafael Caldera. But two political parties, Acción Democrática and the Christian Democratic party, have dominated the modern era.

The birth of the modern political party system occurred during the years immediately preceding and following the end of the Gómez dictatorship. The most significant event during that administration (1909-35) was the discovery and exploitation of Venezuela's vast petroleum reserves in the early 1920s. During World War I agricultural products received higher prices, and the government encouraged and stimulated industry. But the pace of change was greatly accelerated at the war's end, with the discovery of petroleum.

Several authors have described the profound effects of the petroleum industry during the Gómez era.[2] Companies from Great Britain, Holland, and the United States built roads and mapped large areas of Venezuela. Given the nature of the industry, only a small percentage of the labor force was employed by petroleum companies; but these workers did improve their standard of living through high wages compared to the rest of the labor force. Business increased through the industry's foreign imports and domestic purchases. And as agricultural exports declined at a faster rate during the world depression, the petroleum industry took up the slack and possibly saved Venezuela from economic collapse. The Gómez administration benefited considerably from the tremendous increase in national wealth, paying off the entire foreign debt in 1930. Gómez also undertook a broad public works program, building roads, expanding railway and port facilities, and constructing many new public buildings.

Did the discovery of petroleum and the increased economic activity benefit the masses? For the most part, the answer is no. The administration made no allowance for government housing, nor did health and education receive serious consideration. Gómez also decided not to make significant investments in industry or agriculture. In fact, the country's relative standing in the production of basic agricultural products—coffee, sugar, cotton, tobacco, beef—declined steadily after World War I. What, then, happened to the enormous sums that entered the country as a result of increased petroleum exports? Wealth became increasingly concentrated in the hands of a small group—the oil companies, Gómez and his family, some military officers, and the Táchira friends of the dictator who held high government positions. The gains of the few did not bring about any corresponding improvements for the many. Those connected with Gómez and petroleum prospered, but there was no "trickle down" effect for the large number of people engaged in agriculture.

The government used the huge sums acquired from petroleum exports, in part, to begin the modernization process.[3] The infusion of capital into the economy, whether by the government or the petroleum companies, resulted in an acceleration of economic growth; however, the gap between the haves and the have-nots increased, leading to greater political unrest. The dynamics of relatively rapid economic development and increased social mobility were not the only cause of political instability. The Gómez dictatorship was also brutal, with terror, torture chambers, censorship, and the complete absence of civil liberties. The opposition complained that oil income was used to increase the efficiency of the instruments of repression: the army, police, and spy system. Political opposition was the offspring of accelerated economic growth, with accompanying social mobility, and governmental repression. Its birth coincided with the demise of the tyrant.

Political Ferment

The death of Gómez in 1935 unleashed various forces that had long been suppressed. The labor movement, which had been developing in the late nineteenth century, surfaced only after the dictator's death; in addition, many professionals who prospered during the Gómez administration now demanded greater freedom. Venezuela experienced profound political changes similar to those in the Dominican Republic following the death of Rafael Trujillo in 1963. The period immediately following the demise of the dictator was one of violence and bloodshed, with a general demand for greater political freedom developing into a protest movement under student leadership.

This was not the first time the students had led a protest movement; their open criticism of the government had led to the closing of the Central University in Caracas in 1923. Nevertheless, they continued to hold meetings where national problems were discussed. The Federación de Estudiantes de Venezuela (FEV) was dissolved twice, but Gómez allowed it to be reorganized in 1927. The following year, during the "Semana del Estudiante," the FEV turned a supposed period of festivities—social events, the crowning of a queen, cultural discussions—against the regime. Student leaders Jóvito Villalba, Rómulo Betancourt, and Pío Tamayo used the occasion to denounce Gómez. The government reacted by jailing several of the principal speakers; other student leaders went into exile.

Government repression swelled the ranks of the protesting students. Numerous citizens joined them, as mobs roamed the streets; student delegations appeared before municipal authorities with lists of demands. Discontented laborers and junior army officers joined the movement, leading to armed clashes with troops loyal to Gómez. The government gradually brought the situation under control, primarily through the efforts of General Eleazar López Contreras, whom the dictator subsequently appointed as minister of war and navy.

The student leaders who led the movement against the Gómez regime became known as the Generation of 1928.[4] Some had been considerably influenced by the Mexican Revolution of 1910 and the Russian Revolution of 1917. The activity of this "generation" led to the formation of several political parties: the Communist party, Acción Democrática (AD), and Unión Republicana Democrática (URD). During this time the student intellectuals found much on which they could agree. They opposed military dictatorship, and they believed that anti-imperialist nationalism was preferable to what they considered to be United States domination of their country. Above all, they opposed Gómez and the monopolistic and large landowning interests he represented.[5]

The Generation of 1936

Robert J. Alexander has observed that the dictatorship of Juan Vicente Gómez was a turning point in the political development of Venezuela. Two important events occurred during his regime which changed the country and ended the *caudillo* system.[6] One was the discovery and exploitation of the huge petroleum reserves, which eventually undermined the foundations of the old rurally based *caudillo* system of politics; the second was the establishment of a military academy, which began to produce career officers some time before Gómez's death. The end of the *caudillo* system did not result in the end of military dictatorship, but it did mean that military rule would be much more institutionalized, with one leader appearing as the first among equals.

Since the death of Gómez, new forces have developed in the form of political parties, trade unions, peasant organizations, and business and professional groups. The military can seize power, but it must now convince such organizations of the legitimacy of its rule. These groups will support the military, or at least remain neutral, if they believe that doing so will not jeopardize their interests. Although political parties, trade unions, and peasant organizations are sometimes recalcitrant, at least such efforts can lesson friction. However, it has been extremely difficult for the military governments to obtain student support.

Government repression declined after the dictator's death. Student leaders, freed from prison or returned from exile, organized and made their bid for power. They were joined by a new and younger group of student leaders as the country faced the post-Gómez era.

Two days after Gómez's death, riots and demonstrations broke out in Caracas, Maracaibo, and other cities. General Eleazar López Contreras, the chosen successor of Gómez, brought the situation under control. But, contrary to the strong hand he had used with the Generation of 1928 during the Gómez era, the general now took various steps to meet the demonstrators' demands. He dismissed many Gómez followers from the government, permitted political exiles to return to the country, and allowed a certain degree of freedom of the press. After the Venezuelan Congress elected him president for 1936-41, López Contreras continued his efforts to lessen political tension. In 1936 the government announced its "Program of February" which, among other things, created two new ministries, of sanitation and agriculture. The Congress promulgated the Central Banking Law and approved the Labor Law. (When the government decided to create the National Office of Labor, the direction of this new agency was offered to Rafael Caldera. He had impressed several governmental officials with his knowledge of labor problems through his writings as a university student. Since he was only nineteen years old, he was too young to accept the direction of the newly created agency; instead, he occupied the position of deputy director from 1936 to 1938. Caldera contributed to the writing of the Labor Law of 1936 which, with some modifications, remains the core of Venezuelan labor legislation.) The government's program included several other reforms: strengthening the judicial system, granting more funds for education and social security, improving port facilities, and expanding the transportation network.

A new group of students, who ultimately formed the present Christian Democratic party, also became active in the post-Gómez period. This group, which we shall refer to as the Generation of 1936, developed out of a theological-ideological split in the reconstituted Federación de Estudiantes de Venezuela (FEV). (Although the differences between the Generations of 1928 and 1936 were clear, this was not necessarily a "generation gap." Elements active in the student movement of 1928 supported the position of the Generation of 1936, whereas the reverse was true for some who began their activities in 1936. Many students remained in their respective student organizations; others became active in the formation of political parties.) The major issues precipitating the division were arguments over Marxism and communism, the Catholic church and religion. As the controversy developed, these issues became intertwined.

Two considerations should be kept in mind when analyzing the issue of Marxism and communism within the student movement of the late 1930s. The minority who eventually left the FEV to form their own organization believed that Marxist and communist influence was very strong within the FEV. Furthermore, this group's opposition to the Marxists and communists was strong and emotional, no doubt influenced by their religious background. A recent history of the Christian Democrats included the following statement:

> . . . it is necessary to point out that Marxism had penetrated the mass of Venezuelan youth with its dialectical materialism. At the death of Gómez those Marxist currents tried to establish a religious struggle, they grouped around the Venezuelan Federation of Students and men such as Rómulo Betancourt and Jóvito Villalba, who, assuming the leadership of the youthful rebellion, did not hesitate in declaring themselves as Marxists of the first order.[7]

These words of a young party militant of the present Christian Democratic party are indicative of the current belief of many: that the Marxist-communist struggle has been (and, for some, still is) a primary factor in the development of the student movement and even of the political party system. There is ample evidence to indicate that the student leaders of the Generation of 1928 did indeed study works by Marx and Engels during their years of exile and imprisonment (1928-35). These were the years of searching for an ideology relevant to Venezuela's problems. Lengthy discussions took place in prison among those who were to become the future leaders of Venezuela's communist and noncommunist political parties. In the last years of the Gómez regime, the exiles remained in continuous communication as they tried to develop their ideas.

Rómulo Betancourt, who became a founder of Acción Democrática and president of the country, was an important leader of the Generation of 1928 and has often been charged with being a Marxist or communist. He has never denied his association with communism at that time, and he worked with the Communist party of Costa Rica from 1930 until he resigned in 1935. But Betancourt always emphasized the importance of local conditions, and he became increasingly disillusioned with communism.

The exiled student leaders kept in close contact, particularly those who were in Costa Rica and Colombia. Some letters of Betancourt, Raúl Leoni, and other exiled student leaders came into the possession of the Gómez regime. After Gómez's death the López Contreras government attempted to discredit its opposition by publishing some of the correspondence in a *Libro Rojo*, or red book. Betancourt and others vouch for the authenticity of the correspondence, although of course not for the government's interpretation of it. Excerpts of cited letters were intermingled with sections of communist literature, bringing the authenticity of the *Libro Rojo* into serious doubt.[8] Nevertheless, the book's existence confirmed the fears of those students who were concerned with what they believed to be Marxist-communist influence within the student movement.

Consider these few examples from the *Libro Rojo*. In a letter to Valmore Rodríguez, Ricardo Montilla, and Raúl Leoni, 27 January 1932, Betancourt stated that he was a Marxist but that he and his comrades had to use their own tactics of struggle and not follow imported European models.[9] He opposed the idea of an open communist campaign in Venezuela, and he also opposed following the sterile line of the Communist International. Instead, he suggested that they struggle within their own political organization to organize the masses— the Agrupación Revolucionaria de la Izquierda (ARDI)—and let the Communist party follow its own path. The *Libro Rojo* also cited a letter written by Raúl Leoni, another leader of the Generation of 1928 who also became president. The letter, dated 24 November 1931, was addressed to J. T. Jiménez Arráiz. Leoni stated that the group's doctrinal position was of the revolutionary left: "It is clear that we look to interpret our social, political, and economic reality as Marxist and revolutionary, although we do not join the Communist party."[10]

Other examples can be given, such as the programs and positions held by the exiled student group. Those who were designated as Marxists or communists did not always agree among themselves.[11] But the major point, once again, is that the students who eventually left the FEV believed that the organization was controlled by the communists. They were not particularly influenced by the fact that Rómulo Betancourt and his colleagues ultimately denounced the Communist party and were in turn denounced by the communists. Instead, the most important issue at the time was communist influence within the FEV, an issue which was also a major factor in the split within the student movement.[12] The international situation was a factor as well, for this was the period of the civil war in Spain. Most of the FEV supported the republican forces; the minority supported Franco as a leader in the struggle against communism because they feared the effect a communist Spain would have on Latin America.[13]

The second major issue giving rise to the split in the student movement was that of the Catholic church and religion. In the spring of 1936, several recently formed political parties assumed the name of the Bloque de Abril (April Bloc) and presented a joint program to the national Congress.[14] The program, entitled *Anti-proyecto de Ley Orgánica de Educación Nacional*, proposed that education in the country be "lay in character." Although the Congress rejected it without debate, the Caracas newspapers did present the arguments for and against the program.[15] Two of the program's defenders, Raúl

Leoni and Luis Beltrán Prieto Figueroa, stated that religious institutions would be able to organize and conduct private schools under the program. Nevertheless, as a result of the Bloque de Abril program, the question of secular versus religious education became a major issue in Venezuela.

Many people believed that Congress and the president supported parochial schools, while the Bloque de Abril attacked religious instruction and therefore the church itself. Several political parties and labor unions felt that Congress should dissolve itself and schedule new elections. The Bloque de Abril called for the ouster of President López Contreras, and his replacement by a "constitutionally elected president."[16] Developments in the student federation reflected the tension. The Generation of 1936 supported President López Contreras and the Congress, feeling that the government could carry out various reforms peacefully. These young students, under the leadership of Rafael Caldera, were particularly concerned that the Bloque de Abril program would lead the country to chaos. They preferred evolutionary change to a radical transformation of the society and its institutions.[17]

The Split in the FEV

Tension was high when the FEV met on the night of 6 May 1936 in the Teatro Nacional of Caracas. The student organization's leadership had issued a statement attacking the church and its position on education; they also demanded that the Jesuit order be expelled.[18] The leader of the FEV, Jóvito Villalba, criticized López Contreras for not applying the nineteenth-century laws which provided for secular education, and he called for the closing of all religious seminaries and convents. Other speakers also insisted that all religious orders be outlawed.

At that point, according to a witness, "A pale, thin youth arose with tears in his eyes and said to the crowd: 'I ask that the record show that opposed to this motion is a grateful pupil of the Company of Jesus whose name is Rafael Caldera.' " Others arose to make similar statements: Lorenzo Fernández, Lara Peña, Pérez Machado, Eduardo López de Ceballos, and Francisco Alfonzo Ravard. These men were deeply moved by Caldera's plea. The turmoil was such that they had to leave the theater by a rear door, fearing for their lives. The handful of young men went directly to Caldera's home to form a new student organization.[19]

Most of the dissidents who left the FEV had attended Catholic schools; some had been active in several Catholic organizations. One of these groups was the Venezuelan Catholic Youth, formed in 1930 with Pérez Machado as president and Rafael Caldera as secretary. Pérez Machado and Caldera also attended a Congress in Rome in 1933; the youngest participants were Caldera (then eighteen years old) and Eduardo Frei Montalva of Chile. Others who attended were Fernando Belaúnde Terry (future president of Perú), Mario Polar Ugarteche (future second vice-president of Perú), and Venancio Flores (future foreign minister of Uruguay).[20]

One of the most significant speeches at the Congress was delivered by Father Eugenio Pacelli, who subsequently became Pope Pius XII. He told the young participants that the Congress would help form character—that future political leaders of the respective countries would emerge from this Congress. Of the several themes presented, the most important was the need to struggle against communism. Father Pacelli also stated that the church must do more to help the poor.

When the delegates returned to Venezuela, Caldera organized the Sociedad Inter-Americana de Estudiantes Católicos (Inter-American Society of Catholic Students). They also started a magazine, *Nuevos Rumbos*, which lasted for a short time (with Pérez Machado as the director); Lorenzo Fernández, Lara Peña, and Luis Hernández Solís were among the contributors. The magazine defended the church and called for greater emphasis on social action.

Prior to their political organizing, the Generation of 1936 was almost exclusively concerned with theological questions. Unlike the more flexible and accommodating approach taken by the Catholic church today, the Generation of 1936 emphasized the atheistic nature of communism. Furthermore, while this group showed some concern for the poor of this world, they had not yet worked out any theory of social justice. In contrast, several leaders of the Generation of 1928 were Marxists; others were anticlerical. They called for a radical transformation of society, by violence if necessary, to alleviate the misery of the poor. Given these conflicting views, a polarization within the student movement was probably inevitable.

Unión Nacional Estudiantil

The students who attended the meeting in Caldera's home named their new organization the Unión Nacional Estudiantil (UNE). Their first act was to issue a manifesto explaining their position to the Venezuelan people.[21] They announced that the UNE would make no religious or political distinction except to reject communism completely.

The leaders of the Christian Democratic party, in referring to the early student organization from which their party developed, rejected the labels of "left" or "right." With regard to the student split within the FEV, they felt that the left was anticlerical and the right was pro-church and staunchly Catholic; only in this sense could Betancourt, Villalba, and their group be considered leftists, and Caldera, Lara Peña, and others who joined the UNE be considered rightists.[22] They emphasized that the UNE and the political organizations to which it gave birth were not falangist or fascist; rather, its members were concerned about the issue of religion and the influence of communism in the country. The UNE was anticommunist, but it was not reactionary or right wing.[23]

The Christian Democrats are very sensitive to the charge of being "right wing." They point out that the more conservative elements left the party when the leadership, after some hesitation, decided to oppose the Pérez Jiménez dictatorship in the 1950s. They insist that theirs is not a confessional party, and they deny the criticism that they have been aligned with the "oligarchy." They emphasize that the Christian Democrats have always been primarily interested in winning elections, and that they have shared this concern with the nation's other major political parties.

But there are opponents of the UNE and the Christian Democratic movement who assert that the orientation of the UNE was "facist, Nazi, and extreme right wing." The UNE equated the progressiveness of the FEV with communist doctrine. Actually, the FEV was the home of those involved in the social struggle and independence movements. The FEV opposed Franco and supported republican Spain; the UNE supported Franco. Thus Caldera and his followers split from the more progressive elements of the student movement.[24] The UNE addressed itself to what its leaders considered to be the major issues of the day: social and economic problems, international relations, and a position vis-à-vis communism.

A major principle of Christian Democracy, as expressed through the early student organization, was social justice.[25] Based on Catholic social thought, the concept referred to the growth of all members of the society. The Christian Democrats believed that each person should have the opportunity to realize his full potential, but that he should also be sensitive to the needs of his less fortunate fellows by sharing his wealth with them. The rich must not feed on the misery of the poor. The efforts of the society must be directed toward benefiting all its members for the common good, and not toward assisting a select few. According to Christian Democratic thought, a liberal democratic system, with its concept of equal opportunity in an open society, stood the best chance of realizing social justice for its inhabitants. (The Christian Democrats did not seem concerned with the paradox of their support for Franco and their belief in liberal democracy.)

Specifically, social justice called for a more equitable distribution of wealth through fair taxation and social welfare programs. Other ideas included the worker's right to social and economic improvement, an active role of the state to protect the worker, and the social responsibility of private property.[26] The Christian Democrats also believed that, while private property could provide an element of stability for man and his family, the best use of private property was determined by the social good. This might include expropriation with adequate indemnification.[27]

The student organization was also concerned about the relationship between capital and labor, particularly wanting to avoid the Marxist class struggle that would lead to the ruin of production in the economic sphere and the ruin of collective life in the social sphere.[28] Capital, as well as property, had a social function which should be manifested primarily with respect to the worker's rights to economic and social improvement.[29] The state must play an active role in social and economic development (a principle which remains important to the Christian Democratic party today). "The state cannot be inhibited before the relations between capital and labor; on the contrary it should intervene, protecting the one that is economically weaker and defending the superior interests of production and justice."[30]

As previously indicated, the UNE was particularly strong in opposing communism. Criticism appeared throughout the student newspaper and in various pamphlets.[31] Not only did the student leaders criticize communism; they also hoped to eradicate the causes they believed gave rise to it. Social justice, then, was supported as a concept in its own right, and also as an effective means to combat "the communist danger." For this reason UNE members were encouraged to support programs for the family, peasants, workers, and the masses in general.

The UNE students opposed what they believed communism to be. We have already mentioned the problem within the FEV which led to the split of that student organization: there seemed to be the tendency to lump various groups together as part of the communist movement—so-called progressives, various types of radicals, Marxists, and socialists. This type of thinking may have affected Rafael Caldera's analysis of the Mexican Revolution. He distinguished between the two revolutions: the "original revolution" of Madero, and the "socialist revolution" of Lázaro Cárdenas. The latter had "goals of social anarchy . . . which called for the class struggle and the disappearance of the State; it reflected the Marxist dialectic."[32] The influence of this thinking upon UNE students was considerable—they would argue for social justice on the one hand, yet criticize a social revolutionary movement as communist on the other. This inability to distinguish communists from noncommunists continued in the early years of the Christian Democratic party's development. The distinction between communist and noncommunist movements toward the left of the political spectrum was not made until the Christian Democratic movement developed further.

In international relations, the UNE opposed foreign domination by either the Soviet Union or the United States,[33] with most of its criticism directed toward the latter. The development of a policy of anti-imperialism, in the form of anticolonialism, subsequently became a major plank in the Christian Democratic party's foreign policy. The UNE was highly critical of the role of United States petroleum companies in Venezuela and suggested that this situation resulted in foreign control of the economy. They compared this to what they considered to be U.S. colonialism in Puerto Rico, referring to the island as the "Gibraltar of America." They criticized various actions of the United States government: support of the dictator Batista in Cuba, the Platt Amendment, and the occupations of Haiti and the Dominican Republic by U.S. troops.[34] This criticism subsided upon the entry of the United States into World War II, and after 1941 the UNE supported the concept of a hemispheric defense against the Axis.

The UNE did not limit its activities to Caracas, and it was fairly successful in some areas outside the capital. The major organizing effort took place in areas with concentrations of population, secondary schools, and universities. These included several cities and states west of Caracas: Valencia, Barquisimeto, Maracaibo, the Andean states of Táchira and Mérida (the University of the Andes is located in Mérida). The leaders felt that the area east of Caracas, the *Oriente*, was not propitious for organizing.[35]

Political Organizations

Those who formed the UNE intended to have an apolitical organization. They were not certain of the government's attitude toward political parties in the immediate post-Gómez era, and they felt that the students' needs could perhaps best be met apart from political considerations. When it was later noted that parties were indeed allowed to function, some student leaders concluded that political organization would be desirable, while others decided to remain within the UNE and struggle in the schools.

Those who thought the time propitious for political action formed two political organizations in the late 1930s and early 1940s, Acción Electoral and Acción Nacional, precursors of the Christian Democratic party. Acción Electoral concentrated on electing members to the municipal council of Caracas,[36] and was fairly successful in the December 1938 elections, when three of its candidates won: Lorenzo Fernández, Martín Pérez Matos, and Silvio Gutiérrez.

The municipal councils were given the responsibility of electing deputies to the national Congress. Pedro José Lara Peña was elected in January 1939, and Rafael Caldera in January 1941. Although members of Acción Electoral, both men ran on lists presented by a political group called Agrupación Cívica Bolivariana, which had been organized by the López Contreras government to strengthen its position. On 1 February 1942 municipal elections were again held in the Federal

District; Acción Electoral joined the Agrupación Cívica Bolivariana and an organization called Renovación Municipal in presenting common candidates. The three members of Acción Electoral retained their seats. Taking note of the results, the press commented: "To judge from the results known so far, the elections for Municipal Councilmen have favored the rightist political currents (Acción Electoral, Renovación Municipal, and Agrupación Cívica Bolivariana) and have gone against the leftist currents (Acción Democrática, Unificación Democrática, and Unión Municipal)."[37] It might be noted that political coalitions began very early in the development of Venezuela's political party system.

Acción Electoral was not a national party. Although two of its members served in the Congress by means of a political coalition, it limited its actions to the Federal District. Thus the organization took the name "Electoral Action." The outlook of Acción Electoral was not as clearly defined as that of its successor organization, Acción Nacional. Nevertheless, the party's leadership made decisions which reflected the theological-ideological bent of the Generation of 1936. By choosing to work with President López Contreras and his political groups, they opposed the Generation of 1928 and their political parties, of which Acción Democrática was the most prominent. The original struggle within the FEV was now projected, in a more complicated form, to the larger political arena. The issues were the same, however, and the Generation of 1936 continued to oppose communism, as they perceived it, whether within the FEV or among the leaders of Acción Democrática.

Other political organizations were created in various parts of the country for the purpose of supporting López Contreras. In Táchira, for example, the Partido Nacionalista existed for a few years; the state of Mérida produced the Cruzada Cívica Bolivariana. Both groups were absorbed by the Christian Democratic party in the mid-1940s.[38]

On 28 April 1941 the Congress chose General Isaías Medina Angarita to replace López Contreras as president. It was generally agreed that there was more political freedom during the Medina Angarita administration than during that of López Contreras. The new president relaxed the repressive policies pursued by López during the latter part of his administration, permitting opposition political parties such as Acción Democrática to function legally. He also successfully sponsored female suffrage and a modest agrarian reform act.

The leaders of Acción Electoral thought the time had come to form a new political party, one which would be able to organize throughout the country. In April 1942 Rafael Caldera and his followers launched their political movement on a national scale with the creation of Acción Nacional, a party which fused Acción Electoral and the Movimiento de Acción Nacionalista. Caldera became secretary-general of the party; other members of the National Directorate included Pedro José Lara Peña, Lorenzo Fernández, Germán Borregales, Martín Pérez Matos, Miguel Angel Landáez, and Jesús María Pérez Machado.

The party's doctrine, published in a twelve-point program,[39] closely paralleled that of the UNE. Among the most significant principles were the call for a revolutionary movement to establish new and just solutions; social justice in the form of equity in human relations; the elevation of the legitimate rights of the collectivity above individual or class aspirations; the subordination of economic forces to spiritual interests and national necessities; national unification, excluding all international or class propaganda; and a defense of the Catholic religion and the rights of the church. With regard to this last principle, the party leaders emphasized that Acción Nacional was not to be designated as a confessional organization. It was not a Catholic party, but a party of Venezuelan Catholics. They added that the party was sensitive to the development of social justice as supported by the church.[40]

As the UNE and Acción Electoral had done, Acción Nacional assumed an anticommunist position. Communism was rejected on the ideological level. The importance of economic forces in social relations was deemphasized. The Christian Democrats could not accept the Marxist dialectic that economic forces determined history; they also rejected the significance of the class struggle, for the realization of social justice would make the concept of the class struggle inoperative. The party's periodical was quite explicit in seeing the organization as a force to combat communism.[41]

The fortunes and ultimate demise of Acción Nacional were affected by the Medina government and the party members' various attitudes toward the administration. Political parties were allowed to operate, but with serious limitations. One party director recalled that it was difficult to develop political activity because the government restricted the holding of meetings. Since the party could not circulate its message and grow, for the most part it remained limited to the original nucleus.[42]

Government restrictions also affected the party's showing in municipal and congressional elections. The party leaders decided not to participate in the elections of January 1943, which permitted municipal councils to elect deputies to the Congress. The government's hand-picked candidates had a definite edge, due to the administration's financial backing. Two party members who considered running, Germán Borregales and Lorenzo Fernández, were discouraged by the government's maneuvers.[43] The situation did not improve during the elections of October 1944 and January 1945. The party did allow some of its members to run, but they were soundly defeated (as were the candidates of Acción Democrática) by the government-sponsored Partido Democrático Venezolano (PDV). The only elected officials connected with the party were Pedro José Lara Peña and Rafael Caldera. Although they had been elected to the Congress before Acción Nacional was formed, they identified with the party and spoke in its name.

The party was divided in its attitude toward Medina Angarita. The previous organizations—the UNE (still existing) and Acción Electoral—had supported López Contreras during his term of office. The leaders of Acción Nacional, although not completely happy with some of Medina's policies, nevertheless generally supported him. (They formed part of a welcoming committee when he returned from a trip to the United States in the spring of 1944.) The party's periodical stated that Medina's position had coincided with that of the party since its beginning.[44] However, problems arose when former President López Contreras attempted to return to power.

In 1944 the former president announced that he was ready to resume the duties of the presidency because of his concern with the adverse effects of rapid political change. President Medina, desiring to prevent this possibility at all costs, convoked the PDV convention in the summer of 1945 to nominate his own choice for a successor, Diógenes Escalante. (Acción Democrática also supported Escalante.) At this point the PDV and the government supporters split between López Contreras and Medina Angarita. The consensus was that López represented the more conservative elements in the country, while Medina appealed to the more liberal factions.

The turn of events produced serious discussions within the ranks of Acción Nacional, and party leaders differed over tactics. Lara Peña and his followers wanted the party to give its full support to López Contreras, whereas Caldera and his supporters favored a more flexible approach in which individual party members would be able to support the candidate of their choice.[45] Lara Peña admitted that he supported López Contreras at the time, but he felt that Caldera definitely supported Medina Angarita. This opinion was confirmed by Martín Pérez Matos, who was active in the party and also a Medina supporter.[46] Lara Peña and his followers left the party to participate in the formation of the Agrupaciones Pro-Candidatura Presidencial, an organization which served as a front for the presidential ambitions of López Contreras. Its convention of 13 October 1945 chose López as its presidential candidate, indicating that Medina and the PDV were not worthy of popular support.[47]

The demise of Acción Nacional was completed when its deputies in the national Congress left office. Lara Peña's term ended, and he left the party to support López Contreras. Caldera resigned to devote more time to university teaching. The end of the party coincided with the Revolution of 1945 and the assumption of power by a civilian-military junta under Rómulo Betancourt and Acción Democrática.

The Development of Ideas

Christian Democracy is one of the few movements in Latin America which has an identifiable doctrine. Philosophically it is closely identified with the social thought of the Catholic church as expressed in the encyclicals *Rerum Novarum* of Leo XIII (1891), *Quadragesimo Anno* of Pius XI (1931), *Mater et Magistra* and *Pacem en Terris* of John XXIII (1960). The movement has been influenced by modern European writers such as Jacques Maritain, Luigi Sturzo, and Emmanual Mounier. In Venezuela, the young men of the Generation of 1936 who helped shape the Christian Democratic movement were influenced by the early encyclicals and writings. No single force, however, was more significant than the influence of one Jesuit priest.

Manuel Aguirre Elorriaga, S.J.

When Padre Aguirre died in February 1969, the magazine which he had started, *SIC* (*Seminario Interdiocesano Caracas*), dedicated to him a special issue with articles which summarized his background and described his influence.[48] He left Spain for Venezuela in the mid-1920s and became a teacher in the Colegio San Ignacio. (He had not yet decided to become a priest.) Many students who were preparing for their degrees attended his study circles; these included Rafael Caldera, Arístides Calvani, and Lorenzo Fernández. He returned to Europe and spent the years 1929-37 studying and developing his philosophy. During this period he attended the Rome Congress with Caldera and other future leaders of the Christian Democratic movement in Latin America. At the Congress he introduced the young Caldera to Luigi Sturzo.

Manuel Aguirre returned to Venezuela as a priest in 1937. He started the magazine *SIC* the following year, organized study circles, and worked with labor groups. Perhaps I can best describe his role in the ideological development of the Christian Democratic leaders by relating the extensive interview I had with his brother.[49]

Padre Genaro Aguirre believed that his brother's most important impact on the Christian Democratic movement was through his personal influence with Rafael Caldera. Manuel Aguirre was very impressed with Caldera's intellect; the young man was a brilliant student. Manuel Aguirre believed, however, that the young Caldera was concentrating on his own achievements and was not sufficiently concerned with the plight of others; this concerned him, because part of his teaching was to convince his students about the importance of serving mankind. When Padre Aguirre returned to Europe, he began a correspondence with Caldera which lasted for several years, continuing the process of cultivating the young student's intellectual development.

The UNE was formed several months before Padre Aguirre returned to Venezuela. Upon his return, he began classes in Christian social thought for a select group within the UNE; his students included Caldera, Lara Peña, Lorenzo Fernández, and Víctor Giménez Landínez, among others. The priest emphasized two things: first, he wanted his students to learn as much as possible about social philosophy and social action; in addition, he taught them to develop their speaking techniques. Manuel Aguirre also believed that it would be necessary to form a political party in order to realize Christian social thought in practice.

Throughout this period Manuel Aguirre and Rafael Caldera had many discussions, more often systematic than casual. Caldera would often ask the priest to analyze specific problems and situations; subsequent reflection would lead to the integration of the two men's views. Another influence on Caldera was Gil Robles, a deputy in republican Spain before the Franco takeover. Robles's ideas of Christian Democracy and legalism appeared in the newspaper *Debate*.

These intellectual stimuli affected Caldera's thinking in three general areas. First, he was thoroughly convinced that the church's teachings on social justice should be politically implemented. Second, Caldera concluded that the political system best suited to realize social action was democracy, with its emphasis on legality, constitutionalism, and a strong opposition to dictatorship. Here Caldera was influenced by Gil Robles and Manuel Aguirre, particularly by the classes and study circles of the latter. Finally, he placed a strong emphasis on dealing with social problems, such as the factors related to poverty and an inequitable distribution of wealth, through social justice. On this point Padre Aguirre's influence on Christian Democracy in general and on Rafael Caldera in particular was unquestionable.

"From those study meetings," a friend of the Padre's has noted, "I remember the message which Padre Aguirre emphasized that undoubtedly has influenced the orientation of my life: political activism facing social injustice." (These words of Valmore Acevedo Amaya, long-time Christian Democratic leader and former governor of the state of Táchira, appeared in an extensive article written at the time of Padre Aguirre's death.[50]) Valmore Acevedo worked with Padre Aguirre in the Workers' Circle of Caracas. They also organized a circle of studies on social themes with a group of university students, among whom were Luis Herrera Campins, Rodolfo José Cárdenas, Gonzalo García Bustillos, and José Luis Zapata. Padre Aguirre would present ideas and then analyze how social and political events related to them. Politics was considered not an end in itself, but a means to serve the superior ideal of social justice.

Other Christian Democratic leaders paid homage to Padre Aguirre in the commemorative issue of *SIC*, Rodolfo José Cárdenas and Eduardo Fernández among them. President Caldera wrote that he and Padre Aguirre had been friends since he himself was eleven years old. Caldera saw the priest as a man who made "a great human effort so that the people may be oriented toward peace, liberty, and justice."

Manuel Aguirre had always been an anticommunist, but, according to his brother, he reached a point in the 1960s where he thought violent revolution would be the only answer to the plight of the masses. Although he still could not accept communist principles, he did see other dangers which he felt were greater than communism, such as the continuation of human misery. Thus he saw some merit in communist doctrine that led to a reconsideration of his position on communism. (However, this reconsideration did not appear in his writings and probably did not affect the general anticommunist position of the Christian Democrats.)

Let us turn to some of the specific ideas of Manuel Aguirre, keeping in mind that many of these themes have been and are still a part of the Christian Democratic movement. We will refer to his *Esquema de la Doctrina Social Católica* (1940), a book published serially with other of his articles in the magazine *SIC*.[51]

Aguirre felt that certain historical trends contributed to the problems of his day. In particular, he cited the growing secularization of the Western world, general contempt for authority, and tendencies toward economic centralization. He believed Venezuela was a part of this world crisis, with social problems in its mining and petroleum camps, in its cities, and on its haciendas.[52] The most serious manifestation of the social problem was the inequitable distribution of wealth, which exacerbated the misery of the masses. According to Padre Aguirre, the church should consider the economic and social questions as an extension of the church's moral order: "Catholic social doctrine is distinguished from the liberal (doctrine) in that: 1) it admits the social function of property, of capital and of labor, 2) it rejects the materialist concept of life, 3) it accentuates the human dignity of work of the laborer, with its consequences in retribution, until arriving at the fair salary." But not only does Catholic social doctrine reject liberalism, "It is distinguished from the socialist solution in that: 1) it admits the right of property, 2) it rejects historic materialism and, 3) it condemns the class struggle as unjust and barren."[53]

Thus we see the "third position" of Catholic social doctrine and Christian Democratic doctrine, a position that lies somewhere between traditional liberalism and Marxist socialism. This was evident in the church's position concerning property as stated by Padre Aguirre: "Property is indirectly destined to contribute to the well-being of society and comes subject to the dictates of social justice."[54] But social justice cannot be realized through traditional liberalism or Marxist socialism: "As Pius XI . . . indicates, the acceptance and defense of the individual function of property separates us radically from socialism; the defense of the social function of property separates us from economic liberalism, or from individualism. Our position is a middle term, real and objective, founded in the naturalness of man and equidistant from both deviations."[55]

In rejecting traditional liberalism, Padre Aguirre looked to the state to assume an active role in meeting society's social and economic problems. He believed in the socialist concept of partial nationalization, of "major industries which are vital to the economic life of the country and in which a great deal of power had been concentrated,"[56] with just payment to the former owners.

In addition to rejecting traditional liberalism, Manuel Aguirre also denounced capitalism: "Capitalism has been converted in recent times—and in part in the present—into a true economic dictatorship, and at times into a true feudal patron, making demands from its employees, including the personal vote in political questions. Such capitalism is reproachable."[57] Instead, Padre Aguirre called for a harmonious relationship between capital (as distinguished from capitalism) and labor.

Manuel Aguirre was also outspoken and definite in his denial of communism. In 1944 he wrote an article supporting a particular section (Article 32, Paragraph 6) of the constitution,[58] which states: "Communist and Anarchist doctrines are considered contrary to the independence, political form and social peace of the Nation; those who proclaim, propagate or practice them will be considered as traitors to the Country and will be punished according to the laws." He admitted that this section might be abused, but he considered it worth the risk. In the struggle against communism, all Catholics must stand up and be counted. Catholic doctrine concerning liberty of thought and action should apply to all except the communists.

When President Medina Angarita assumed an anticommunist position, Padre Aguirre strongly supported him: "To struggle against Communism, as a political philosophy, the people have their faith and love for liberty, which is incompatible with . . . dictatorship and slavery without rights, characteristic of the dictatorship of the proletariat."[59] Not only did Padre Aguirre oppose Venezuelan communists, but he opposed international communism as well: "We have never believed in the truthfulness of men who do not admit the eighth commandment of the law of God. (We do not) believe concretely in the sincerity of Russian democracy, or Soviet religious tolerance, of the dissolution of the Third International. . . ."[60]

Padre Manuel Aguirre was the symbolic as well as the real link between the theological-ideological dimensions and the student-political organizational dimensions of early Venezuelan Christian Democracy. He was a Jesuit priest who believed that Catholic social thought must be expressed through political action. The leaders of the Generation of 1936 attended his classes at a time when they were active in student organizations and fledging political parties. Thus students who were steeped in religion and engaged in organizational efforts were receptive to the ideas of Padre Aguirre, a friend and teacher during their early development.

While the anticommunism expressed through the student and political organizations reflected Padre Aguirre's views, the students also began to evidence greater sensitivity to social problems, undoubtedly analyzed in depth in Padre Aguirre's classes. Although adamant in their anticommunism, the Generation of 1936 also saw the need for a more equitable distribution of wealth and a positive role of the state. Anticommunism by itself would not bring about social justice.

Perhaps such questions contributed to the split in Acción Nacional. Apparently those who agreed with Caldera developed misgivings about López Contreras; no longer could they support his repressive policies and maintenance of the status quo. They began to lean toward Medina Angarita, in the hope that his policies might alleviate the human misery which they saw around them. Thus, within the theological-ideological-organizational linkage, we can observe a conceptual evolution: a more positive approach to problems, as exemplified in the ideas of Padre Aguirre and Rafael Caldera.

The ideological pillars of Christian Democracy in Venezuela were developed in the period 1936-45. To be sure, there have been theoretical refinements through the years; new writers have emerged in Europe and Latin America, and new ideas have come forth with new generations in the Christian Democratic movement. Basically, however, the doctrine of the early student movement and short-lived political parties has remained intact. The Generation of 1936 gave birth to Christian Democracy in Venezuela, presented it with a doctrine, and began to nurture their political party in a nation feeling the convulsions of revolutionary change.

CHAPTER 2

Revolution and Dictatorship

W H E N M E D I N A ' s hand-picked successor, Diógenes Escalante, became ill and retired from the political scene a few months before the
1945 presidential election, the struggle between López and Medina
intensified. The new candidate of President Medina, Angel Biaggini,
the minister of agriculture, was not acceptable to the major political
party, Acción Democrática. The party leaders generally supported
Escalante's ideas, but they felt that Biaggini would be a puppet of
Medina and would not make the changes that AD wanted and Escalante had promised. Nor did they want López Contreras to return.
This development led Acción Democrática to an agreement with
some of the younger military officers who had formed the Patriotic
Military Union (UPM). This new alignment of forces and the division of the old guard between López and Medina resulted in the Revolution of October 1945.[1] The new Junta Revolucionaria de Gobierno
consisted of five civilians (four from AD) and two military men. It
called for elections to be held in October 1946 and 1947, in order to
select representatives to write a constitution and to elect a new president, members of Congress, and other legislators.

The UNE, along with Rafael Caldera and his supporters, enthusi-
astically supported the revolution, and Caldera accepted the position
of attorney general in the new government. However, on 13 April
1946 Caldera resigned, highly critical of the alleged AD attempt to
break up a Christian Democratic meeting in Táchira. Caldera stated
that AD could not separate its party actions from that of its government, and that, because of this and the particular incident of the
Táchira meeting, he had no choice but to resign.[2]

Caldera and his supporters felt that they had to work toward the
formation of a new political organization to meet the demands of the
time. A group of university leaders and professionals who had been
active in the UNE, Acción Electoral, and Acción Nacional held a
series of meetings late in 1945[3] which led to the formation of the
Comité de Inscripción Electoral (CIE). The organization lasted until
13 January 1946; on that day, the members of the CIE and others
met to form the Comité de Organización Política Electoral Independiente (COPEI). One meeting took place on the first floor of the
Ugarte laundry in Plaza Candelaria in Caracas, while a simultaneous
meeting that also founded COPEI took place in San Felipe. In a moving speech, Caldera stated that all Venezuelans must identify with the

ideals of the Revolution of 1945. The revolution must succeed; it must not become merely another coup d'état.[4]

Those who formed COPEI realized there were many independents who did not want to join a political party. That is why they chose the name COPEI, which included the word "independent."[5] Its leaders insisted that, rather than establishing a political party, they had founded an electoral committee to prepare for the forthcoming elections. It was interesting, however, that the electoral committee held its First National Convention in September 1946. That convention's manifesto concluded by explaining that its leaders had intended to make COPEI a political party from the beginning, but decided not to take this step at the outset. Instead, this decision would be made after the elections for the Constituent Assembly. Thus COPEI was to be a "partisan group of transcendent projections dedicated to the service of Venezuela."[6]

Comite de Organizacion Politica Electoral Independiente (COPEI)

Shortly after COPEI's formation, its leaders circulated literature which attempted to explain their position. One of these documents, which listed various principles of the newly formed political organization,[7] made it apparent that the ideas developed by the precursors of COPEI would be a major influence. Stressing such themes as anti-communism and social justice, the leadership also made it clear that COPEI would support religion and the Catholic church. The First National Convention declared: "We must consider religion, particularly the Catholic religion, as one of the most estimable forces within the national panorama. . . . We should not offend the religious sentiment of the majority of Venezuelans. . . . Religious teaching should be facilitated in the public schools, but parents are not obliged to have their children participate if it is against their convictions."[8]

The commitment to such principles did not prevent the leadership from supporting goals of the revolutionary movement which had toppled the dictatorship. At the First National Convention, COPEI leaders stated that the organization had a public obligation to struggle for achievement of the October Revolution's promises. They explained that COPEI was formed so that the elections promised by the government would be fulfilled by the free participation of the citizens.[9]

At the Third National Convention of COPEI, in March 1948, the Comité de Organización Política Electoral Independiente was transformed into a political party, conserving the name COPEI. Rafael Caldera was elected secretary-general and Lorenzo Fernández deputy secretary-general. It is interesting to note that Caldera's announcement of his candidacy for the presidency preceded the electoral committee's transformation into a political party. At the convention, the party declared its program of eighteen principles which had been included in its electoral platforms of 1946 and 1947.[10]

Early Development

Two factors had a direct effect on the development of COPEI in Caracas: opposition to Acción Democrática by a certain element of the population, and the belief of many that COPEI was a defender of the church.

Francisco Peña Blanco, *hijo* (son), a former Copeyano and labor leader, felt that opposition to AD was particularly significant in COPEI's early development.[11] He and others, such as Germán Borregales, believed that Rómulo Betancourt and other AD leaders represented communism, and that AD was dangerous because it opposed the doctrine of the Catholic church and thwarted the development of the individual.

Expanding upon this view, José Luis Zapata, who has held various leadership positions in the party, believed that many looked to COPEI in order to express their own personal reaction against AD.[12] According to this interpretation, there was a great deal of emotionalism at the time (1945-48), and reactionaries who were not necessarily Copeyanos (i.e., members of COPEI) supported the party. They wanted to defeat AD, and they saw COPEI as their only vehicle. Zapata believed that AD presented a radical government in 1945-48. There was a great deal of demagoguery at the time; Betancourt would deliver fiery speeches that the people would discuss for months. During this period political meetings were filled with agitation, shouting, threats, and violence.

Furthermore, according to Zapata, the anti-AD feeling contributed to class differences between the structures of the two political parties and led to a general political polarization. AD had the support of most peasants and workers; COPEI appealed to the professionals and the small bourgeoisie. (COPEI attracted peasants only in the Andean states of Mérida and Táchira.) Compromise between these two poles was extremely difficult, if not impossible.

The second factor in the development of COPEI in the capital, presenting the party as the defender of the church, was closely related (in fact, intertwined) with the anti-AD bias. It was the opinion of two priests, both of whom I found very sensitive to political developments in the country, that the background of the Copeyanos and the attitude of the Adecos (members of AD) during the latter's three years in power were important elements in the political conflicts which developed.[13] It must be remembered that COPEI grew out of the Catholic schools (*colegios*); its leaders were strongly influenced by the social doctrine of the church and Padre Manuel Aguirre. Many others continued to identify with COPEI as the defender of the church, although one could argue whether it was the church's policy to assume this attitude. Nevertheless, COPEI and the church were close in their positions, and both were strong in the Andean states. According to this view, the positions of the party and the church were very close due to the historical circumstances.

Certainly the relationship between COPEI and the church was a factor in the party's founding and early development in the Andean state of Táchira. A well-known priest there, who asked that his name not be used, felt that a very strong relationship existed between COPEI and the church in this early period. The peasants would see the party name Social Christian–COPEI; they would identify the word "Christian" with the church, and would vote for the party. In general, they were not aware of the party's program or the election issues.

The church strongly supported COPEI in Táchira; indeed, it was not uncommon for priests to tell their parishioners, from the pulpit, to vote for the party. Many believed that AD was against the capitalists, the church, and foreign clergy. There was only one reasonable course in the face of such a danger: organize a political party as Christians.[14]

During this early period in Táchira, the party had a very conservative orientation—even a reactionary one, according to its critics. This was caused, in part, by many opportunists who flocked to the party's banner. One organization in Táchira, the Partido Nacionalista, had supported the candidacy of López Contreras; it joined COPEI after the October Revolution of 1945. Such groups made it difficult for COPEI to avoid the conservative-reactionary label at the outset.[15]

However, we should add another perspective in discussing the party's early conservatism. Conservatives joined the party, which led to a particular philosophical bent. But what were the attitudes of party leaders? Did they accept the influx of new conservative members reluctantly? Or did they welcome them with open arms to strengthen their own conservative leanings? These questions cannot be answered with certainty. The party leaders were interested in winning elections, and they welcomed the opportunity to increase the number of party militants. It is also safe to assume that the philosophy of the newcomers was at least acceptable. Some of these elements were to leave a few years later, when the party leadership decided to oppose the Pérez Jiménez dictatorship.

An interesting development took place in the other major Andean state of Mérida, where important families were decisive in the foundation and early development of the party. Two of these families, Picón and Parra, had alternated in power prior to the October Revolution. The psychology of the *caudillo* was a factor here, and in the 1946 and 1947 elections important family names headed the COPEI electoral lists. In the 1947 election for the Constituent Assembly, for example, Parra Pérez headed the Copeyano list. He was a prominent doctor in Mérida, and his family had a great deal of influence. It might be added that priests from well-known families were also presented as COPEI leaders.[16]

Electoral Flurry: 1946, 1947, 1948

Three elections took place during 1946-48: 1) 27 October 1946, the Asamblea Nacional Constituyente (National Constituent Assembly), to write a new constitution; 2) 14 December 1947, the president, Congress, state legislative assemblies, the municipal council of the Federal District, and the federal territories; 3) 9 May 1948, municipal councils of the twenty states. COPEI participated in each.

Five political parties participated in the 1946 election: AD, COPEI, URD, the Communist party (PCV), and the Socialist party (PS). Actually, two communist groups participated, the PCV (the "Reds") and the Partido Revolucionario Proletario (the "Blacks"), with the PCV dominant. There was a great deal of violence in the 1946 election, resulting in several dead and wounded. Some pertinent statistics from this election appear in Table 2.1.[17]

A further breakdown of the statistics indicated that AD took first place throughout the nation, except in Mérida and Táchira, which were taken by COPEI and the smaller allied parties. COPEI received 57 percent in Mérida and 60 percent in Táchira. The election results also meant that AD would have overwhelming control of the National Constituent Assembly, indicated in Table 2.2 for some key areas.

Two general conclusions can be drawn from the 1946 electoral statistics. For one thing, the political strength of AD throughout most of the country was overwhelming; the political party which led the October Revolution and began to initiate basic reforms received electoral successes for these efforts. But we must also note the political strength of COPEI in the Andes, particularly in Mérida and Táchira. COPEI also scored fairly well in a third Andean state, Trujillo, receiving 29 percent of the vote. Of COPEI's 185,347 votes, 110,850 came from the three Andean states, as did fifteen of the party's nineteen representatives to the National Constituent Assembly.

As indicated in some of the interviews already cited, it can be as-

TABLE 2.1. Results of the 1946 Election

Party	Votes	%
AD	1,099,601	78.43
COPEI and allies	185,347	13.22
URD and allies	59,827	4.26
PCV and allies	50,387	3.62
Socialist	2,087	0.14

TABLE 2.2. Representatives to the National Constituent Assembly, 1946

	AD 137	COPEI 19	URD 2	Communist 2
Federal District	12	2		1
Lara	12	1		
Mérida	3	5		
Táchira	3	7		
Trujillo	8	3		
Zulia	12	1		1

sumed that there was a direct relationship between the strength of the church and the strength of COPEI in the Andes. COPEI's identification with the church was a decisive factor in the party's success there, particularly in Táchira, where many priests were active. Táchira was also an agricultural state, with a population consisting mostly of small farmers. Here we see the strength of COPEI in a conservative rural area. In 1946 the party leaders decided (successfully, as it turned out) to concentrate on Táchira.

Although admitting that he could not prove his contention, one political analyst at the time believed that AD and the October Revolution appeared as a threat to the people of the Andes. Many considered the revolutionary movement an effort to eliminate Andean influence, particularly in Táchira, from public life.[18]

The regional committee of COPEI in Táchira issued an analysis of the party's favorable showing in that state,[19] while confessing that COPEI never thought it would win throughout the country. The party organized in seventeen states; it did not organize in three others, or in the two federal territories. Because some states were considered more important than others, organizational efforts lasted anywhere from two to seven months.

COPEI published an electoral platform for the 1946 election,[20] presenting twenty principles which, for the most part, reiterated the ideological position already mentioned. During the National Constituent Assembly's debates, party representatives had the opportunity to develop these ideas in a public forum; several major speeches appeared in the press and, at Caldera's urging, were transmitted by radio. Some of the nineteen representatives to the 1947 National Constituent Assembly were priests; the others included well-known party leaders such as Caldera, Lorenzo Fernández, and Edecio La Riva Araujo.[21]

Perhaps the perennial religious issue caused the most bitterness during the several months the Assembly was in session. Both Lorenzo Fernández and Rafael Caldera appeared as strong defenders of the church's role during these sessions; from the very beginning, Fernández argued for the clergy's right to become involved in politics.[22] The debates frequently became quite vehement, and often the representatives of AD and the Communist party were in opposition to COPEI.

The COPEI representatives feared that the AD majority would insist upon constitutional restrictions on the church. Caldera strongly opposed the suggestion that religious officials be appointed by the government, pointing out that the church had been a political arm of the Venezuelan government, and that the new constitution should guarantee it independence regarding its own laws and the nomination of its own authorities. According to Caldera, it was unjustifiable and absurd to keep the Catholic church in a state of subjection. But he saw no immediate end to this conflict: "This debate," he said, "will continue in Venezuela until the church has liberty and justice."[23] Caldera also argued for religious instruction in the schools. He wanted to eliminate the constitutional phrase which stated that "education is the essential function of the state." Instead, he wanted the people to view the family as the fundamental educator.[24]

COPEI supported the constitution of 1947, but the party criticized those articles pertaining to executive power, agrarian reform that "threatened property," and nationalization of judicial power (which was "contrary to democracy and could lead to extreme totalitarianism").[25] The most criticism was directed against religious restrictions dealing with teaching and the schools; the Copeyanos felt that the private schools would be inferior.

Of course, other issues were discussed in the writing of the constitution. For example, Lorenzo Fernández and Luis Roberto Riera called upon the large landowners to parcel out their land among the peasants.[26] But the religious issue seems particularly significant, in that it contributed to the tense relationship between AD and COPEI in this early period.

One other factor that deserves mention here concerns the bitterness between representatives of COPEI and the Communist party. The communist newspaper, for example, strongly criticized COPEI for opposing the Ley de Patronato Eclesiástico; it cited COPEI's attitude as part of an international offensive of Catholicism, an attempt to substitute the new Catholic order for the overthrown Hitler order. According to the communists, this was evidence of the Vatican's policy of influencing the politics of various countries. As a result, the communists cited the coincidences of the "Copeyano religious newspaper" of Caracas with all the fascist, falangist, and Hitlerite propaganda.[27]

It was significant that the Communist party and AD appeared as the primary opposition to COPEI during the Constituent Assembly sessions. The communists and Adecos agreed on almost every issue, which strengthened the resolve of those Copeyanos who would not, or could not, distinguish between the two. And so the polarization of political forces continued to intensify, until the major parties joined forces to overthrow the Pérez Jiménez dictatorship in 1957-58.

In the election of 14 December 1947, the people of Venezuela were able to choose their president by direct election for the first time.[28] They also had a new constitution, promulgated on 5 July 1947. Many of the smaller groups which had participated in the 1946 election did not participate this time; indeed, there seemed to be generally less interest. (There were also fewer violent incidents.) In view of the 1946 results, many felt that an AD triumph was a foregone conclusion. The religious question, particularly in Mérida and Táchira, was again a major factor. COPEI had appeared as the defender of the church during the National Constituent Assembly debates, and in Táchira the church was accused of interfering in the election.

The results (shown in Table 2.3) were again a triumph for AD. Three parties or coalitions competed in the presidential election: AD, COPEI and the UFR in Mérida, and the Communist party. The URD did not offer a candidate.

T A B L E 2.3. Results of the 1947 Presidential Election

	Votes	%
Rómulo Gallegos (AD)	871,752	74.47
Rafael Caldera (COPEI)	262,204	22.40
Gustavo Machado (CP)	36,587	3.2

Once again the geographical strengths and weaknesses of COPEI were apparent: the range was 6 percent in Sucre to 66 percent in Táchira. On a national scale, COPEI won in Mérida and Táchira and received second place elsewhere.

COPEI did not do quite as well in the elections for legislative bodies. (Here it was a four-way race, because URD presented candidates.) COPEI received 20 percent of the vote, leading in Táchira and Mérida, and running second in the Federal District, Apure, Aragua, Barinas, Bolívar, Carabobo, Falcón, Guárico, Lara, Miranda, Portuguesa, Trujillo, Yaracuy, and Zulia. As a result, Senate representation was as follows: AD, 38; COPEI-UFR, 6; URD, 1. Two of the COPEI senators were from Táchira, two were from Mérida representing the UFR (which eventually merged with COPEI), and the other two were given to the party through a quotient reflecting its total votes. The Chamber of Deputies figures were: AD, 83; COPEI-UFR, 19; URD and allies, 5; Communist, 3. And for the state legislative assemblies: AD, 244; COPEI-UFR, 50; URD, 9; Communist, 3.

Two facts should be mentioned in regard to the 1947 election. First, the COPEI vote for president was 22 percent, and for the legislative bodies 20 percent. Perhaps accounting for the difference was the widespread popularity of Rafael Caldera. Furthermore, because the URD did not field a presidential candidate, we can assume that some of the Urredistas or sympathizers voted for COPEI.

The other fact emerges from comparing the total votes in the 1946 and 1947 elections (see Table 2.4).

T A B L E 2.4. 1946 and 1947 Vote Totals

1946	1,402,011
1947 for president	1,170,543
1947 for legislative bodies	1,183,764

In the face of this smaller voter turnout, the percentage of COPEI voting strength increased. In 1946 COPEI and its allies received 13 percent, but in 1947 the COPEI-UFR effort showed an increase of 9 percent for the COPEI presidential candidate and 7 percent for the candidates to legislative bodies. Furthermore, COPEI received 185,347 votes in 1946. With a lower voter turnout in 1947, the party's candidates received 262,204 for president and 240,186 for the legislative bodies.

Several possible reasons can be cited for the increase in voter strength. In 1947, COPEI appeared as the main opposition and principal beneficiary of dissatisfaction with AD. Furthermore, Rafael Caldera had become a national figure as a result of the proceedings of the National Constituent Assembly. We should also consider the non-Marxist anti-AD vote, which seems to have gone to URD in some areas and to COPEI in others.

The voting in the 9 May 1948 election for municipal councils did not result in a significant change in any party's voting strength. (See Table 2.5.)[29]

Relations With Acción Democrática

According to Samuel P. Huntington, "Two groups which see each other only as archenemies cannot form the basis of a community until those mutual perceptions change. There must be some compatibility of interests among the groups that compose the society. . . . The obligation is to some principle, tradition, myth, purpose, or code of behavior that the persons and groups have in common."[30] In the evolving relationship between AD and COPEI, the respective party

T A B L E 2.5. Results of 9 May 1948 Election

	Votes	%
AD	491,762	70.09
COPEI-UFR	146,197	21.1
URD	27,007	3.9
Communist	23,524	3.4

leaders ultimately concluded that political democracy was in their mutual interest. Once this point was reached, perhaps during the years of exile under a dictatorship, their competitive political relationship could rest on a more solid basis. But the basic rules of the game were not sufficiently accepted in the period 1945-48. As a result, the relationship between AD and COPEI was extremely bitter, and the tenuous structure of political democracy came tumbling down in a coup d'état.

In its very first issue, the party newspaper *COPEI* printed an editorial critical of AD, accusing it of putting pressure on COPEI, particularly in the interior. AD had committed various antagonistic acts, such as arresting Copeyanos for distributing party literature.[31] For its part, the newspaper of AD, *El País*, accused COPEI of preparing a civil war with the forces of López Contreras.[32] Accusations were traded back and forth. A few months later the COPEI newspaper accused AD of making a pact with the communists. According to the Copeyanos, the two had joined forces to attack COPEI; an example of this collusion was their support of Decree 321 of the revolutionary junta, which strengthened the government's control over the church and religious teaching. In effect, they were sowing the seeds of anticlerical discord in their effort to close the Catholic colleges. Such were the tactics of the "ADECOMUNISTAS."[33] The Táchira Copeyanos also linked the communists with AD: "We refer to people of the Communist party called Acción Democrática."[34]

Decree 321, published on 30 May 1946, was intended to reform the examination system. Instead of basing students' grades on yearly examinations, work through the year would also be taken into account. The decree distinguished between examinations in public and private schools and outlined complex rules for each, specifying who could be excused from examinations, explaining how to average work to obtain a final grade, breaking down private institutions into Type 1 and Type 2 (depending upon the percentage of courses taught by instructors and professors), and so forth. The apparent intent of the decree was to reform the examination system while imposing stricter control over private schools. Although Betancourt subsequently suspended the application of Decree 321 and replaced it with a new decree, the damage had been done.

COPEI's leaders decided to call a mass meeting in the Nuevo Circo, one of the well-known buildings in central Caracas. Major events such as circuses, rallies, and the like had been held in this building. The meeting took place on 18 June 1946,[35] but bedlam broke out shortly after it began. In the fighting and shooting, several people were wounded and two were killed. COPEI issued a statement accusing AD and the Communist party of breaking up the meeting. Afterward, those who sympathized with COPEI passed resolutions and petitions. A group of women publicly repudiated the Revolutionary

Junta of Government for not creating a favorable climate for the electoral process.[36]

The tense political climate was not limited to the Caracas area. In the first edition of their newspaper, the Copeyanos of Lara complained that the government had jailed nine party members.[37] The Táchira Copeyanos were also very critical of AD, the government, and what they considered to be the rise of communism in the country.[38]

In June 1947 the party newspaper *COPEI* was replaced by *El Gráfico*, founded and at first directed by Miguel Angel Landáez. The newspaper continued the general line of its predecessor in its strong criticism of AD and the government. For the first several years of the newspaper's existence, a barrage of criticism was directed against Decree 321. The paper strongly supported striking students who opposed that decree and the allegedly inferior position of private schools.

During an attempted coup d'état in 1947 (numerous attempted coups occurred between 1945-48), COPEI assumed a public position opposing that effort and supporting the government. The party's representatives in the National Constitutional Assembly issued a resolution to this effect: "The national evolution, to which we aspire, will not succeed with a succession of coups d'état, which, besides altering economic and social life profoundly, discredits us before world opinion and sows desperation in the hearts of Venezuelans, and weakens confidence in the capacity of democracy to solve peacefully the political problems of Venezuela."[39] This support for the government, however, proved only a brief respite; the party newspaper soon continued its harsh criticisms.

Toward the end of 1947, *El Gráfico* ran a series of articles by Luis Herrera Campins explaining COPEI's position and the broader question of the party's opposition to AD.[40] Herrera Campins began the series by stating that no one doubted the sincerity of Rómulo Gallegos (the AD presidential candidate), but no one believed in the sincerity of AD, either. He went on to charge the governing party with many acts of violence, including the persecution of priests. Not only was COPEI against the violence of AD, he said, but it was also active in the ideological struggle between Marxism and Social Catholicism: "The destiny of COPEI will assure the struggle against Marxism."

The Copeyanos were somewhat cautious in criticizing President Rómulo Gallegos, perhaps recognizing his prestige as one of the country's best-known authors. However, their criticisms did indicate that he was controlled by the "sinister" forces of AD and Rómulo Betancourt. It was also suggested that the president was timid in allowing the persecution and agitation of AD to continue. Caldera, addressing himself to this point in a speech to the Chamber of Deputies, stated that the president must assert himself with a strong hand in order to stop the abuses in the country.[41]

On 21 November 1948, *El Gráfico* announced that President Gallegos had suspended constitutional guarantees. The party newspaper, along with other periodicals, was closed and did not publish for several days, 22-25 November. On 24 November the Gallegos government was overthrown by a coup d'état.[42]

Perhaps the military intervention was inevitable. The period was one of intense ferment, with the regime facing periodic threats and unsuccessful conspiracies, and many military leaders were probably concerned with the deteriorating condition of "law and order." For approximately ten days before the coup, intense negotiations had taken place between the military and the government. President Gallegos rejected the military's final demands: inclusion of more officers in the cabinet, ministerial representation for COPEI, sending Rómulo Betancourt into exile. It was interesting that the military might have felt more secure with COPEI, on the surface at least, as part of the government. It might also be argued, however, that the military leaders had reached the point of no return, and that they presented to the government demands which they knew would be rejected.

The COPEI party newspaper continued to be critical of AD and its former government. When it resumed publication, *El Gráfico* left no doubt about the COPEI position on recent political developments: AD had caused the coup. In a press conference Caldera stated that "the delicate situation developed through recent events was the undoubtable consequence of the accumulation of errors and injustices committed by Acción Democrática in its three years of government."

Shortly after the coup, COPEI published an official position paper[43] listing various criticisms of the AD governments, the revolutionary junta, and the Gallegos administration. They attacked the sectarian policy fomented by one group; according to COPEI, this resulted in an arbitrary system of government, exemplified by the violation of their dictated constitution almost at the moment of its birth. It was very dangerous, furthermore, to maintain an irregular armed militia of partisans to supplant the army.

COPEI also criticized AD for building a climate of hate which divided the people, asserting that this clearly reflected the communist origins of AD's leaders. As a result, the administration of justice became a partisan instrument, and opposition leaders were assassinated. Rómulo Gallegos might be an honorable man, but he could not control the violations of his party. AD, then, lost the support of the people, opening the road to a military takeover.

I had the opportunity to speak to several Copeyanos, Adecos, and independents who were in the country at the time. COPEI's political opponents felt that COPEI was much more conservative during 1945-48 than it is now. According to one, the party supported Franco and the extension of his influence in Venezuela; thus we can understand the COPEI label "fascist." And there was no doubt that the party played a role in the overthrow of the Gallegos government.[44] This interview brought out two major elements in the AD-COPEI relationship: the supposed conservatism of COPEI as it affected that relationship, and the party's role, if any, in the 1948 coup d'état. As far as the question of conservatism is concerned, the party *can* be viewed as conservative in its early years of development, COPEI protests to the contrary. The party leaders who denied this cited the Social Christian doctrine, but of perhaps greater significance were the groups and individuals who comprised the party: "As the government tended to become an exclusive AD preserve, COPEI began to absorb landowner and church elements, thus becoming increasingly rightist in character and increasingly antagonistic towards the regime."[45] And, as we have mentioned, many people looked to COPEI as the defender of the church, which helps explain the political significance of the revolutionary junta's Decree 321. Those who were violently opposed to what they considered to be constitutional restrictions on the church supported COPEI. They were not necessarily Copeyanos, and many of them left the party after a short time. But this situation resulted in a polarization of political forces, and in the irreconcilable perceptions of COPEI and AD at the "fascist-communist" poles.[46]

There was a difference of opinion concerning COPEI's role in the 1948 coup, even among the Adecos. One military officer stated that several groups cooperated with the military in the coup: URD, some Copeyanos, and big business interests.[47] However, a well-known Adeco felt that COPEI might have cooperated with the military, but that there was no proof.[48] Another well-known political figure, a former Adeco who was a leader of MEP, believed that COPEI had an indirect role in the coup. By their harsh criticism of AD and the Gallegos government, the Copeyanos helped create an environment for it. One cartoon in *El Gráfico* had even depicted people waiting for the *mango* (the AD government) to fall.[49]

Referring to the COPEI position, Miguel Angel Landáez emphasized what he believed to be the excesses of AD as the major factor in the tense relationship between the two parties. Given this political reality, the COPEI opposition was firm but not conspiratorial. Although COPEI did not work toward a coup, its opposition did contribute to the general environment which led to the military takeover in 1948.[50]

While we can safely assume that both AD and COPEI contributed to the tense environment, it is difficult to say which party struck the first blow. Perhaps the Revolution of 1945 itself, and the political immaturity of the recently formed parties, made a clash between AD and COPEI inevitable. The more conservative elements of COPEI, committed militants or those "passing through," felt threatened by the AD reforms. They saw no role for themselves, with the political base of the ruling party now residing in the middle and lower classes, rather than in the elite. They believed the government was leading the country down the road to communism.

Differing attitudes toward religion and the church also contributed to the AD-COPEI confrontation. According to the Copeyanos, AD was persecuting the church—but the Adecos saw COPEI as representatives of the Vatican and the church's most conservative thinking. The relationship deteriorated to a Christ versus anti-Christ polarization. Consider the words of Rafael Caldera in 1946; after criticizing AD and the infamous Decree 321, he concluded with the following: "It is not only for Catholicism, but for the well-being and progress of our country as well that we desire the triumph of our ideas. For throughout the world Catholics are making clear that no one loves his country more nor serves it better than he who bears Christ in his heart."[51]

Other factors, aside from party rivalry, were particularly significant in causing the overthrow of the government.[52] The former followers of López Contreras and Medina Angarita opposed the regime; foreign economic interests felt threatened; the church, landowners, industrialists, manufacturers, and petroleum firms all had specific grievances. The attitude of the military was crucial, because officers were concerned about AD's efforts to proselytize within the armed forces. Added to these factors was the perennial plotting of Pérez Jiménez.

The fact that COPEI perhaps played a marginal role in the overthrow of the government did not alleviate the AD-COPEI animosity. The Adecos were particularly incensed when they observed what they believed to be COPEI cooperation with the government during the early years of the military dictatorship.

Military Dictatorship, 1948-1952

The military dictatorship lasted until 1958. For the purpose of analysis, however, I have chosen to divide this period into two sections. During the first, 1948-52, COPEI continued to exist as a political party. One major figure of the military junta was assassinated, and Marcos Pérez Jiménez made his bid for undisputed power. During the second part, 1952-58, the Copeyanos were in exile or in prison, and Pérez Jiménez led the country.

In his book, Rodolfo José Cárdenas explained the three alternatives which faced COPEI at the beginning of the new government.[53] The right wing, led by such people as Gómez Mora and Barrios Mora, wanted the party to incorporate itself into the new military government. This group left the party when the majority would not support its position, and, according to Cárdenas, became COPEI's worst enemies. A second group called for total and immediate opposition to the government; its supporters included university students, labor leaders, and those who had founded the Juventud Revolucionaria Copeyana in 1947.

As an official position, the party adopted the suggestion of a third group. This policy, which they referred to as "dynamic prudence" (to be "expectative and vigilant"), lasted from 1948 to 1950. Its supporters included Pedro Del Corral, Rafael Caldera, Lorenzo Fernández, Pérez Díaz, Edecio La Riva, Miguel Angel Landáez, and Víctor Giménez Landínez. Their idea was to move the party, imperceptibly, from a position of neutrality to one of opposition. A gradual approach was necessary, according to Cárdenas, because the Andean supporters of COPEI, who were strongly anti-AD, would find it difficult to understand a policy of strong opposition to a government which had just overthrown the Adecos. Admittedly this would be a difficult period for the party, but a patient strategy would prove beneficial in the long run.

However, as later events showed, the strategy wasn't worth much. Along with the communists, URD, and AD, COPEI was destined to experience persecution. It appeared that the policy of "dynamic prudence," at least from the time of the coup until 1950, resulted in the party's collaboration with the government. Several Copeyanos were appointed governors and judges, and the party refrained from criticizing the government for a time. Although COPEI was treated less severely than other political parties, it was not long before it began to criticize developments within the country. *El Gráfico* was suspended several times, and the party strongly protested the detention of Luis Herrera Campins for having written articles critical of the administration.[54]

Such developments caused the party to convey an official communication of protest. The document quoted a section of a telegram sent by the government to the party, citing reasons for the arrest of Herrera Campins: "the newspaper . . . reached the extreme in publishing notes of a political character written by Herrera Campins, constituting disrespect to the authorities and prone to sow alarm with the general public." It was signed by Doctor Miguel Moreno, secretary of the military junta.[55] Caldera went to Miraflores to talk with Colonel Delgado Chalbaud, head of the junta; Miguel Angel Landáez, director of *El Gráfico*, spoke with Manuel Vicente Tinoco, chief of the censor office. Herrera Campins was released shortly thereafter.

In its communication, the party criticized government restrictions, pointing out that these were increasing each day. The authors particularly complained about the government's interference in party activities. The police detained several Copeyanos, such as Delgado Emán, secretary-general of COPEI in Yaracuy, for "lack of respect"; they also detained Jorge Saad, president of municipal administration and president of COPEI in the Nirgua district. In addition, the police closed the party headquarters in that district. The communication urged the government not to obstruct the COPEI efforts to influence the many people who considered themselves to be Adecos. COPEI pointed out that both it and the government would benefit from the

former's opposition to Adeco Marxism, for such Marxism could return through governmental repression: "We must struggle against
international Bolshevism; governmental detention of Copeyanos
causes jubilation in Adeco-communist ranks." Among the communication's signatories were Pedro Del Corral, president; Rafael
Caldera, secretary-general; and Lorenzo Fernández, deputy secretary-
general.

The Copeyanos became quite concerned that the junta might not
return power to civilian elements. In a series of articles entitled
"Consignas," Caldera cautioned the military government to become
not a political force, but a guarantor of order. It should prepare for
the return of the institutional life of normality. Freedom of the press
should be restored as soon as possible, because it was important to
hear various views.[56]

COPEI continued to work on party organization and development
during this period. In Táchira, for example, a party document indicated the intensive work of the local organization on various levels:
the parliamentary wing, the FFC (Frente Feminino Copeyano), the
JRC (Juventud Revolucionária Copeyana), the FTC (Frente de Trabajadores Copeyanos).[57] The party also reported an improved financial
position. As far as its attitude toward the government was concerned,
the regional organization would faithfully follow the instructions of
the National Committee, collaborating with the government and not
allowing any differences to favor the "Marxist" URD in the state. The
document concluded by announcing that regional conventions had
taken place in Lara, Barinas, Trujillo, Mérida, Falcón, Zulia, and
Táchira.

The Copeyanos continued to carry out party activities as best they
could. A party convention of the Federal District took place in the
spring of 1950 to choose delegates to the Fourth National Convention.[58] The party also attempted to expand its activities in the Andean
states. A radio program, "Radioperiódico Venezuela," discussed Copeyano activities in Trujillo, Mérida, and Táchira. The programs included talks of party leaders such as Caldera and Herrera Campins.[59]

Government persecution continued to increase, particularly after
the assassination of Delgado Chalbaud in 1950. On 24 October 1951,
several professors at the Universidad Central de Venezuela wrote to
the government protesting a decree which allegedly violated university autonomy.[60] Their document also listed pressures which were
directed toward Caldera: the police frequently went to his office; he
was sent to prison at the Cárcel del Obispo; after leaving prison, he
was kept under permanent surveillance; several attempts were made
to bomb his home. Those who signed the document included Rafael
Caldera, Edgar Sanabría, René de Sola, and Juan Quintana Archila.
Caldera also made a speech to an assembly of law professors who had
decided not to attend classes because of government interference in
the UCV. This led to the publication of a second document.

The Election of 1952

After the assassination of Delgado Chalbaud, the junta decided to promulgate an electoral statute and hold an election for a Constituent Assembly. The government passed a restrictive political party act in conjunction with the electoral law, and the two leading parties not banished, COPEI and URD, were forced to campaign under very difficult conditions.[61] Prior to the election, COPEI issued a position paper on the situation within the country.[62] (The document appeared in the form of a long letter from the party's National Committee to the governing junta.)

Persecution of Copeyanos continued as the election appproached. The minister of the interior again ordered the detention of Luis Herrera Campins, who was subsequently expelled from the country. The police detained various members of the party's regional directorate in Táchira. COPEI of Táchira protested in a letter directed to the president of the junta, but the censor refused to allow the letter to be published.[63] Given the political climate, many of the party's faithful questioned the wisdom of participating in the elections. The party leadership, however, insisted upon such participation; to support its position, it published an extensive document two months before the elections.[64]

The junta organized several groups into a pro-government Frente Electoral Independiente (FEI), the third party in the campaign. AD was not allowed to participate in the election; however, it appeared that the AD underground, led by Alberto Carnevali and with the concurrence of Rómulo Betancourt, secretly urged AD supporters to vote for URD. The election was held on 30 November 1952. The next day the Supreme Electoral Council published preliminary figures, based on approximately one-third of the votes; URD led the FEI by almost 150,000 votes, while COPEI was far behind. Later returns showed the FEI badly trailing URD, and the government then suspended all election news coverage. Pérez Jiménez subsequently announced that the junta had resigned and handed over power to the armed forces, which then designated him interim president. On 13 December the government published the electoral results given in Table 2.6.

T A B L E 2.6. Results of 30 November 1952 Election

Government	
FEI	788,031
Grupo de Iván Rodríguez (Falcón)	12,125
Opposition	
URD	638,336
COPEI	300,359
Other sectors	48,358

COPEI figures, however, placed the government party and supporters in third place: URD (with support of the illegal parties), 1,190,000; COPEI (with their own lists and without agreements), 500,000; FEI and other governmental groups, 190,000.[65]

Aftermath of the Election

During the following year (1953), COPEI continued to issue publications and engage in party activities, although severely limited by the government. One of these documents analyzed the 1952 election. Written by Pedro Pablo Aguilar in his capacity as the party's regional secretary of organization for the Federal District,[66] it offered some frank self-criticism of COPEI's electoral efforts there. COPEI also published an official position paper explaining the party's refusal to attend the Constituent Assembly.[67]

Although COPEI and URD decided to boycott the Constituent Assembly, some delegates of both parties did attend the sessions. The Assembly, controlled by the government, promulgated a new constitution which was acceptable to the military; it elected Colonel Marcos Pérez Jiménez constitutional president for a five-year term beginning 17 April 1953.

The party leaders followed through with their threat to expel members who attended the Constituent Assembly.[68] Juan Blanco Peñalver was an elected alternate from the state of Aragua; when he joined the Assembly on 9 January 1953, the party's regional committee issued a public statement expelling him. This act provoked the police to detain some Copeyanos who refused to attend the Assembly, such as Godofredo González and Armando Nieto Ontiveros. Some Copeyano delegates did not wait for the party to expel them: Francisco Peña Blanco, *hijo*, who had been elected to the Assembly on the COPEI *plancha* (list), renounced the party and became a supporter of Pérez Jiménez.[69]

In light of the 1952 election and the official party position advocating the boycott of the Constituent Assembly, it became increasingly difficult for COPEI to continue its activities as a legal political party. It was able to publish only a few more documents before its leaders were sent into exile or to prison. One of these documents was a discourse by Caldera to the party's regional convention in the Federal District.[70] Caldera complained about the censorship in the country. For example, there was nothing in the newspapers about the COPEI convention in the Federal District; the press even refused to publish a notice to the party militants to attend the convention. The print media did announce that one party leader, Godofredo González, was expelled from COPEI, but the party was not allowed to publish the fact that this was not true. Caldera complained about other government abuses but concluded that, in spite of these transgressions, it was the first duty of all Copeyanos to preserve the party: "its reality, its organization, its moral force."

It finally appeared that the government was encouraging the development of a sympathetic faction within COPEI to compete with the official party leaders and their colleagues. This situation was of such great concern to the party leaders that they felt compelled to issue a clarification, one of the last documents published by COPEI during this period.[71] All political activity was outlawed shortly thereafter. Although COPEI was never declared illegal by the government, as AD, the URD, and the Communist party had been, it became impossible for the party to carry out its normal activities. Those COPEI leaders who were not already in prison went into exile. Caldera lived in Caracas for several years under the wary eye of the police. Eventually he was confined, and finally forced to leave the country.

An Overview of the Period

In *Latin American Christian Democratic Parties*, Edward J. Williams has made the following observation:

> Perhaps Venezuela provides the most striking historical example of military support of a Social Christian party. During the short-lived democratic experiment between 1945 and 1948, the military showed a marked preference for the COPEI party over Betancourt's Acción Democrática. They sought COPEI participation in the government and, after the military coup in 1948, COPEI was permitted to continue functioning. It is true, of course, that this incipient cooperation soon ended because of COPEI's rejection of the brutal military dictatorship. . . .[72]

In attempting to explain the possible reasons for the military attitude toward COPEI, Williams pointed out that the military felt safer with a party more conservative and Catholic than with the other two major political forces, AD and URD. He also observed the interesting similarity between COPEI and the military in their socioeconomic and geographic areas of recruitment and strength. Both were based on the Andean states; indeed, we have already remarked on the strength of the church and COPEI's electoral successes in this area. Writing in 1964, another observer noted that perhaps 90 percent of the country's officers had likewise come from the Andean states.[73]

When the junta was under the leadership of Delgado Chalbaud (1948-50), COPEI cooperated but also felt free to criticize those government actions which the party could not accept. It was the view of one military officer, active during this period, that the Delgado Chalbaud government was working to return the country to democracy.[74] If this was indeed the case (although it would be difficult to document), perhaps this influenced COPEI's political leaders to cooperate.

The government sought the counsel of the party from time to time; however, according to a Copeyano, this cooperation was not an official party position, and individuals cooperated with the government at their own choosing.[75]

After Delgado Chalbaud's death in 1950, the party's opposition to the government became more pronounced. Was this a preconceived plan to move from a position of "neutrality to one of opposition," as Rodolfo José Cárdenas stated in his book? Or did the party take this position as a result of the change of Venezuelan leadership from Delgado Chalbaud to Pérez Jímenez? I am inclined toward the latter view. As one Copeyano observed, repression became more obvious after Delgado Chalbaud's assassination, and the party had no choice but to move into opposition.[76] Furthermore, people were expelled from COPEI for cooperating with the government in the second period of the dictatorship (1952-58), but not in the first (1948-50).[77] However, we should also add that the apparent rigged election for the Constituent Assembly took place in 1952, during the second period of the dictatorship.

COPEI assumed the position of an opposition party during the 1952 campaign. After the election the government refused to meet the party's demands, and party leaders instructed their elected representatives not to attend the Constituent Assembly. Discipline had to be imposed at this point, to convince some recalcitrant militants that cooperation was no longer advantageous to the party—or, perhaps, to the country. This was a difficult period as far as party unity was concerned; several Copeyanos were expelled or departed of their own accord.

A dramatic event occurred following the 1952 election, and only the influence of Rafael Caldera prevented a serious split in one crucial state. Shortly after the election, Caldera and Víctor Giménez Landínez traveled to Mérida to attend the party's regional convention.[78] The major question during the convention was whether or not Copeyanos should attend the National Constituent Assembly. They arrived about 10:00 A.M., and Caldera continued talking to everyone until 6:00 P.M. There was no doubt that Caldera dominated the convention, and all but three local party members agreed with his position. The latter were expelled.

Within a year after the 1952 election, most party leaders were imprisoned or in exile. This did not mean, however, that their activities stopped. On the contrary—whether in prison or in foreign countries, they studied, they resisted, and they prepared.

CHAPTER 3

From Exile and Prison to
Political Democracy

THE COPEYANOS conceded that Acción Democrática offered the major resistance to the Pérez Jiménez dictatorship. Nevertheless, available information allows us to identify examples of Copeyano resistance as well. Some of these efforts occurred within Venezuela, while members in exile carried on other activities. Between 1952 and 1958, individual party members studied and debated ideological questions, and the party shifted from a conservative to a more moderate and progressive orientation. Let us first turn to the activities of some exiled Copeyanos.

Activities of the Exiles

In July 1953 several Copeyanos met in Santiago, Spain, to form an exile newspaper, TIELA (Triángulo de Información Europa-Las Américas).[1] It was directed primarily by Copeyanos, although several students and European Christian Democrats helped in the effort. A member of Acción Democrática, Humberto Egui, also aided the Copeyanos by hiding the mimeograph machine. However, the work in Spain became too dangerous, and TIELA was moved to Rome under the direction of Herrera Campins with the collaboration of Guido Díaz Peña.

Various issues of the newspaper criticized the repression of the Pérez Jímenez dictatorship, discussed questions of ideology, and provided information concerning events in Venezuela. This was important because of the strict press censorship at home during the period. One issue explained the tacit understanding between the opposition parties in their struggle against the government; it also announced the arrest of Rafael Caldera.[2] Smuggled into Venezuela and distributed rather widely, TIELA became a major focal point in the resistance efforts of the dispersed Copeyanos.

The exiles also attended international congresses of the worldwide Christian Democratic movement. The first International Christian Democratic Congress to be held in Latin America took place in Santiago, Chile, in 1955. Several Copeyanos also attended the World Conference of Christian Democratic Parties in Paris in 1956.[3] At the Paris conference, Herrera Campins met Eduardo Frei Montalva of Chile for the first time. These meetings proved to be very important for the Copeyanos because they were influenced by the general leftist trend in Latin American Christian Democratic thought, particularly as it had been developing in Chile on such matters as more extensive land reform, national control of industry, and the need to develop a foreign policy more independent of the United States. In addition, they had an opportunity to share their ideas with others who might translate the doctrines of Catholic social thought into political action.

Activities within Venezuela

From 1953 to 1958, the government declared all opposition political activities illegal. Nevertheless, some Copeyanos continued to be politically active through various organizations.[4]

Trade Union Movement

Although operating under severe restrictions, several individuals remained active in labor circles. These included the Copeyano Enrique Aristeiguieta, and Arístides Calvani, a Copeyano sympathizer at the time. Some labor leaders attended the study circles conducted by Padre Manuel Aguirre. The Frente de Trabajadores Copeyanos maintained a small "central labor body" directed by COPEI, and the party controlled some unions throughout the dictatorship.

Liceos (Secondary Schools)

One party militant who was actively engaged in the resistance believed that the most intense opposition to the government took place in the secondary schools, rather than in the universities.[5] More frequent strikes and greater individual efforts occurred at this level. Students of all political beliefs cooperated in the resistance: present and future Copeyanos, Adecos, Urredistas, and communists.

Comité Estudiantil de Resistencia or Frente Universitaria

This group of students, who operated on the university level, engaged in strikes and acts of violence to overthrow the government. They formed a committee which represented the four major political parties: COPEI, AD, URD, and the Communist party. The Copeyanos in the group included Hilarión Cardozo, Pedro Pablo Aguilar, Gonzalo García Bustillos, José Luis Zapata (before his exile), Horacio Moros, and José de la Cruz Fuentes. The students led two major strikes, one in 1952, which resulted in the closing of the Central University, and another on 21 November 1956.[6]

Venezuela Universitaria

The university students who comprised this group were more concerned with discussing policies of the government, occasionally through invited speakers, than with direct confrontation through strikes. Enrique Pérez Olivares helped organize the group, which did not become active until 1957. Its activity increased toward the end of the dictatorship, when the young people who joined the party that year, the Generation of 1958, took over the direction of Venezuela Universitaria.

The Copeyanos would take advantage of any event or activity to talk about politics and plan their next moves. The wedding of Pérez Olivares, for example, turned into a conspiratorial meeting.

There are differences of opinion concerning the extent and intensity of COPEI resistance during the dictatorship. The party's political opponents believed that COPEI limited its activities primarily to the Caracas area. Paz Galarraga, for example, stated that while he was in prison in the state of Zulia for six and a half years, he never heard of COPEI resistance in that part of the country. Raúl Leoni mentioned AD's contacts with URD and the Communist party during the resistance, but AD-COPEI contacts did not take place at least until 1955 and probably later.[7] However, Copeyanos such as José Luis Zapata believed COPEI's resistance spread throughout most of the country.

We can point to the party's activities in some states of the interior. COPEI had been the first political force in Táchira, and, according to one observer, the party led the resistance in that state.[8] When party members took to the streets, several, such as Edilberto Escalante, ended up in prison. The party also penetrated the labor movement and began a peasant organization to struggle against the dictatorship. In Mérida, Copeyano resistance did not meet the government forces head on, but there was defiance nevertheless. Party members met in homes and criticized the administration; seven Copeyano professors refused to sign a document in support of the government.[9]

COPEI was not very active in Lara, which permitted AD to assume leadership of the resistance.[10] The Adecos, with 80 percent of the vote in the 1948 election, comprised the principal political force in the state. Although the nucleus of a COPEI organization continued to exist, and the militants paid their dues, many Lara Copeyanos lived in Caracas.

Contrary to the view of Paz Galarraga, the COPEI secretary-general of Zulia believed the Copeyanos offered some resistance there, although it certainly was not systematic or organized.[11] Some individuals, such as Landrade Labarca and Esteva Ríos, did actually oppose the government. In 1957 a group of young people who eventually joined COPEI were led by some Jesuits as they engaged in propaganda against the government; the group's members included Manuel

Guanipa Matos and José Rodríguez Iturbe. However, none of these activities could be classified as violent resistance.

In summary, then, various Copeyanos did resist the Pérez Jiménez dictatorship. This was primarily an individual or group effort, rather than a conscious party policy. The resistance was not organized, and, to use the word of one Copeyano who was involved in student activities during the period, the party's attitude seemed to be one of passive resistance, at least during the first years of Pérez Jiménez's rule. COPEI did not turn to active resistance until 1956-57, with the jailing of Caldera and the cancellation of promised elections.[12]

Experience in Prison

Many party members served prison terms during this period, some for several years. In early 1953 the government cut off COPEI from all means of publicity—press, radio, public meetings—and then placed the National Directory and several state executives in prison.[13] Caldera returned to the university to assume his position as professor of sociology, but, as mentioned earlier, he spent two periods in prison prior to his 1957 exile.

Pedro Grases, an author, active Copeyano for many years, and long-time associate of Caldera, believed that imprisonment was of great importance to some party militants. Many party leaders developed intellectually, returning to civilian life with tremendous motivation and a special approach to politics and revolutionary change. According to Grases, the present COPEI youth has not had this experience, although they talk of revolution.[14]

Rodolfo José Cárdenas is a veteran of the Pérez Jiménez prisons. In 1953 he was incarcerated for eight months. According to Cárdenas, many young Copeyanos never studied before they went to prison. Besides broadening their intellectual horizons, they also developed a strong sense of unity and mutual respect.[15]

How did they spend their long periods of time in prison? What effect did the experience have on their intellectual and political development? Valmore Acevedo Amaya spent two periods in prison: 1952 in Caracas, and 1955-56 in the interior.[16] During the former he was joined by Rodolfo Cárdenas and Horacio Moros; José Luis Zapata and Luis Herrera Campins came somewhat later. The prisoners arranged their time as if they were in a university, with classes, conferences, and lectures for three hours a day. These sessions were frequently conducted like seminars. The party members also had the opportunity to read a great deal, and they became well versed in the works of such writers as St. Thomas Aquinas and Jacques Maritain. Because political prisoners were not separated, the Copeyanos and future members of the party struck up friendships with imprisoned members of the Communist party and Acción Democrática. The Copeyanos and Adecos had many conversations, and these led to identification of shared interests against the dictatorship and political cooperation in the post-dictatorial period.

The Beginnings of an Ideological Shift

Several factors combined to produce a shift in the thinking of COPEI's leaders and future leaders. We have already mentioned the interaction of the exiles with Christian Democratic leaders of other countries through international conferences. Another significant factor was the change in the government produced by the rise of Pérez Jiménez. When he solidified his control after the 1952 election, the COPEI leadership decided to go into opposition. Many of the more conservative elements of the party, who had joined in the late 1940s "to oppose communism and defend the church," left, either to work with the government or to return to their nonpolitical pursuits. These more conservative elements therefore became less influential in the orientation and decision-making of the party. The experience in prison constitutes a third factor. The young party militants grew intellectually; they broadened their minds to consider opposing ideas. They also began to appreciate the advantages of cooperation with other political parties—a tactic which they had rejected earlier, except when expedience required forming pacts with local political groups for electoral purposes. If they were to cooperate with other political parties toward larger ends, compromise would be necessary; a rigid ideological position would no longer be possible. Changes within the Roman Catholic church were also a factor, as the more conservative influence of Pope Pius XII was replaced by the comparatively liberal views of Pope John XXIII. His thinking affected the Christian Democratic parties of Europe, as well as those of Latin America.

Perhaps this period produced a shift in emphasis, rather than an ideological shift per se. Christian Democratic ideology remained, as it had through the years, but COPEI began to emphasize its more positive aspects. Party leaders began to place greater importance on the health of the country's political institutions, rather than on the anticommunist struggle and defense of the church. For without political democracy, there was no COPEI.

The exiled AD leadership held several meetings which led to a change in AD's attitude toward other parties. Betancourt urged his followers to deemphasize AD's leftist and sectarian nature, a change which would be essential if cooperation with COPEI and URD was to become a reality. Thus a new orientation of both AD and COPEI was necessary to provide the linkage with coalition politics of the post-dictatorial period.

Movement to Overthrow the Government

Acción Democrática provided the major resistance to the dictatorship during 1952-58, although COPEI participated to a lesser degree. In a sense, the same could be said for the period 1957–January 1958, which resulted in the government's fall. Civilian elements, allied with younger military officers, played the most significant role; nevertheless, some Copeyanos did participate. Within Venezuela and outside the prisons, AD had contacts with the Communist party and URD in the resistance.[17] There were also AD-COPEI contacts in the unions and among students.

In Europe, the first official contact between AD and COPEI occurred in 1955, in Italy, between two political exiles: the Adeco Jaime Lusinchi and the Copeyano Luis Herrera Campins.[18] Other contacts occurred between Adecos and Copeyanos during the next two years. On an intermediate leadership level, the Generation of 1945 (those who had entered the Christian Democratic movement just prior to COPEI's formation) began to meet with leaders of AD and other political parties in Europe and, subsequently, in Venezuela. Pérez Olivares, for example, met with Jóvito Villalba in New York.[19] These meetings led to an agreement between the leadership of the major political parties shortly before the overthrow of the government.

Huntington's analysis can be applied to the AD-COPEI relationship at this point:

> For attitudes must be reflected in behavior and community involves not just any "coming together" but rather a regularized, stable, and sustained coming together. The coming together must, in short, be institutionalized. And the creation of political institutions involving and reflecting the moral consensus and mutual interest is, consequently . . . necessary for the maintenance of community in a complex society. Such institutions in turn give new meaning to the common purpose and create new linkages between the particular interests of individuals and groups.[20]

The development of such a political community between AD and COPEI began with preliminary contacts in Europe. While common opposition to the dictatorship brought the leaders of the two parties together, mutual perceptions would also have to change if the parties were to have a sustained, mutually beneficial political relationship. No longer could AD see COPEI as the "fascist, reactionary defender of the church"; no longer could COPEI equate AD with communism. These perceptions began to change during the dictatorial period of prison and exile, and the new relationship was tested and strengthened in the immediate post-dictatorial period. This, in turn, would provide the linkage to institutional political democracy.

Shortly after Pérez Jiménez assumed control of the country, it became apparent that many were discontented with his regime.[21] Opposition developed among most sectors of the civilian society: organized labor, urban slum dwellers,[22] the rural element, the business sector, the Roman Catholic church, students and intellectuals. A series of events, several of which involved Copeyanos, led to the government's fall. Perhaps it was Monsignor Rafael Arias Blanco, Archbishop of Caracas, who struck the first blow. His pastoral letter of 1 May 1957 was highly critical of Venezuelan socioeconomic conditions; he listed the serious problems of the working class and described the wretched conditions in the *barrios*. His letter was read in churches throughout the country, leading to government repression of the church.[23]

Shortly thereafter, in June, representatives of AD, COPEI, URD, and the Communist party met and formed the Junta Patriótica (Patriotic Junta). That clandestine civilian organization agreed to overthrow the government by whatever means necessary. Arms were smuggled into the country and distributed to junta supporters. The organization succeeded in attracting representatives of other groups, such as business, labor, students, and clergy; it issued anti-government propaganda[24] and was a generally effective focal point for the opposition.

Through the rest of 1957 pressure on the government continued to build. The term of Pérez Jiménez was to expire in April 1958; according to the 1953 constitution, elections were scheduled for December 1957. Instead, the government announced that a plebiscite would take place. Pérez Jiménez would be the only candidate, and the electorate could indicate approval or disapproval of him for another five-year term. At this time a pamphlet entitled *Frente a 1958* was circulated. Written by the Copeyano Luis Herrera Campins, it pointed out that the idea of a plebiscite violated the dictatorship's constitution, which called for periodic presidential elections. Herrera Campins urged that an election take place. The government should present its candidate, and the united opposition would present Rafael Caldera.[25] The pamphlet made the government very wary of Caldera and his presence in the country; shortly before the plebiscite took place, he was jailed and exiled.

The government had good cause for concern about Caldera's possible candidacy, for AD had considered supporting him in a presidential election.[26] Indeed, when Caldera arrived in New York, several Adeco leaders were at the airport to greet him. In December, Caldera, Rómulo Betancourt, and Jóvito Villalba met in New York to coordinate their efforts.

The plebiscite took place in Venezuela on 15 December 1957. The government announced the following results:[27] Affirmative, 2,374,-790; Negative, 364,182; Invalid, 186,013. The Junta Patriótica issued several communiqués declaring the results of the plebiscite a fraud. Two weeks later, a revolt by the air force and some army units almost succeeded in overthrowing the government.

The exiled political leaders decided to include the Communist party in their plans. In December they announced that a committee had been formed in Mexico to struggle against the Pérez Jiménez dictatorship;[28] the members were Caldera, Betancourt, Villalba, and Gustavo Machado of the Communist party. The committee's stated purpose was to coordinate political action of the four parties. AD held its presidency, and COPEI the vice-presidency; the Communists agreed not to be in the directive group, "so as not to arouse the suspicions of the anti-Marxists."

The government was overthrown on 23 January 1958, in events which have been described in various works.[29] Several Copeyanos were involved, although the major leaders were either in exile or in prison at the time.

Filling the Political Void

The first attempt to establish a junta failed because of protests against some of its members. On 25 January a civilian-military Junta de Gobierno was established under the provisional presidency of Rear Admiral Wolfgang Larrazábal. One major function of the junta was to prepare the country for elections later in the year. The Copeyanos supported the junta, and, in spite of an attempted coup by General Castro León, the elections took place on schedule.

Under the provisional government, the trade unionists of the major political parties formed a federation, the National United Trade Union Committee (Comité Sindical Unificado Nacional). The executive committee was divided among the parties: AD, 6; COPEI, 2; URD, 2; PCV, 1; Independents, 1. This development helped COPEI to extend its influence in the labor movement:

> The COPEI trade union group that had existed during the dictatorship was dissolved, and the small unions that had been under the influence of the party merged with those controlled by the other political groups to form *sindicatos únicos*. In elections in these united unions, which were held throughout the year (1958), the four parties with some following in the labor movement—Acción Democrática, COPEI, URD, and the Communists —agreed on slates that were more or less automatically victorious. This represented a net gain for COPEI in the labor movement, since according to the rules followed during this period, all parties were represented on union executive committees and in a very large proportion of the unions COPEI had few if any followers, so it was represented among union leadership far out of proportion to the popular following it then had in the various labor organizations.[30]

The major concern of the most prominent political leaders—Betancourt, Villalba, and Caldera—was to prevent another coup d'état and to insure civilian control of the government. They met in New York after the overthrow of Pérez Jiménez and created the Venezuelan Civilian Front, so named to maximize cooperation between the major political parties. They also agreed to search for a unity candidate whom they could support as president. But when they returned to Caracas (Caldera arrived in February), it proved impossible to agree upon a single candidate. Negotiations continued until a few weeks before the election. The idea of a four-man presidency (of Larrazábal, Betancourt, Caldera, and Jóvito Villalba) was also discussed. In spite of several summer meetings, a few of which the Communists attended, AD, URD, and COPEI chose their own candidates. URD decided to support Wolfgang Larrazábal. Caldera, fearing that the unity of the political parties might dissolve, invited the principal leaders of AD and URD to his residence, Punto Fijo. (The homes in Caracas have names, rather than street numbers.) The meeting produced the Pact of Punto Fijo, 31 October 1958.

In the pact Caldera, Betancourt, and Villalba committed their respective parties to abide by the results of the forthcoming election and to defend the new government against any threats.[31] They also agreed to establish a government of national unity. Each of the three parties would be represented in the cabinet; through this tactic they would be able to avoid "systematic opposition which would weaken the democratic movement." The signatories agreed to a common minimum program, stipulating that no points in the individual party programs would conflict with it. This was spelled out more clearly in a subsequent agreement. The Copeyanos who signed the Pact of Punto Fijo were Caldera, Lorenzo Fernández, and Pedro Del Corral. The subsequent agreement was signed by the three presidential candidates: Caldera (COPEI), Betancourt (AD), and Wolfgang Larrazábal (URD). In it we see the programmatic goals on which the three parties could agree.[32]

In the area of political economy, COPEI representatives found the stipulations consistent with their own ideology. For example, they did not find it difficult to agree that the state should assume a major role for national development. According to the agreement, the state was to stimulate and protect private initiative; specifically, there would be agrarian reform which would "guarantee and stimulate private property to fulfill its economic and social function." Among the other areas of agreement, the three parties supported the idea of a national petroleum organization. They also presented a broad outline of foreign policy: "Establishment of diplomatic and commercial relations with all countries in agreement with the superior exigencies of the national interest."

The agreements were particularly significant in the evolving AD-COPEI relationship. Not only were the two parties able to agree on cooperation and the desirability of a coalition government in the post-dictatorial period, but they were also able to find areas of ideological similarity. Perhaps AD and COPEI had always had areas in which their respective ideologies could be expressed in similar programmatic goals, but the clarification of this fact required conversations among political prisoners and exiles, and a commitment to political democracy under civilian leadership. Adecos and Copeyanos will argue which of their respective parties is right, left, center, or some variation thereof. But as their leaders began to search for areas of agreement, attempting to lessen the friction between them and to strengthen the post-dictatorial underpinnings of political democracy, the areas of ideological coincidence came into sharper focus.

1958 Election

True to its promise, the Junta de Gobierno conducted elections on 7 December 1958 for the presidency, Congress, state legislatures, and municipal councils. Table 3.1 shows the major results.[33]

A comparison of the 1947 and 1958 presidential races for COPEI indicates that the party fared better in 1947 (with 22.4% of the vote) than in 1958 (with 15.17%). The lower percentage occurred almost everywhere, even in Mérida (61.64 versus 53.26%) and Táchira (66.34 versus 52.28%). However, in a few states and territories COPEI strength increased in 1958: Apure, Cojedes, Miranda,

T A B L E 3.1. Results of 7 December 1958 Election

For President	Votes	%
Rómulo Betancourt	1,284,092	49
Wolfgang Larrazábal	800,716	30
Rafael Caldera	396,293	15

For Congress Party	Senate	Chamber of Deputies
AD	32	73
URD	11	34
COPEI	6	19
*Communists	2	7

State Legislative Assemblies	
AD	193
URD	68
COPEI	46
PCV	5

* The Communists supported Larrazábal for president.

Portuguesa, Yaracuy, and the Federal Territories of Amazonas and Delta Amacuro.

There were several reasons for the poorer COPEI electoral showing. The candidacy of Wolfgang Larrazábal, one of the popular heroes in the overthrow of Pérez Jiménez and the president of the Junta de Gobierno, was a major factor. In fact, the popular vice-admiral of the navy also affected AD's electoral strength, which dropped from 75 percent in 1947 to 49 percent in 1958. This was an example of the psychology of *caudillo* politics: people voted for Larrazábal the man, rather than for URD the party.

AD made inroads into COPEI strength in 1958, particularly in Mérida and Táchira. The fact that AD had offered the major resistance and opposition to Pérez Jiménez undoubtedly gave it electoral benefits. Another factor was that the Venezuela of 1958 was different from that of 1947. The electoral census indicated 1,621,687 people in 1947 and 2,913,801 in 1958. The fact that a greater percentage of the voting population was urban was bound to hurt COPEI, whose strength rested primarily upon the rural base of the Andes. If the party was to make a better showing in future elections, it had to extend its influence throughout the country and appeal to the growing urban population.

Coalition Government

In his book on the development of mass political parties, organizations, and the management of conflict in Venezuela, Daniel H. Levine considers the period of the Betancourt administration (1959-64) to be crucial in the stabilization of a party system.[34] Although COPEI and AD had not settled all of their differences, they expressed those conflicts through their respective parties and thereby acknowledged the legitimate bounds of competition and dissent. Yet COPEI went further than merely avoiding violent forms of action against the government: it actually joined in the administration of the country, thereby broadening the base of the government's support. COPEI continued its support even in the face of serious threats to the administration, making it possible for a democratically elected president to finish his term of office and to hand over power to a democratically elected successor (for the first time in the country's history). COPEI made a major contribution to the stabilization of the party system and, consequently, to the strengthening of political democracy.

As Levine points out, COPEI was aided in its efforts for political accommodation by the actions of AD and the church. The issue of the government's attitude toward religion and the Catholic church had been a major point of contention between AD and COPEI during the *trienio* (1945-48). It was apparent that AD had assumed an anticlerical position during its three years of power in the 1940s. However, after the fall of Pérez Jiménez, the Betancourt government "substantially increased the subsidy traditionally paid by the government to the church." This movement toward accommodation was strengthened through decisions taken by the church. The Catholic schools began to participate in the deliberations of teachers' organizations, under the control of AD, which had been anticlerical. The AD leadership now urged the teachers to cooperate with the church. In his inaugural address, Betancourt promised to revise the church-state relationship with a view toward eliminating the subordination of the former to the latter. Although the country permitted civil divorce, the new policy resulted in a *modus vivendi* between the Vatican and Venezuela in 1964.

The role of COPEI was crucial in the growing accommodation between AD and the church. There was also a growing bond in the sense that the two relationships, AD-COPEI and AD-church, mutually affected and reinforced each other. It was in the interest of COPEI to encourage cooperation between AD and the church, because the strengthening of institutional ties would enhance the development of the new political democracy. The Copeyanos often served as mediators in seeking better relations between the other two groups.

On a government level, COPEI received three ministries of fifteen in President Betancourt's first cabinet. The Copeyanos were Lorenzo Fernández, minister of development, and Víctor Giménez Landínez, minister of agriculture; Andrés Aguilar, minister of justice, was a political independent who was close to COPEI. Other Copeyanos replaced their colleagues when the cabinet was reconstituted. Godofredo González became minister of development in 1961, and, a year later, Miguel Angel Landáez became minister of justice. COPEI also held up to six governorships.

AD, COPEI, and URD cooperated in the labor unions and student organizations, agreeing upon the principle of proportional representation and guaranteeing representation for each political party regardless of its strength. From 1960 to 1962, AD-COPEI cooperation in organized labor greatly reduced communist influence there, with the result that the communist-controlled unions left the CTV to form the CUTV.

Without the support of COPEI, it is doubtful that the government could have withstood the onslaught of the left and prevented a coup d'état. The most radical wing of AD was expelled from the party and formed the MIR (Movement of the Revolutionary Left) in 1960. A sizable number of students also left AD to join MIR; in coalition with the communists, they controlled student organizations in the Central University of Venezuela and at other universities. These groups engaged in guerrilla warfare in the early 1960s, and it was not until the 1963 election that the main effort of the guerrillas was blunted.[35]

Levine's assessment of the period, particularly as it affected the AD-COPEI relationship, is very perceptive:

A system of mutual guarantees has been evolved and accepted among major sectors of the society. Mutual confidence was promoted by the decision to form and maintain a coalition government in the 1959 to 1963 period, and was further reinforced by the common threat posed by leftist revolutionary warfare, which drew many old enemies together in common defense. The system of mutual guarantees has permitted the legitimation of conflict between these sectors, with increasing use of common methods and arenas of conflict.[36]

Initial Opposition to the Coalition

Some AD, COPEI, and URD militants opposed the idea of a political coalition. Caldera recognized the problem expressed by some who did not want to strengthen their political adversaries, and he explained that he saw the coalition as operating in a transitory way.[37] Within COPEI the opposition, particularly strong in Táchira, contributed to the tension of the early coalition government. However, at the inception of the Betancourt administration, the top leadership of the three parties cooperated, and in time the problem was overcome.[38] (Under Betancourt the government reduced opposition within the Táchira COPEI by always appointing a Copeyano as governor.) This did not mean that there were no difficulties within the coalition, but at least opposition to the mere idea of political cooperation did not become a major problem.

AD-COPEI Tension

Tension and differences of opinion existed throughout the Betancourt administration; even the secondary leadership periodically expressed dissatisfaction. However, Caldera and Betancourt always managed to carry the day within their respective parties.

On a national level, Raúl Leoni believed that there was some cooperation between AD and COPEI, but that there were very real difficulties. In part this stemmed from what Leoni considered to be the reactionary tradition of COPEI, leading to very clear political, social, economic, and cultural differences. He also pointed out that COPEI resisted certain reforms of the Betancourt administration and even threatened to leave the government if Venezuela established diplomatic relations with the Soviet Union.[39] Prieto Figueroa said there was no doubt that AD had problems with COPEI. He believed this was caused by COPEI resistance to certain reforms, especially efforts to control inflation, and devaluation of the *bolívar* (the monetary unit). According to Prieto, COPEI resisted these reforms because of its association with the oligarchy and big business.[40]

The general Adeco criticism of COPEI—reactionary, associated with big business—was not heard too much during the Betancourt years. Ever since the fall of Pérez Jiménez, it has been common for one to hear and read such accusations around election time. In regard to another subject, however, the Copeyanos were quite explicit: Caldera stated on several occasions that the party would indeed leave the government if AD insisted upon establishing diplomatic relations with the Soviet Union.[41] It is doubtful that Betancourt seriously contemplated renewing such diplomatic relations.

The party newspaper pointed to various problems of the AD-COPEI coalition. In one article Luis Herrera Campins complained that AD bypassed the COPEI minister of agriculture and worked through other institutions such as the Instituto Agrario Nacional (IAN) and the Banco Agrícola Pecuario. He also was not happy with AD's treatment of the COPEI minister of development.[42] Other issues of the newspaper complained about AD discrimination against Copeyanos in the ministry of public works and the ministry of education. In the former, COPEI accused AD of dismissing many URD and COPEI workers in order to employ more Adecos.[43]

During the political coalition AD-COPEI wariness also existed on a state level. In Mérida, an AD official stated there was a great deal of tension.[44] Although the COPEI governors cooperated with the Adecos, particularly with the first governor, Febres Pobrere, the general "majority complex" of COPEI led to difficulties. Being in such a strong position, the Copeyanos would not give due consideration to AD and treated the Adecos as if they were not very important. The Copeyanos admitted to AD-COPEI tension in Mérida but considered their relations with URD to be good.[45]

The COPEI secretary-general in Zulia believed there was a great deal of AD-COPEI tension in that state.[46] COPEI militants, remembering their experiences in 1945-48, opposed the AD government. The problems became so great that the Copeyanos left the state government within four months and only reentered after receiving pressure from Caracas. But the tension did not abate. Most opposition came from the COPEI youth group, the JRC. Many of these young people entered COPEI in 1958-59, and they thought AD was too traditional. Interestingly, this was a reversal of the JRC attitude during 1945-48; at that time the youth leaders had equated AD with communism.

AD-COPEI Cooperation

The examples of interparty cooperation outweighed the incidences of tension and possible misunderstanding. The importance of that fact cannot be overemphasized, particularly after URD decided to leave the coalition.[47] Politicians and the media referred to the period as the *guanábana*, after a Venezuelan fruit which is green on the outside (COPEI's color) and white on the inside (AD's color).

The Copeyanos had considerably altered their public expressions concerning AD. Party leaders had to express these views to convince some of their recalcitrant partisans that AD-COPEI cooperation was the backbone of the coalition government. Speaking at a press conference for American and Canadian journalists, Caldera explained that philosophical differences between the two parties were no longer so great.[48] COPEI had a spiritualist interpretation of history; the interpretation of AD was Marxist. But the Marxist interpretation of AD had been readopted in accordance with the party's experiences and through the evolution of the old Marxist philosophical ideas. For example, whereas there had been strong differences between the two parties over private and public education in 1946, now they were able to harmonize their ideas. COPEI accepted the state's obligation and right to control the educative process in its general lines, and AD admitted the important role of private education. On this point AD probably made the greater move toward accommodation. Christian Democratic doctrine had always accepted a major role for the state in the life of the country; Caldera was merely restating the party's position that the state had the primary responsibility for public education. In contrast, when AD supported the role of *private* education, it *reversed* its former position. However, it was not a large price to pay for strengthening the coalition government.

AD and COPEI worked very closely in the Congress during this period.[49] Raúl Leoni became president of the Senate, and therefore of Congress; Caldera presided over the Chamber of Deputies and also served as vice-president of Congress. This arrangement lasted until 1962, when Leoni and Caldera decided to step down to concentrate on respective party activities. It was at that point that the coalition lost control of the Chamber of Deputies. Two of the political groups which left AD (the MIR and ARS) joined the Communist party and the URD, giving the opposition the majority in the lower house. In addition, the coalition of AD and COPEI barely retained control of the Senate (27-24) for the remainder of President Betancourt's term. Prieto Figueroa replaced Leoni as president of the Senate and the Congress; Manuel Vicente Ledezma of the ARS was named president of the Chamber of Deputies.

The major legislation of the coalition government, however, had been passed prior to 1962. One item, agrarian reform, directly involved COPEI, since it was accomplished under a Copeyano minister of agriculture. The reform involved granting unoccupied government lands to landless peasants, coupled with expropriations. By the end of the administration, approximately four million acres had gone to the *campesinos*.

COPEI strongly supported the government against several serious incidents of violence: an attempted invasion from Colombia in 1960 directed by the former minister of defense, three military uprisings by individual units, and guerrilla warfare. Various issues of the party newspaper condemned the communists and the MIR, who had joined forces. The party supported the government's suspension of constitutional guarantees, although it indicated that this was only a temporary necessity, and that the government should be prudent. COPEI labor organizations supported the government, while the party's student organization joined with AD in campus elections to defeat the student alliances of MIR-PCV-URD. COPEI never wavered in its commitment to the coalition government and stood with AD against the danger of insurrection. Nevertheless, in October 1962, Caldera made a speech against Betancourt's idea of ousting the communist and MIR representatives from Congress. Caldera's position prevailed, and this proved to be the most serious disagreement between the two men.

On the national level, the major political figures of AD and COPEI believed the cooperation was the major ingredient in the successful coalition government. Gonzalo Barrios of AD felt that COPEI made a major contribution to the effectiveness of the Betancourt government;[50] both he and Caldera worked together with their respective parliamentary groups in the Chamber of Deputies. Miguel Angel Landáez, minister of justice for sixteen months (1962-63), admitted to sharp differences between the parties, such as on the question of the *bolívar*'s devaluation; but generally he believed the cooperation was very good. In his view, President Betancourt gave the Copeyanos in the government a great deal of freedom. There were many discussions, and President Betancourt and Caldera used to meet periodically.[51]

However, the success of the coalition would not have been possible without military support. According to José Luis Zapata of COPEI, the party's influence with the military probably discouraged a number of attempted coups; he also believed that COPEI's influence in Táchira was very significant in defeating the attempted coup there. Zapata felt that certain elements of the military suspected Betancourt because they believed he was either a communist or had worked too closely with the communists. COPEI's presence in the coalition alleviated these fears.[52] Paz Galarraga, a power in AD during the coalition government, believed that, at the beginning of the administration, COPEI had no military contacts to speak of. The party began to develop cells in the military, however, and these proved useful in securing military support for the government.[53]

Cooperation between AD and COPEI proved very effective on the student level. In a sense, this cooperation contributed to polarization of the youth groups, for there was not much communication between the Marxist left (MIR, the youth of the Communist party, and the URD) and the youth groups of AD and COPEI. According to a Copeyano youth leader who was active at the time, both sides contributed to the polarization.[54] The Marxists and communists opposed the institutions and refused to work within the political system; the COPEI youth group, the JRC, would consider no dialogue with the communists. The period 1961-62 was particularly difficult, with violence on the campuses and in the secondary schools. In the face of violence, the cordial relationship between the AD-COPEI student groups resulted in several important student election victories and in increasing influence for the respective political parties.

Cooperative efforts were also very successful on the state level, although there was some resistance in Táchira. According to a COPEI founder in that state, it was difficult for the Copeyano peasants to accept cooperation with AD,[55] because they still viewed the Adecos as too far to the left. COPEI leaders explained that cooperation was necessary if democracy was to succeed, and when the peasants saw the material benefits that were forthcoming—public works, roads, schools—they understood and cooperated. Under the leadership of Copeyano governors such as Ceferino Medina Castillo and Valmore Acevedo Amaya, political cooperation existed on all levels.

Contrary to the political situation in Táchira, the states of Zulia and Lara were under AD administration. In Zulia, the governor was an Adeco and the secretary a Copeyano. According to the AD view of the working relationship, there was equitable distribution in the prefects, despite overwhelming AD strength in the state.[56] In Lara, the Copeyanos felt that the coalition was very successful.[57] Governor Eligio Anzola Anzola had considerable power within his party and was popular in the state. Rafael Montes de Oca, a Copeyano, was the secretary of government. The relationship between the two was excellent. Montes de Oca, rather than an Adeco, served as acting governor many times due to Anzola's poor health. The coalition's majority in the state legislature worked well until it was weakened by the first split within AD.

Growth in COPEI's Strength

COPEI benefited considerably from its participation in the Betancourt government.[58] Particularly after URD left in 1960, COPEI increased its number of governors and other bureaucrats. This was significant, because the party was then able to facilitate its organization of local groups in parts of the country where the Christian Democrats had little or no representation. Party members also received considerable patronage. COPEI was given posts in the public administration, many of which the incumbents were able to hold after the party left the government in 1964.

Perhaps the most important gain for COPEI was its increased influence in the labor movement. Through its functional organization concerned with labor, the Frente de Trabajadores Copeyanos, the party trained many young people in the strategy and tactics of union leadership. It established a training school for trade unionists in Caracas in 1962, sponsored by the Copeyano trade unionists in Venezuela and by the Confederación Latino Americana de Sindicalistas Cristianos.

Such developmental efforts proved to be successful. Speaking to the Ninth National Convention of the party, Caldera reported that COPEI had increased its strength in Venezuela's principal labor organization, the CTV, to 36 percent.[59] Several Copeyanos were directors, including Dagoberto González, Francisco Urquía, José Camacho, and Rafael León León. According to a COPEI labor leader of the period, the party penetrated the industrial and petroleum organizations. Party leaders took advantage of the political climate of cooperation, hoping to change the mentality of the workers: to show them that, contrary to propaganda, COPEI was not rightist and reactionary.[60]

As a result of its participation in the government, COPEI increased its influence with labor in the state of Táchira. Padre Manuel Aguirre was very effective in his work through CODESA, a Christian labor organization not affiliated with any political party, but with many Copeyanos as members.[61]

The 1963 Election

As the 1963 election approached, the leaders of AD and COPEI had to decide whether to try to establish a new coalition by supporting a single candidate, or to reject the idea and nominate their respective standard-bearers. Caldera and other party leaders were inclined to continue the coalition, but many militants within the COPEI rank and file felt they could not support an Adeco president for another five years. Faced with this fact, the National Committee called for the formation of a National Democratic Front,[62] to consist of the democratic parties, workers, peasants, students, intellectuals, businessmen of "modern mentality," etc. Its purpose would be "to safeguard the republican institutions and the democratic system from the dangers of the extreme right and left."

However, the AD leadership was not interested in this tactic. COPEI then sent a communication to AD suggesting Caldera as the presidential candidate of National Understanding (*Entendimiento Nacional*); he would serve as the candidate of an AD-COPEI-Independents alliance.[63] But again AD was not interested.

In a final effort, despite opposition within the rank and file, COPEI suggested that an Adeco might again be acceptable as the presidential candidate of the AD-COPEI coalition. However, COPEI insisted that it be consulted as to which AD candidate would represent the coalition in the election.[64]

Rómulo Betancourt, concerned about maintaining the democratic system, suggested to AD leaders that they name a list of possible candidates and let COPEI choose one. But the leaders rejected his idea, and the party convention nominated Raúl Leoni, a member of the Generation of 1928 and long-time confident of Betancourt. COPEI again nominated Rafael Caldera. In contrast to previous elections, Caldera's name did not appear on a slate for election to the Chamber of Deputies; he probably felt that democratic government would now survive, and that it would be advantageous to devote himself more actively to party affairs. Furthermore, he would appear more serious about his presidential possibilities if he had no "fall back" position of certain election to the Chamber of Deputies.

The program which COPEI presented during the campaign was consistent with its previous positions. Perhaps the most interesting part was Caldera's call for the construction of 100,000 houses per year—interesting in that it would be repeated in the 1968 electoral program. When the party won the presidency in that year, President Caldera was obliged to make a major effort to fulfill his two-time electoral promise.

On 1 December 1963, Raúl Leoni won the presidential election. The presidential vote and percentages of the major candidates were as follows:[65] Raúl Leoni (AD), 957,574 (32.80%); Rafael Caldera (COPEI), 589,177 (20.18%); Jóvito Villalba (URD), 510,975 (17.50%); Arturo Uslar Pietri (IPFN, Independientes Pro-Frente Nacional), 469,363 (16.08%); Wolfgang Larrazábal (FDP, Fuerza Democrática Popular), 275,325 (9.43%). COPEI had increased its electoral strength since 1958, from 15 to 20 percent. Ordinarily 20 percent of the vote might not be particularly significant, but it was relatively close to the 32 percent for Leoni. COPEI passed from third place in 1958 to second in 1963, having become the main electoral force in the Andean states; it also placed second in six states, compared to two in 1958. COPEI's electoral strength increased throughout the country, declining slightly in the Federal District, Táchira, and Delta Amacuro. The strength of the popular journalist Arturo Uslar Pietri was a major factor in those areas.

COPEI had become a national political party. It increased its strength in the rural and urban areas and doubled its vote in six states. In fact, its strength increased in all of the electoral zones except the Central-North, where it declined by less than 1 percent. Finally, COPEI's strength decreased somewhat in the three Andean states, while it increased in the rest of the country; the party still received a majority in the Andes region, but its electoral strength was now much more balanced on a national level.

The Leoni Government

Before Leoni was inaugurated, AD and COPEI engaged in negotiations to determine whether their coalition could be continued for the life of the new administration. When these efforts did not prove fruitful, Leoni determined that his first cabinet would be made up of Adecos and independents. The Copeyanos then decided to go into opposition.

Several factors came out of the negotiations. Caldera's public pronouncement, that the party would not join a governmental coalition because the Adecos would only offer COPEI the same three ministries and six governorships, should not be taken too seriously.[66] If AD had wanted COPEI to join the administration, it could have offered more political plums. Instead, the leaders of both parties probably viewed COPEI's position as one of developing strength. The Copeyanos had been strengthened considerably by their participation in the Betancourt administration. The government had survived and political democracy was assured, at least for the immediate future. Because the danger of guerrilla warfare had subsided, the Leoni administration would be in a much better position than its predecessor to complete its term. AD would govern without COPEI and would try to recoup some of the inevitable political losses to the Copeyanos which had occurred during the Betancourt administration.

Leoni might have argued that the Copeyanos demanded more than he was willing to give,[67] but I do not believe this was the major factor. The Adecos also argued that COPEI's obstructionist policies during the Betancourt administration made it impossible for the Copeyanos to participate in the next government; Paz Galarraga maintained that this was his reason for opposing a role for COPEI.[68] According to Paz, it was difficult for President Betancourt to initiate some of his reforms because of COPEI's opposition, and Paz wanted to be certain that the Leoni government would be able to realize its program.

From the COPEI viewpoint, the party would not benefit to any great degree from participation in the Leoni government, since major political inroads had already been made during 1959-64. According to the Copeyanos, the party would strengthen its position for the 1968 election by remaining in opposition.[69]

I agree with Robert J. Alexander that the role played by COPEI during the Leoni administration was of major importance for Venezuela's political maturation.[70] Notwithstanding the period of the *trienio*, this was the first time that a major opposition party had not been engaged in plots to bring down the government. Although some Adecos might disagree, COPEI gave the country its first example of loyal opposition. The reasons for COPEI's attitude were both ideological and tactical. First, the party was committed to political democracy; its experience under the Pérez Jiménez dictatorship had served to reinforce that commitment. But the party leaders were also optimistic about their chances in the 1968 election. They believed that COPEI could win on its own, and they wanted the Leoni government to finish its constitutional term of office.

During this period, the party continued to develop its grassroots support. Younger leaders were trained to work in and assume the leadership of peasant and labor organizations. COPEI made a great effort to increase its strength throughout the country, particularly in the eastern states, where it had failed to garner much more than 5 percent of the vote.

At the outset of his administration, President Leoni formed a coalition with two smaller parties, URD and FND (Frente Nacional Democrático), which the press referred to as the government of the *Ancha Base* (Wide Base). The arrangement lasted until the spring of 1966. COPEI decided upon a posture relative to the government: *Doble A*, or Autonomy of Action. Caldera explained the new policy at the party's national convention, and it was further developed in an article by Herrera Campins.[71] Autonomy of Action allowed for conversations with AD and other political parties, in order to reach understandings regarding legislation and the officers for congressional posts. Under the policy COPEI would support President Leoni in matters of great importance for the country. The party would not take an intransigent position and thereby contribute to "excessive radicalizing of Venezuelan politics"; instead, it would offer just criticism for the defense of the democratic system. COPEI would support initiatives and measures of the governing party or any other party which it felt might benefit the country. Autonomy of Action, then, committed COPEI to support the democratic system while allowing the party a free hand in criticizing the government. There would be criticism without conspiracy.

Although COPEI terminated its coalition with AD at the end of the Betancourt administration, the Copeyanos reached agreements with other political parties on the state level during the Leoni regime.[72] COPEI and FDP (Fuerza Democrática Popular) signed an agreement to control the legislature of Yaracuy. After AD lost control, the other two parties divided the official positions as follows: president, COPEI; secretary, FDP; comptroller, COPEI; attorney general, FDP. In Barinas, the Copeyanos made an agreement with the FND (Frente Nacional Democrático) to name the directors of the state legislature: president, an independent; first vice-president, COPEI; second vice-president, FND; secretary, COPEI.

Taking an overall view of the Leoni administration, COPEI's position of Autonomy of Action was one of loyal opposition. However, looking back on his term in 1971, former President Leoni did not believe that COPEI was responsible in opposition.[73] He stated that, when COPEI was participating in the Betancourt administration, the party agreed to government investments in certain areas of the country. President Leoni subsequently discussed the matter with Caldera, who said he would study it. Leoni has asserted that the benefits of the law would not have been realized until 1969, and that he wanted it for the future, rather than for his own government. Eventually a law was produced, but with major modifications demanded by COPEI. President Leoni also mentioned his government's proposed fiscal reform, which would have increased the taxes on the petroleum companies and the nation's wealthier elements. According to Leoni, this program was opposed by COPEI because the party did not want to antagonize the oligarchy that supported it. As a result, when the COPEI government succeeded the Leoni administration, it was forced to wrestle with fiscal reform.

A former Adeco who was very influential during the Leoni administration, Prieto Figueroa, pointed out that a new force, the *desarrollistas*, was making itself felt around 1965. According to his view, COPEI and the *desarrollistas* under Pedro Tinoco opposed financial reform. Prieto believed that COPEI represented the oligarchy and big business, and that the *desarrollistas* represented national and international banking interests. Notwithstanding these criticisms, many Adecos agreed with their 1968 presidential candidate, Gonzalo Barrios, that the opposition of COPEI was strong but loyal, in that there was no Copeyano conspiracy.[74]

Autonomy of Action for one Copeyano, Valmore Acevedo, signified systematic opposition in the form of constructive criticism.[75] But it was low-key opposition, not the violent opposition of the past, because COPEI did not want to provoke the return of a military dictatorship. Valmore Acevedo also drew an interesting comparison between COPEI's opposition through Autonomy of Action and AD's opposition to the Caldera government (1969–74). AD had the experience of being the former governing party; COPEI had not had this pleasure. Thus AD in opposition had more strength than COPEI in opposition, as was exemplified by AD's position in the CVP (Venezuelan Petroleum Corporation). When the COPEI government assumed power in 1969, Copeyanos were appointed to first- or second-echelon positions in the corporation; the remainder were Adecos. Furthermore, AD was the strongest party in the labor movement and the Congress, and this reality made itself felt in such areas as congressional legislation and developments in the labor movement.

Let us now consider the election which brought the presidency to COPEI.

The 1968 Election

Some elements of the party's secondary leadership seriously questioned the wisdom of nominating three-time loser Rafael Caldera;[76] they threatened to oust him from COPEI leadership if he lost in his fourth presidential bid. However, approximately one year before the election, a serious split within the ranks of Acción Democrática convinced many Copeyanos that their own party would have a very good chance if they rallied around Caldera.

The schism within AD involved various reform measures and the party's 1968 presidential nominee,[77] and resulted in a sizable group leaving the party and forming the Movimiento Electoral del Pueblo (MEP). The newly formed party nominated Prieto Figueroa as its presidential candidate, drawing votes away from AD.

As the election approached, COPEI made agreements with several political groups. It formed an electoral front with the Movimiento Democrático Independiente (MDI) and the Liberal party,[78] signing a pact in which all three parties agreed to join their parliamentary forces into a bloc of ten senators and forty-seven deputies. They also agreed to form a mixed commission to develop a platform of "programmatic coincidences."

Shortly before the election a group of independents, identified as the *movimiento desarrollista* and under the direction of Pedro R. Tinoco, declared its support for Caldera.[79] After the election President Caldera appointed Tinoco as finance minister. The *desarrollistas* represented certain Venezuelan and foreign business interests. COPEI also made an agreement with the industrialist Eugenio Mendoza, who had contributed a considerable amount of money to the party's campaign in exchange for a major voice in deciding who would hold the ministries of housing, finance, and development. (There was also evidence that Mendoza contributed to Acción Democrática.[80]) Another agreement was reached between COPEI and Miguel Angel Capriles, the owner of a newspaper chain and several magazines. COPEI promised Capriles that he could designate eleven persons to run for Congress on the Copeyano lists, that he would be assured of a seat in the Senate, and that his brother would be appointed ambassador to Canada if Caldera won the election. The COPEI administration fulfilled each of these promises.

I discussed these agreements and their implications with several people representing COPEI, AD, and URD.[81] The spokesmen for URD and AD believed the agreements confirmed the fact that COPEI had close ties with the oligarchy. A URD deputy added that COPEI's policies were strongly influenced by three wealthy Venezuelan families: Capriles, Mendoza, and Vollmer.[82] An active Copeyano who was a member of the Chamber of Deputies and of the party's National Committee told me that he certainly did not like the arrangements made in the 1968 election campaign, when the Capriles chain contributed publicity and Mendoza gave money; however, he felt that COPEI had to make these arrangements in order to win the election. Once the party controlled the executive branch, it could build its strength through labor, peasant, and various organizations. The Copeyanos would also have the opportunity to realize their program, something which they could never do without control of the government.

The reality of Latin American politics makes such arrangements generally acceptable. Rather than pass moral judgment (a useless exercise in this case), we should ask ourselves whether COPEI was able to realize its programmatic goals once it assumed the presidency.

COPEI ran a well-financed campaign.[83] According to the statutes, national and regional organs fixed membership dues, and the more wealthy were asked for special contributions. Private interests, however, including large landowners and industrialists, were the most important source of funds. The major interest groups—the church, peasants, and organized labor—made very little contribution. Although favoring Caldera, the Roman Catholic hierarchy decided to remain officially neutral. The economic status of the peasants restricted their importance as a source of funds, and the COPEI labor organization comprised less than 15 percent of all union members. On the other hand, foreigners, particularly the Christian Democrats of Germany and Italy, gave important financial support to COPEI. Additional foreign contributions came from the Venezuelan subsidiaries of international petroleum corporations: Creole, Shell, and the lesser producers.

One other question concerned COPEI in the 1968 election: Did the party have an understanding with Pérez Jiménez? The former dictator won in his bid for the Senate from the Caracas area, although he was not allowed to assume his seat because of a contrived technicality (he did not return to the country to register). Pérez Jiménez supporters had to choose another major candidate for president, and according to one active Copeyano, Caldera won the 1968 election because of the Pérez Jiménez vote.[84] This observer pointed out that Pérez Jiménez received approximately 400,000 votes for the Senate, half of which went to Caldera for president. Caldera received about 200,000 votes more than COPEI in general, and these were fundamentally Pérez Jiménez votes.

I tend to agree with the view of Paz Galarraga, certainly no Copeyano sympathizer.[85] Paz conceded that half of the Pérez Jiménez vote went to Caldera, with the rest spread among the other candidates, although he did not believe there was any agreement between COPEI and Pérez Jiménez. Indeed, it was impossible to have such an agreement, because there was no disciplined vote. Because most of the Pérez Jiménez vote was in protest against the government, much of it naturally fell to Caldera for president.

On 1 December 1968, Rafael Caldera won the presidential election with a plurality. The vote was as follows: Rafael Caldera (COPEI, MDI), 29% ; Gonzalo Barrios (AD, several small groups), 27% ; Miguel Angel Burelli Rivas (URD, FDP, FND, MENI), 22% ; Luis Beltrán Prieto Figueroa (MEP, small groups), 19% ; other candidates, 3%. Burelli, former ambassador to the United States and highly respected in the country, ran as an independent with the support of URD and its allies. He and Pérez Jiménez represented the anti-government and anti-major-party sentiment. The former dictator, running under the party label of his newly created Cruzada Cívica Nacionalista (CCN), did well in the Federal District in his race for the Senate.[86]

In most states, COPEI ran stronger in the urban than in the rural sectors. The urban sectors gave the Copeyanos 23 percent of the vote, compared to 21 percent for AD. In the states of Carabobo, Lara, Yaracuy, Miranda, Portuguesa, and Zulia, COPEI was stronger with the urban voters, while AD won in the rural areas.

Several conclusions might be drawn from these results. The CCN vote indicated that anti-major-party and anti-government sentiment was stronger in the urban areas. As previously mentioned, Pérez Jiménez appealed to certain elements of the middle class; in addition, the poorer elements in urban slums might also have supported the former dictator, hoping to find jobs and seeing a way out of their desperate situation. COPEI's strength in the urban areas might also have been based on other factors, such as the fact that party organizational efforts were stronger there. Eighteen of the country's twenty-three rural areas favored AD, but that support was not quite enough to offset COPEI's strength in the urban areas.

Of the twenty-one electoral areas, COPEI won in eleven and AD in eight. The Copeyanos carried the states of Mérida, Táchira, Trujillo, and Barinas. However, AD was the leader in congressional, state legislative, and municipal races. Because Caldera ran ahead of COPEI, the party was a minority in the Congress. AD controlled the largest bloc of seats, making some kind of political accommodation essential if COPEI was to enact any of its legislative program.

In considering COPEI's rise to the presidency, I believe that the factors listed by Robert J. Alexander are valid.[87] Of the major factors, we should emphasize careful attention paid to organizational work and extensive training of party leadership. Furthermore, the break with the more conservative elements during the Pérez Jiménez dictatorship allowed the party to broaden its electoral base after 1958. But I would place greater emphasis on the AD-MEP split than Alexander does. This was the major factor which preordained the COPEI victory. Alexander also points out that COPEI maintained its unity in the post-dictatorial period, whereas the other two major parties suffered debilitating splits—AD in 1960, 1962, and 1968; URD in 1963 and 1967. COPEI did experience factional problems, particularly during and after the Leoni administration, but they did not result in an open schism. Consequently, the party leadership could concentrate on organizational development and increasing its influence with the voters.

During 1952-68, two factors largely determined the course of COPEI's development. The first, which affects the development of all political parties, was the political environment. As the title of this chapter indicates, a period of exile and imprisonment was followed by one of political democracy. COPEI matured within this set of circumstances, both influencing and being influenced by the political environment. The party's attitude toward the AD administrations strengthened political democracy in Venezuela. The requirements of opposition to the dictatorship and support of political democracy enabled the party to shed its more conservative elements and move toward the center of the political spectrum.

Within this environment, COPEI's political fortunes were inter-woven with the development of Acción Democrática. The Copeyanos shared in the successes of the Adecos and took advantage of their failures. They benefited from their participation in the Betancourt administration, and improved their stature and political influence by serving as the loyal opposition to the Leoni government. AD's failure to maintain party unity in the post-dictatorial period was a major factor in bringing the presidency to COPEI.

CHAPTER 4

Organization and Function

L E T U S now analyze the structure and major functional organizations of COPEI. We will consider its principal ideological and political disputes over the years, and then set the 1973 electoral defeat in this broader context.

Structure and Organization

The statutes of organization were first presented and approved at the Third National Convention on 22 March 1948. Modifications of the statutes have been made from time to time, affecting either national or regional party matters. (The following discussion is based on the Tenth National Convention, held on 9 April 1967. See the Appendix for a more complete summary.)

The statutes stipulate that party members are expected "to participate in the courses, seminars . . . that the party may organize to improve the ideological and political formation of the militancy." COPEI is one of several Latin American Christian Democratic parties that sponsor and have working agreements with institutes and schools throughout the continent. The Venezuelans sponsor the Luigi Sturzo Institute and the Caracas-based Instituto de Formación Democrática Cristiana (IFEDEC).

In June 1970, a second center of IFEDEC began in the state of Zulia,[1] financed by individual donations and by the labor movement. According to Lesbia Hernández Márquez, the administrative secretary, IFEDEC was independent of COPEI and received no help from the party. In Zulia, professors offered courses which lasted from one week to thirty days. The students were members of the party's labor, peasant, and youth groups; also in attendance were Copeyano university professors, as well as party professionals and technicians. Seminar topics included Internal Revision of the Party; Information, Public Opinion, and Propaganda; Policy and Administration of Municipalities. The National Agrarian Institute gave a course for Copeyano peasants and technicians, and it was announced that "the technicians of the other political parties could also attend." Sra. Hernández stated that IFEDEC in Caracas and Zulia cooperated through broad collaboration and frequent interchange of professors and students. IFEDEC in Zulia was an extension of the IFEDEC-Caracas activities, not a competitive organization. Thus the two organizations had a parallel relationship.

The statutes also state that any Copeyano may present his point of view to the various party organs; however, he must not present his views—"criticisms and observations"—outside. The statutes stipulate that, once a decision is made by the majority, the individual member must abide by that decision. The problem of expressing opposing views is further elaborated upon in a section dealing with discipline. A party member can be subject to discipline because of "infractions against the statutes, regulations, directed orders, political lines, fixed action of certain organs." The punishment may consist of a warning, release from duties for two years, suspension for two years, or definitive expulsion. The National Committee can also "cause the retirement, temporary or definitive, of any party militant who exercises public functions: representatives, administrators, and those with political positions. Anyone who attacks the action of the National Committee will be suspended as a militant of the party." The statutes are quite detailed in spelling out the procedures to be followed when disciplinary action is taken—the requirement of a two-thirds vote for suspension; appeal; actions of the regional and national committees; functions of the regional and national disciplinary tribunals; and so forth.

The National Committee, directing the activities of the party through a National Secretariat, is the party's highest executive authority. Key party leaders are members of the committee, including the president and two vice-presidents of the party (the president's role is largely ceremonial), the secretary-general, and the secretaries general of the party's functional organizations. Among its powers, the National Committee can appoint and remove party officials, initiate disciplinary action, propose candidates for public office, and convoke the National Convention or an Extraordinary National Convention.[2] During the Caldera administration, key members of the National Committee met weekly with President Caldera to discuss party actions and to coordinate government-party activities and positions.

The principal member of the National Secretariat (which coordinates the daily activities) is the secretary-general. According to the statutes, the secretary-general has "as his charge the immediate direction of the work of the National Committee, the National Secretaries, and the fractions, services or specialized groups." If he has a majority of the National Committee supporting him, the secretary-general can be the most powerful person in the party. (Of course, if the nation's president is a Copeyano, it is crucial that the secretary-general have his support as well.) The National Secretariat includes the national secretaries who have specific tasks within the party aimed at decentralizing administrative work. There are twenty-one national secretaries: a political formation secretary, an agrarian secretary, etc. Thus the party is organized functionally, in the form of units and specialized groups.

The statutes specify that each regional organ is functionally autonomous. Although they do have influence in the selection of regional and municipal candidates, they are created by the National Committee and are expected to carry out national party policy on regional and local levels.

Party organization follows the political and territorial division of Venezuela—national, regional (the states), and district and municipal committees.[3] There are also village or *barrio* organizations under a committee. Two types of organization operate within the party: vertical and horizontal. The vertical organization involves communication from the highest authority to the lowest: this communication can be "ascending"—first calling assemblies of the base of the party, followed by a municipal convention—or "descending"—when the "orders, instructions, political tactical lines, and strategies of the party are filtered from the National Convention to the Committee of Base in a direct descending line." The horizontal organization involves the functionally independent groups; a predetermined number of party members perform specific activities in accordance with special regulations. When the two systems are joined, the result is a mixed system of organization. The regional systems maintain the same organization throughout the country, with slight modifications in the Federal District and the Federal Territories.

The statutes list financial sources for the party. Congressmen and members of other national bodies are expected to pay a percentage of their salaries which is fixed by resolution or by the National Convention. State legislators and members of municipal and district bodies contribute a percentage fixed by national or regional conventions. Contributions also come from regional committees and individual party members, with special contributions for electoral campaigns.

One can rank the source of funds in order of importance to the party.[4] Most funds come from members holding elected or appointive positions which they have obtained by having their names on a *plancha* (list), or through patronage. The second major source, of course not mentioned in the statutes, is foreign and domestic industries, particularly during electoral campaigns. The smallest contributions come from the regional organizations.

The statutes list the party's regionally and nationally organized groups. They include the state legislative and the national parliamentary groups. These groups are expected to follow the general line of the national and regional committees. All Copeyano senators and deputies belong to the parliamentary group, which functions as a legislative caucus; it publishes important political positions and reports, usually in pamphlet form. All political parties represented in Congress have parliamentary groups with offices located in the parliamentary building in downtown Caracas. (After each election, the parties receiving the most votes are given the largest suites of offices.)

The statutes list six functional organizations: Frente de Trabaja-dores Copeyanos (labor, FTC), Juventud Revolucionaria Copeyana (youth, JRC), Frente Feminino Copeyano (women), Movimiento Agrario Socialcristiano (peasants, MASC), Movimiento Magisterial Socialcristiano (teachers), and Movimiento de Profesionales y Técnicos Socialcristianos (professionals and technicians). The first two are the most important, although the MASC has gained importance in recent years.

The functional organizations were created by the party and, like the other groups, are expected to follow the general line of the national and regional committees. Shortly before the 1968 election a COPEI pamphlet stated, "We are members of COPEI, but we also belong to a professional college, a trade union, the JRC, a center of students, and so forth. These groups should not be converted into instruments of the party because this would destroy the social forces. The party is an intermediate body."[5] In practice, however, the functional organizations have been answerable to and controlled by the party; this situation has led to difficulties with specific organizations, particularly the JRC. (After the 1973 election, it was again suggested that the functional organizations be made more autonomous and representative of social forces.)

Although this chapter will concentrate on the FTC, the JRC, and to a lesser degree the MASC, we should point out that the other functional organizations do issue publications, put forth candidates in elections, and hold periodical meetings and congresses.[6] Throughout the years they have strongly supported the party's general positions, whether the anticommunist position of the women's group in the late 1940s, or the 1958 call by Copeyano teachers to educate their colleagues in Christian Democratic doctrine so that the ideas and philosophy of the movement could be expressed through teaching. The professionals and technicians organized in 1967 with their first national directorate under the leadership of Hugo Pérez La Salvia, subsequently Caldera's minister of mines and hydrocarbons. Consisting of various groups including engineers, physicians, nurses, psychologists, radiologists, and veterinarians, their literature said they would help the party and penetrate the professional colleges with Christian doctrine.

Movimiento Agrario Socialcristiano (MASC) and Other Peasant Organizations

It could be said that COPEI was active within a segment of the Venezuelan peasantry since the party's inception in 1946. We recall that the party's early electoral efforts concentrated on the peasantry in the Andean states of Mérida and Táchira, and to a lesser extent in the other Andean state of Trujillo. For some time following the overthrow of the Pérez Jiménez dictatorship in 1958, the party's primary electoral support continued to consist of Andean peasants. In the post-dictatorial period, party leaders began to think beyond immediate electoral necessities and moved toward the long-range organization of the peasantry.

During the Betancourt coalition (1959-64), COPEI increased its influence with the peasantry. The Copeyano minister of agriculture, Víctor Giménez Landínez, presented the 1960 Agrarian Reform Law to the Congress. The party had made some limited efforts to organize the peasants through the COPEI labor group (the FTC), but leaders concluded that COPEI's influence with the peasantry could be increased still further through a new functional organization devoted exclusively to the peasants. In 1958, the decision was made to split labor-peasant organizational efforts by forming the Movimiento Agrario Socialcristiano (MASC). Party leaders also began to concentrate on organizing peasants throughout the country, and in 1962 they called the first regional meeting of the Social Christian Peasant and Agrarian Leagues of Lara.[7]

The MASC represented COPEI in the reestablished peasant federation, Federación Campesina de Venezuela (FEDECAVE). As with their efforts in the labor movement, each party tried to win control of as many state peasant organizations as possible, thereby increasing its strength in the national peasant federation, FEDECAVE. COPEI did so primarily through the AD-COPEI coalition of the Betancourt administration. Interparty peasant politics during that period have been recounted elsewhere.[8] Regardless of some AD-COPEI tension (such as subsequent COPEI concern over the "socialistic program" of agrarian reform), COPEI continued to increase its strength with the peasants; this influence extended into the Leoni administration. In 1966 the MASC called an assembly, the Primera Asamblea Campesina del Movimiento Agrario Social Cristiano.

During the Caldera administration (1969-74), COPEI continued to increase its strength with the peasant sector on the national and state levels, despite interparty competition. It was only natural that the party would benefit from the COPEI government's programs, such as PRIDA, which concentrated on increased productivity of the rural areas. (Greater influence with the peasantry, however, did not prevent a COPEI defeat in 1973.) The national secretary of MASC, Teófilo Borregales, was pleased with the projects of the National Agrarian Institute (IAN), which, he believed, would show "a new concept of the integral promotion of the peasant family."[9] Borregales had great hopes for PRIDA (Integral Program of Agricultural Development), through which he hoped that the peasant would be incorporated into the nation's cultural, social, and political process. According to one MASC official, COPEI was taking partisan advantage of these governmental programs and activities.[10] On one occasion, the ministry of public works (MOP) sent this official to the city of Maracay on business involving the planning of a road. While he was not sent as a party member, everyone knew he was a Copeyano.

The party continued to increase its influence in FEDECAVE, particularly after the AD-MEP split in 1968. As in the labor movement, AD wanted to limit MEP's influence with the peasantry, and AD-COPEI cooperation was its vehicle. In the labor organization, the CTV, the two parties worked very closely, similar to the *guanábana* of the Betancourt administration. In FEDECAVE, however, the AD-COPEI relationship might be more aptly categorized as a series of general agreements.[11]

During the Caldera administration, COPEI increased its influence with the peasantry in a number of states, notably Mérida, Yaracuy, Aragua, and Falcón. Using political tactics similar to those demonstrated in the various state legislatures, the Copeyanos operated through state affiliates of MASC, forming pacts with different political parties in regional peasant conventions. The details of the pact depended upon the balance of political power in the particular states.[12] (The regional conventions send delegates to FEDECAVE.) In Yaracuy the party formed a pact with URD and MEP to oppose AD, which was the major political influence with the peasants. But in Aragua the MEP controlled a majority of the peasants, and COPEI and AD formed a pact. In Mérida COPEI was the overwhelming peasant force, and the Copeyanos wanted to maintain good AD-COPEI relations. COPEI included AD on their various electoral lists, or *planchas*, so there would not be a Copeyano steamroller.

Besides wishing to increase COPEI's influence with the peasantry, the party's peasant leaders wanted to increase peasant and MASC influence within COPEI. The peasant interest did have a party voice through Duplat Pulido and Alirio Cruz, who were on the National Committee, and Duplat Pulido and Marquez Pulido, who were in Congress. But the party's peasant leaders felt that that voice should be strengthened.[13] The problem centered on the MASC-COPEI relationship. Although it was created as a functional organization of the party, Duplat Pulido believed that MASC had taken on a life of its own.[14] According to Duplat, the politicians were afraid that party organs would develop their own strength; this was not part of the Latin American or Venezuelan tradition, which exemplified strong centralization according to the Spanish heritage. Regardless of the politicians' fears, Duplat believed that MASC influence within COPEI was growing.

One could argue whether or not this analysis was correct, pointing on one hand to the relatively strong influence of the labor and youth organizations within the party, or, on the other, at statistical analyses of population trends which indicate that Venezuela was becoming more urbanized and that, therefore, peasant influence within the parties was declining. Our discussion is not concerned with this question. Instead, let us look at the peasant organizational efforts of some Copeyanos outside COPEI. They expressed a great deal of enthusiasm for these nonparty organizations as vehicles to improve the condition of the peasants, and perhaps to provide them with a more effective political voice throughout the country.

Instituto de Servicios Rurales (ISER) and Fundacion para el Desarrollo Rural y la Educacion Campesina (FUNDECA)

Although COPEI was increasing its influence with the peasants through the MASC, many Copeyano peasant leaders were dissatisfied with the national peasant federation, FEDECAVE. Because of the partisan conflict within FEDECAVE, they believed it could not be an organization which would fight for the peasants. In addition to the MASC, these Copeyano leaders wanted to create other peasant organizations, separate from the political parties, through which the peasants could participate in their own social, cultural, and economic development. More than a change of government, they hoped to bring about a change of attitude on the part of the peasants and their leaders.[15]

The COPEI peasant leaders used three approaches in their organizational efforts with the peasants. First, they brought attention to government organizations and activities such as the National Agrarian Institute (IAN), the National Peasants' Bank (BAP), and PRIDA. Second, the illiterate peasants, who were termed *marginados* (on the margin of the society), comprised approximately 32 percent of the population; the MASC concentrated on organizing this group. Finally, private organizations were used.[16] In 1963, several COPEI peasant leaders formed the Instituto de Servicios Rurales (ISER), an organization which would concentrate on providing such rural services as running water and electricity. In 1968, Duplat, Víctor Giménez Landínez, and others formed the Fundación para el Desarrollo Rural y la Educación Campesina (FUNDECA) to concentrate on developing the educational, cultural, and overall capabilities of the peasants.

The founders of ISER and FUNDECA developed various projects and raised money from two sources. First, projects were sold to some government agencies, such as the IAN and BAP; second, they received loans and grants from the international Christian Democratic organization. Periodically they sent proposals to the Christian Democratic organization of West Germany for approval. In contrast to AD practice, wherein the government financed peasant organizations, the Copeyanos wanted the nongovernment organizations to raise their own funds.

The Copeyanos believed that AD was paternalistic and demagogic in manipulating the illiterate peasants. Adeco technicians allegedly did all the work themselves, with the peasants merely onlookers. In the ISER and FUNDECA projects, however, peasants participated and worked with Copeyano technicians. But political considerations were never far from the Copeyanos' minds. First they would send technicians to work on a particular project; these were later followed by political activists, who asked the peasants to think carefully the next time they voted and reminded them of the improvements that had taken place under the COPEI government.

Thus the MASC was a political arm of COPEI, but ISER and FUNDECA were concerned with social, economic, and cultural questions. An early FUNDECA pamphlet stated that agrarian reform and rural development would fail unless the peasant was transformed into the protagonist of change and progress. With this in mind, FUNDECA was not simply another organization; rather, it was interested in the development and the education of the peasant so that he could improve his life through his own efforts.[17]

Although the founders of ISER and FUNDECA wanted their organizations separate from COPEI and wished to have political considerations minimized, I have concluded that ISER and FUNDECA did indeed have evident political overtones. They were private organizations directed primarily by Copeyanos; Duplat stated that it took him approximately five months to convince people that he was not acting as a Copeyano, and that other political parties were also represented in the FUNDECA leadership.[18] However, the role of Copeyano political activists within the organizations was clearly defined. Political considerations aside, ISER and FUNDECA appealed to those peasants who might not have wanted to join a party. They were organizations directed toward the improvement of the peasants' condition; if, while members, they met political activists who extolled the virtues of COPEI, this did not dissuade the peasants from the belief that the technicians and perhaps even the political activists were trying to improve their lot.

Frente de Trabajadores Copeyanos (FTC) and the Confederacion de Trabajadores de Venezuela (CTV)

The birth and development of the COPEI labor movement is an important part of the history and evolution of Venezuelan labor that grew out of the late nineteenth century guilds.[19] In the early twentieth century, under the Gómez regime (1909-35), some labor groups, such as the mutualist societies, had a Catholic orientation. In the post-

Gómez period the newly formed political parties created and incorporated modern trade union movements into their organizations. This is very different from the experiences of Western Europe and the United States, where trade union movements were born and developed apart from the political parties.

In 1947, during the AD *trienio*, the unions under AD leadership reconstituted the central Venezuelan labor organization and formed the Confederación de Trabajadores de Venezuela (CTV). Those Christian Democrats interested in labor matters attended courses taught by Padre Manuel Aguirre through the Círculo Obrero de Caracas (COC). According to one of his former students, Padre Aguirre's influence in labor matters was total, and he provided the first labor education for many future Christian Democratic labor leaders.[20]

The Christian Democrats created their own political party in 1946, and the following year the party leaders formed COPEI's labor group, the Frente de Trabajadores Copeyanos (FTC). The newly created labor organization held its first public demonstration on 1 May 1948, in the Plaza Capuchinos, and FTC labor militants were involved in violent encounters with labor followers of AD and the communists.[21]

Despite the tension during this period, FTC leaders went ahead and held discussions concerning the most appropriate political tactics. A central question was the future relationship between the FTC and the CTV: although the Adecos created and dominated the CTV, it was a Venezuelan labor organization and included industrial unions and peasant leagues. The 1948 coup put an end to such discussions, and the CTV as well as the political parties were declared illegal during the dictatorship. From 1948 to 1958, Padre Aguirre continued to hold courses in Gómez's former home, Ocumare de la Costa. (The courses continued in the early post-dictatorial period and dealt with such matters as trade unionism, civic formation, the family, and civil rights and responsibilities.)

When COPEI attempted to cooperate with Pérez Jiménez at the beginning of his regime, the FTC leaders followed suit. In 1950, for example, they opposed a proposed strike of petroleum workers, declaring that the strike would be suicidal for the country's labor movement and that it would play into the hands of the Marxists.[22]

During the dictatorship the FTC created twelve separate trade unions throughout the country, in the face of government persecution. These included the Sindicato de Trabajadores Organizados del Petróleo (STOP), located in the state of Falcón, and the Unión Venezolana de Empleados y Obreros (UVEO). In 1950, in order to coordinate nationally the efforts of the various Christian Democratic trade unions, they formed the Comité Pro-Federación de Trabajadores de Venezuela (COFETROV). Although it was illegal, COFETROV managed to hold clandestine national conventions. Its leaders included Arístides Calvani and Valmore Acevedo. Many of its directors were persecuted, and several of them, in exile, participated in a 1954 congress in Santiago, Chile, creating the Confederación Latino Americana de Sindicalistas Cristianos (CLASC). When the Labor representatives of the various parties formed a General Strike Committee in 1957, Dagoberto González represented COFETROV and the Christian Democrats.

Following the dictatorship, the CTV was reconstituted, and the Copeyanos once again addressed the question of the CTV-FTC relationship. In 1958, Padre Aguirre and those who had been attending his courses formed the Comité de Sindicatos Autónomos de Venezuela, which subsequently became the Confederación de Sindicatos Autónomos de Venezuela (CODESA). This Christian labor organization consisted mainly of Copeyanos, with some independents and a few members of AD and URD. The members were allowed to vote for their respective political parties, but they were expected to defend Christian trade unionism.

The question of labor relations was even more complicated for Copeyanos. Was the party's labor group, the FTC, to have a working relationship with the Venezuelan CTV, the Christian CODESA, or both? Rafael Caldera and Padre Aguirre differed on tactical matters.[23] Caldera believed that the FTC should operate through the CTV and that it should attempt to increase its influence, perhaps even becoming the major force in Venezuela's largest labor organization. The FTC would compete with the labor groups of other parties within the CTV, making temporary alliances when necessary. Aguirre, in contrast, believed that the FTC should work with CODESA, avoiding the interparty competition of the CTV, and build the Venezuelan Christian labor movement. A compromise was finally reached: the FTC would work through the CTV, and individual Copeyanos would be permitted to join CODESA. The various Christian trade unions either disbanded or joined CODESA, and the FTC turned its attention to the CTV.

The FTC-CTV relationship was based on AD-COPEI cooperation. During the *guanábana* of the Betancourt administration, COPEI, AD, and URD formed a pact within the CTV to run candidates on a single slate and to divide the CTV executive positions. At the Third Congress of the CTV in 1959 (the other two congresses were held in 1936 and 1947), COPEI emerged as the third-strongest political force, with approximately 14 percent of the delegates: AD, 561; Communist party, 210; COPEI, 152; URD, 142. COPEI was awarded two positions on the fourteen-member Executive Council.

For the next ten or fifteen years COPEI increased its strength in the labor movement, primarily due to three developments: FTC's improved organizational efforts, conflicts and splits within the other parties, and through the efforts of the Caldera government. We recall that URD left the coalition government, and that the AD-COPEI agreement formed the political basis of the Betancourt administration. The

Copeyanos also increased their influence with labor when the Venezuelan labor movement split several times during the 1960s.

In the Fourth Congress of the CTV, held in December 1961, the AD-COPEI coalition defeated the slate of the Communist party (PCV), MIR, and URD. Four Copeyanos served on the eleven-member Executive Council: Dagoberto González, secretary of organization and statistics; Francisco Urquía Lugo, secretary of labor; Elio Aponte, secretary of culture; and José Camacho, secretary of studies and planning. COPEI controlled approximately 30 percent of the delegates and slightly more than 30 percent of the Executive Council.

Shortly thereafter, upon losing all their leadership posts, the MIR and the PCV withdrew from the CTV and formed their own organization. This was followed by an internal AD split: the *arsista* group left AD, and its labor wing joined the PCV-MIR forces to form a rival labor organization, the Central Unica de Trabajadores de Venezuela (CUTV). When the PCV left the CTV, COPEI automatically became the second force behind AD. When groups began to split from AD, the Adecos became more dependent than ever upon their agreement with the Copeyanos.

We should recall too that COPEI decided to leave the coalition and go into opposition vis-à-vis the Leoni administration. Due to its weakened position following the 1963 election, the AD government sought agreements with URD and smaller parties; these agreements helped determine the alignment of political forces in the Fifth Congress of the CTV, held in November 1964. The numbers of delegates were: AD, 538 (70%); COPEI, 107 (14%); URD, 95 (12%); FDP, 10 (1%); FND, 12 (1.5%). COPEI strength had obviously declined in the Fifth Congress. The party as a whole might have benefited through its position as the loyal opposition to the Leoni government, but the FTC leadership concluded that the party's labor group still needed a pact with AD. When AD split again in 1968, giving rise to a new political party (the Movimiento Electoral del Pueblo, or MEP), the stage was set for a new AD-COPEI agreement.

Although the next congress of the CTV was not scheduled until 1970, the effect of the 1968 AD split was felt within the CTV almost immediately. Several key AD labor leaders declared themselves to be members of MEP; these included CTV President González Navarro and Carlos Galúe, the secretary of labor representation. The Executive Council reflected the new political situation: AD, seven members; COPEI, two; MEP, two; URD, two; FND, one; and FDP, one. Although a majority of the national directorate remained with AD, most regional directors went with MEP.

In 1968 the COPEI candidate, Rafael Caldera, was elected president. The period 1968-70 was crucial for the realignment of political forces, particularly within the labor movement. The AD leadership decided that they must weaken MEP at all costs. Since almost half of the votes in the 1968 election were cast by organized labor, they would carry the battle to MEP within the CTV. If AD was to wrest the CTV leadership from MEP at the forthcoming labor congress, a new agreement with COPEI would be necessary. COPEI had proven its trustworthiness in the past; URD had not. Furthermore, AD-COPEI cooperation would be easier under a COPEI administration. But what would be the price of Copeyano cooperation?

The Sixth Congress of the CTV

Shortly before the congress opened, José González Navarro, president of the CTV and a former Adeco, then a member of MEP, granted an interview to the editor of a prominent magazine.[24] He proposed that the first force in the CTV would receive the presidency, the second force the position of secretary-general, and the third the various secretaries in order of quality, with some representation provided for the smaller forces. González stated, "We cannot accept the fact that people without sufficient force within the labor movement become directors. . . . We will not accept alliances which propose solutions." He hoped to retain the presidency by having MEP emerge from the congress as the first force. On the other hand, if AD won a majority of the delegates, González hoped that MEP would at least receive the very important position of secretary-general.

The MEP labor leader was frustrated on both accounts. Although MEP became the second force behind AD, the Copeyano price for cooperating with AD to defeat MEP was high: Copeyanos were to receive three positions on the fifteen-member Executive Council, and the position of secretary-general. The terms were not difficult for the Adecos to accept. Not only would they have a working majority with COPEI on the Executive Council, but they would deny the secretary-general position to MEP.

At the congress that met in October 1970, the delegate strength of each party was as follows: AD, 34 percent; MEP, 31 percent; COPEI, 18 percent; URD, 11 percent. Two opposing slates were presented in the election. The AD-COPEI slate was led by the Adeco labor leader Francisco Olivo; the MEP-URD-FDP-FND slate was led by José González Navarro. Olivo's slate won, 478 to 396.

The results of the congress found COPEI in a strengthened position as far as the CTV was concerned, but in a somewhat weakened position because of an internal dispute within the party's labor group, the FTC. Within the CTV, the party was represented on the Executive Council by Rafael León León, secretary-general; Francisco Urquía Lugo, secretary of organization; and Ramón Darío Godoy, secretary of labor. The party had increased its strength from 14 to 18 percent over the previous congress. COPEI controlled three National Labor Federations affiliated with the CTV (compared to twenty-six for AD and nineteen for MEP): FETARANJAS (agricultural development), RA-DIOTELE y BAFISTAS (the communications media), and FETRAI-NOS (public works). Overall, COPEI's influence within the CTV was greater than the party's strength with organized labor as a whole. The agreement with AD gave COPEI a greater voice in the labor hierarchy than its relative numbers might indicate.

The Copeyano Conflict over the CTV Secretary-General and Control of the FTC

The magazine *Elite* described the disputes within the FTC as to which Copeyano should be secretary-general of the CTV and who should lead the FTC.[25] Rafael León León and Francisco Urquía Lugo wanted the CTV secretary-generalship. Sectors supporting Dagoberto González, the head of the FTC, opposed Urquía Lugo and accused him of having abandoned his work within the CTV. For their part, the followers of Urquía Lugo accused León León and Dagoberto González of having used official money to buy the votes of Copeyano labor directors in order to elect León León. According to León León, the rumors were obviously false, because he received 150 out of 166 votes in a party labor caucus. The secretary-general of COPEI, Arístides Beaujon, reprimanded Urquía Lugo and said that, for the prestige of the party, he must accept another position on the CTV Executive Council.

Urquía Lugo also wanted to replace Dagoberto González as head of the FTC. Rather than attack Dagoberto directly, he attempted to become CTV secretary-general himself and thus to defeat Dagoberto's candidate, or to defeat Dagoberto's selection for deputy secretary-general of the FTC. He failed in both efforts.

Thus AD emerged from the Sixth Congress in a much stronger position than COPEI. The Adecos had replaced the MEP president of the CTV with their own party militant, Francisco Olivo. They also had become the first force in the CTV, skillfully working with COPEI to defeat the MEP-led slate. Although they had to give the Copeyanos a certain number of seats on the Executive Council and the position of secretary-general, they did not fear a challenge by COPEI within the CTV. Their major concern was MEP, and they had three years (1970-73) before the next election to build on their Sixth Congress victory and to increase their influence within the labor movement. In what proved to be frosting on AD's cake, the Copeyanos had weakened their own position within the labor movement because of an internal conflict.

The Copeyanos wanted to deemphasize the importance of their intraparty dispute over the position of CTV secretary-general. According to Rubén Darío González, deputy secretary-general of the FTC and a supporter of León León within the CTV, both candidates were able men.[26] He pointed out that Urquía Lugo came from the old school, had good contacts with the old leaders, and also had charisma. But times had changed; the CTV secretary-general should be a young person who had good rapport with the younger leaders and who could offer new alternatives.

Urquía Lugo considered himself to be a fighter for labor independence.[27] Although he tried to keep politics to a minimum, he realized that his image as a fighter would be disadvantageous for one who was CTV secretary-general. He stated that the position required someone who was more able than he to moderate between the different groups. Urquía praised the character and ability of Dagoberto González and León León.

Dagoberto González said he supported León León for CTV secretary-general because it was necessary to give positions of responsibility to young people who would produce results.[28] He believed that Darío González, as deputy secretary-general of the FTC, would probably give him more trouble than the old guard; however, change could not be held back.

The Seventh Congress of the CTV

The increase in AD labor strength following the 1973 election was reflected in the CTV Congress, 25 April-1 May 1975.[29] AD and COPEI again presented a combined slate—but this time the Adecos did so for political reasons, because they could have won a majority of the Executive Council alone. AD won 52 percent of the delegates and eight of the fifteen seats on the Executive Council; COPEI won 20 percent of the delegates, and MEP 19. The increase in AD strength was primarily at the expense of MEP, which dropped from 31 percent in the Sixth Congress to 19 percent in the Seventh. The Adecos claimed they controlled all the labor federations except petroleum's, where a COPEI-MEP coalition was in control.

The new Executive Council membership was AD, eight; COPEI, three; MEP, three; URD, one. The Adeco José Vargas became president. The three Copeyanos appointed to the council were Rafael León León, secretary-general; Francisco Urquía Lugo, secretary of employment and professional formation; Rubén Santiago Santiago, secretary of technical education and contracts. Thus, for the sake of maintaining as much AD-COPEI cooperation as possible, the Adecos decided that the Copeyanos should retain the position of CTV secretary-general.

The FTC-CTV Relationship: Conclusions

According to COPEI's labor leadership, the FTC was a bridge between the CTV and COPEI.[30] Rather than allowing only transmission of orders from COPEI to the CTV, the COPEI-FTC relationship was a two-way street. The FTC tried to persuade the party regarding the positions on labor that the Christian Democrats should present in the CTV. Thus the COPEI labor leadership saw a CTV-FTC-COPEI linkup, as exemplified by the official positions of Darío González and Urquía Lugo. Depending upon COPEI strength within the CTV during a given period, they might simultaneously belong to the CTV Executive Council, the FTC National Directory, and the COPEI National Committee (see Chart 4.1).

Although one might disagree with this interpretation of the FTC's role, it was clear from the outset in 1959 that the FTC wanted to increase COPEI's influence within the CTV, utilizing cooperation with AD whenever possible. In the post-dictatorial period, as shown in the 1975 congress, COPEI's normal delegate strength within the CTV has been approximately 20 percent. We use the word "normal" guardedly. Most such CTV congresses have not taken place under normal conditions, due to a party coalition immediately following Pérez Jiménez's downfall, guerrilla warfare, the withdrawal of the communists, and splits within AD (the *arsista* faction and MEP). However, we look at the 1975 congress as normal because AD regained much of its labor strength from MEP: Adecos were 52 percent of the delegates, and COPEI captured 20 percent of the seats.

Although at times it was advantageous for COPEI to cooperate with AD within the labor movement, the tactic held serious risks for the Copeyanos, due to an internal struggle over the party's candidate for CTV secretary-general and the confrontation between the national FTC and its Zulia affiliate.[31] Given the results of AD-COPEI cooperation in the labor movement since 1959, we conclude that the Adecos received greater political benefits than the Copeyanos.

Chart 4.2 depicts the relationship between the various Christian Democratic organizations. Most deal with the labor movement, but peasant organizations have also been added in order to provide a composite view. Starting from the top of the chart, the CMT (Confederación Mundial del Trabajo) is the international Christian Democratic labor organization. In Latin America, CLAT (Central Latino-Americana de Trabajadores), formerly CLASC (Confederación Latino Americana de Sindicalistas Cristianos), is the primary labor organization, and FCL (Federación Campesina LatinoAmericana) is the primary peasant organization. We recall that, in Venezuela, the Christian Democratic labor leaders decided to separate labor activities through COPEI's labor group, the FTC (Frente de Trabajadores Copeyanos), and the nonparty CODESA (Confederación de Sindicatos Autónomos.) Shortly thereafter, they formed CUSIC (Comité Unitario de Sindicalistas Cristianos) to help the FTC and CODESA avoid friction and establish common strategies. CUSIC is in charge of the international representation of the FTC and CODESA and represents them in CLAT. A similar agreement was made with the peasant organizations. Peasant activities were divided between COPEI's peasant

CHART 4.1. CTV-FTC-COPEI Interrelationship

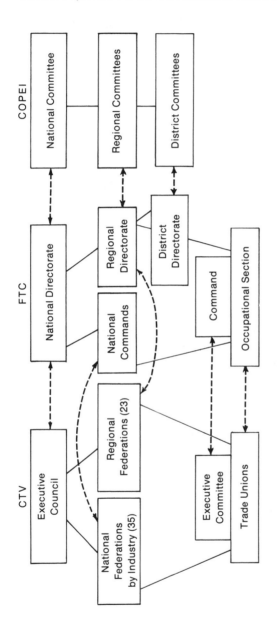

SOURCE: Dagoberto González (1971). When I was in his office, González drew the chart.

C H A R T 4.2. FTC and Other Christian Democratic Organizations

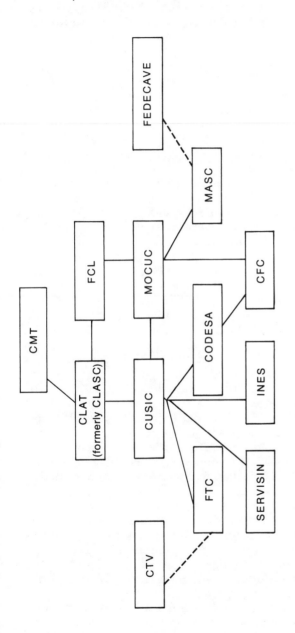

S O U R C E S : Ramón H. Silva T., *Introducción al Estudio del Sindicalismo Venezolano*; Chi-Yi Chen con la colaboración de Enrique Brücker, *Economía Social del Trabajo—Caso de Venezuela*.

group, MASC (Movimiento Agrario Social Cristiano), and CODESA's peasant organization, the CFC (Comité Pro Federación de Ligas Campesinas). Both organizations belong to MOCUC (Movimiento Campesino Unitario Cristiano), which in turn is affiliated with the FCL. The MASC operates within FEDECAVE (Federación Campesina de Venezuela), and the FTC operates through the CTV. The leaders of CUSIC also formed two organizations to service both the FTC and CODESA: INES (Instituto Nacional de Estudios Sindicales) and SERVISIN (La Central de Servicios Sindicales). Finally, some Copeyanos are active in yet another organization, MONTRI (Movimiento Nacional de Trabajadores Independientes). (Since MONTRI does not have a direct relationship with the other organizations, it is not shown on the chart.)

Let us look more closely at some of the organizations and their relationships. A perusal of CODESA's statutes clearly indicates an ideological coincidence between CODESA and the FTC;[32] tactically, however, the two organizations were very different. According to their agreement, CODESA was to concentrate on the creation and development of new trade unions, while the FTC was to work within existing trade unions and the CTV. In practice, the FTC leadership was aware that CODESA competed with the CTV as confederations and, at times, CODESA trade unions competed with FTC trade unions.[33] In theory, CUSIC was supposed to deal with administrative problems, and CLAT and CMT were to deal with political problems. In practice, political problems were frequently sent to CUSIC as well.[34] We can cite two examples. When the Communist party left the CTV in the early 1960s, the communists wanted CODESA to join their party in forming a new confederation. Some of the CODESA leaders wanted to accept the Communists' offer; this caused serious friction within CODESA and between CODESA and the FTC. CUSIC eventually prevailed upon CODESA to reject the idea. Another continuous problem, often sent to CUSIC, involved the directors of CODESA who were Copeyanos but who competed with the CTV for influence in the labor movement. When they criticized the CTV, they forgot that they were criticizing the FTC as well.

COPEI has three institutes, two for training political directors (IFEDEC and the Luigi Sturzo Institute) and one for training labor leaders (INES). The Luigi Sturzo Institute differs from IFEDEC in that it emphasizes Latin American over Venezuelan questions. According to the Copeyano leadership, the party is not simply concerned with arousing emotions or electoral action; "We are forming people and that is what is valuable in politics."[35]

INES (Instituto Nacional de Estudios Sindicales) developed out of the Christian trade union movement. We recall that from 1945 to 1960 Padre Manuel Aguirre conducted courses for future Christian Democratic labor leaders; these were organized and offered by each existing

Christian labor organization. Conversations in 1958-59 led to the formation of CUSIC, and shortly thereafter INES was formed (on 15 May 1960, the same day that the encyclical *Rerum Novarum* first appeared). Over the years INES has conducted courses for Venezuelans and other Latin Americans, graduating thirty to forty labor leaders a month. The courses normally deal with doctrine, labor legislation, or one's place in society, and last from one to fifteen days. INES has its own library and publishes a variety of materials.

While stating that the organization agreed with the general policy and strategy of the FTC, INES also tried to incorporate the internal administrative structures of both the FTC and CODESA.[36] This involved choosing professors and utilizing programs; an FTC member served as director and a CODESA member as deputy director for a period, and then reversed positions with other personnel. The same idea held true for lower administrative positions. In addition, INES periodically signed agreements with other organizations such as the Instituto para Capacitación y Recreación de los Trabajadores (INCRET), an organization originally formed by the government and placed under CTV authority. The agreement called for cooperative educational programs for labor leaders throughout the country; jointly offered courses that lasted from one to three years and dealt with the economic, cultural, and civic problems of workers.[37]

The FTC and COPEI

Let us look more closely at the labor group's role in the party and examine the FTC-Caldera government relationship. As we have stated, FTC leaders believed that the primary mission of COPEI and the FTC was to serve the common good. The trade union had professional functions, while those of the party were primarily political.[38] Although the FTC was a functional organization of the party, labor leaders believed that a high degree of autonomy would serve the best interests of both the FTC and COPEI. But the FTC leadership also believed that the political parties hampered the natural development of the labor movement by converting trade unions into "vulgar instruments of partisan proselytism."[39]

The FTC directors decided long ago to accept the constraints of party control over their body.[40] We have seen that they carried out the party line while simultaneously trying to increase labor influence without COPEI. According to the FTC leadership, their own participation and cooperation in the party's various decision-making organs guaranteed that the policies adopted by the party would be carried out.[41] They also looked to the party's secretary of political formation to provide specialized political education for Copeyanos and FTC militants.

The FTC leadership had hard evidence that the labor group's influence within the party was growing. In 1963, there was only one trade union deputy in the Congress; with Caldera's victory in 1968, the number increased to twelve. Urquía Lugo pointed out that he was deputy secretary-general for regional matters of COPEI. By selecting a labor leader to hold this position, the party broke with tradition and provided an important opening for the FTC within COPEI.[42]

Other labor leaders observed that FTC influence within COPEI was growing, regionally and nationally, but they believed there was much resistance to the objectives of the trade union struggle as they defined them.[43] Rubén Darío González wanted a truly revolutionary party which would be sensitive to the anguish of the workers, and whose objectives would include the elimination of any capitalist influence. In spite of resistance to their beliefs, Darío González thought that he and the younger leaders would win because they were gaining in representation at the national conventions, as well as in the legislative assemblies and municipal councils.

The FTC took the position that it had common cause with COPEI and "lines of coincidence" with the Caldera government. Although it supported the Christian Democrats, the FTC claimed to defend the autonomy of the trade union movement before the industrialists and the Caldera government.[44] However, as a functional organization of of COPEI, the FTC was naturally very limited in its manner of expressing autonomy. At times the FTC supported a strike of public employees and called for greater governmental efforts to alleviate the unemployment problem, but for the most part labor supported the Caldera government's programs and policies. For example, the Fifth FTC National Assembly supported, among other things, the nationalization of gas, the regulation of the sale of vehicles by quotas, the government's negotiations with Colombia, and service contracts with the petroleum companies and the policy of no more concessions.[45]

We have mentioned elsewhere that COPEI's influence within the Venezuelan labor movement increased during the Caldera regime. As the government signed many collective contracts and increased wages, it was only natural that Copeyanos would benefit, but many FTC leaders were not satisfied with the FTC-government relationship. Some pointed out that although the FTC voice was increasing within COPEI, the labor group had no influence within the Caldera government.[46] According to this view, the powerful interests, such as the local oligarchy and the foreign monopolies, had penetrated the administration; they were joined by the *desarrollistas*, who strongly pressured the government and prevented changes in society which the FTC believed were necessary.

In some states the local FTC leadership did not believe the COPEI regime was improving their position within the labor movement. In Zulia, the FTC depended upon its own efforts and received little help from the government.[47] In Táchira, the COPEI-controlled regional government did not help the FTC to increase its strength in the labor movement.[48] The government hired too many non-Copeyanos, particularly in the ministry of public works. Thus the Táchira FTC leadership believed that their hopes of increasing COPEI's labor strength on the regional and national level had not been attained.

Juventud Revolucionaria Copeyana (JRC)

Throughout its history, the Copeyano Revolutionary Youth (JRC) has been concerned primarily with ideological questions. In the following discussion we shall treat some of these ideological questions and note their effect on the development of the JRC, the relationship between the JRC and COPEI, and the relationship between the JRC and the Caldera government.

The party created the JRC as a functional organization on 24 December 1947. The original National Provisional Directorate included Valmore Acevedo Amaya, Eduardo Tamayo, Luis Herrera Campins, Rodolfo José Cárdenas, and Rafael Jacobo Alfonzo. Shortly thereafter, the National Committee of COPEI published a pamphlet which explained the role of the JRC, the requirements for membership, and the national party's control over its youth affiliate.[49]

Early Ideological Position

We can discuss similarities and differences between the JRC and the UNE, the earlier (1930s) youth organization of Caldera and his associates. We recall that the UNE was not political; it was a Catholic organization formed to oppose what its leaders considered to be Marxism in the Venezuelan student movement. Thus it was an anticommunist organization, but with a Catholic rather than primarily Christian Democratic political orientation.

The JRC, on the other hand, was formed as a functional organization of COPEI. Like the peasant and labor affiliates, it was political from the beginning, and its battles were to be fought in the schools, universities, and streets. At the outset, the JRC was clearly anticommunist. During the politically violent period of the *trienio* (1945-48), the party newspaper stated that the JRC was as anticommunist as its parent organization.[50] Various JRC publications in the 1940s and early 1950s repeated the anticommunist theme. Reflecting the party position, a JRC publication from Táchira identified the common enemy: "the Marxists of Acción Democrática and their communist vanguard. We struggle against the traitors who violated the promises of the October Revolution."[51] After 1959, the JRC continued to express its anticommunist orientation, albeit to a lesser degree than in 1948-52.

Early Development

The following Copeyanos, most of whom rose to positions of party leadership, served as national secretaries or secretaries-general of the JRC in this order: Luis Herrera Campins, Rodolfo José Cárdenas, Hilarión Cardozo, Eduardo Fernández, Alvarez Paz Pumar, Abdón Vivas Terán, Oswaldo Alvarez Paz, José Rámon Solano, Julio César Moreno, and Donald Ramírez (Ramírez was elected in 1976).

Herrera Campins and Rodolfo Cárdenas directed the JRC until the fall of the dictatorship in 1958. During that period several student leaders were jailed or exiled, but, regardless of the difficulties, the JRC managed to hold its First National Convention in 1952 and continued clandestine operations in several universities, *colegios*, and *liceos*. The party newspaper announced various organized activities in the states of Lara, Miranda, Portuguesa, Táchira, and Yaracuy.[52] Since the student leadership was harassed by the government, Caldera periodically directed JRC activities. One of his letters announced that the party's National Committee had chosen Francisco Sánchez Carrillo to be a member of the JRC National Directorate. The other members of the directorate were Gonzalo García Bustillos, Eduardo Gómez Tamayo (who was also director of the Copeyano university group), Pedro Pablo Aguilar, Horacio Moros, José Luis Zapata Escalona, Arnoldo Matheus Camacho, Pedro Contreras Pulido, and Carlos Léañez.[53] We have outlined Copeyano efforts in resistance to the dictatorship elsewhere in this study. Several members and future members of the JRC participated in strikes, street demonstrations, and the like.

When the dictatorship fell, Venezuela entered the period of the *guanábana* which reflected AD-COPEI cooperation (1959-64). As we have seen, the student movement was polarized between the Marxists and communists (the Communist party and ultimately the MIR) and the youth groups of AD and COPEI. The AD students and the JRC worked together in opposing the insurrectionist tactics of the Marxists and communists. During that period the JRC was anticommunist, and there was no dialogue between the JRC and communist-led students.[54]

Although the JRC supported the party position during the *guanábana*, the JRC and COPEI were on opposite sides in the 1964 student strikes.[55] At issue were the university's efforts to oust perennial repeaters and hangers-on; COPEI supported the administration, while the JRC supported the strike. AD denounced the strike, and its students returned to class. COPEI and the JRC also continued to be at odds over other issues and ideological questions.[56]

Ideological and Political Conflicts

The year 1965 was crucial for internal JRC alignments and JRC-COPEI relations. The difficulties that surfaced that year were to persist, in varying degrees, until the 1973 national election.

At its Third National Convention in 1965, the JRC assumed a radical posture. Three groups with different ideological positions were born: the Araguatos, the Avanzados, the Astronautas. One recognized leader of the Araguatos was Delfín Sánchez; his views reflected the classical Christian Democratic doctrine that we have analyzed elsewhere in this study, and the Generation of 1936 (including Caldera) supported him for a leadership position within the JRC. Sánchez claimed that his ideological position did not differ significantly from that of the Avanzados and Astronautas;[57] he believed they agreed on the goals listed in the eighteen points of COPEI's 1946 platform, but that they differed on the means to realize those goals. Sánchez added, however, that he did not agree with the party-sanctioned positions of the students.

Because Delfín Sánchez considered himself to be a Christian Democratic revolutionary, he felt free to criticize "Yankee wars" and United States military presence in the Panama Canal Zone, Puerto Rico, Guantánamo Bay in Cuba, and Vietnam. He also criticized the U.S. invasion in the Dominican Republic in 1965, the Soviet invasion of Czechoslovakia in 1968, and the factors leading to the deaths of the Kennedys and "Che" Guevara.[58]

Although he did not like to consider himself part of any particular group, Julio César Moreno often represented the views of the Avanzados, and they supported him within the JRC. His views were "advanced" in the sense that he did not want the JRC to be an anticommunist organization; instead, he saw it as more like the Tomic wing of Chile's Christian Democratic party, which had advanced toward socialism but remained distinct from Marxist socialism.[59] Occasionally the Avanzados and Astronautas presented their views jointly, as in the pamphlet "Juventud para el Cambio." They called for a revolutionary movement that would struggle against status, and for the creation of a different society. The pamphlet stated that the orientation of COPEI must change to prepare for the new era.

Several students were recognized as leaders of the Astronautas, including Abdel Muhamad, Carlos González, Joaquín Marta Sosa, Rafael Iribarren, Saúl Rivas Rivas, and Oliver Belisario. The older party leaders and their followers considered these young men to be radicals whose views were outside the main stream of Christian Democratic thought.[60] The Astronautas expressed their opinions in a series of letters and position papers circulated at the JRC convention, and in several interviews and articles that appeared in the media.[61] They addressed themselves to the questions of democracy, the party, the communists, and communitarian society. For the most part, their views on these topics challenged the Generation of 1936 and those who accepted that generation's interpretation of classical Christian Democracy.

In one of the political doctrines circulated at the JRC convention, the Astronautas rejected liberal democracy, claiming it had failed because it had not satisfied the fundamental necessities of the people. Needless to say, this criticism could never be acceptable to the party leadership: without the ideological foundation of liberal democracy, COPEI would not be a Christian Democratic movement.

The Astronautas were highly critical of COPEI as a political party. A document signed by Joaquín Marta Sosa, Germán Ahrensburg, and Rafael Iribarren accused party leaders of pursuing a negative and opportunistic policy through agreements with powerful forces, such as the industrial sectors and the clergy. COPEI leaders allegedly tried to make the party their tool, thereby forgetting the importance of the popular sectors. Furthermore, the Astronautas claimed that COPEI's militancy was marginal because the party was controlled by regional *caudillos*; i.e., the political life of COPEI was decided at a "high level" and without the real participation of functional organizations. In a letter written by Iribarren to José Antonio Pérez Díaz (deputy secretary-general of COPEI) and to the other members of the National Committee, the Copeyanos were warned that they must exorcise Caesarism. (The Astronautas were not the only ones to criticize what they considered to be one-man domination of COPEI. Throughout the years, others had accused Caldera of overwhelming the party.)

The Astronautas rejected the heretofore anticommunist orientation of the JRC. In an article in the magazine *Momento*, they stated that the party "must erase the barriers that separate the Social Christians from the communists. The enemy is on the right, not on the left." We must remember that the Astronautas stated this position in 1965. Although the Copeyanos had cooperated with the communists and other parties to overthrow the dictatorship, during the Betancourt administration, in the face of a serious guerrilla movement, they again assumed an adamant anticommunist position. By 1965 COPEI was the loyal opposition to the Leoni government, and was not as anticommunist as it had been during the *guanábana*. Nevertheless, COPEI was not ready for rapprochement with the communists. Not until Caldera's term (1969-74) did the Copeyano position change toward the communists. Thus the Astronautas' call was premature.

The concept of the communitarian society had been discussed by the Christian Democrats before the Astronautas emerged as an identifiable group. The Generation of 1936 accepted the idea that private property had to be used responsibly and possessed a social function. But in rejecting the idea of communitarian property, that generation thereby rejected the Astronautas' idea of a communitarian society.[62] In their discussion of the communitarian society, the Astronautas broadened the analysis and introduced new ideas. (Those who opposed the Astronautas believed that their view of communitarianism did not differ significantly from Marxism.) The Astronautas saw the communitarian society as a substitute for the capitalist regime. The class conflict, identified with capitalism, would be eliminated, because capital and labor would no longer be divided between employer and employee. The land would be given to those who work it, and private property would develop toward socialization for the dignity of man. However, conciliation between the classes would not be the final goal, because it would only lead to a false class unity within the capitalist structure. To avoid this danger, the Astronautas called for a new, classless society. In a subsequent document, coauthored by the Avanzados,[63] the Astronautas stated that Christian Democracy must be defined as socialist because it would otherwise lean toward capitalism. The debate that began in 1965 continued, and subsequent JRC conventions and documents addressed themselves to the question of communitarian society.[64]

Other JRC groups also had opinions on communitarianism. Expressing the Araguatos viewpoint, Delfín Sánchez saw the communitarian society as an alternative to socialism and capitalism.[65] The emphasis would be on individual human development in a personal rather than collective sense, directed toward the common good. He found building toward the communitarian society preferable to discussions about utopia. Beyond that, Sánchez believed one could not outline the communitarian society in detail.

Julio César Moreno stated the Avanzado position,[66] asserting that socialism is a stop along the road that is necessary before the advanced socialism of a communitarian society can be attained. This was not Marxist socialism, because the communitarian society would be pluralist, allowing different types of property in addition to permitting individual liberty. Nevertheless, socialism was an integral part of the picture, and it was improper to speak of the communitarian society without communitarian socialism.

Abdón Vivas Terán also identified with the Avanzado position.[67] He believed that the communitarian society was a global concept involving political, social, and economic changes. In the economic structure, communitarian socialism would replace capitalism; it would feature communitarian ownership of the means of production, a social plan or central planning for the economy, and self-management in industry, similar to the Yugoslavian example. Politics would be expressed in terms of participatory rather than representative democracy. Socialism would be implemented strictly in an economic sense, and would entail social property and central planning.

In comparing the interpretations of these three groups, we should note that each admitted that its concept was theoretical. They also agreed on the need for some type of system to replace capitalism. For the Astronautas, that system would be based on communitarian property and would lead to a classless society. The Araguatos were not explicit concerning the form their system would take, and their ideas did not differ significantly from those of classical Christian Democratic doctrine. Although the Avanzados leaned toward the Astronautas view, particularly in some of the documents the two groups coauthored, their spokesmen presented yet another system, calling for a non-Marxist socialism that would allow for different types of property relationships within the communitarian society. Furthermore, their advocacy of participatory rather than representative democracy implied some type of decentralized decision-making.

Given the different ideological currents that had emerged within the JRC, and the ensuing intraparty and public debates, Caldera deemed it most appropriate to address the Third JRC Convention in his capacity as secretary-general of COPEI.[68] He underlined the importance of liberal democracy for the Christian Democratic movement, and stated that COPEI should neither have an anticommunist complex nor be "philo-communist." The party must deal with the communists objectively, as exemplified by the COPEI directors' approaches to the communist leaders. Caldera expressed concern that some elements within the JRC sympathized with President Nasser's Egyptian model, reminding the convention that the Nasser regime was a dictatorship and not worthy of Copeyano emulation. He discussed at length the concept of property and pointed out that "private property was an institution of natural right, immutable in time and inextinguishable in the light of Christian Democratic doctrine." Caldera closed his speech by stating that youth was important, but that it should not be converted into a party within the party.

As the controversy developed among the three groups and with COPEI, the Third JRC Convention held an election for national secretary and deputy national secretary. For the first time candidates ran on slates representing the three ideological currents: Araguatos, Alvaro Páez Pumar and Oswaldo Alvarez Paz; Avanzados, Abdón Vivas Terán and Rubén Darío González (the slate included Julio César Moreno); Astronautas, Joaquín Marta Sosa and Saúl Rivas Rivas. The Avanzados edged out the Araguatos by two votes. The election pointed to two developments: although close ideologically, the Astronautas and Avanzados decided to field their own slates, rather than to combine; and strength within the JRC in 1965 was almost equally divided between the Araguatos and Avanzados, with the Astronautas running third.

Caldera's speech to the convention did not end the JRC-COPEI controversy. Toward the end of the year several members of the JRC, including Vivas Terán and Marta Sosa, were invited to appear on Venezuelan television with visiting dignitary Robert F. Kennedy.[69] The COPEI leadership gave permission for Vivas Terán to appear on the program, but it did not want Marta Sosa to participate. The JRC leadership rejected the party's position, and the two took part in the program; they were joined by other university students, some of whom were not members of the JRC. In all, there were seven: Vivas Terán, Marta Sosa, Douglas Dáger, Adelis Romero, Narciso Romero, Rodolfo Porro Aletti, and Carlos Torres Bracho.

During the program Marta Sosa made a fervent attack on the United States and discussed such items as the use of dogs against black students; killings by the Ku Klux Klan; the fact that the fascist John Birch Society was allowed to exist; the exploitation of man by man in the United States; and the desperate war policy of President Johnson in Vietnam. Marta Sosa also asserted that the revolution for the Christian Democrats in Latin America signified the elimination of private property.

This led to a violent campaign within COPEI. The National Committee met, and Caldera proposed that Vivas Terán be dismissed as national secretary of the JRC and suspended from all activities. The Copeyanos divided over the issue; those who supported Caldera's position included Daniel Scott, Urquía Lugo, Pedro Pablo Aguilar, and Hilarión Cardozo. Several supported Vivas Terán, including Contreras Pulido, Briceño Salas, Rodolfo José Cárdenas, Herrera Campins, Leonor de Brandt, Carlos Felice, and Felipe Montilla. Manual Duplat and a few others did not support either side. The majority eventually accepted Caldera's position, and the National Committee appointed Oswaldo Alvarez Paz to become national secretary of the JRC. After ratifying his ideological position, Vivas Terán accepted the party's decision. He went to Williams College in the United States, remained for two years, and received a master's degree in economics. (Throughout the proceedings, the majority of the JRC and of the party's university directors supported him.)

Problems within the JRC and between the JRC and COPEI continued. Toward the end of 1966, Edecio La Riva Araujo, COPEI vice-president and national senator, made a speech in the Senate criticizing the government for lack of a coherent policy on guerrillas and urban violence. He stated that the Central University of Venezuela was harboring guerrillas, and that the Communist party was receiving annual payments through the university.[70] Three JRC members—Piñera, Muhamad, and Carlos González—publicly attacked La Riva's views concerning the university; they went before the disciplinary tribunal and were suspended from all party activities.[71]

The party leadership allowed the JRC to choose a new national secretary (also called secretary-general), and José Ramón Solano was elected. But a new crisis soon arose when the JRC directors signed a document "against imperialist penetration in Cambodia and the extension of the war to that zone."[72] The document was also signed by youth representatives of other parties and groups, including MEP, URD, FDP, PCV, MIR, and the Christian Left. They declared a "Week of Anti-Imperialist Solidarity" during which they held a series of meetings to protest the U.S. invasion of Cambodian territory and the war in Vietnam. A fourth identifiable group within the JRC then emerged, the Auténticos; in their call for socialism and on some other positions, it was difficult to distinguish between them and the Astronautas.

The COPEI National Secretariat met with Caldera, and a meeting of the National Committee followed. The party leaders were particularly disturbed by the JRC repudiation of alleged brutal repression against peaceful student manifestations, and by the signing of the document with other leftist groups. Several JRC members were suspended: Carlos Eduardo Febres and Alexis Ortiz of the Auténticos, Orlando López of the Astronautas, Rafael Domínguez Daly of the left wing of the Avanzados, and José Ramón Solano, the secretary-general of the JRC, also of the Avanzados.

The National Committee of COPEI established an intervention committee, under Hilarión Cardozo, to direct the JRC during an interim period. Although some Copeyanos, such as Oswaldo Alvarez Paz and José Rodríguez Iturbe, wanted to extend the intervention to the regional committees, meaning a "reorganization to the depth" of the JRC, the intervention commitee did not agree. Instead, Cardozo and most other committee members saw their role as stabilizing the situation until a new election for JRC directors could be held.

The JRC's Sixth Convention

The struggle among the various groups reached a climax at the Sixth Convention, held in December 1970. The most important candidates for JRC secretary-general were Delfín Sánchez of the Araguatos and Julio César Moreno of the Avanzados. Sánchez claimed that the differences between Moreno and himself were political, rather than ideological;[73] they agreed on such questions as the need for social justice, but differed on the desirable pace and intensity of change. He believed that a specific historical moment would complete each change, and did not want to use violence to accelerate the process. For his own part, Julio Moreno believed there were profound differences between Delfín Sánchez and the Araguatos and himself.[74] Sánchez and his followers allegedly supported the capitalist system and wanted to use the JRC as an anticommunist instrument. Moreno accused them of holding to dogma, and of not realizing that conditions and policies must change.

Rafael Isidro Quevedo and Luis Eduardo González also appeared as candidates at the last minute.[75] González represented some discontented Araguatos. Quevedo was a professor of agronomy at the Central University (UCV); he represented a group of Astronautas who did not feel that Moreno's position was radical enough to offer a real change within the JRC. (Other Astronautas supported Moreno.) But he really wanted representation on the JRC directorate and asked for four of the eleven positions a few hours before the convention opened. The request was rejected by all the slates and, although several delegates voted for him, he ended his candidacy one day before the balloting.

Thus we see two developments at the convention: the Auténticos did not make an impact, while the Astronautas were divided in their support for the candidates, reflecting an ideological split within that group. (Yet another group of Astronautas called themselves the Christian Left; their model was the MAPU of the Chilean Christian Democratic party, which left that party to support Salvador Allende.) In order to be elected, the candidate had to receive 111 votes. The totals were as follows. First ballot: Julio Moreno, 104; Delfín Sánchez, 91; Rafael Quevedo, 30. Second ballot: Julio Moreno, 117. According to COPEI statutes, the results of the JRC election had to be officially sanctioned by the party's National Committee before the youth wing's directorate could be named. When the ballots were counted, there were approximately six votes more than there were delegates. This was not enough to change the election results, but the question was raised by several Copeyanos who were extremely unhappy with developments within the JRC. José Rodríguez Iturbe, Oswaldo Alvarez Paz, Alberto Silva Guillén, and Alvaro Páez Pumar asked that the election be declared illegal at a special meeting of the party's National Committee. But other committee members concluded that this would be very unwise; among them were Arístides Beaujon (the party's secretary-general), Pérez Díaz, Edecio La Riva, Herrera Campins, Eduardo Aguilar, Eduardo Fernández, Lisando Estopiñán, and Hilarión Cardozo. At one point José Rodríguez reportedly became very upset, shouting at Beaujon and calling Cardozo a traitor.[76] The National Committee heard the report of Hilarión Cardozo, as chairman of the intervention committee, and proclaimed Julio Moreno secretary-general of the JRC. Delfín Sánchez and his delegates proposed in vain that Moreno's victory not be recognized.

For all practical purposes, the battle that had begun in 1965 was over.[77] The Avanzados dominated the new National Directorate, taking seven of the eleven positions. The remaining four positions consisted of three for the "Grupo Caracas," who supported Julio Moreno, and one Astronauta, Rafael Isidro Quevedo. No Araguatos were represented. The deputy secretary-general was Rafael Domínguez Daly, who had previously been suspended by the party. In a sense, the election results were a· defeat for Caldera, because the Generation of 1936 and their allies had supported Delfín Sánchez and the Araguatos. The JRC was now under the leadership of the more left-wing and progressive forces. Early recognition of that situation explained the vote of the party's National Committee. Caldera's supporters—Pérez Díaz, Edecio La Riva, Eduardo Fernández, and Hilarión Cardozo—joined Herrera Campins, a spokesman for the party's left wing who wanted to accept the results of the JRC election. Other Caldera supporters—José Rodríguez Iturbe and Oswaldo Alvarez Paz—could not yet reconcile themselves to those results.

After the Sixth Convention

Disagreement continued over issues of socialism and communism as they related to Christian Democratic doctrine. The National Committee of COPEI decided that Copeyanos should not use the concept of socialism within regular party channels. It was reported that Eduardo Fernández, a young party leader and Caldera supporter, had stated that he was against the use of socialism as an economic expression of Christian Democracy, and that "socialism" as a word had lost prestige. When asked to respond, Julio Moreno said that "democracy," "justice," "liberty," and "development" were also words that had lost prestige.[78] However, some regional JRC members continued to perceive the youth affiliate as an anticommunist organization. In Mérida, for example, the leadership acknowledged that there should be dialogue between the Christian Democrats and the communists, but they insisted that the JRC should continue as an anticommunist organization.[79] In Zulia, a cross-section of the membership admitted that the JRC could unite with the communists in support of certain programs, but they too viewed the youth affiliate as basically anticommunist.[80]

We recall that Vivas Terán, in a losing effort, had presented himself as a candidate for secretary-general of COPEI. The national JRC leadership and most regional affiliates had supported him; they had also supported the presidential candidacy of Herrera Campins, who lost the nomination to Lorenzo Fernández. Numerous directors of the labor affiliate (FTC), such as Rubén Darío González, worked with the JRC in these efforts.

The major theme of Vivas Terán's candidacy was that the party should commit itself to a deeper and clearer ideology.[81] As the candidate for the JRC malcontents, he praised the Christian Democratic ideology but criticized the party leaders for expressing it in terms too general to have meaning for most people. He wanted Christian Democracy to be specifically related to the real problems of poor and oppressed people of the Third World; to achieve those ends, it must be truly revolutionary and must demand basic changes in the political, economic, and social spheres.

The JRC and the Caldera Government

Vivas Terán saw the Caldera administration as a reform government "in a period of transition in which foundations were being created to exercise a more profound revolutionary process." Christian Democracy should build on the foundation of the Caldera government, bringing about the definite ascent of popular power, changing the structures of property (i.e., into the communitarian society), and altering people's attitudes to permit them to take the necessary steps along the revolutionary path. Thus Vivas Terán saw the period of transition provided by the Caldera government as tactical within the general revolutionary strategy. He believed his revolutionary position complemented the reform objectives of the Caldera regime.

Although the leadership of various groups within the JRC agreed that the Caldera government was reform minded, rather than revolutionary, several of the JRC rank and file could not accept this fact. Once the Christian Democratic government assumed power, they insisted that it carry out a revolution according to their own idea of "true" Christian Democracy. This was one major reason for the conflicts between the JRC and the Caldera government. The Astronautas and the left wing of the Avanzados insisted, for example, that the government enact the youth's conception of the communitarian society. Redistribution of wealth and nationalization of industry must be realized immediately! Of course, this was not to be.

Several JRC members complained that their organization had to defend unpopular measures of the government. For example, they (and other students) strongly opposed the stationing of troops in the Central University at Caracas. But the particular measure that caused the most serious problems was the University Reform Law, which was perceived by the students and the university's rector as severely restricting, if not eliminating, university autonomy. We have mentioned the document, signed by several JRC directors, members, and other students, criticizing the invasion of Cambodia and the war in Vietnam. Part of that document also criticized the University Reform Law. The JRC affiliates in Mérida and Lara produced similar documents; in addition, the JRC paid for newspaper advertisements that defended university autonomy and offered support for the Central University's rector.

The Aftermath

The organized youth of Venezuela often finds itself opposed to the government, even when the government is Christian Democratic and the JRC is the potential opponent. This does not mean that the JRC consistently opposed the Caldera government, although the JRC did take strong exception to the University Reform Law. The primary challenge was ideological. The struggle that took place within the JRC and between the JRC and COPEI concerned the very nature of Venezuelan Christian Democracy, indicating that the challenge to the party was more serious than the challenge to the government.

Some JRC sectors, especially the Araguatos, continued to support the government and party positions. But because the majority of the JRC, and particularly the leadership, supported the Avanzados, the Generation of 1936 (and, more important, the ideas motivating it) did not control the JRC. This factor was confirmed at the Seventh Convention, in 1976, where an integrated slate of Avanzados and Astronautas won the election for JRC officers and the directorate. Donald Ramírez of the Avanzados was elected secretary-general, and Gehard Cartay of the Astronautas was chosen as deputy secretary-general.[82]

Different Groups and Generations within COPEI

It can be said that the conflicts within the JRC and between the JRC and COPEI reflected the disputes within the party. It can also be said that the conflicts within the JRC paralleled those within COPEI. The party differences through the years have involved different generations and disagreements over tactics (i.e., whether or not to cooperate with Pérez Jiménez; the advisability of joining the *guanábana*). Although the media labeled groups within COPEI as Araguatos or Avanzados, the party did not develop a significant group of Astronautas.

Three major generational groups—1936, 1945, and 1958—can be found within COPEI; perhaps we could even add a fourth, 1965, which became active as the conflicts within the JRC came to a head. It remains to be seen whether the 1965 members comprise a new group of activists or are merely a section identifying with one or the other major generational groups.

We have discussed the Generation of 1936 at length. Its members have held major party positions and were important in various Venezuelan administrations. Throughout most of COPEI's history, this generation has controlled the party. Besides Caldera, its members include José Antonio Pérez Díaz, Godofredo González, Pedro Del Corral, Edecio La Riva Araujo, Lorenzo Fernández, and Dagoberto González. As in the case of other generations, the Generation of 1936 certainly is not ideologically monolithic. Using the United States Republican party for comparison, Dagoberto González would be with the Senator Jacob Javits wing and Edecio La Riva with the Senator Barry Goldwater wing. In general, however, the Generation of 1936 has been more conservative than the other generations.

The Generation of 1945 includes Pedro Pablo Aguilar, Luis Herrera Campins, Hilarión Cardozo, Francisco Urquía Lugo, and Arístides Beaujon. Perhaps the only thing this generation has in common is that they began their partisan activities around the same time. Tactically and ideologically they have often gone their own ways and have formed opposing alliances. For example, Cardozo worked with Caldera and most members of the Generation of 1936 to secure the presidential nomination for Lorenzo Fernández, thereby opposing the candidacy of Herrera Campins. Beaujon and Pedro Pablo Aguilar competed for the position of secretary-general.

We can make similar observations about the Generation of 1958. Included in this group are Rodolfo José Cárdenas, Hugo Briceño Salas, Eduardo Fernández, José Rodríguez Iturbe, Oswaldo Alvarez Paz, José Ramón Solano, Delfín Sánchez, Abdón Vivas Terán, and Julio César Moreno. We have already discussed the competition within this generation for the position of JRC secretary-general. Eduardo Fernández and Alvarez Paz have usually supported Caldera on the issues, while Julio Moreno has usually been on the opposing side. Vivas

Terán and Rodríguez Iturbe are far apart ideologically, especially on such questions as the communitarian society.

Thus, internal differences have involved a combination of factors, and the lines between groups are not as clearly drawn as they are in the Italian Christian Democratic party. In Italy, the various groups are represented on different party committees. COPEI does not seem to be moving in that direction, partly because coalitions shift from issue to issue, and also because of the effects of the 1973 election.

After the guerrilla violence of the early 1960s, the three generations moved closer together. This harmony was short lived, however, and friction soon developed over several issues. In 1967, at the Tenth National Convention of COPEI, forces headed by Rodolfo José Cárdenas and Hugo Briceño Salas (Generation of 1958) opposed those of Edecio La Riva (Generation of 1936) for control of the National Committee.[83] The two groups agreed that Caldera should remain as secretary-general and run for president in 1968, and that Lorenzo Fernández should be the first vice-president of the party. But the more progressive forces wanted to replace La Riva with Professor Pedro Contreras Pulido as second vice-president. Caldera remained neutral. The effort to replace La Riva did not succeed at that time, but a few years later he was replaced as vice-president and removed from the National Committee for a time. There was also some tension over reform of the party's statutes concerning admission of new members, and it was reported that José Curiel attempted to create a structure parallel to the traditional party.

An active party militant commented that the power struggle within the Chilean Christian Democratic party started about a year after Eduardo Frei won the election; in Venezuela, the struggle within COPEI started approximately a month after Caldera's victory.[84] The Eleventh National Convention of COPEI had only three days (1-3 August 1969) in which to choose a secretary-general to replace Caldera. Three candidates were nominated. José Antonio Pérez Díaz, a member of the Generation of 1936, was president of the Senate and of the National Congress; he also became acting secretary-general after Caldera won the presidency. Although a member of the Generation of 1936, he was supported by the progressive forces associated with Herrera Campins. Godofredo González, the second candidate, was also a member of the Generation of 1936; he was supported by forces associated with Caldera. The third candidate was Arístides Beaujon, a member of the Generation of 1945 and deputy national secretary of functional organizations. The voting was as follows. First ballot: Beaujon, 243; Pérez Díaz, 234; González, 168. Second ballot: Beaujon, 336; Pérez Díaz, 305.[85]

Beaujon's victory was most unexpected. Tending to party affairs, he had made many trips to the interior, where he built his base of support while many talented party leaders were busy forming the government. (Pérez Díaz, for example, was organizing the Congress and did not have time to travel to the interior.) At the convention, the Generation of 1936 divided its loyalties between two of its own candidates. Others voted for Beaujon because they saw his victory as an opportunity to begin to wrest party control from the founding generation.

Beaujon's victory was a defeat for Caldera, as his candidate, Godofredo González, ran a poor third. Shortly thereafter, the Caldera forces reasserted themselves in three key party elections. The first was for national secretary of organization,[86] a position which became vacant when José Curiel joined the Caldera administration in the ministry of public works. When the National Committee met in the fall of 1970 to elect a replacement, it was immediately apparent that two opposing groups supported different candidates. One group consisted of Edecio La Riva, Arístides Beaujon, Francisco Urquía Lugo, Eduardo Aguilar, Luis Guillermo Pilonieta, Lisandro Estopiñán, Rafael Clarencio González, Milagros Valentino, Teófilo Borregales, Ventura Quero, and Andrés Monterola; their candidate was Pablo Malpica Matera. The other group, which consisted of Pérez Díaz, Pedro Pablo Aguilar, Luis Herrera Campins, Godofredo González, Hilarión Cardozo, Eduardo Fernández, Oswaldo Alvarez Paz, José Rodríguez Iturbe, Dagoberto González, Felipe Montilla, and María de Guzmán, supported Adolfo Melchert.

There were twenty-one voting members of the National Committee. Some were absent—Godofredo González was ambassador to the Vatican; Pedro Del Corral had been ill; José Ramón Solano had been suspended. When this occurred, the *suplentes* voted in their place, starting with Hugo Briceño Salas as the first *suplente* and so on, in order. However, a *suplente* could not vote in place of José Solano because of his suspension. The *suplentes* who voted in this case were Hugo Briceño Salas, Lisandro Estopiñán, and Luis Guillermo Pilonieta. The *suplentes* were important, because the National Committee was almost evenly split between the two candidates. The first vote ended in a tie of nine votes each, with abstentions. Caldera intervened at that point to urge the committee to agree upon a candidate, and Melchert won on the second ballot by one vote.

Several conclusions can be drawn from this election. Members of the three major generations, conservatives and progressives, supported the winning candidate. The coalition included Herrera Campins on the left and Rodríguez Iturbe on the right. Those opposed to Beaujon, some of whom supported Caldera, were now in control of some of the party machinery, which would enable them to challenge the Beaujon forces on the national and regional levels. Thus, while it was a partial victory for Caldera and a defeat for Beaujon, the third group, identified with Herrera Campins, was also strengthened. The contending forces prepared for the next encounter.

By the time of the party's Twelfth National Convention in August

1971, Beaujon's position had been seriously weakened. Because the relationship between President Caldera and the secretary-general was cool and formal, Beaujon's followers did not gain much by supporting him. They saw that the Calderista forces could form coalitions and defeat Beaujon's candidate for national secretary of organization. At the Twelfth National Convention they deserted Beaujon, and Pedro Pablo Aguilar was elected the new secretary-general on the first ballot.

COPEI in the Post-1973 Electoral Period

Effects of the 1973 Election

Ironically, COPEI's overwhelming loss strengthened party unity, because the various forces concluded that their only chance for success required them all to remain within COPEI. Had the election been close, for example, the Herrera Campins forces might have been tempted to join the Movimiento al Socialismo (MAS) and build a new political party. Instead, they decided to work within COPEI, in the hope that Caldera and the party would now be ready to support a candidate of the left, Herrera Campins, for president in 1978. Thus AD's major victory minimized the threat of a COPEI split.

The party leaders decided to postpone their regional conventions until late 1974, and the National Convention until late 1975. This meant that Pedro Pablo Aguilar would continue as secretary-general, and there would be no early struggle over his position. Caldera also believed this would allow him time to reassert himself within the party.

Control of COPEI and the Nature of the Party

Traditional Latin American *caudillo* politics have often witnessed the establishment of a political party to foster a particular leader's ambitions. Because the party could not survive without him, that leader received more or less unquestioning obedience from other leaders and from the rank and file. Throughout most of its history, many political observers considered COPEI to be Calderista. However, we should not think of the party in terms of traditional Latin American *caudillo* politics: it was not created to foster Caldera's ambitions, and it can survive without him. Instead, we define the Calderista party as possessing several components. First, there is the overwhelming personage and, at times, domination of Caldera. Second, most power lies in the hands of his followers, primarily the Generation of 1936, but including Caldera supporters from other generations. Finally, individual members remain loyal to Caldera, and the party adopts his positions and doctrinal interpretations. Of course, Caldera did *not* always get what he wanted, and at times his candidates for secretary-general of the party and of the JRC were defeated. In the main, however, the party followed his wishes.

Because it was Calderista, tensions developed within COPEI. New generations had their own ideas and set different priorities; many new leaders have emerged, particularly since 1958. As new people assume important positions, there arise controversies and struggles for leadership. One spokesman for the more radical group within the Generation of 1958 said that his generation wanted a new party that would go with the rhythm of the Venezuelan people. He believed it was time for the youth to assume positions of leadership, and that the Generation of 1936 would have to recognize the changes within the party, or else it will fail.

But Caldera did not hand over control of the party to other leaders. He decided to try to retain control, partly because he wanted very much for COPEI to win the 1978 election; he did not want the 1973 election to be seen as a repudiation of his government.

Immediately after the 1973 election, the party continued to be Calderista, but with some variations. The Calderista forces comprised several major elements including Hilarión Cardozo and the Zulia group, José Curiel and the MOP group (the former minister of public works—MOP) and the Luis Alberto Machado group, the "Caesars," under the leadership of the former presidential secretary. The non-Calderista forces included the followers of Arístides Beaujon, the former secretary-general (a group which could claim very little power), and the followers of Herrera Campins (a very significant group). Another group comprised the supporters of secretary-general Pedro Pablo Aguilar. Since Caldera had supported his candidacy for secretary-general against Beaujon, many considered the Aguilar group to be Calderista.

The Secretary-General and Presidential Candidate

Throughout 1974 and 1975, the different groups negotiated and campaigned to get their men slated for the positions of secretary-general and president in the 1978 election. Once again party politics dictated that the struggle for the two positions be interrelated. Potential candidates made trips throughout the country as the political lines began to be drawn. During early 1974, Eduardo Fernández, a member of the Generation of 1958 and a Caldera supporter, was already building his support within the party. Herrera Campins had not yet asserted himself, because he was in a difficult position: he knew that Caldera did not want him to be the presidential candidate, and he also knew that, to have any chance for the nomination, he had to have the secretary-general's support. He would have to either receive the nod from Pedro Pablo Aguilar, or else support someone else to replace him as secretary-general. It was a difficult situation, because Aguilar was a Caldera supporter. Or was he?

Sometime in 1975 Caldera made a crucial decision. He let it be known that he did not like the way Pedro Pablo Aguilar had handled the 1973 election (he probably was looking for a scapegoat), and that he wanted him replaced as secretary-general. His candidate for the position was the former minister of public works, José Curiel. So Aguilar had two choices: he could bow to Caldera's wishes, or align with one of the party's other forces to defeat Caldera's candidate. Pedro Pablo Aguilar and Herrera Campins reached an agreement to support each other. If they were successful, Aguilar would be re-elected secretary-general, and Herrera Campins (who had just turned fifty) would be nominated for president in 1978.[87]

At the party's Fourteenth National Convention, December 1975, Pedro Pablo Aguilar easily defeated José Curiel, 810 to 332 votes,[88] handing Caldera and his supporters a major defeat. But Caldera had one more card to play. Instead of a party convention to choose the 1978 presidential candidate, he proposed a *Gran Congreso Nacional*, consisting of both party and non-party members (independents, business interests, and so forth). By this device he hoped to deny the nomination to Herrera Campins. However, the National Committee voted his idea down.

By early 1976, the combined Herrera Campins–Pedro Pablo Aguilar forces had triumphed in nearly all of the state conventions and in the party's six functional organizations. Realizing that his supporters would lose out in the next national convention, Caldera reportedly reached an understanding with Herrera in January 1976. They divided the party's National Committee almost evenly between their respective supporters, and Caldera agreed to support Herrera for president. Thus, COPEI would be united behind Herrera's candidacy in 1978.[89] Two Herrera supporters—Deputy Rafael Montes de Oca and Senator Juan José Rachadell—took over the functions of deputy secretary-general, replacing Eduardo Fernández, a Caldera supporter. At the Fifteenth National Convention (17-19 August 1977) Herrera Campins was unanimously nominated for president.

The Aguilar-Herrera alignment means that their forces constitute a major, if not *the* major, element within COPEI. Because of this development, the party can no longer be considered Calderista. There are still Calderista groups, but the Aguilar-Herrera forces have the upper hand, and the Beaujon forces are no longer significant.

With Luis Herrera Campins running for president, and subsequently winning the election, COPEI might shift to the left; Herrera has always been well toward the left within the party. COPEI's struggle against itself—the revolutionary slogans versus the moderate to conservative actions—might come to an end. Now that Herrera is president of Venezuela, Caldera's influence within COPEI might decrease further. But in the 1983 election Caldera will be eligible to run for president, and he probably will receive the nomination if he wants it. We witnessed a similar situation with Acción Democrática: Rómulo Betancourt could have had its presidential nomination in 1973 if he had wanted it, but he decided not to run, and instead supported Carlos Andrés Pérez. Thus, for COPEI as well as for AD, the Generation of 1945 is now in a position of power.

In November 1979, as this book went to press, Eduardo Fernández defeated Pedro Aguilar as secretary-general, 801 to 712 votes (*Latin America Weekly Report*, 16 November 1979.) The party's National Committee, functional organizations, and regional organs will probably reflect the Calderistas' strengthened position within COPEI. Shortly afterwards, Caldera pointedly said he wanted the Herrera government to fulfill its election program, particularly with regard to housing, delinquency, and rising prices. Although one might conclude that the prospects are for a long war of attrition between the Calderistas and Herreristas, the strength of Caldera's 1983 candidacy will partly depend upon the Herrera government's performance. Thus Caldera would not want possible government-party friction to hinder unduly President Herrera's effectiveness.

The Functional Organizations

The party's labor organization (FTC) overwhelmingly supported Herrera Campins. Shortly after the 1973 election, approximately 85 percent supported Herrera, 10 percent were with Beaujon, and the other 5 percent were spread among other groups.[90] Since the Fourteenth National Convention, Herrera's support has increased.

The FTC and other functional organizations have been studying ways to restructure the party in this post-electoral period. One such study was undertaken by a commission, working through CUSIC, whose members included Dagoberto González of the FTC and William Franco of CODESA, the Christian labor organization. According to the CODESA president,[91] the commission's purpose was to bring together the various workers' organizations—labor, technicians, teachers, etc. —to attain social power. The people would have that power and would express it through their own organizations, distinct from the party. The party would coordinate the efforts of the people's organizations. In a document on social power that he presented to COPEI's National Committee,[92] Franco and his colleagues rejected the party's practice of setting policies and strategies and then calling upon the functional organizations to carry them out. Instead, they wanted COPEI to carry out the people's wishes as expressed through their intermediary bodies. Another section of the document stated that true political power, based on the people and expressed through their organizations, was to be distinguished from the administration of the state; the state, and the party, were merely convenient vehicles for realizing the people's wishes. Franco acknowledged that certain Cope-yanos would resist the idea because their own power would be threat-ened, but he believed the party had no choice. If COPEI was to regain power, it would have to base its policies on the people's social needs. The people's organizations, rather than the party, were truly sensitive to those needs. COPEI was too concerned about winning elections and maintaining control over the functional organizations to do much about those broader social needs.

As we have observed elsewhere, the idea of social power and the role of functional organizations in the attainment of that idea is nothing new in Christian Democratic thought; leaders of the function-al organizations have often complained that their peasant, youth, and labor bodies have been mere appendages of the party. What is new, however, is that these Copeyanos maintain that the only road to fu-ture victory involves weakening party control and strengthening func-tional organizations. In a sense, they are calling for a pluralistic party (in function as well as form), rather than a centralized party ap-paratus.

The key question, which Franco recognized, is: Who will have power? The realization of social power within COPEI would require drastic changes in power relations. For the foreseeable future, party policies will be determined by coalitions, such as the alignment of the Pedro Pablo Aguilar and Luis Herrera Campins forces. However, if the advocates of social power ever win a majority of the National Convention delegates by working at the base of the party, this conclu-sion will have to be reassessed.

The party's youth group (JRC) has been affected by two develop-ments within COPEI: the party's apparent leftward ideological shift (COPEI's only alternative was to attempt to place itself to the left of AD) and the strengthening of the Herrera Campins forces. In the next section, we shall observe specific legislative and foreign policy initiatives taken by the Caldera government during its final year. While these moves may have been opportunistic, they resulted in a governmental and party shift to the left. The Copeyanos believed this diminished the ideological gap between the party leadership and the JRC.[93] Conflicts over such questions as socialism, private property, and the communitarian society were softened; in 1975, for example, after a world conference of Christian Democratic parties in Rome, Eduardo Fernández suggested that COPEI would adapt its ideology to accept the principles of a communitarian society.[94]

In spite of the greater JRC-COPEI ideological compatibility, we can expect the JRC to continue asserting itself regardless of the wishes of party leaders. When the Caldera government announced an extension of the labor law shortly before Carlos Andrés Pérez assumed the presi-dency, the JRC demonstrated against the country's leading business organization, FEDECÁMARAS, because business was opposed to the extension of the law. The party leaders were not happy with the demonstration, which they believed to be instigated by Julio Moreno, but they did not try to stop it. The JRC leadership must face the fact that the Movimiento al Socialismo (MAS) is the major force with the students, and that the Adecos are second. Thus, JRC demonstrations assume militant positions to attract greater numbers of students. Momentary tactical alliances in some high schools, of little political significance, have been motivated by the same goal.

The Araguatos, Avanzados, and Astronautas still exist, but the tripartite division no longer represents ideological differences.[95] Instead, it is another manifestation of the internal power struggle, and of recent differences over the choice of a presidential candidate. Because ideological questions are no longer emphasized, the three groups are now much less cohesive internally. Several "directors" have changed their group affiliations, and many (possibly a majority) do not identify with any group. As of January 1979, the major leaders were: Paciano Padron of the Araguatos; Donald Ramírez, the present JRC secretary-general, of the Avanzados; and Gehard Cartay, JRC deputy secretary-general, of the Astronautas.

Julio César Moreno resigned as JRC secretary-general. He accepted a bureaucratic position in the government and subsequently was elected to the Chamber of Deputies in the Congress. Differences over tactics within the Avanzados led to his resignation. One group sought a rapprochement with the then recently elected party secretary-general, Pedro Pablo Aguilar; they were opposed by Julio Moreno, who maintained that his sole loyalty was to Herrera Campins. This attitude led to his downfall. In contrast, the primary cause of Ramírez's victory as JRC secretary-general was his public support of Herrera Campins's presidential candidacy.

Thus, the confrontation within the JRC and between the JRC and COPEI has ended. Many looked to Herrera Campins as a long-standing revolutionary; others believed he was the only candidate who could defeat Acción Democrática in 1978. One salient characteristic of the last party convention and of the pre-convention campaigning was a scarcity, if not total absence, of ideological argumentation.

PART II

The Caldera Government

CHAPTER 5

Political Reality

THE 1968 election left the leadership of Acción Democrática confused and bitter. For the first time since 1958, the party did not control the executive branch. Although they had a majority in the National Congress, state legislative assemblies, and municipal councils, the Adecos were not ready to sit down with President Caldera and discuss arrangements for governing the country. They needed time to develop appropriate tactics in their unaccustomed role as the major political opposition.

Nor were the Copeyanos prepared to approach AD. In their euphoria following the election, they decided that the cabinet would consist of Copeyanos and perhaps a few independents. Under no circumstances would they devise a government that would favor AD; instead, they would try to seek understandings with smaller political parties in order to insure congressional passage of major portions of their program. But political reality indicated that AD and COPEI needed each other. The Adecos needed COPEI if they were to regain their predominant position in the labor movement; the Copeyanos needed AD, the strongest party in Congress, if they were to enact any of their programs.

Alliances

In 1968, COPEI reached a parliamentary understanding with two other political parties, MEP and FDP.[1] They were able to take the presidency of the Congress from AD and bestow it on an independent proposed by COPEI. (The same person holds the position of president of the Senate and president of the Congress. In case of the removal of the president of the Republic, he assumes the presidency on an interim basis until a new election is held.) The three parties also took the presidency of the Chamber of Deputies from AD and gave it to a representative without political affiliation.

During 1969 they succeeded in cementing the parliamentary understanding into a formal alliance. They also acquired the support of the Cruzada Cívica Nacionalista (CCN), apparently because CCN antipathy toward AD encouraged its leaders to seek an understanding with the other political parties. Although COPEI could count on the votes of the CCN in Congress, the Copeyanos insisted that the Pérez Jimenistas were not a formal part of the alliance, and they received no concessions.[2]

The year 1969 was not a fruitful one in Congress, with each political party blaming the others for the fact that no significant legislation was passed. We should remember that AD was still very strong in the Congress, comprising the largest political bloc. The alliance required nearly unanimous support to overcome what amounted to an AD congressional veto, and this unanimity proved to be almost impossible to attain.

Perhaps the alliance's failure was due largely to the political newness of FDP and MEP, which were established in 1962 and 1968 respectively. True, the party leaders had political experience as former Adecos; but they now represented relatively new parties, whose militants had not developed working relationships with COPEI over the years. As we have seen, the AD-COPEI relationship developed over a period of thirty years, evolving from one of extreme conflict to one of governmental cooperation and a commitment to make the democratic system work. The FDP-MEP-COPEI relationship had no such firm basis or commitment to a higher principle.

How did the Copeyanos, party leaders and militants, perceive MEP and FDP? I have no hard evidence, but I would imagine that the Generation of 1936, which controlled the party, had misgivings about the alliance. FDP had been formed from the MIR, the guerrillas who made a serious effort to overthrow the government in the early 1960s. MEP leaders were proclaiming that their party was socialist and would work with other parties on the left. Given the anticommunist background of the Copeyanos, cooperation with these new allies was probably very difficult.

During early 1970, AD was negotiating for a three-way pact with MEP and URD. According to the proposed agreement, Jóvito Villalba of URD would have been president of the Senate and the Congress, and the three parties would have had to announce the agreement publicly, so that no one could demand concessions later (as MEP had done with COPEI in 1969). When MEP refused, the agreement did not materialize.[3]

In late 1969 and early 1970, as they were negotiating with other political parties, representatives of AD and COPEI also held conversations with each other; so approximately one year elapsed before the two principal parties could sit down and work out an agreement. Perhaps that year of relative political inactivity, as far as governing the country was concerned, was necessary. The experience confirmed a political reality which had existed since 1958: the effective functioning of political democracy in Venezuela required at least minimal AD-COPEI cooperation.

Coincidencia

The situation in 1970 was somewhat similar to that in 1959. In the earlier period, AD and COPEI shared both the legislative and executive responsibility to insure that political democracy would not fail. As a result of that arrangement, COPEI increased its political strength in the country. In the later period, representatives of AD did not join the executive branch, although the two parties worked closely in Congress and on other levels. AD increased its political strength, particularly at the expense of MEP. (In the 1968 AD-MEP split, the principal AD labor leaders joined MEP. Shortly after the 1968 election, AD lost control of the petroleum union to MEP.) The Copeyanos knew that AD-COPEI cooperation during the Caldera administration would increase the political strength of the Adecos, but they had no choice. Furthermore, the leaders of COPEI felt more secure in working with AD, which had moved closer to the center of the political spectrum, than with MEP. The Copeyanos also believed they could offset any AD gains because their own control of the executive branch insured them control of patronage jobs and government contracts.

The period of AD-COPEI cooperation during the Caldera administration was referred to as the *coincidencia*, which indicated that AD and COPEI would cooperate where their interests coincided. The formal *coincidencia* began on 8-9 March 1970, when the two parties agreed on the division of congressional officers and committee chairmen.[4] They also worked out agreements in various state legislatures and municipal councils. Since the total AD-COPEI memberships comprised approximately 66 percent of the Senate and 55 percent of the Chamber of Deputies, their cooperation insured the passage of legislation.

While AD and COPEI were developing the *coincidencia*, MEP and URD decided to join forces and form the *Nueva Fuerza* (New Force), known later as the Popular Front. The principal leaders attempted to emulate the model of Salvador Allende of Chile, in which a group of leftist political parties formed a coalition to elect Allende president in 1970. The Communist party subsequently joined the Venezuelan coalition.

For a time there seemed to be a polarization between the parties of the *coincidencia* and those of the Popular Front, but the latter eventually split when they could not agree on an acceptable candidate for the 1973 election. The Communist party and MEP supported the secretary-general of MEP, Paz Galarraga; the URD could not agree with this decision and nominated its founder, Jóvito Villalba, a member of the Generation of 1928. As one political leader put it, the Popular Front collapsed because everyone wanted to be an Allende.

Before its demise, the Popular Front gave rise once again to the issue of Marxism and communism. However, the concerns were not the same as those of the earlier AD-COPEI confrontation, when harsh mutual recriminations and even violence occurred. Some noncommunist leaders of the Popular Front were quite explicit in stating that their coalition would not be Marxist, even though the Communist party was a member.[5] But AD and COPEI were highly critical of what they considered to be Marxist and communist influences in the Popular Front. The Adecos were very concerned with the apparent strength of MEP, and their criticism of the Popular Front often tied the Mepistas to the communist bogey: "[The Popular Front] is nothing more than a propagandistic projection which I have shown as an invention of the 'dialectic' of the old communist guard and of the secretary-general of MEP."[6]

Thus *coincidencia* witnessed the coming together of AD and COPEI as the major noncommunist political element in Venezuela. In a sense, this was a continuation of the AD-COPEI position of the early 1960s, when the two parties opposed a serious violent guerrilla movement. According to their opponents, there were no differences between AD and COPEI, because both were the parties of status.

Throughout the Caldera administration (March 1969-March 1974) AD and COPEI were able to agree on the officers and committee chairmen of Congress. Although AD won the December 1973 election, the parties continued to cooperate during the last few months of President Caldera's term, and they again agreed on new congressional officers for the 1974 session.[7]

Another interesting phenomenon of Venezuelan politics during this period was the ease with which some political parties cooperated in some states and opposed each other in others. Although AD and COPEI cooperated in Zulia, they were often on bitter terms in Bolívar. In Zulia, the state which produces most of the country's petroleum, the parties agreed to cooperate in naming the officers of the legislative assembly and the municipal councils. They were opposed by the smaller political parties—MEP, FDP, URD, and CCN.[8] To insure their control of the municipal council of Maracaibo, the principal city in Zulia, AD and COPEI offered the council presidency to a member of FDP. In other Venezuelan cities AD and COPEI formed pacts with FDP or with URD, but they did not form any agreements with MEP.

Thus the *coincidencia* manifested something old and something new. Old was the kaleidoscopic nature of Venezuelan politics, in which various political alliances were made because local situations indicated they would be *conveniente* (convenient). New was AD's effort, with the support of COPEI, to weaken MEP. This was particularly evident in the labor movement, where COPEI supported Adeco efforts to regain control of the Confederación de Trabajadores de Venezuela (CTV) from MEP.

Tension in the Coincidencia

The political position of AD during the Caldera administration was similar to that of COPEI during the Leoni regime. Both parties considered themselves to be the loyal opposition (designated Autonomy of Action in one case, and *coincidencia* in the other), which meant that they would support the political system but would remain free to criticize the government and offer alternatives when they deemed it appropriate. As the major political opposition, the respective party leaders were obliged to devise policies which would strengthen their positions for the next election. The attitude of the Adecos in the *coincidencia* was determined partly by their desire to regain the presidency in 1973. This contributed to AD-COPEI tension, particularly during the last two and a half years of the Caldera administration.

The Copeyanos expected AD criticism of their policies,[9] but they distinguished between AD's opposition and that of the Popular Front, which they believed actually tended to weaken the political system. They accused the Popular Front of fomenting strikes and student disturbances which led to periodic violence.

Although it rarely took a violent form, the AD opposition was very strong. At a party meeting in February 1971, the Adecos apparently decided to switch to a "hard line" vis-à-vis COPEI,[10] and they strongly criticized the government's handling of several small guerrilla movements and a wave of kidnappings. This criticism was tantamount to a frontal attack on the government's policy of pacification. (As part of the pacification policy, the government removed certain political restrictions on the Communist party; it also encouraged the guerrillas to lay down their arms without reprisals, and to participate in the political system.) Carlos Andrés Pérez, the secretary-general of AD at the time, led the attack. He was particularly critical of the pacification program of the minister of interior, Lorenzo Fernández, who was the likely 1973 COPEI presidential candidate. Thus, beginning in the spring of 1971, AD attacks on COPEI and the government intensified. Approximately two and a half years before the election, a campaign was underway. I would not accuse the Adecos of merely playing electoral politics, since their criticisms were in part based on their perception of AD's role as the major political opposition. Nevertheless, the timing and intensity of those criticisms were affected by the forthcoming election.

Other areas of friction developed betwen the partners of the *coincidencia*. In a full-page advertisement in the newspaper *El Nacional*, AD made several attacks on COPEI and the Caldera government. The Adecos brought up the old accusation that COPEI had won the 1968 election with financial help from the West German Christian Democrats, with the fact that the German publication *Der Spiegel* published a story making the same claim adding credence to the AD position. COPEI denied the accusation. Other articles on the page strongly criticized the government's housing policy and blamed the government for the considerable unrest at the Central University of Venezuela (UCV). In addition, the COPEI governor of Anzoátegui was accused of having a "blind pride" in causing political problems in his state.[11] Various editions of COPEI publications accused AD of electoral politics, of attempting to discredit the government and to strengthen AD's political position for the 1973 election.

Did these events mark the end of the *coincidencia*? In one sense, it continued until the end of President Caldera's term, for AD and COPEI cooperated in choosing congressional officers and passing major pieces of legislation. However, the principal laws were passed during the first half of Caldera's term. For the final two and a half years the Adecos and Copeyanos apparently concluded that they would only keep the government's machinery functioning. They did, however, maintain open lines of communication, and the principal leaders met periodically: Carlos Andrés Pérez of AD; Arístides Beaujon, secretary-general of COPEI; Pedro Pablo Aguilar, deputy secretary-general who succeeded Beaujon; and Hugo Briceño Salas, the Copeyano financial expert. Although the gulf between AD and COPEI widened during the last part of the Caldera administration, both parties still wanted political democracy to function.

According to some political opponents, the *coincidencia* actually began in 1958 and continues today. Regardless of the differences between AD and COPEI, both were committed to the present system and to the major interests in the country.[12] The Adecos and Copeyanos tended to ignore such comments, however. AD asserted that their opposition was very responsible, and they provided the only support for COPEI during Caldera's administration; in fact, they maintained that, without their support, the democratic system and the COPEI government would have fallen.[13] For their part, the Copeyanos strongly criticized AD's role during the *coincidencia*, pointing out that the situation was one of permanent tension between the two parties. They likened AD's position to that of a doctor who gave his patient medicine to help him feel better but who did not cure him: the Adecos wanted to maintain the system, but they would do everything possible to minimize the effectiveness of COPEI. The Copeyanos pointed to the necessity of constant negotiations with AD during the entire Caldera administration, maintaining that AD always wanted something in return for its support, and that it was necessary to proceed "drop by drop" in order to accomplish anything.[14]

If we distinguish between the form and spirit of the *coincidencia*, we can conclude that it continued formally, with the functioning of Congress and periodic conversations of the respective leaders. The latter proved effective in determining the boundaries of political competition beyond which the democratic system might be jeopardized.

But the spirit of the *coincidencia* waned considerably during the latter half of the Caldera administration. This surprised neither the Adecos nor the Copeyanos, who knew that the exigencies of an electoral campaign could not dictate otherwise.

Pressure Groups

Before we consider the performance of the Caldera government and the steps taken in the name of *El Cambio* (COPEI's campaign promise of change), let us identify some of the groups which might have influenced the government. We are not concerned here with every pressure group; rather, our concern is with certain groups which might have had more influence with the Caldera government, because it represented the Christian Democratic movement, than with other governments. For example, the most powerful pressure group representing the business, industrial, and producing community is the Federation of Chambers of Industry and Commerce (FEDECÁMARAS), made up of associations of oil interests, agriculture, and commerce. But there was nothing about the FEDECÁMARAS-Caldera government relationship that differentiated it from the relationship with previous AD governments. Although the culmination of government-FEDE-CÁMARAS friction over Venezuela's entry into the Andean Pact was reached under the Caldera government, the struggle had been going on before Caldera became president. Other pressure groups, however, might have had a more direct relationship with the Caldera government than with its predecessors.

Historically, a few of these groups have affected COPEI as a political party, while others only related to the Caldera government. The government's support of or opposition to specific kinds of legislation, and its success or failure in realizing significant changes in the social, political, and economic structure of the country, were determined largely by its own predilections, and by those of the groups which influenced it. (The major political influence on the government, Acción Democrática, will be considered later.)

The Church

During the Caldera administration, government officials and Catholic church leaders wanted to avoid giving an appearance of undue church influence in government matters. COPEI might have been accused of being the political arm of the church in the party's early years, when its electoral base rested primarily in the conservative Andean states. However, as Caldera's victory indicated, COPEI could claim to be a plurality party because it had broadened its base. And COPEI accomplished this largely without the church's help. But how far did the party have to move ideologically to win the election? COPEI's critics would answer that the party might have used appealing campaign slogans, but it was still under church influence. However, one must take into consideration the changing nature of both COPEI and the church. The pastoral letter of Paul VI, stressing the need to deal with social and economic development and the problems of the poor, were in sympathy with the changes within COPEI and the thinking of President Caldera. Perhaps, ideologically, COPEI did not move very far from the church; however, they both moved a considerable distance from their earlier, more conservative positions.

Some observers did not agree with this conclusion, pointing out that the Generation of 1936 was still close to the classical position of the church. As a result, conflicting views concerning private property and the question of socialism were a major cause of the party's problems with its youth. Because COPEI used different tactics to win the presidency in 1968, there was no longer a question of moving away from the position of the church.[15]

Both positions possess some elements of validity. One might argue that the Generation of 1936 was close to the church's classical position, and that this caused strains within COPEI and the government. Certainly, as we indicated in analyzing the 1968 election, a variety of factors contributed to Caldera's victory, particularly the AD-MEP split. Philosophically, the Generation of 1936, speaking through President Caldera, agreed with the change in the church's position over the last fifteen years or so.

In discussing the church, we should also consider the attitude of certain priests. Approximately 80 percent of Venezuela's priests are foreigners, and many of them have worked in the *barrios* for years. Several of the priests with whom I spoke felt that the Caldera government was doing little to alleviate the problem of human misery. In fact, they saw little difference between the efforts of the AD governments and those of the COPEI. Furthermore, there was no consensus among individual priests concerning political support: some favored COPEI, but others supported AD and URD.[16]

In Táchira, the church more openly identified with the Caldera government than it did in the rest of the country;[17] Monsignor Rafael Arias Blanco publicly supported the government and COPEI. The COPEI-dominated state government even supported Catholic schools out of the state budget. Politically, the peasants still identified COPEI with the church and voted for the Copeyanos in large numbers (a pattern which was broken in the 1973 election), and the workers normally voted for AD. Thus, during the Caldera administration, the church-government relationship in Táchira was very close.

In Mérida, the church made a conscious effort not to support COPEI officially.[18] In the past the church had supported some Copeyanos over others for various government positions and appointments, and this had led to friction within the party. The church hierarchy also recognized that some of the state's priests supported AD. Nevertheless, the strong COPEI majority in the state legislature did allocate state funds for Catholic schools on a yearly basis.[19]

The Case of Padre Wuytack

An astute political observer told me that the work of various priests in the *barrios* was bound to benefit COPEI, since the people would identify the efforts of COPEI and the government with representatives of the church, whom they saw almost daily. One of these representatives was a Belgian priest, Padre Francisco Wuytack. He was imprisoned several times and finally expelled from Venezuela in 1970.[20]

Padre Wuytack lived and worked in the Parroquía de la Vega, where he officiated in the Capilla de Nuestra Señora del Carmen. He believed that direct action by the people, rather than petitions and letters to governmental officials, would dramatize the plight of the poor and bring some relief. The act which finally led to his expulsion occurred in front of the Congress building. Padre Wuytack declared a hunger strike as he led approximately two dozen followers of the Para Cristo (For Christ) movement in a demonstration protesting rising unemployment and general misery in the *barrios*. The demonstrators specifically asked for a law on unemployment. Padre Wuytack had not requested government permission for the demonstration because it had been denied on other occasions, and he thought it would be useless to ask again.

Lorenzo Fernández, the minister of interior and COPEI's presidential candidate in 1973, was authorized by President Caldera to handle the situation for the government. Fernández has since stated that it was one of the most painful decisions he ever had to make. Cardinal José Humberto Quintero and the church hierarchy supported him, agreeing that Padre Wuytack had disrupted public order. President Caldera pointed out that Padre Wuytack was a foreigner who consistently broke the laws. Because he led popular demonstrations without the required license, the government had no choice but to expel him. The outcry from younger priests, students, opposition parties, and most of the press was intense and prolonged.

Opus Dei

Formed in Spain in 1928 by Monsignor Escrivá de Balaguer, Opus Dei's purpose is to provide the church with a vehicle for participation in secular activities. At one time, the majority of the cabinet in Franco's Spain were members.

The Spanish priest Odón Moles Villaseñor introduced Opus Dei in Venezuela in 1952. Since its meetings are secret, the extent of its organizational efforts can only be surmised.[21] Observers differed concerning Opus Dei's influence in the country; some believed it was not a significant factor, while others felt that the movement was increasing rapidly.

Opus Dei also competed for influence with the Jesuits. The latter were considered to be more progressive, with a greater sensitivity to the problems of the poor. The Jesuits, through the influence of Padre Aguirre, were very influential within COPEI during its early years. One might also argue that the Jesuits are more influential than Opus Dei due to the power of the Jesuit magazine *SIC*. The Jesuits were important in the Andean states, while Opus Dei was more active in other areas—a factor which should be taken into account when we consider the conservatism of the Andean peasants. Because they were conservative, more often than not they voted for COPEI because they identified the party with the church. As far as voting behavior was concerned, we need go no further. But one might question the degree of conservatism of the Andean peasants by considering the opposing Jesuit–Opus Dei influence.

Why would one consider Opus Dei to be conservative? Critics of the Caldera government answered in part by identifying various groups and individuals who they felt not only had a conservative influence on the government by their presence, but who actually cooperated to forestall government changes. One would categorize a group by the company it kept: Eugenio Mendoza, the *desarrollistas*; Opus Dei, the oligarchy. According to this view, Opus Dei reinforced the conservative nature of the government which was consistent with COPEI's natural orientation.[22] A more widely accepted conclusion was that members of Opus Dei shared views with the more conservative business elements, placing primary emphasis on development of heavy industry and various infrastructure projects. Since they believed capital was primarily needed in these areas, rather than in the agricultural sector or in low-cost housing, questions of structural change and social justice received very low priority.

Opus Dei pursued the objectives of penetrating COPEI and gaining influence within the Caldera government. Not surprisingly, Opus Dei became a decisive force within COPEI. During the competition over the party's 1973 presidential nominee, several cabinet ministers supported Arístides Beaujon, the secretary-general. This support was, in part, a result of Opus Dei influence.

We can identify several party and government officials who were members of Opus Dei during the Caldera administration. José Rodríguez Iturbe, an important figure within Opus Dei, was head of COPEI's secretariat of political formation.[23] Enrique Pérez Olivares, minister of education, was said to have been the strongest voice for Opus Dei in the Caldera cabinet. The son of Lorenzo Fernández, the minister of interior, was also a member. Others identified with Opus Dei included Rafael Tomás Caldera Pietri, the president's son; General Martín García Villasmil, the minister of defense; Haydée Castillo, the minister of development; Arístides Calvani, the foreign minister; Colonel Juan Manuel Sucre Figarella, chief of the *casa militar*; Luis Alberto Machado and Eduardo Fernández, office of the secretariat of the presidency; Luis Enrique Oberto, chief of Cordiplan (Oficina Central de Coordinación y Planificación de Venezuela); Eduardo Acosta Hermoso, president of IVP (petrochemicals); Hugo Pérez La Salvia, minister of petroleum and hydrocarbons; and Julio Sosa Rodríguez, ambassador to the United States. Some members of the political opposition felt that most government officials contributed financially to Opus Dei.[24]

President Caldera's attitude must be considered a crucial factor in determining Opus Dei's influence within COPEI and the government. The president, who dominated both the party and the executive branch during his administration, was not a member of Opus Dei and could not be manipulated by the movement. Although he did visit Opus Dei representatives when he was in Spain, there is no evidence that he encouraged the spread of the movement's influence within COPEI or the government. Caldera must have known which Copeyanos were members, but this factor did not necessarily influence his decisions in making cabinet appointments or in making his wishes known about personnel changes within COPEI. Because of his overwhelming authority and his sensitivity to allegations of church influence within the government and COPEI, we can conclude that Opus Dei's ability to place individuals in key positions was somewhat limited.

Can we identify Opus Dei's influence in the determination of specific government policies? The political opposition's consensus was that Opus Dei's influence could be identified in three areas: key individuals who were members, an alliance with the *desarrollistas* in the cabinet and bureaucracy, and government policies toward private education. With regard to private education (by which we mean schools operated and supported by the Catholic church), it was difficult to discern a definite influence on the government's policies. Specifically, was the government's support of private education determined by the predisposition of the Generation of 1936? By the influence of Cardinal Quintero? By Opus Dei, speaking through Enrique Pérez Olivares as minister of education? Or by some combination of these factors? I am inclined to say that each played some role. (Incidentally, several leaders of other parties—MEP, URD, and AD—had children enrolled in private schools.)

Besides playing an active role in Venezuelan politics for over forty years, Luis Beltrán Prieto Figueroa is well recognized as a scholar and leader in educational matters.[25] (Prieto is also probably one of the most anticlerical figures in Venezuelan politics.) He believed that Opus Dei influenced the government's educational policy. By the summer of 1971, the government had appropriated eighteen million *bolívares* for private schools. (At the time, five *bolívares* equaled one dollar.) Taking the example of educational policy in Guayana, located in the country's eastern region, Prieto stated that the head of the development corporation there was a member of Opus Dei; through his influence, a large quantity of public funds were being diverted into private schools, at the expense of the public school system. Prieto also believed that unrest at the Central University of Venezuela (UCV) was caused, in part, by the government's effort to weaken public and favor private education.

The Church as a Pressure Group: Conclusions

The analysis of church influence has covered the church in a general sense, the expulsion of Padre Wuytack, and Opus Dei. In a general sense, church influence was more indirect than direct. Perhaps the degree of emphasis on certain policies, such as government aid to church schools, was a result of church influence, in particular states. Or one might propose that the government's commitment to the concept of International Social Justice corresponded with the wishes of the church hierarchy. (For that matter, the foreign policy of the AD administration of President Carlos Andrés Pérez was also concerned, in part, with alleviating the plight of the less developed countries.) But I cannot prove that any particular government action or inaction was due to church influence.

The expulsion of Padre Wuytack raised serious questions concerning Christian Democracy's doctrine and the actions of a Christian Democratic administration. Must COPEI's espousal of Christian Democracy always be divorced from the actions of the Caldera government? Did the party really mean what it said about revolution? Or was it merely content with some limited reforms from the top?

The last question, too, was raised in considering Opus Dei's influence. The government's critics believed that any hopes of a Christian Democratic revolution under Caldera were bound to be shattered because of Opus Dei's great economic power and its influence in Cordiplan and the ministry of development, and because of Caldera's apparent reluctance to discourage the spread of Opus Dei influence.

Did the government's relationship with the church, the expulsion of Padre Wuytack, and the influence of Opus Dei weaken public support for COPEI and the government? I am not aware of any polls dealing with these questions, but the consensus of political observers is that the answer was no. People who supported the Christian Democrats continued to do so; the opposition was based on other factors.

The Oligarchy

In his excellent study of Venezuelan elites, Frank Bonilla has stated that the country did not have an oligarchy.[26] Elites could be identified; but they were to be distinguished from an oligarchy, in which a small group traditionally controlled the government and forced it to follow policies primarily for the benefit of its members. According to Bonilla, the country had long known a separation between economic and military sectors on the one hand and political and cultural sectors on the other. Throughout its history, Venezuela has experienced a continuous turnover of people in high places; power was held for only a short time, and an organic sense did not develop among elite groups.

The political opposition, however, believed that several members of the cabinet and the bureaucracy owed their positions to an oligarchy. Specifically, they claimed that Eugenio Mendoza controlled the heads of the ministries of housing, finance, and development. They claimed that the Vollmer family controlled the minister of education, and that the oligarchy also determined the policies of the minister of communications and the directors of the central bank and the workers' bank.[27]

It is simplistic to state that big business supported and strongly influenced the government. As we have previously pointed out, Eugenio Mendoza has been known to contribute financially to both AD and COPEI. Furthermore, the business community itself is not necessarily unified on political matters. David J. Myers observed this fact in his study of Caldera's 1968 electoral victory:

> Venezuela's business community is divided into several powerful clusters. The Mendoza and Phelps groups inclined toward Dr. Caldera while the Zuloaga and Vollmer interests [believed] a Social Christian victory would give the former unacceptable influence. Consequently, the Zuloaga and Vollmer interests became the core of Burelli Rivas financing.

> The Zuloaga family was associated with the economic group which centered around the Vollmers, one of Venezuela's oldest and most prestigious families. The Vollmers derived their initial economic strength from ownership of the sugarcane producing area surrounding Caracas. In more recent times, however, the Caracas Electric Company and the National Brewery have been cornerstones of the Vollmer economic empire.[28]

The Mendozas, Vollmers, and Zuloagas were not "oligarchs," as the critics would have us believe. They are relatively *nouveaux riches*, with a variety of economic interests in industry, commercial agriculture, and so forth.

The political opposition also charged that oligarchical influence caused government programs to favor major business interests, both national and international (U.S.). This was particularly evident in the budget proposals of the minister of finance, Pedro Tinoco, and the developmental projects of the minister of development, Haydée Castillo. (Most ministers, including those of finance and development, were replaced by President Caldera before the end of his term.)

Considered to be an important component of the oligarchy, the *desarrollista* (developmentalist) group was formed by some professionals and businessmen around 1965. Most *desarrollistas* openly supported Caldera and COPEI in 1968, while others formed their own Democratic Independent Movement (MDI); the latter supported Caldera for president and ran its own candidates for Congress, the state legislatures, and the municipal councils. President Caldera appointed one *desarrollista* leader, Pedro Tinoco *hijo* (son), as his first minister of finance. Much of the press criticized the appointment, accusing Tinoco of representing the Chase Manhattan Bank and Standard Oil of New Jersey in Venezuela.[29] The appointment also led to tension within COPEI, and several groups—youth, labor, and those supporting the presidential candidacy of Herrera Campins—expressed their displeasure over the finance minister's actions.

The *desarrollistas* had more influence during the first part of President Caldera's five-year term than later, when they ran into enormous obstacles. In part, this was due to Tinoco's replacement as finance minister; but it was also apparent that the ruling party had many interests to represent. The *desarrollistas* began to flirt with other political groups, including AD, and finally they and the Caldera government agreed to an amicable parting of the ways. In 1973 they did not support COPEI, and Tinoco ran as a presidential candidate in his own right, trying unsuccessfully to woo the Pérez Jiménez vote.

The Army

Observers differed concerning relations between the military, particularly the army, and COPEI and the government.[30] One view was that the government did not have to pay special attention to the military, and that President Caldera had a great deal of freedom of action. The military was content to receive approximately 9 or 10 percent of the federal budget (a lower percentage than in most Latin American countries, but from a larger budget). Since the Caldera government assumed office during a relatively peaceful period—not in the immediate aftermath of a coup d'état, like the AD governments had in 1945 and 1958—it did not have to grant special privileges to the military, in the form of housing and other benefits. Except on the policy of pacification, these observers did not believe that the government consulted with the military regarding particular policies. In fact, they pointed out, the Caldera government appointed its own military man as minister of defense and did not continue with the officer who had served under the Leoni government.

Another observer has pointed out that various groups in the military sympathized with particular political parties, but that they had to be quiet in order to avoid being reported by the intelligence agencies. If the government or COPEI tried to proselytize, other political parties would be encouraged to do the same; the army would ultimately be politicized, as it had been during 1936-58. President Caldera exhibited no favoritism, and the armed forces were more apolitical than ever. In fact, the military preferred it this way, because promotions could be based on time in rank and on ability, rather than on political connections.

Others believed that the government and COPEI did indeed try to proselytize the armed forces, particularly the army. One observer told me about two activities, the Movimiento de Cursillos and the Movimiento Familiar Cristiano. Several Copeyanos would meet with young military officers in the homes of party members, hoping to persuade them to study the tenets of the Catholic church and Christian Democracy. Such efforts were not very successful. Another proselytizing effort involved COPEI's attempt to work with the right wing within the military. Other groups within the military supported Pérez Jiménez, however, and opposed COPEI's efforts.[31]

Certainly President Caldera did not have to discuss most of his government plans with the military. However, being an astute politician, he did not pursue a policy that would antagonize the military, and he took the officers into his confidence when he deemed it necessary. For example, he discussed with them his thinking about appointing a new minister of defense. Frequently, too, he praised the military in public speeches, on television, and in the press.

The military accepted the results of the 1968 election, and Rafael Caldera assumed the presidency. Since the military was indeed more apolitical during his administration, the effectiveness of possible proselytizing was seriously in doubt. In short, the government and COPEI did not need to proselytize the military; conversely, the military was probably better off if it avoided or minimized such efforts.

Did the military, as a pressure group, influence the government? I think not. Like his predecessors, President Caldera used prudence in dealing with the military. One might argue that, because the Peruvian-type mentality (modeled after the so-called former left-wing military government in Perú) did not exist in Venezuela, the government tended to refrain from attempts to institute radical reforms. This is merely a conjecture, however, and I believe other factors, some of which we have already discussed, were much more crucial in determining the government's actions.

Internal Problems and Developments

The government faced several problems inherited from its predecessors (the guerrilla movement, for example), while others reflected the political reality of the period (i.e., the relative strengths of various political parties and groups in the Congress). Problems also resulted from actions which were necessitated by the demands of governing.

These problems, and the administration's efforts to deal with them, in turn affected the relations with political parties and other groups.

Makeup of the Cabinet

When President Caldera named those who would serve in his first cabinet, the political opposition immediately expressed its disapproval. The major complaint was that the cabinet was too narrow in its composition. President Caldera appointed Copeyanos and technicians who were considered to be independents; he did not choose anyone from the other parties. In view of his narrow electoral victory, the political opposition believed that the cabinet failed to provide the president with the broad political base he would require in order to govern effectively.

We have mentioned the ministers who were appointed as payment for political debts. The president also decided to ask senior COPEI leaders to join the cabinet: Lorenzo Fernández became minister of interior; Arístides Calvani, minister of foreign affairs; Víctor Giménez Landínez, minister of agriculture.[32] This made it easier for younger party leaders to rise to positions of power. Before the end of his term, President Caldera replaced and shifted all the ministers except Calvani.

The appointment which caused the most bitterness was that of the minister of finance, Pedro Tinoco, "former director of Chase Manhattan Bank's Venezuelan subsidiary and a long-time spokesman and lawyer for the United States oil companies."[33] Joining the political opposition, several COPEI party militants and congressional representatives denounced his fiscal and revenue proposals as favoring upper-income people. Such developments contributed to government-COPEI tension.

President Caldera did not appoint Adecos to his cabinet because he did not want a coalition government with Acción Democrática. He felt that AD would oppose the government as the party tried to strengthen its position for the forthcoming elections. AD representation would cause too much dissension and hinder governmental effectiveness. The president preferred that the differences with AD remain between the executive branch and the Congress, rather than within the administration. He also realized that AD did not look favorably upon successful programs of his government, because they would result in increased COPEI influence. Nor did President Caldera want coalitions with other political groups because they would lead to too much divergence.[34]

As we have stated previously, the country experienced a changed political environment during the Caldera administration. Presidents Betancourt and Leoni had needed to seek cooperation from other political parties in order to stabilize the political situation, whereas the fear of a possible coup d'état in the one case, and of increased guerrilla warfare or possibly civil war in the other, did not exist to the same degree under Caldera. Because the country did really not need a coalition government, the president selected his cabinet accordingly. Furthermore, it is doubtful whether the Adecos had any desire to participate in Caldera's government.

Patronage

When a political party does not control the executive branch, patronage is not a serious problem. The party may have some positions available for its followers, as COPEI did during the Betancourt administration; but because party militants knew the positions were few, they did not expect COPEI to deliver the spoils. On the other hand, when their candidate won the presidency, many expected to be amply rewarded for their years of party work. Because there was a limit to the number of positions the government could offer, friction developed within COPEI and between many disappointed Copeyanos and the government.

At the outset, the government decided to minimize interparty friction by allowing most AD, MEP, and URD technicians who had been working in the bureaucracy before 1969 to retain their positions.[35] This decision was particularly significant as it related to AD, which had been in power for the preceding ten years. The government had to use many AD bureaucrats in order to function, and while it appointed several Copeyanos to direct bureaus and agencies, more Adecos than Copeyanos were in lower administrative positions. In the ministry of public works, for example, Adecos continued to hold important technical positions. The government convinced party leaders of the necessity of its actions, but many rank-and-file Copeyanos were bitter nonetheless.

The patronage problem was not limited to Caracas. In Lara, several Copeyanos criticized the government on this matter. An activist in peasant affairs accused the power structure of not allowing party representatives from the rural areas to participate in the government.[36] According to Armando Acosta, the problem started after COPEI won the 1968 election. Whereas there had previously been little friction, now various Copeyanos were scrambling for jobs, and the party's rural sector was not in the running. Acosta did not believe that the problem was due to a scarcity of projects in the state—on the contrary, additional projects required an increased labor force. But nonparty laborers and *Copeyanos* from outside the rural sector were receiving the jobs. Why did such a situation exist under a COPEI government? Armando Acosta answered his own question by stating that personal relationships were too important: party leaders favored their friends when assigning party work and employment on governmental projects.

A member of the party's teachers' movement in Lara disagrees within these views.[37] Pablo Pérez González asserted that all elements of the party participated in the government; he also stated that the government was employing both Copeyanos and non-Copeyanos. He admitted that the opportunities for the Copeyanos were limited, but felt that this was due to members' failure to qualify for positions in the professions, mechanics, and industry. A local priest, who prefers to remain anonymous, expanded upon this view.[38] According to him, the unemployment rate was too high, but this reflected the fact that the people were passive and did not know how to work. He knew of several youngsters recently employed by the Lara government who certainly were not capable or prepared. But the fault also laid with the government's desire to stay in power, which meant that budget priorities were in industry, particularly petroleum, and the army. The rural people were taken less seriously, according to this priest.

The patronage problem involved several interrelated factors: the limited number of positions, the ability of certain Copeyanos to fill those positions, and the Caldera government's overall national policies. As was shown in Lara, greater emphasis on the industrial rather than the rural sector, whether by design or because COPEI was a minority in Congress, could antagonize important rural elements and adversely affect COPEI in the next election.

Appointment of the Minister of Defense

A few weeks after he assumed office, the newspaper *El Nacional* reported that President Caldera's appointment of the minister of defense was his first important and sensitive decision.[39] The president decided to appoint General Martín García Villasmil, thereby bypassing General Pablo Antonio Flores, a military official under the Leoni administration. Flores felt that he should have received the appointment because of his seniority. (In the latter part of the Caldera administration, Admiral Jesús Carbonell Izquierdo replaced General García Villasmil as defense minister.) In order to avoid a conflict, Caldera appointed General Flores to be inspector general of the armed forces, and to report directly to him. A recent analysis has stated that this action eliminated General Flores's base of military and political power.[40]

According to several observers, most army officers were Adecos. Caldera had to look for neutral officers, but many of them were not very competent. General García Villasmil was not well liked, and the army in particular did not want him to be minister of defense. Many feared the general because of his growing influence and his ability to place his men in key positions. However, for reasons I have not been able to determine, no one in the military liked General Flores, either.

Toward the end of August 1969, President Caldera ordered the arrest of three high military officials for criticizing governmental policies in public. At a news conference he remarked that discipline in the armed forces had been lax in the past, but that it had greatly improved under the new minister of defense.[41] General Flores used the incident to express his disagreement with such remarks about the military; he called a number of his colleagues and spent several days visiting commands and units of the armed forces to organize support for his position. President Caldera ordered General Flores arrested by civil authorities. When Flores's appeal to the president failed, the general increased his efforts to win the support of his military colleagues. Then, in a surprise move, the president and the minister of defense rescinded the original order and instead ordered that Flores be arrested and tried by military authorities. The military court declared Flores guilty of conspiring against the highest authority of the country. He was arrested personally by a group of high officials and sentenced to two years in prison.

I believe the conclusion drawn by Kenneth F. Johnson and María Mercedes Fuentes was most perceptive. Although I question their view that the incident demonstrated that the possibility of a coup d'état was now past in Venezuela, I agree that the vitality of the legal institutions was apparent. As these authors pointed out, "Instead of negotiating behind the scenes with the military to avoid a *coup*, Caldera chose the more difficult course of action. He demanded respect for his constitutional authority and for the free functioning of the legal institutions. *This in itself is a revolutionary achievement in the contemporary history of Latin America.*"[42]

The authors also stated that Caldera was capable of exercising strong executive power, despite COPEI's minority position in Congress and his own narrow electoral victory. General Flores had risen through the military ranks under the previous AD governments, and some Adecos accused President Caldera of trying to purge military officers loyal to former Presidents Betancourt and Leoni. The Caldera administration vehemently denied the charge, and as a result of the incident the president's popular image was much stronger than it had been when he entered the Palacio de Miraflores. This was fortunate, because he would need all the political strength he could muster to face myriad problems.

Unrest and Violence

Venezuela experienced various degrees of unrest and violence during most of Rafael Caldera's presidency. For purposes of analysis, we can divide the topic into several (admittedly overlaping) parts: the general level of unrest throughout the country, police actions, student actions, and the guerrilla movement.

The Caldera government faced a residue of unrest and violence from previous administrations. In March 1969, the press reported the following incidents: a hunger strike in Cárcel Modelo, a letter to former President Leoni asking the whereabouts of twenty-three people who had disappeared, a hunger strike of two laborers at the entrance of the ministry of labor, and airborne army pursuit of a band of guerrillas in the mountains of Vigirima.[43] One could not pick up a newspaper without reading about murder, robbery, or a demonstration. In the spring of 1972, the press reported that the police and national guard, together with special anti-riot units, faced large groups of demonstrators who were trying to reach the central part of the city. All strategic points were occupied by forces armed with tear gas, shields, and masks; large water-throwing trucks were also in position. Before the violence subsided, some young people were killed, while others occupied the halls of Congress.[44]

The government tried to crack down on violence and crime through Operación Vanguardia, an energetic police action.[45] The operation caught the criminal elements unprepared, and for the first few months of 1970 it appeared to be successful. Several shootouts occurred between police and criminals, when the latter were either caught committing crimes or discovered in their hideouts. In one month twenty-two criminals were killed. But the criminals counterattacked through bank robberies, kidnappings, assassinations, and even a sensational robbery of the Palacio de Miraflores.

The opposition to Operación Vanguardia was considerable, particularly that emanating from the opposition political parties and most of the press. Middle-class elements who had often been the objects of crime, particularly in Caracas, supported the idea at first; but eventually many of them joined the chorus of opposition, which accused the police of carrying the operation to an extreme. When Operación Vanguardia came to an end, the results were less than the government had hoped for, but the criminal elements had learned that there were limits which, if trespassed, would cause the government to act vigorously.

Much of the unrest and violence centered around student reaction to the University Reform Law. Cosponsored by AD and COPEI and passed by the Congress in November 1970, the law amended the Law of the Universities. According to Daniel H. Levine,

> The major reforms were: 1) prohibition of the re-election of the rector (and provision for executive removal of rectors who fail to comply with the provisions of Law); 2) imposition of stricter auditing procedures on university budgetary operations; 3) tightening the legal definition of regular students . . . and 4) redefinition of the meaning of autonomy. . . . These reforms were approved by Congress and rejected by the UCV authorities. The Congress then named a provisional university council, headed by the Minister of Education. The rector, Dr. J. M. Bianco, resigned in protest, and in late October 1970, the UCV was occupied once again by the police and the National Guard. . . .[46]

Student strikes and violence spread throughout the country—in

Mérida, Valencia, Maracaibo, Barquisimeto, and Cabimas. In its search of the UCV, the army reported that it uncovered arms and explosives in several buildings. In mid-November, President Caldera charged that Castroite guerrillas had stored the arms at the university. Other university officials joined Rector Jesús María Bianco in resigning, and they refused to appear before the national council to explain the problems facing the UCV. The opposition parties—MEP, URD, and the Communist party—accused the government and AD of supporting fascist tactics in dealing with education.[47]

The government, supported by the military and by Acción Democrática, won the showdown; eventually troops left the UCV campus, and classes resumed under a new rector. But this did not put an end to the student problem. In the spring of 1972, the *Times of the Americas* reported that the police killing of a girl on the campus led to violent demonstrations and the closing of many schools throughout the country. The following year *Latin America* reported:

> Hardly a week now passes without one high school or another going on strike. The reasons behind the strikes are, generally, not complex. Overcrowding in schools, a rigid, old-fashioned syllabus, harassed teachers and lack of funds have caused the strikes, rather than any political motives. In fact, difficulties in getting into higher education, particularly universities, have been the major irritation in the last few months, but neither the university authorities nor the government have seen fit to tackle the problem. This week, however, the riots were provoked by the visit of William Rogers, and particularly by the fact that his main purpose was to discuss the Orinoco heavy oil belt.[48]

Student unrest and violence, which reached a peak during the controversy over the University Reform Law, reflected the next stage in the development of AD-COPEI relations. As we have mentioned, the parties cooperated during the first part of the Caldera administration in order to pass major pieces of legislation. As during the *guanábana*, they stood together to face a crisis. Admittedly, the university reform controversy was not as serious as the guerrilla movement of the early 1960s; but it might have become more serious, had the two major parties not cooperated. Whether the president was an Adeco or a Copeyano, crisis management demanded AD-COPEI cooperation.

The crisis also exemplified the country's growing political polarization. The lines were clearly drawn between the parties of the *coincidencia* and the Popular Front, as far as university reform was concerned. AD and COPEI had the votes to pass the measure in Congress, but the growing polarization became more clearly evident in the 1973 election. A final by-product of the university reform controversy was its impact within COPEI. As we have mentioned, the controversy caused bitter feelings for some within the party's youth wing, the JRC.

The government was more successful in dealing with the guerrilla movement. As in the case of the students, the problem did not disappear during the Caldera administration. Nevertheless, the government's policy, when added to the actions of the Betancourt and Leoni administrations, went a long way toward diffusing the guerrilla movement as a major national problem. In his inaugural address of 11 March 1969, President Caldera offered amnesty to the insurgents in exchange for a respect for democratic processes and an end to violence. The government would buy airline tickets for those who wished to leave the country. The president followed up his offer with specific steps: he would legalize the Communist party,[49] and subsequently the MIR; a presidential decree would free twenty people detained for subversive acts, including communist leaders Pompeyo Márquez, Teodoro Petkoff, and Guillermo García Ponce. The minister of interior, Lorenzo Fernández, directed the government's program under the name of "pacification."

Not content with merely offering amnesty, the government offered to negotiate with the guerrillas. Douglas Bravo, the Marxist leader of the largest known guerrilla band, sent a message through Cardinal Quintero which stated that he would agree to negotiate. Hostilities between the army and the guerrillas were suspended for a month, and the negotiations were successful. Members of various guerrilla groups left the hills. Some became ordinary citizens; some fled the country; others, charged with minor crimes, were tried and received light sentences; some entered politics as members of the MAS, MEP, or the Communist party. One group of guerrillas announced the formation of a party to support COPEI's presidential candidate.[50] However, Douglas Bravo himself did not accept the government's offer of amnesty.

The pacification program broke the back of the guerrilla movement. Orlando Castro Hidalgo, former Cuban intelligence agent, testified before the United States Senate that the offer of amnesty had been a death blow to the guerrillas. He referred to Orestes Guerra Matos, a member of the Central Committee of the Cuban Communist party, who said that the guerrillas were tired and dispirited due to their lack of victories since the moment when Caldera became president.

The pacification program succeeded partly because of external developments. Under President Caldera, Venezuela established or reestablished diplomatic relations with various communist countries, including the Soviet Union. The official Soviet position of peaceful coexistence, which generally opposed the export of the revolution through violence, coincided with the pacification program's aims. The Cuban government's decision—made in response to strong Soviet pressure—to curtail the support of insurgent groups clearly hurt the Douglas Bravo–led FALN, and made it easier for the guerrillas to consider the promises of pacification.

Incidents of guerrilla violence decreased throughout the country. In Lara, Governor Rafael Montes de Oca believed the pacification program was a success and served as the outstanding example of the government's promise of *El Cambio*.[51] However, a priest who lived for many years in the state (and asked to remain anonymous) differed from this view.[52] Commenting on the situation in Guárico, where he had worked for some time, the *padre* agreed that guerrilla activity was practically eliminated. This was significant, because Guárico had had more guerrilla activity than any other town in the state. Still, as far as the inhabitants were concerned, the government's promises were not fulfilled. The same problems continued to exist, or became worse with time: there was still a lack of adequate roads; a decline in agricultural production took place; there were very few schools. Many people were leaving the town to seek employment elsewhere. The Lara government was approached for help, to no avail. Although the pacification program dealt with a *symptom* of unrest and violence, in the form of the guerrilla movement, other government programs under *El Cambio* would have to deal with the *causes*, if the guerrilla movement was not to take root again on a major scale.

The guerrilla movement did continue, albeit to a lesser degree, during most of Caldera's administration. Compared to the previous administrations, the number of guerrillas killed by government forces was much less: not more than ten during the five-year period.[53] Be that as it may, the press periodically reported guerrilla activities and new outbreaks of violence. In the spring of 1973, the press also reported the MIR's return to legal political life through a presidential decree.[54]

The Adecos and Copeyanos differed concerning which party should take the major credit for the pacification. The AD position was that the guerrilla movement had been seriously weakened, if not destroyed, under the Betancourt administration; according to this observer, President Leoni had already stopped the repression, and his government had enacted a pacification program without publicly proclaiming it.[55]

The Copeyanos, for their part, maintain that the pacification program certainly was not an AD policy. The AD governments generally followed a policy of suppressing the guerrillas, but they were not psychologically prepared for a pacification program. President Leoni released a few prisoners who had important relatives, but it was COPEI that had a pacification policy demonstrated through various actions: legalization of the Communist party and the MIR, incorporation of the guerrillas into the political system, a foreign policy resulting in an exchange of ambassadors with the Soviet Union and improved relations with Cuba.[56]

The Caldera government was proud (and justly so, in my view) of the pacification program's results. The government's specific internal and foreign policy decisions significantly weakened the guerrilla movement. The contrast between the policies of the Betancourt and Leoni governments and those of the Caldera administration was evident: for the most part, the former relied on repression, which resulted in fear on the part of the guerrillas; the latter relied on pacification, which resulted in the voluntary integration of many guerrillas into society and the political process. There can be no doubt that the pacification program was very successful. Unrest and violence due to the guerrilla movement were much less at the end of the Caldera administration than at its beginning.

Executive-Congressional Relations

The AD-COPEI relationship was the primary factor determining the course of executive-congressional relations. That the Adecos wanted to limit the effectiveness of a Copeyano president was most evident during two periods: 1969, prior to the *coincidencia*, and during the last part of the Caldera administration, after major pieces of legislation had been passed. In all fairness to AD, both parties' later actions were influenced by the forthcoming 1973 election.

Other factors also affected executive-congressional relations. As indicated by Table 5.1., none of the eleven parties represented in the Congress had as much as one-third of the vote in both houses. As Professor Lott has noted, the Congress had a wide political spectrum, ranging from the Communist party on the left to the followers of Pérez Jiménez on the right. The government's proposals were subject to a broad range of discussions by groups within and without the Congress. The executive branch had to resort to constant negotiations, and the key to the government's realization of its goals (or a reason-

T A B L E 5.1. Party Composition of the Venezuelan Congress, 1969

	Senators	Deputies
Democratic Action (AD)	19	63
Social Christian Party (COPEI)	16	59
People's Electoral Movement (MEP)	5	25
National Civic Crusade (CCN)	4	21
Democratic Republican Union (URD)	3	20
Popular Democratic Force (FDP)	2	10
Democratic National Front (FND)	1	4
Revolutionary Party for National Integration (PRIN)	1	4
Union for Advancing (UPA)	1	5
Social Democratic Party (PSD)	0	1
National Action Movement (MAN)	0	1
	52	213

s o u r c e : *Venezuela Up-to-date*, 12 (Spring 1969). Cited by Leo B. Lott, *Venezuela and Paraguay*, p. 313.

able representation thereof) was an accommodation with Acción Democrática.

At times it was not possible to reach such an accommodation. AD-COPEI differences were evident in the dispute over presidential power to make judicial appointments, with long-range effects on executive-congressional relations.[57] (This dispute took place prior to the AD-COPEI accommodation under the *coincidencia.*) In 1969, AD pushed a bill through Congress which transferred the power to appoint judicial officials below the Supreme Court level from the minister of justice to a special committee; said committee was made up mostly of members from AD, with a few from URD. President Caldera vetoed both the original bill and a modified version resubmitted by Congress. He then resorted to his constitutional privilege (Article 173, Constitution of 1961) by asking the Supreme Court to rule on the constitutionality of the law. The Court upheld the law 8-7, providing the first example in Venezuelan history where a president was rebuffed by both Congress and the Court. As Professor Lott has remarked, the dispute showed that Congress can prevail over the executive branch—if the former is firm in its resolve, has the votes, and is willing to carry the battle to the end.

An Adeco told me that the necessity for almost constant executive-congressional negotiations was a positive result of the Caldera administration. One might argue that negotiations toward consensus over major issues of national policy are healthy, and that the more often the country experiences such endeavor, the better it will be for the development of political democracy. In this sense, executive-congressional relations under Caldera may be viewed in a positive manner. (However, the reader may also recall the comment of Eduardo Fernández, that the necessity of step-by-step negotiations hindered the effectiveness of governing.) I would argue that the question of executive-congressional balance depends upon the political situation of the period. Apparent balance (or the congressional dominance, according to some critics) was unique to the Caldera period, and would not necessarily exist to the same degree at other times. For example, under President Carlos Andrés Pérez (1974-79), the Adecos controlled both the executive branch and Congress. One cannot then talk of negotiations and balance in the same sense.

Let us now turn to Congress and consider the more important legislative accomplishments during the Caldera administration. We will be concerned with a major question: Which laws could be attributed primarily to the Caldera government, and which ones primarily reflected the influence of the opposition, particularly Acción Democrática?

CHAPTER 6

Governing Reality

IT WAS APPARENT from my various conversations with Adecos, Copeyanos, and representatives of the smaller political parties that different views existed concerning COPEI's legislative role. One young Copeyano told me that the government was opportunistic, exemplifying the phrase *Al son que le tocan baila.* This signified that the government danced to the tune of others when assuming a strong nationalist position, or when supporting legislation initiated by other political parties and already backed by public opinion. However, the government had to utilize this tactic, because COPEI members were a minority in the Congress.[1] Others pointed out that COPEI exercised the administration of the state, but that AD actually governed.[2] This was an exaggeration, because both parties were involved in the governing process.

Several significant laws were passed during the Caldera administration. We have discussed the amendment to the Law of the Universities, initiated by AD with COPEI support. Other laws pertained to petroleum, foreign investments, nationalization of electric energy, creation of a national petroleum tanker fleet, suffrage, and banking. Still others focused on basic industries and the promotion of national development: the Corporation of the Development of the *Oriente*, credits for the Petrochemical Industry (*El Tablazo*), credits for the Steel Industry (SIDOR), and credits for the National Agrarian Institute (IAN). Additional legislation dealt with agricultural development (PRIDA), labor, and education.

The Adecos took the position that most, if not all, major legislation was initiated and brought to fruition primarily by AD and to a lesser degree by the Popular Front (MEP-URD-Communist party). They complained that COPEI merely continued programs initiated by AD, and that Congress seemed stronger than the presidency because Congress had to assert itself or nothing would be accomplished.[3] The Copeyanos strongly disagreed, admitting that they had continued some AD programs, but asserting that they had modified others and had initiated some of their own. The party claimed that their approach to legislative requirements was patriotic, and that they did not need any pressure from AD. COPEI wanted to place such resources as petroleum, iron, and electrical energy into the hands of Venezuelans, and the Copeyanos criticized the Adecos for not having done more of this in the past.[4]

We shall now attempt to determine the degree of COPEI influence in shaping legislation. We might point out, however, that the political environment makes it difficult to identify a party's imprint on a specific piece of legislation. The maneuvering involved in the development of a foreign investment law is a case in point.[5]

Major Pieces of Legislation

The government established a commission, consisting of members of different parties and well-known people in business and financial circles, to study the best possible way of approaching a foreign investment law. The Copeyanos prepared an investment law while the commission was deliberating, but MEP, URD, and AD prepared their own bills, even though they were also represented on the commission. The result was that the final bill did not originate in the commission. Instead, it came from the Congress, and reflected the give and take of negotiations between COPEI and the other political parties having bills of their own. COPEI claimed that it was a major architect of the law that eventually passed, but the opposition likewise claimed that honor.

A consideration of the banking law will help us to clarify two questions regarding this specific legislation: Did Congress make a conscious effort to strengthen the government's role in the economy, and thereby to bolster the so-called tendency toward statism? And how did this legislation affect the relationship between the foreign business community and the Venezuelan government?

On 30 December 1970, the *Official Gazette* published Extraordinary Issue No. 1454: General Law of Banks and Other Credit Institutes. Passed unanimously by Congress, the law ordered a 20 percent limit on the equity that foreigners could hold in Venezuelan banks. Limitations were placed on banks not meeting this requirement; a bank could carry obligations on call equal to no more than six times its capital and reserves, it lost the capacity to carry savings accounts and issue savings bonds, and it could no longer sell foreign currency directly or indirectly to the Central Bank. According to the press, the government believed that greater local control over banking would assure it of credits for expanding new export-oriented businesses.[6]

Foreign banking interests included First National City Bank of New York, Royal Bank of Canada, Chase Manhattan, and the Bank of London. For the most part they reacted negatively to the law.[7] Felipe Casanova, president of the National Banking Council, stated that the law could cause excessive government intervention in the activities of private commercial banks. Sources close to the banking industry said that the law failed in its attempt to broaden participation in the country's economic activities. Instead, the law made it possible for four powerful commercial groups to concentrate in their hands all but complete control of the country's banking industry. The stock sold by banks which exceeded the legal restriction, according to stock market sources, was snapped up by these four groups, giving them control of yet another segment of the nation's economy.

Hector Hurtado, the former head of Cordiplan (the government agency in charge of coordination and planning) under Acción Democrática, wrote the original draft of the law. The drafters also leaned heavily on the Mayobre Report, written by José Antonio Mayobre, former minister of finance under AD. In addition to dealing with petroleum, the report offered suggestions for greater Venezuelan control of banks and insurance companies.[8] Although COPEI representatives were directly involved in the deliberations which led to passage of the banking law, the major impetus for the law and the philosophy behind it clearly came from AD.

The foreign bankers made several miscalculations.[9] They did not realize that the question of foreign banks in Venezuela was primarily a political issue, rather than an economic one. Given the rising tide of nationalism in Latin America in general and Venezuela in particular, the COPEI government had to insist on greater local control of banks once AD took the initiative. Foreign bankers were not accused of bleeding the country and removing most of their profits. Rather, Latin America of the 1970s indicated that the time had come for them to leave. Although the foreign bankers assumed that the Venezuelan business community would join them in their fight, local businessmen by and large did not feel threatened by restrictions on foreign banking interests. In fact, several major local commercial groups saw an opportunity to increase their own stake in the country's banks. Nor did the foreign bankers make any direct effort to seek public support for their own cause. They believed that no law discriminatory to their interests could possibly be passed as long as Pedro Tinoco was minister of finance. Because of his past experience in the management of Banco Mercantil y Agrícola, an affiliate of Chase Manhattan Bank, they were certain that he would not allow their interests to suffer. But they were wrong—Tinoco could not help them.

The banking law had a traumatic effect on the foreign business community. No longer could they count on their friends in government and local business to protect their interests; no longer would their financial stakes in the country be invulnerable; and no longer could they withstand the crescendo of nationalism. Other foreign financial interests—petroleum and iron mines—closely observed the process that brought the banking law into being, and they did not like what they saw.

Those who claimed to see "supranationalistic" tendencies among the country's leaders also pointed to the banking law. According to this view, supranationalism was equated with legislation giving the government greater control over the economy. Clem Cohen wrote:

It is clear to me why this trend exists among the leaders of MEP, URD, FDP, and the other splinter groups. They are trying to fill the political void left by the absence of a viable extreme-left force. The Communist party has split and the once rampant MIR is now more a memory than a reality. In search of the "leftist" vote, the so-called "New Force" parties have swung rapidly in that direction.

Why the ruling Social Christians and the opposition Acción Democrática appear to be heading in the same direction is quite another matter and deserves a closer scrutiny. . . .[10]

Several political leaders to whom I spoke denied, for various reasons, that there was a conscious effort to fill a political void on the extreme left. According to a Communist party spokesman, the various laws actually reflected the right-wing position: they might have been considered radical by foreign investors, but their purpose was to maintain and solidify the present system.[11] A political leader of URD pointed out that COPEI did not initiate any major legislation, and that the Copeyanos had made no effort to fill a political void on the extreme left.[12]

The COPEI leaders did not see any need to fill such a political void.[13] They felt that the extreme left—e.g., the guerrillas and the MIR—were no longer a threat. Nor did the Copeyanos believe that the Communists seriously challenged the major political parties. The party had never appealed to a significant number of people, as indicated by its poor electoral performances, and it certainly had never been a party of the masses. The Copeyanos admitted that the Communists had some support in the high schools and universities, but the "communist" students became bourgeois upon graduation. (However, the Communist party split during the Caldera administration, giving rise to the MAS.)

There was another side to the left-wing question. In September 1970 Salvador Allende, the Marxist candidate, won the presidential election in Chile. Perhaps Venezuela's leaders did not consciously attempt to fill a political void on the extreme left, but did they nevertheless try to prevent a recurrence of the Chilean phenomenon by supporting legislation which appealed to those toward the left of the political spectrum? One view, expressed by a young COPEI technician, was that the Caldera program was like that of the Chilean Christian Democratic president, Eduardo Frei: he was all too ready to propose programs which he hoped would be popular. But, according to this man, President Frei's program raised the aspirations of the Chilean people, who subsequently felt cheated when their hopes were not realized. The situation, if repeated in Venezuela, could result in a COPEI defeat in 1973. But in that case the victor would be Acción Democrática, and not a Marxist coalition as occurred in Chile. The young technician went on to point to the effect of the Chilean election on COPEI, observing that it did not necessarily mean that the party had to move to the left; rather, it indicated that the Caldera government had to complete a fundamental part of its program, as promised. This would involve the problem of the *coincidencia* because of AD's congressional strength. The Adecos, aware of this, would not allow the government to succeed in realizing its program.

Valmore Acevedo, the long-time COPEI leader, did not believe the Chilean election affected the Caldera government's legislation. Rather than reflecting any attempt to move to the left because of the Chilean election, the laws indicated Venezuela's political maturity. More of the country's resources would be in the hands of Venezuelans, enabling them to run their own affairs. The political leaders did not say that there would be no foreign interests; instead, they called for "Venezuelanization," or more local participation, which reflected the Venezuelan brand of nationalism.

I am more inclined to agree with the young technician. The Chilean election probably affected Venezuela's political leaders in varying degrees, whether it signified greater efforts by the Caldera government to realize its program, or action by the congressional leaders to fashion laws that would appeal to the left and thereby help diffuse unrest. We should also note that more than half of Venezuela's eligible voters were under thirty years of age—a fact which was never far from the thoughts of the country's leaders.

Petroleum Legislation

Background

Substantial petroleum exploration did not begin until 1921. By the end of the decade, petroleum accounted for over 90 percent of the foreign exchange—the same level as today. The petroleum industry also provides 67 percent of the government's revenue and 20 percent of the gross national product. Because it is capital intensive, the industry employs less than 2 percent of the labor force. Before nationalization, 80 percent of the country's petroleum was produced by two giant companies: Exxon Corporation (formerly Standard Oil of New Jersey), operating through its 95 percent-owned subsidiary, Creole Petroleum Company; and Royal-Dutch Shell. The Gulf Oil Company held 50 percent of the stock in Mene Grande Oil Company, the country's third-largest oil producer, with the remaining 50 percent held equally by subsidiaries of Exxon and Shell. There were several smaller companies, including the government-owned Venezuelan Petroleum Corporation. Created in 1960, the CVP accounted for 1 or 2 percent of the total petroleum production.

In January 1976 the government of President Carlos Andrés Pérez nationalized the petroleum industry, culminating a long struggle between the sovereignties of government and the petroleum companies. "In a nutshell, the heart of petroleum policy [by the government] in the years since 1959 has been the struggle to find ways of achieving the goals of income, conservation, control, and ultimately domestication of the industry, while not sacrificing the other objectives of economic growth and regime consolidation and legitimization."[14] Over the years, the petroleum companies took the position that they were taking risks and making heavy investments of money, talent, and equipment. This gave them the upper hand, and they felt that they had the right to dictate how much money the government should make from the sale of petroleum. The companies also threatened the government by suggesting that they could move their equipment and investment of several billion dollars elsewhere. The government, for its part, argued that the oil belonged to the nation, not to the petroleum companies, and that once it left the ground it could not be replaced; therefore the government must have a stronger voice in the determination of petroleum policy and prices. The fact that the companies operated under concessions, or contracts signed with the government to exploit thousands of acres of land, did not alleviate the growing conflict. Although due to expire in 1983, the concessions would not revert to the government until that time. The government would not wait.

A key figure in the dispute was Juan Pablo Pérez Alfonzo, who served as minister of mines and hydrocarbons under Betancourt. He has written many articles and books and has spoken frequently on the subject. Betancourt and Pérez Alfonzo were the principal architects of the AD petroleum policy, which, after 1958, COPEI and most other parties broadly shared.

Pérez Alfonzo argued that the government should stop granting new concessions and instead sign service contracts with the petroleum companies, through which the latter would work for the government in exploring and exploiting petroleum. He also insisted that the government support legislation which would enable it to make greater profits on the sale of petroleum, because the taxes that the companies paid to the government were not adequate. Pérez Alfonzo accused the companies of undercharging for their petroleum by selling to other companies in which they themselves had interests. Rather than basing taxes on the selling price of petroleum, the government should assess by reference prices, which would be pegged above the market price and would therefore bring greater income to the government. Once the reference prices were established, the government would increase taxes on the petroleum companies. Pérez Alfonzo also believed that the government's position vis-à-vis the companies would be strengthened through cooperation with other petroleum-producing countries; he strongly supported the formation of an Organization of Petroleum Exporting Countries to control the world's petroleum supply and regulate prices. For those who argued against the idea of a monopolistic petroleum supplier's organization, Pérez Alfonzo pointed to the Texas Railroad Commission in the United States, which controls approximately one-third of that country's petroleum production. The minister was also concerned about the enormous investment in petroleum equipment in Venezuela, realizing that if the government had no control over the billions of dollars of machinery, pipelines, and refineries, it would have no leverage when dealing with the companies that could move away, leaving the country with gigantic holes in the ground. Furthermore, Pérez Alfonzo believed the government should limit petroleum production, forcing prices up. It was better to leave much of the petroleum in the ground, because it could not be replaced. He also thought that the government would spend the additional income from taxes foolishly in bureaucratic schemes. Such a move would adversely affect the economy.

Franklin Tugwell has outlined the efforts of the Betancourt and Leoni administrations to strengthen the government's position vis-à-vis the petroleum companies. The limited success of these efforts was due to one crucial factor: world demand for petroleum was not strong enough in those days, and prices continued to fall. As we mentioned, the Betancourt administration established a state oil corporation, the Corporación Venezolana de Petróleo (CVP), "with the goal of building managerial experience in oil matters within the Venezuelan public sector." In 1960, primarily through the efforts of Pérez Alfonzo, the Organization of Petroleum Exporting Countries (OPEC) was established by Iraq, Kuwait, Saudi Arabia, and Venezuela. OPEC was not very effective during the first ten years of its existence. In addition to the relatively weak world demand for petroleum, the internal divisions and unpreparedness of Middle Eastern and, subsequently, North African members prevented the organization from being much more than a creation on the drawing board.

Regardless of the limited successes of the Betancourt government, the petroleum companies were concerned. They did not like the government's efforts to force them to keep petroleum prices high, and they wanted more concessions. The companies then adopted counterpressures of their own, decreasing their investments in Venezuelan petroleum and moving sizable funds to Canada, the Middle East, and North Africa, thereby reducing the rate of petroleum production. Exploration and drilling activity declined, employment fell, and the Venezuelan budget contracted. A second strategy involved efforts to form an alliance with the Venezuelan private sector. The foreign and private interests created their own Chamber of Petroleum Industry, which then jointed FEDECÁMARAS, the powerful association of chambers and producer organizations. Despite these counterpressures, the Betancourt administration refused to grant new concessions.

The conflict between the government and the petroleum companies intensified during the Leoni administration. Although politically weaker as a result of the 1963 election, the executive branch resorted to a variety of tactics to strengthen its position. These included the idea of a retroactive tax that would make it possible for the government to collect additional taxes on petroleum which had allegedly been sold at levels lower than those obtainable elsewhere. This "excess profits" tax applied to earnings in excess of 15 percent of net fixed assets. The government hoped to increase the taxes on domestic companies as well, but this proposal only strengthened the alliance between the petroleum companies and private enterprise. Eventually, the government and the companies reached a compromise. According to Tugwell,

> The companies agreed to pay some 700 million bolívares ($155 million) to the government in return for the abandonment of its back tax claims. Further, they agreed to pay taxes in the future on a set of Tax Reference Values (TRVs) to be negotiated with the government, which would be higher than prevailing prices and which would increase gradually for a period of five years. (Before this agreement, taxes were paid on actual or "realized" prices.) For its part the government agreed to modify its tax reform as it applied to the petroleum companies by eliminating the "excess profits" tax. Although the companies would still have to face another increase, roughly from 65% to 68% of profits, the government thereby agreed to eliminate from the law the single item most feared by the companies. The agreement reflected accurately the new bargaining positions of the contenders. Weakened politically, anxious for continuation of the growth of fiscal income, and facing parliamentary immobilism, the government gave way on an important tax issue. In return, it received needed funds and an important new policy instrument.

At first it appeared that the Caldera government was not going to rock the boat. True, the government did not offer new concessions, and it chose to move ahead with the service contract system. But President Caldera was not very enthusiastic about OPEC; he favored a steady growth of income from oil, rather than conservation and the defense of international prices. In the face of a continuing decline of petroleum prices, the government concentrated on the expansion of production to increase national income. The oil company executives were delighted.

But all was not serene. The country's political leaders continued to complain about the hemispheric system of preferential treatment, whereby the United States established an import quota system and gave preference to petroleum imports from Mexico and Canada while placing Venezuela in the same category as suppliers from the Middle East, North Africa, and elsewhere. According to an anonymous U.S. official, policymakers decided to favor "White Anglo-Saxon Canada"; they also had to include Mexico (which was believed to have relatively limited petroleum resources at the time), using the rationale that the United States would favor overland petroleum imports. Furthermore, U.S. producers had to be protected. Venezuela could not be included in the system of preferential treatment because it was the largest producer in the hemisphere; as one United States official told me, this would be tantamount to allowing Brazil into a coffee-producing agreement intended to protect United States producers. Pérez Alfonzo had believed that Venezuela would be included in the preferential system, and he bitterly denounced the U.S. government policy. As late as October 1970 a Copeyano political leader complained about his country's exclusion.[15]

I said "as late as 1970," because that was the year of noticeable change in the world petroleum picture. Demand rose significantly: it was estimated that the 15 billion barrels a year consumed by the United States would increase to approximately 27 billion barrels by 1980. As a result of the closing of the Suez Canal following the 1967 Middle East war, Venezuelan oil became much more important in the United States market—particularly in the northeastern states, which are on a shipping line from northern South America. OPEC began to flex its muscles, and the member states of Iran, Algeria, and Libya made greater demands on the foreign producers in their respective countries. At about this time the leadership of Acción Democrática also made a decision concerning the country's petroleum policy. Reacting to the pressure of a faction led by Pérez Alfonzo, the Adecos decided to promote a more aggressive stance. They saw their opportunity when the executive branch presented its budget and tax reform proposals to Congress.

Budget and Tax Reform

The controversy over income and spending that culminated in specific petroleum legislation lasted for about a year. The political opposition strongly denounced the 1970 budget, the 1971 budget, and tax reform. The budget proposals were presented against a background of relatively poor national economic performance in 1969.[16] Prices, which had remained stable for years, suddenly jumped by more than 3 percent. The increase in the gross national product declined from 6 percent to almost 5 percent. The Caldera government had inherited an unusual burden of public works projects from the preceding administration, and found it difficult to maintain them because of the decline in petroleum exports, primarily to the United States.

In 1960 the United States imported a total of 371,575,000 barrels of oil, of which 172,887,000 came from Venezuela, chiefly in the form of heating fuel for the northeast market. A total of 41,349,000 barrels were imported from Canada. In 1969 the United States imported a total of about 490 million barrels, of which an estimated 120 million came from Venezuela and almost 200 million from Canada. As a result, the petroleum companies decreased their efforts to find new oil fields in Venezuela, and reserves of known petroleum declined.

With these factors in mind, the executive branch presented its 1970 budget proposals to Congress.[17] The opposition-controlled finance committee of the Chamber of Deputies slashed Finance Minister Tinoco's original request by 40 percent, and he had to resubmit new proposals after the congressional recess. This time the administration submitted two budgets: the regular budget, and a supplementary budget to cover the cost of public works. The opposition again denounced the proposals, fearing that the supplementary budget would cause a deficit of 10 billion *bolívares* over the next five years. Finally, a special session of Congress approved a budget 6 percent higher than that of the previous year. We should remember that AD and COPEI had not yet agreed to the *coincidencia*; once they reached a political agreement, the administration's budget proposals received more sympathetic hearings in Congress.

The following year, Minister Tinoco presented the administration's 1971 budget, which called for a deficit of 800 million *bolívares* (180 million dollars) to be offset by nine new taxes designed to raise 962 million *bolívares* (215 million dollars). Since the constitution clearly stated that the budget must be balanced, the administration argued that tax reform was the only alternative. (Only a reported 3 percent of the population officially declares its income taxes, and only 1 percent of that number actually pays.) The Caldera government knew that it was presenting a politically dangerous proposal, but it believed it could convince the majority of Congress, particularly AD, of the logic of its position.

Although the cabinet approved the proposed tax reform, elements within COPEI were vehemently opposed. The Copeyano Senator Edecio La Riva Araujo argued that the new taxes would result in economic sacrifice for groups with the lowest incomes. (Since he was identified with the more conservative elements within COPEI, many were surprised to learn of La Riva's position.) Several younger Copeyano technicians made a press declaration opposing their party's tax reform proposals, agreeing that the poorer consumer sectors would be unduly burdened. The *técnicos* also felt that such actions would jeopardize the party's political base with the masses, as far as future elections were concerned, and they wanted the party to assume a position more politically advanced than that of AD. One enraged Copeyano told me that Caldera forced the party to accept tax reform proposals which only served to advertise his domination of COPEI, or *Calderismo*.

The leadership of Acción Democrática strongly criticized the administration's proposals also. The AD secretary-general, Carlos Andrés Pérez, opposed the idea of a new sales tax because it would be applied to articles indispensable to the consumer, such as clothing.

This would result in a higher cost of living "which would be a set-back to people of all social strata. Taxes should be distributed in a selective way so as to tax people with high incomes more heavily than people with lower incomes. This in turn will create a fairer and more proportionate tax distribution for all."[18] In the same vein, Pérez objected to the proposed income tax increase of 10 percent for all private enterprises. Instead, he called for progressive criteria to be followed, so that enterprises would contribute in proportion to their revenue. Finally, AD's secretary-general took the COPEI administration to task for exempting foreign petroleum companies from the proposed tax reform; he accused the companies of receiving excess profits, in some cases as high as 43 percent. According to Pérez, such enormous profits had negative repercussions on the country's economy, and their existence necessitated a total reevaluation of the status of Venezuelan petroleum.

COPEI's long-time critics pointed to the administration's tax proposals as proof of their major charge against the Copeyanos: regardless of their professed ideology, the party leaders were more sympathetic to the interests of foreign and domestic business enterprises than to those of the masses. Given the nature of the tax reform proposals (referred to as the Tinoco Plan), it was difficult for the party to refute the charge. While the Copeyanos might argue that one must distinguish between the party and the government, the tax reform proposals originated in the administration, and their content was largely influenced by Pedro Tinoco. COPEI, the party, was not responsible for what transpired. But as far as the critics and the press were concerned, COPEI had spoken true to form.

The administration and the party had an opportunity to redeem themselves when Congress rejected the Tinoco Plan. The only alternative left was to raise additional income and eradicate the budget deficit. It was now necessary to increase the taxes on the petroleum companies. Who would initiate the legislation? What positions would be taken by the administration and the Congress?

A Tax Increase on the Petroleum Companies and the Unilateral Fixing of Reference Prices

Although the international petroleum situation changed from a buyer's to a seller's market by 1970, it took time for this new reality to be accepted worldwide. Government officials, business interests, and consumer and supplier countries continued to think in terms of import quotas and competitive pricing. While the Venezuelan Congress debated the proposal to increase taxes on the petroleum companies, several events took place reflecting "the old thinking about petroleum" and affecting the climate of that discussion.

In late 1969, President Nixon appointed a commission under the chairmanship of Secretary of Labor George P. Schultz to determine whether to continue the current system of importing foreign oil or to substitute a new system of tariffs. In the spring of 1970, Venezuelan oil cost approximately $2.00 a barrel in Caracas.[19] It took $.25 to ship a barrel to the northeastern United States ports by tanker. The importer paid a tariff of $.10 a barrel and $1.25 for a "ticket" to import each barrel. The total number of tickets awarded throughout the industry represented, in effect, the quota. For example, if a refiner in the Midwest did not want foreign oil, he could trade his tickets to an importer; the importer would pay him in domestic oil, and use the tickets to bring in cheaper overseas petroleum. About one-third of the tickets were being exchanged in this manner.

Although President Nixon expressed his disapproval of certain basic points of the Schultz Commission report, and its recommendations were not enacted into policies, the Venezuelan press and many political leaders nevertheless denounced the suggestions as evidence of U.S. imperialism and economic control. Among its recommendations,[20] the Schultz Commission called for lowering United States oil prices to $2.50 per barrel, in addition to substituting import duty tariffs for quantitative quotas. The United States and Canada were urged to cooperate closely in the utilization of petroleum, gas, and electric power. The Canadians must be encouraged to increase their production, and Canadian oil should have unlimited entry into the U.S. market. The report also stated that the United States should consider constructing a vast complex of pipelines throughout North America, including Canada, Alaska, and the United States mainland. The United States must control the quantity of Venezuelan oil imported, in order to maintain the $2.50 per barrel price. New exploration in Latin America, which could include new areas in Venezuela, was also encouraged.

The specific Venezuelan complaints over the Schultz Commission's report involved the suggested price of $2.50 per barrel and the restricted U.S. market for their petroleum. Although Venezuela received less than $2.50 per barrel at the time, the press and political leaders argued that the new suggested price was inadequate. They also pointed out that the restrictions on imports merely served to strengthen the hemispheric system of preferential treatment by favoring Canada and further restricting Venezuela.

President Caldera made a trip to the United States in June 1970, with the expressed purpose of receiving a greater share of the United States market for Venezuelan petroleum. He had ample opportunity to express his government's position through an address to a joint session of Congress, discussions with President Nixon, a press conference in Washington, and attendance at a special meeting of the Organization of American States (OAS). In a speech at a National Press Club luncheon, Caldera voiced his country's major complaint:[21] in the last ten years, Venezuela's petroleum exports to the United States had dropped by 30 percent, and prices by more than 20 percent. He attributed the decrease to Washington's policy of import controls, whereby a total quota was assigned to foreign imports, and oil companies were free to select their suppliers within that quota.

Speaking to the joint session of Congress, President Caldera said:

> . . . the idea that a wealthy nation can be oblivious to the plight of other nations is obsolete. . . . Venezuela, for example, exports petroleum. Our economy is largely based upon our petroleum exports. Any decision related to the access of Venezuelan petroleum to the North American market has grave repercussions on our possibilities for livelihood and development. In the last decade the relative position of our petroleum in the United States market has deteriorated. Our people cannot understand being made the object of discriminatory treatment.

> . . . a just and non-discriminatory treatment, that can guarantee a secure place for Venezuelan petroleum in the North American market and a reasonable participation in its expansion, goes beyond the terms of a simple commercial arrangement. It is a condition for the fulfillment of the development programs of a neighboring and friendly country and a key to the direction that future relations between the United States and Latin America will take.[22]

The Venezuelan press generally lauded the president upon his return. The editorials were pleased with his above-quoted speech (in English), during which he expressed Venezuela's position in blunt terms. Although several opposition leaders accused the president of traveling to the United States with hat in hand, he favorably impressed President Nixon and several important senators, and the trip did bring positive results. Shortly after Caldera's return, the United States eased the oil import quotas.[23] This action resulted in an increase of 100,000 barrels a day of foreign crude oil and 40,000 barrels a day of home heating oil for the states of the Northeast. The United States also announced that the new supply of fuel for the Northeast would come from sources within the hemisphere, meaning primarily Venezuela.

If President Caldera had waited a year, he probably would not have needed to travel to the United States. By the summer of 1970, several developments took place which made Venezuela petroleum more attractive and expensive.[24] As the debates over petroleum legislation continued in the Congress, the country's political and business leaders watched these events with great interest.

By July, it was evident that there was a worldwide tanker shortage. The closing of the Suez Canal necessitated a long trip around Africa, and enough tankers simply were not available; this resulted in a quadrupling of freight charges within twelve months. Libya cut back production approximately 550,000 barrels per day to chastise several United States companies operating there. Palestinian guerrillas in Syria knocked out the Trans-Arabian pipeline, which had usually carried 475,000 barrels per day to a Mediterranean port in Lebanon. The tanker shortage and cutbacks by Middle East producers intensified the effects of the increase of world demand: 9 percent greater in 1970 than in 1969. During this period a number of Libya's European customers came to Venezuela to purchase crude oil, thus lifting Venezuelan output from 3.5 million to almost 4 million barrels a day.

The message was clear in the Chamber of Deputies: the world demand for petroleum was increasing; it would continue to increase for the forseeable future; the country's petroleum policy must reflect the new situation. Jesús Bernardoni, a COPEI deputy from Zulia and one of the party's petroleum experts, stated that the nationalist awakening of the Middle East and African countries had affected Venezuela. COPEI should place itself in this nationalist vanguard.[25]

According to a member of the Chamber of Deputies, the original legislation—to increase taxes on the petroleum and mining companies and to authorize the executive branch to unilaterally fix reference prices—was introduced by Acción Democrática; COPEI was the only political party to vote against it at that time. The Copeyanos subsequently assumed a nationalist line and supported the opposition's idea.[26] However, COPEI's position was weakened, because the Copeyanos were divided over the question.

Before the new legislation was introduced, the petroleum companies paid taxes on a graduated scale with a 20 to 52 percent range; the average was closer to 50 percent for many companies. The bill introduced in the Chamber of Deputies proposed a modification of the law to tax the companies at an across-the-board rate of 60 percent, and to make the increase retroactive for 1970. Acción Democrática also proposed that reference prices be unilaterally fixed by the government, thereby eliminating the previous practice of government versus company negotiations to arrive at a price. COPEI's representative on the special congressional oil committee, Deputy Jesús Bernardoni López, strongly supported the bill in his address to the Chamber of Deputies during the first reading. Another COPEI deputy, Herrera Campins, took the same position, stating that the bill reflected "the strengthening of the nationalistic conscience of the country at a favorable moment."[27]

But the head of COPEI's parliamentary wing, Pedro Pablo Aguilar, called for a modification of AD's bill. He proposed to the Chamber of Deputies that "instead of a single tariff of 60 percent for the nation's tax income from oil companies' profits, the national executive should be given more flexibility to either choose from the 60 percent measure or the original progressive levels of collecting income originally established. . . ." Aguilar argued that AD's bill would endanger and harm the success of service contracts because they would be less attractive for the petroleum companies. Similar concern prevailed in the business community, particularly from Pedro Tinoco, FEDECÁMARAS, and Pro-Venezuela's National Front for the Defense of Oil.

The controversy led to strains within COPEI. Dagoberto González, head of the party's labor organization (FTC), stated that the workers supported Aguilar's position. But Deputy Bernardoni said he would defend his prior position "irrespective of pressure from individuals of the COPEI parliamentary wing or any other group or cabinet." He insisted he would support the original bill and threatened to renounce his post on the special oil committee if he was pressured.

Why did Pedro Pablo Aguilar try to modify the bill and, in the view of his critics, attempt to water down the legislation so it would be more acceptable to the petroleum companies? The British news agency, Reuters, carried a report that one of the major petroleum companies—Shell, Creole, or Mobil—had pressured Tinoco into firm opposition to the tax increase. This pressure, in turn, influenced the president's position. My conversations with various Copeyanos corroborated the report. Pressure also was applied in the following manner: representatives of Creole, Nicanor García and Lander Marqués, spoke to Tinoco; he then spoke to Caldera, who issued an order to Aguilar. The executive branch did not plan to increase the tax on the petroleum companies, and at one point Aguilar offered to postpone the matter. But the opposition (AD, certain influential Copeyanos, MEP, URD, FDP, CCN) stood firm. Caldera then assumed a nationalistic position because he knew public opinion was moving in that direction (thus showing his skill in incorporating the opposition's view as his own). The law was passed unanimously by the Congress.

To summarize, the bill that became law in December 1970 called for a flat 60 percent income tax on oil and mining companies and an immediate change of the reference price system—programmed until the end of 1971—giving the executive branch unilateral authority to fix export prices. The government's total take from the oil companies was boosted to approximately 80 percent, including all taxes, and the scrapping of the old reference price system eliminated the legal requirement to consult with the companies before fixing such prices. Politically, the legislation was advantageous for AD and a setback for COPEI. The storm of protest caused by the Copeyano attempt to modify the original proposal was more than the party could handle. Caldera managed to extricate the party and his government from the immediate controversy, but his Johnny-come-lately nationalistic position was fodder for AD in the 1973 electoral campaign.

The petroleum companies made a major effort to defend themselves, but this time they received little support from their allies in the domestic sector. As Tugwell has pointed out, "This was due in part to the fact that oil taxes were replacing proposed domestic taxes, but it was also due to resentment on the part of Venezuelan economic elites at the companies' separate agreement with the AD government in 1966."[28] The companies stated (correctly) that the new law would jeopardize the existence of small companies; they also argued that the government's relatively high profit share had been hobbling the development of the petroleum industry, and that the new legislation would make the companies even more reluctant to explore and develop new reserves. And they were particularly bitter that the tax increase would be retroactive.

The United States also reacted negatively. The Venezuelans had been arguing for years that their petroleum exports should be given the same preferential treatment as those of Canada and Mexico, basing their argument, in part, on the fact that Venezuela provided a secure and continued petroleum source for the United States market. The U.S. ambassador at the time, Robert McClintock, questioned the Venezuelan contention:

> The United States President is required to take into account national security in formulating a national oil import policy. Therefore, any regional preferences . . . must be based on the security of the source of the oil. Security does not only mean relative immunity from possible military threats but, most importantly, its continued availability. In other words, a secure source is one where the United States, as an important importer of oil and gas, can be able to count on production to meet rising needs in future years. In the specific case of Venezuela, and taking into account the recent tax legislation and the "ex parte" fixing of reference prices, only the future will reveal whether investment capital can be found in sufficient quantity to keep up further production, which alone can provide security of source.[29]

Such statements did not frighten Venezuelan political leaders. The worldwide petroleum scene had changed, and they knew it. The Copeyanos also recognized that, as petroleum prices began to rise, the bargaining power of the Venezuelan government would increase accordingly. "Although the initiative for policy changes remained in the legislature with the faction led by Pérez Alfonzo, Caldera and COPEI leaders gradually began to fall in step, assuming a more nationalistic posture and attacking the foreign corporations more frequently in public statements."[30]

The Organization of Petroleum Exporting Countries (OPEC)

Before considering the next major piece of petroleum legislation, we should note two developments: changes within OPEC, and the rise in petroleum prices. The OPEC changes were significant because Venezuela's new petroleum policies had a direct effect on the organization, and the latter, in turn, supported the efforts of the political leaders in Caracas.

President Caldera believed that efforts to raise petroleum prices would have a greater chance of success if the OPEC member states followed suit. On numerous occasions he stated that a price war among the producer countries would only benefit the petroleum companies and the consumer countries:

> The presence in this meeting of representatives of exporters . . .
> shows not only the opportunity of dialogue, but the conviction
> that the times in which our exports were used in the game of
> suicidal competition, through those who maneuvered us against
> our own interests, are now past. . . . We have taken the exact
> measure of the injustices of which we have been the object, in
> order to demand our rights, and that it would be suicide on our
> part to become competitors in lowering our prices. . . .[31]

While the controversy over petroleum legislation was reaching a climax in the Congress, in December 1970, OPEC was holding its twenty-first meeting in Caracas. Several resolutions reflected the turn of events in Venezuela and charted new directions for the producer countries. One of these stated that reference prices should be determined by the governments of the member countries, and that they should be adjusted periodically to offset inflation in the industrialized consumer countries, which resulted in higher prices for manufactured goods. Responding directly to President Caldera's concern, OPEC agreed to establish a uniform general increase in reference prices. Interestingly, though, OPEC did not go quite as far as Venezuela in taxing the petroleum companies: the member states established a 55 percent minimum on the net income of the companies. In February 1971, OPEC met in Teheran and supported the shah's proposal to unilaterally raise the price of oil.[32]

Thus Venezuela reemerged as a major policymaker in OPEC, bridging the gap that had separated the radical newcomers, Libya and Algeria, from the veteran South American oil giant. Strengthened by victories over the petroleum companies and by recognized leadership in OPEC, the government proceeded to raise petroleum prices.

Rise in Petroleum Prices

From the consumer countries' point of view, the escalation in petroleum prices of Venezuela and OPEC during the last years of the Caldera administration was phenomenal: the price of Venezuelan petroleum rose from $2.00 per barrel at the beginning of 1971 to $14.00 per barrel at the beginning of 1974. With approximately the same yearly quantity of petroleum exports (3.5 million barrels per day in February 1974), the country's total tax income rose from $1.5

TABLE 6.1. Venezuelan Tax Reference Price Increases in U.S. Dollars, 1973

January	$ 3.07
March	3.34
April-June	— —
July	4.11
September	4.40
October	4.89
November	7.24
December	7.44
January 1974	14.08

SOURCE: *Latin America Economic Report,* 15 February 1974.

billion dollars in 1970 to $10 billion in 1974. In 1973 alone, the ministry of mines and hydrocarbons announced price increases of more than 400 percent. The significant jump toward the end of the year was no doubt caused by the Middle East war that erupted in October.

As the figures indicate, the Caldera government was relatively cautious in raising petroleum prices; not until the summer of 1973, with approximately five months remaining until the presidential election, did the tax reference price double its 1971 figure. For whatever reasons, President Caldera denied his administration the opportunity to utilize additional billions of dollars which the following government would have at its disposal. The rise in petroleum prices was in accord with one of the suggestions of Pérez Alfonzo; however, his second suggestion—the lowering of petroleum production—was not followed to any significant degree by Caldera. This would have to await the administration of President Carlos Andrés Pérez.

Although they provided the legislative foundation on which to increase the country's income by raising the tax reference prices, the Caldera administration and the political opposition realized that the battle was not yet won. The petroleum companies owned vast facilities throughout the country; they could decrease petroleum production and the government would have no recourse. They could even damage equipment and the government would not be able to lift a finger. The companies controlled the concessions, most of which were not due to expire until 1983. This situation proved intolerable for the government, and Congress once.again confronted the problem.

The Reversion Law

As early as 1962, Pérez Alfonzo expressed concern about the petroleum companies' assets. He believed that refineries, pipelines, and buildings should be subject to eventual reversion to the nation; it made no difference whether the assets were located within the concession area (such as drilling equipment), or outside it (such as the multi-story office building of Shell Oil Company in Caracas). Nor would he allow shifts in assets, such as moving equipment from Venezuela to Nigeria, without the specific permission of the ministry of mines and hydrocarbons. As minister, he had fined several petroleum companies for demolishing antiquated buildings or fixtures without prior written permission from his ministry. A case involving Shell Oil Company went to the Supreme Court, which ruled in favor of the company because the equipment in question was not in the concession area. However, Pérez Alfonzo never accepted this distinction.

While the oil reversion bill was being debated in Congress, Pérez Alfonzo "asserted that there was nothing 'confiscatory' in the legislation, insisting that since 1917 the large companies had amortized two-thirds of their five billion dollars investment in the country, while piling up ten billion in profits. He further argued that the oil giants earned 30 percent on their fixed profits in Venezuela compared with only 11 percent in developed nations."[33]

Although Acción Democrática addressed itself to the question of reversion over the years, MEP and URD introduced the bill in Congress in summer 1971. Both COPEI and AD supported the proposal of the Popular Front. The Hydrocarbons Reversion Law

> stipulated that properties owned by the companies in Venezuela would revert to state ownership when concessions ran out; that unexploited concessions land would return automatically within three years if not utilized; that companies would have to post a bond, amounting to 10 percent of the value of their installations so as to guarantee that the industry would be in good working condition when the government took it over; and, finally, that company operations in the country would thereafter be supervised by the government in the sense that plans for such things as exploration and drilling would have to be submitted in advance for approval.[34]

Commenting on the law's significance, an official of Creole told me that it was a question not of the petroleum companies paying more money to Venezuela, but of control and power with regard to decision-making.[35] The petroleum companies would probably drill for a few more years if they were certain of finding oil, but they would operate on a day-to-day basis and would avoid long-term planning. (These observations were made prior to the 1973 Middle East war.) The official also believed the consensus among petroleum officials was that the companies would not suffer too much if the reversion law was applied under a COPEI government, but they were concerned about AD's possible return to power in 1974.

The Creole official pointed out that this was the second example of a breach of contract under the Caldera government. First, the companies and the Leoni government had agreed that reference prices should be fixed by both parties through 1971; second, the contracts signed in 1943 stipulated that most petroleum concessions were to run until 1983 without significant changes. He believed the 1943 contracts needed clarification with regard to assets reverting to the state, but this could have been worked out without the emotionalism that accompanied the reversion law.

As might be expected, the petroleum companies argued strongly against the law. The Shell director of public relations stated that his company would be particularly punished, because Shell had considerable investments outside the concessions area. He presented other concerns which were shared by the petroleum companies: investment would be discouraged, the 10 percent guarantee fund would freeze large amounts of potential investments, and short-term fiscal and political pressures would discourage long-term planning. Concluding his remarks, he said, "However, leaving questions of national sovereignty aside, no one will argue with this thesis: for there to be any demand there must be some real promise of supply on a continuing basis and on a scale big enough to interest potential buyers. It is the international oil companies' success in developing adequate and continuing supplies that has given Venezuelan oil its position in world markets, and only continued investment will keep Venezuelan oil in the picture."[36]

Efforts by the United States government to pressure Venezuela were feeble and futile. It was at that time that President Nixon called for the United States to become independent of foreign energy supplies by 1980. A bill introduced in the Senate to punish Venezuela by prohibiting imports of natural gas, crude oil, and its derivatives died in committee. The Venezuelan political leaders did not consider these developments to be very serious, since it appeared that they had gained the upper hand. But the petroleum companies had one more card to play.

From the passage of the reversion law in summer 1971 until early 1973, the oil companies made a deliberate decision to cut petroleum production. Within a year production had dropped more than 18 percent, seriously affecting the 1972 budget, which had been drawn up on the assumption that oil output would remain at the 1970 level. When Pedro Tinoco was replaced as finance minister by Enrique Oberto, the country had a budget surplus. Shortly after his appointment, however, Oberto had to borrow 700 million *bolívares* from the Banco Central, and he was forced to look for ways to cut the budget.

Most foreign press reports rejected the companies' standard answers, which argued that the sharp decline in freight rates in the spring of 1972 favored the Persian Gulf producers, and that a mild winter on the East Coast had led the United States to import less oil.

The first explanation had validity, but the second did not. According to *Latin America,*

Total oil imports into the United States rose sharply in the first quarter of 1972, being over 30 percent higher than in the first quarter of 1971. As the Venezuelan share of the total fell from 25 to less than 15 per cent, the whole of the increase was provided by other producers—mainly Saudi Arabia, Libya, Nigeria, Indonesia, Iran, and Canada. But even if this had not been the case and imports of heavy oils used for heating had gone down (Venezuela is the major exporter of these), this would not have been reason enough for an 18.6 per cent decline in Venezuela output in the first four months of the year [1972].
[According to the reversion law], any quarterly decline in company output below the level in the corresponding quarter of 1970 leads to a higher price—and hence taxation—on the whole output of the quarter. The larger the decline, the higher the official price, but only up to a decline of 10 per cent; thereafter the penalty stays the same with no further increase in the official price. It is therefore quite conceivable that some of the international oil companies have decided that it is no more unprofitable to reduce output by 20 or 30 per cent than by 10.[37]

From 1970 to 1972, Venezuela had slipped from first to third place among the world's oil producers (behind Saudi Arabia and Iran). Discoveries of substantial oil reserves elsewhere contributed to the change.

In February 1973, after approximately eighteen months of increasing hostility between the oil companies and the government, Creole Corporation announced that it would significantly increase its oil production for the year. I am not certain for the reasons behind this policy change, considering that the Middle East war did not break out until seven months later. Perhaps Creole was reacting to the worldwide petroleum situation, or perhaps it favored COPEI in the forthcoming election and wanted to strengthen the Copeyanos. Whatever the reasons, the announcement was a welcome relief to the administration. Venezuela's petroleum war was all but over.

In 1973 the outbreak of war in the Middle East [October] and massive increases in prices recast entirely the bargaining relationship between the government and the companies in Venezuela. The companies lost two of their key remaining bargaining cards: the ability to bring economic sanction to bear on the government by cutting production or lowering prices, and the ability to threaten the future of the industry by withholding capital investments for exploration, drilling, refining, and general upkeep.[38]

A high-ranking official of Mobil Oil Company offered what I considered to be an objective analysis of the country's petroleum policies.[39] He believed that emotionalism governed the enactment of petroleum legislation, because the politicians, not the technocrats, determined the events. The latter chose governmental service as a career; they were apolitical, dedicated, and incorruptible. Many technicians and economists in the ministry of mines and hydrocarbons probably opposed the petroleum legislation. However, the 1973 election was approaching, COPEI had a minority in Congress, and AD felt that it would return to power in 1973 if it could get credit for the legislation. AD brought off a political coup when COPEI hesitated.

The Mobil official also accused the government of "turning the screws" on the consumer countries when production declined and prices rose. The result would be relatively painless in those countries, resulting in a price increase of a few cents per gallon of gasoline. He did not believe the petroleum companies would be hurt badly. They might cut back production to pressure the government, but economically the companies were in a healthy state, and the government could push them further. After all, the companies could pass on the tax increases to consumers in the United States.

The companies had two major complaints, said the Mobil representative: the red tape resulting from the petroleum legislation, and the policy that *everything* must now revert to the state. The original legislation allowed for the reversion of much of the equipment, but the new legislation included everything: refineries, trucks, airplanes, even typewriters and office equipment. Furthermore, the companies had to pay 10 percent of the value of that equipment, as determined by the government, into a fund as a guarantee against removal. The money was supposed to be returned, but none of the petroleum companies expected to see any of it. And finally, in 1971 this observer compared the government's actions with those of the Arab states and Iran in the Middle East. The latter did not want to take action that would hurt old investors too much, because this might discourage new investors.

Considering the political impact of the tax increase, the unilateral fixing of reference prices, and the reversion law, it was obvious that COPEI was not the major force. Acción Democrática, and to a lesser extent the Popular Front, had led the drive. But as we observed, COPEI was now firmly in the nationalist camp, calling for greater Venezuelan control over the country's resources. Because it came too late, the massive increase in income from higher petroleum prices did not particularly benefit the Caldera government. By the beginning of 1973, petroleum prices had risen only approximately $1.00 per barrel, compared to the increase of approximately $12.00 per barrel by the beginning of 1974. The administration did present an investment plan to spend additional funds, but AD was not going to allow additional government spending to benefit COPEI in the forthcoming election.[40]

Service Contracts

As long ago as 1958, the Venezuelan government announced it would not grant private companies any more concessions for petroleum exploration. Instead it sought to substitute service contracts, under which the government would hire the private companies to explore, extract, process, and sell oil for the CVP, the government petroleum corporation. Not until 1967 did Congress pass laws authorizing negotiation of the contracts.

In 1971, Shell, Mobil, and Occidental signed service contracts to exploit a large tract of oilfields in the southern Lake Maracaibo region of western Venezuela. Creole Corporation looked with disfavor on the service contract idea and did not sign during Caldera's term. According to the terms of the contracts negotiated between the government and the companies, the latter's exploitation rights were limited to twenty years (compared to forty years for the concessions), and the government would collect up to 85 percent of the profits (compared with 75 percent under the old system). The companies were required to pay a bonus to the CVP before and after petroleum exploration. In addition, all equipment investments were to be made by the companies; the companies' payment was in the petroleum they were allowed to keep and market. The CVP could not lose, whether or not petroleum was found, because the first bonus for exploration would already have been paid.

By March 1974, when President Caldera left office, petroleum company officials had mixed feelings about the service contracts. Drilling was expensive, they came up with many dry wells, and they did not find as much petroleum in South Lake Maracaibo as they had hoped. Shell, in particular, was unhappy, and stopped drilling wells when the price was around $3.00 per barrel. However, Mobil and Occidental had some success by the spring of 1974. According to a Mobil official, the company was drilling at 6,000 feet, the deepest in Latin America; this paid, because of the high world price for petroleum. Thus Mobil was making money under the service contract and found it not a bad arrangement. The company also made seismic studies for the government, discovering that there appeared to be petroleum off Falcón and down the coast near Trinidad.[41]

Again, it was an AD administration that was the architect of the service contracts. The contracts coming to fruition were negotiated and signed under the Caldera government, but the Copeyanos followed a concept and policy previously established by Adecos.

Nationalization of the Gas Industry

Nationalization of the gas industry was one bill initiated by the Caldera government. Although it had been discussed for years, President Caldera put his prestige behind the bill, and it was passed in the fall of 1971. Even in this case AD led the opposition, urging modification of the original COPEI proposal. Although the Copeyanos suggested that the petroleum companies be paid for the gas, the opposition won the day by arguing that, according to a constitutional interpretation, the gas belonged to the state, and compensation was thus not justified.

The law included the construction of two plants for producing liquid natural gas, to be exported mainly to the United States by 1974. It also called for the creation of a state-owned methane tanker fleet. Pipelines were constructed to bring gas to Caracas, and the government successfully pressured the petroleum companies to leave the gas in the ground, rather than burn it. According to an official of one major petroleum company,[42] the government and the political parties must look to the future, well into the 1980s, and determine budget priorities relative to the development of the gas industry. While he felt that Venezuela had enough trained people, on all levels up to the boards of directors of the petroleum companies, utilizing trained personnel could be a major problem, because the government "followed the practice of putting its cronies into certain positions."

The petroleum companies did not react as vehemently to the legislation as they had to the other laws. A Mobil official told me that his company would lose some business, but apparently the industry at large was reconciled to the takeover. Their major concern was to salvage what they could through profitable activities.

The Internal Market Law

The Caldera administration's final piece of petroleum legislation was the "Law Reserving to the State the Exploitation of the Domestic Market of Hydrocarbon By-Products," introduced by three parties— MEP, URD, and Communist—and passed by Congress in June 1973. According to Article 3, "The public interest service reserved to the State . . . shall be exerted by the National Executive through the Venezuelan Petroleum Corporation. The activities of storing, transportation, distribution, and dispensing of the hydrocarbon by-products on the domestic market shall be exercised by the Venezuelan Petroleum Corporation either directly or through agreements it enters into with natural or juridical persons domiciled in the country."[43]

In an article published in *Business Venezuela*, a publication of the American Chamber of Commerce of Venezuela, Kim Fuad of United Press International described the legislation's background. Under President Raúl Leoni, a decree was issued in 1964 calling for the "negotiated turnover" of 33 percent of the gasoline and derivatives market by 1968. In practice, the decree was never completely implemented because the foreign companies demanded compensation for their capital investment and "anticipated profits." Arguing that "anticipated profits" were impossible to estimate, in the absence of an agreed-upon time base, the CVP rejected the approach. This "frustrating experience" with the Leoni decree, Fuad wrote, was not forgotten by the lawmakers, who rewrote the bill to give it more teeth. The estimated worth of the country's internal market was $200 million a year. Under the internal marketing law, all petrol and other oil product outlets would be supplied by the CVP by 1976. There were 1,800 petrol and other oil product outlets in Venezuela, 90 percent in private hands and the remainder owned by the major oil companies and the CVP. The law stipulated that all of them would be supplied by the CVP within three years, even though the state company did not have the refinery capacity to do so with its own oil. Thus the products being sold under the labels of the private oil companies, mainly Creole, Shell, and Mobil, would continue to come from these companies' refineries, but would be transferred to the CVP at a price fixed by the government, and then from the CVP to the outlets.[44]

We can draw two observations from the law: the quantity of petroleum derivatives and their dollar amount was small compared to the country's total production, and the major business continued to be exporting. Some gas stations changed names from Shell or Creole to CVP, but the government's petroleum corporation did not refine enough gasoline for internal use, and it had to rely on the petroleum companies. Politically, COPEI once again followed the lead of others. The original in-fighting between the government and the petroleum companies occurred under the Leoni administration; the Popular Front introduced the internal marketing law.

CHAPTER 7

El Cambio

DID THE ELECTORAL campaign promise of *El Cambio* (The Change) prove to be a myth? Or could the Copeyanos rightfully claim credit for bringing about significant innovations? The Copeyanos would answer the question by pointing out that *El Cambio* meant more than legislation. Let us consider their explanation of change under a COPEI president.

Luis Herrera Campins described COPEI's efforts to realize *El Cambio*.[1] He believed that a major component of change involved the style of President Caldera: "The Government of Change has passed from 'presidentialism' of imposition to 'presidentialism' of persuasion." This could be observed through the president's open political manner, which included extensive travel throughout the country, frequent press conferences, weekly television discussions entitled *Habla El Presidente* (The President Speaks), and numerous meetings with various groups. President Caldera also looked to independent sectors for one-third of the appointive positions for the cabinet, state governments, and directors of autonomous institutes.

Throughout the Caldera administration, the Copeyanos continued to emphasize what they considered to be the positive results of "the dialogue": "We want to pass from a formal and superficial form of democracy to a participatory, substantial, and profound form of democracy. We want to pass from a society where there is no fundamental consensus, because only secondary questions are discussed rather than fundamental questions, to a society of strong consensus because it is based on the profundity and liberty of dialogue."[2]

Herrera Campins listed the pacification policy as another important component of change. He also praised the government's foreign policy under Minister of Foreign Affairs Arístides Calvani, who refused to yield to pressures from the great powers, particularly the United States.

The Copeyanos pointed to their educational policy as another example of constructive change. They praised the minister of education, Héctor Hernández Carabaño, and his successor, Enrique Pérez Olivares, for improving the basis of primary and secondary education. They believed the accomplishments were particularly significant because they were made in the face of teachers' strikes and university violence.

Considering improvement in public administration as an important part of *El Cambio*, Herrera Campins pointed to accelerated economic development, monetary stability, acceptable price levels, and an increase in international reserves. He also referred to the administrative reform that sought to maximize regional development and internal integration. According to President Caldera's Decree of Regionalization, Venezuela was divided into eight zones of development, each under a development corporation. Each region had a representative of Cordiplan (Central Office of Coordination and Planning) and a regional committee of coordination.

The Copeyanos included the changed petroleum situation as part of *El Cambio*, referring to the legislation and service contracts as "nationalistic and non-partisan policies." As our previous discussion has indicated, however, COPEI could not take the major credit for the new petroleum policy.

The government's labor policy was also included as part of *El Cambio*. The Copeyanos were particularly pleased with the increased number of collective contracts, federations, and trade unions. In his final message to Congress, President Caldera stated that the economic and social conditions of the workers had improved markedly under his administration.[3]

The Copeyanos considered the results of their efforts in the agricultural sector to be a very important component of change. Through the ministry of agriculture and the National Agrarian Institute, they promoted exports, improved credit, and distributed land to thousands of peasant families. But political problems arose over COPEI's agrarian reform program, the Programa Integral de Desarrollo Agrícola (Integral Program of Agricultural Development or PRIDA) proposed by the Caldera government during its first year in office.[4] COPEI proposed an investment of 816 million *bolívares* (approximately $181 million) in the agricultural sector over a four-year period, from the budget, to be supplemented by a $75 million loan from the Inter-American Development Bank. The money would be used to change the agrarian reform of the AD administrations "from a social process of distributing the land to an economic process that would increase production—credits, housing, electricity, water, roads, warehouses." COPEI envisaged as its main goal the incorporation of the farmer into the economic, social, and political life of the country via a series of projects destined to consolidate the process of the ten-year-old agrarian reform program. The funds would be applied in four zones: Andes, Central-West, Central, and Northeast.

Acción Democrática opposed the plan from the outset, and the Adecos boycotted a congressional session called in December 1970 to discuss PRIDA. The AD leadership insisted that they opposed PRIDA on economic rather than on political grounds, and that they would support the idea once certain modifications were made. Until that time, they would also oppose the IDB loan.[5] One modification upon which the Adecos insisted, at least publicly, was that the program should be realized in a *minimum* of four years (instead of a maximum, as originally suggested).

PRIDA was finally approved, and the IDB loan authorized, in the spring of 1971. The eight programs comprising the project were farmer settlements, agricultural research, extension programs, credits, construction of silos, drainage, roadways, and a program for training farmers in more efficient agricultural techniques. Besides the $75 million loan, several agreements for technical assistance were signed between the IDB and the ministry of agriculture, the Agricultural and Livestock Bank (BAP), the National Agrarian Institute, and the Foundation for the Capacitation of Applied Research to Agrarian Reform (CIARA). Under the terms of the agreement, Venezuela would begin repaying the loan after the first five-and-a-half years of a twenty-year period at 4 percent interest.[6]

It was apparent that AD's opposition to PRIDA was not based solely on economic grounds, and that political concerns were probably more important. AD opposed PRIDA and the IDB loan because the party leaders feared that, through these, COPEI would increase its influence in the agricultural sector, thereby winning a significantly higher percentage of peasant votes in the 1973 election. The Copeyanos believed that AD's position toward PRIDA reflected that party's attitude as expressed in Congress throughout the Caldera administration: "We support COPEI only if it benefits us and in exchange for something we want." This, according to the Copeyano leadership, was the Adeco interpretation of *coincidencia*. AD's price for the support of PRIDA was the creation of a commission, with AD participation, to steer the bill through Congress. Thus PRIDA would have an AD-COPEI stamp of approval.[7]

Herrera Campins listed industrialization under the Caldera government as a part of *El Cambio*. He expressed the government's wish to increase the quality and quantity of goods produced for both the foreign and local consumer markets. Venezuela did achieve positive results in heavy industry. The state-owned steel corporation, Siderúrgica del Orinoco (C. A. or SIDOR), finally began to show a profit by 1968, although this cannot be attributed solely to the Caldera government. Faced with complaints about poor quality pipes and electric furnaces, the government revamped the entire steel complex, instituted cost accounting, and brought in the best technicians available. The improved quality and quantity of steel production meant that Venezuela was able to provide all of its own steel plate and other flat products, and it now rates with Argentina, Brazil, and Mexico among the largest steel producers in Latin America.

By the end of the Caldera administration, the then-seventeen-year-old petrochemical industry came into its own. Under the government-owned Instituto Venezolano de Petroquímica (IVP), the country witnessed a significant increase in the production of textiles, plastics, and fertilizers. The most dramatic development was in the huge El

Tablazo complex on the shore of Lake Maracaibo in the heart of the country's petroleum industry.

This is not to suggest that all is well in the area of consumer products; indeed, Venezuelans of various political stripes continue to complain about the shortcomings of the petrochemical industry. The wealthier people make yearly trips to the United States and Europe to visit their dentists, doctors, and buy their children's clothes for the forthcoming school year. Foreign imports find a ready market, and the high-priced import shops of Caracas's Chacaíto complex do a thriving business. The want ads emphasize the desirability of buying second-hand United States furniture, washing machines, and clothing. Venezuelan-produced goods have a reputation, particularly among the middle and upper classes, for being shoddy. There are many stories of T-shirts and pajamas shrinking a full size after the first washing, of wooden bed frames that come apart and peel, and of short-lived electrical appliances. This situation did not improve much during the Caldera administration; no government can solve the problem of poor labor efficiency and lack of a work ethic.

In the *Programa de Gobierno* (1969-74), the incoming administration explained the concept of *Promoción Popular* (Popular Promotion): "To rise above the state of marginality so that the channels for the distribution of the benefits and services of society and for the participation in decision-making may be open to the popular sector." Like the program of the former Christian Democratic government in Chile, Popular Promotion was COPEI's effort to organize coordinated development programs in the urban slum areas. Its effects were limited, in part, because AD feared an increase in COPEI's political influence in the *barrios*.[8] The Adecos at first led the congressional effort to block the spending of appropriations by government agencies, and adequate financing was not available in the 1970 budget. However, once the *coincidencia* came into being, Popular Promotion was able to make progress. The wife of the foreign minister, Doña Adelita de Calvani, did a creditable job in the secretariat of Popular Promotion.

The COPEI newspaper periodically referred to work in the *barrios*. One issue described efforts in Barrio El Observatorio del 23 de Enero, where the Banco Obrero (Workers' Bank) was developing a program for approximately three hundred houses; Urbanización Andrés Eloy Blanco received better water facilities, electricity, and street improvements. But work still needed to be done to improve the garbage service and to broaden the *colegio* to handle more students.[9]

During the 1968 electoral campaign COPEI promised that, if victorious, its government would build 100,000 houses per year as dramatic evidence of *El Cambio*. Only in its last year was the government able to reach that figure. Halfway through his term, President Caldera expressed his disappointment:

The affirmation made years ago, that to seriously take care of the housing problem there would have to be *no less than* 100,000 units built per year, was engraved in the collective conscience in such a way that it demanded the construction of the 100,000 dwellings. I must say that the goal proposed in my *Programa de Gobierno*, and more specifically in the *IV Plan de la Nación*, have not yet been reached. What has been accomplished is still far away from achieving our needs.[10]

From all available evidence, the government's failure to reach its total goal of 500,000 houses was not caused by AD's opposition. Other priorities, such as huge investments in industrial development and the infrastructure, and the sheer magnitude of such a monumental task as building 100,000 houses per year, made the realization of its goal an impossibility.

There were several other areas which the Copeyanos included under *El Cambio*: the law to reform attainment of administrative careers through civil service examinations, development of the country's electrical energy capacity, public works, improvement in sanitation and social assistance, and the initiation of a national petroleum flotilla. Perhaps one of the most dramatic expressions of the effort to realize change was the administration's program of "The Conquest of the South." Driving from Maquetía airport to Caracas, one could see numerous signs urging young people to seek their fortunes in the south, a vast area along the Brazilian border comprising 45 percent of the country's land area but accommodating less than 3 percent of the population. "The Conquest of the South" was initiated by the government in 1969 through CONDESUR (South Development Commission, under the ministry of public works) to realize the following objectives: "1) To carry to all corners of the region the fiscal, administrative, cultural, and economic presence of the Venezuelan State; 2) To raise the sociocultural and economic level of its inhabitants, without interfering with the values of the indigenous culture; 3) To study the exploitation of the natural resources."[11]

As might be expected, one's view concerning the success or failure of *El Cambio* depended upon his political affiliation. Generally, the opposition parties had a negative impression of the government's programs, while the Copeyanos were very positive and enthusiastic.

In Zulia, representatives of MEP believed that *El Cambio* was all talk. Only minimal change could be observed, such as completion of the airport which had been started by an AD administration. The condition of the people had not changed; in fact, the condition of the Guajiro Indians had worsened. In its attempt to create jobs, COPEI used the government in Zulia for political purposes, but even there it was dragging its feet. Approximately 50,000 *bolívares* had been approved for the state, but little happened. There could not be much change because many of the Zulia *latifundistas* were relatives of the National Agrarian Institute agents, and many government officials were involved in contraband.[12]

The Adecos remarked that *El Cambio* in Zulia was a joke. For the most part COPEI was following AD plans, such as by making improvements in Parque Urdaneta. In fact, COPEI's only significant accomplishment involved changing the name of the airport. Others admitted, however, that COPEI did begin to renovate Saladillo, the old part of the city of Maracaibo, and various projects were underway there. In general, however, very little had been accomplished since 1968.[13]

The COPEI governor of Zulia believed one had to look to the state's infrastructure to see evidence of *El Cambio*.[14] The party's secretary-general in Zulia elaborated upon this view.[15] According to Guanipa Matos, there were many examples of *El Cambio* in Zulia. President Caldera showed a preference for the state, and he made more visits there than to any other part of the country. The secretary-general admitted this was politically wise, for in his view no one could win the presidency if he lost Zulia. Betancourt, Leoni, and Caldera all lost in Caracas, but won in Zulia. In 1968 there was a 30,000 vote margin for Caldera, and Zulia made that difference.

The secretary-general pointed to other evidence. Of the eight zones established for regional development, Zulia was the only state that had a zone to itself, the Corporación de Desarrollo de la Región Zuliana. True, AD had begun the state's petrochemical development; but the rhythm had since quickened, and more money had been invested by the COPEI administration. The federal government had encouraged agricultural reform, and public administration had become more honest. And finally, for the first time, the state was receiving just treatment in the light of the wealth from petroleum resources that it provided for the entire country. More money was plowed back into Zulia in the form of large infrastructure investments in roads, marketing, and agricultural facilities.

Guanipa Matos believed that the problem of the Guajiro Indians was more complicated than COPEI's critics would admit. Many Guajiros crossed the border from Colombia in what amounted to a peaceful invasion, but a high percentage did not have proper papers. The administration established a *defensa social* to help them. Under this program, those without proper papers were repatriated. (Many of them were from "antisocial groups" who were involved in robberies and other crimes.) Some of the Guajiros became peons on the *haciendas*, and they were left alone. Others found domestic service employment in Maracaibo; many of these would send money home and leave after about a year. A large group attended schools in Venezuela—the *liceos*, universities—and became Venezuelan citizens. COPEI found that many of the Guajiros were well prepared, compared to the poor of Venezuela, and the party recruited them.

The Táchira Copeyanos were generally pleased with the benefits of *El Cambio*.[16] From the FTC's point of view, various projects created more jobs, and the workers had more hope. The Caldera government also handled collective contracts better than had its predecessors. Wages were raised, salaries for those in public works improved, and, following a strike, teachers had their salaries increased. The peasants received better dispensaries, water facilities, housing, and schools. But not all government programs could be applied in Táchira. For example, the agricultural reform program, PRIDA, had less significance there than in other parts of the country, because tractors could not be used effectively in the Andes.

The FTC representative in Táchira expressed concern about some members of the Caldera administration, asserting that many were honest and capable, but that some had given political payoffs to industrialists. We have already discussed one side of this coin when analyzing COPEI's agreement with various groups and individuals during the 1968 electoral campaign. The post-election payoffs merely completed those agreements.

Similar remarks were made by Copeyanos and their political opponents in Mérida, where the governor believed that *El Cambio* could be observed in several areas.[17] The housing situation significantly improved in the peasant sector, more roads were built to isolated communities, and school construction was accelerated. In contrast to the observation voiced in Táchira, the Mérida governor believed that PRIDA helped the state considerably, with an investment of 80,000 *bolívares*.

A member of COPEI's youth group, the JRC, had an interpretation different from that of the Copeyano governor.[18] While he agreed that one could observe the newly constructed plazas, water facilities, housing districts, avenues, and rural dispensaries, he thought a great deal more needed to be accomplished. The hospital could be put to better use through more credits. PRIDA was limited because of the great need for peasant housing, and the state definitely needed more industry. This young man concluded that the Caldera government would not be able to realize the promises of change because of its minority position in the Congress; it might build more primary and secondary schools than the previous governments had, but *El Cambio* would not bring about significant improvement in the human condition.

The Adecos in Mérida took a very dim view of The Change and the actions of the Caldera government that only continued projects already instituted by previous AD governments.[19] Caldera's administration claimed it was improving the school situation, but 70 percent of the funds came from the Alliance for Progress. Some buildings were being changed to dispensaries, but in many cases this was very impractical. Many illicit lotteries only enriched the government and further exploited the poor. Furthermore, the Adecos believed the COPEI government was very repressive. The military man chosen by the Copeyanos to be in charge of the police did not know the local people; he lived luxuriously while giving orders to beat up and jail students. Troops took over the University of the Andes by force, resulting in three known deaths. Even local Copeyanos joined in a demonstration against this seizure, resulting in one death and fifty wounded.

AD was convinced that funds collected by Mérida's COPEI-dominated government were used to strengthen the local party apparatus. The municipal councils allegedly swelled the bureaucracy by hiring many Copeyanos, who, in turn, contributed part of their salaries and bribes to COPEI. Such activities had an air of legality through the Institute of Municipal Councils, INCOAT, which was controlled by COPEI. Public works were supposed to be authorized under INCOAT, but the Copeyanos allegedly participated in a great deal of graft and kickbacks. Many of the appointees received high salaries and did no work. Even some local Copeyanos opposed such excessive corruption. As far as AD was concerned, such activities constituted *El Cambio* in reverse, because conditions had worsened considerably.

The Copeyanos of Lara were proud of the changes in their state. One party leader believed that the local government's projects had increased COPEI's strength,[20] but these were primarily projects involving work in the *barrios*, labor contracts, and more jobs—rather than national programs. The central government did commit itself to extending an expressway through Lara's principal city, Barquisimeto, which would ultimately benefit the city and the state. But *El Cambio* would not be complete until more workers became involved.

The governor saw evidence of change in various ways,[21] citing many studies and projects which indicated the beginning of an infrastructure. As we have mentioned the success of the pacification program was significant in Lara, where several different guerrilla groups had been operating. He also believed that the government was using its power efficiently, and that the people had faith in it.

Another COPEI leader, Dr. Carlos Zapata, believed that *El Cambio* in Barquisimeto resulted from the efforts of the city's municipal council,[22] and that the COPEI majority made a great effort to avoid conflict. This removed the council from national political problems and resulted in good administration. The council also tried to improve conditions for the inhabitants of the *barrios*, and COPEI formed various committees to oversee the work.

The municipal council had increased taxes by one-third over the preceding two years, for projects which included parks and city-owned markets. The national government did not help to any appreciable degree, and the municipal council, with some help from the state government, was doing 99 percent of the work, including raising the money. Thus I think we can say that *El Cambio* in Lara was largely a local rather than a national effort. This did not hold true for the pacification program, however, which was conducted primarily under the auspices of the central government. Dr. Zapata believed that the regional COPEI organization was interested in local rather than national problems, except when the latter directly affected Lara. For example, the additional national income from increased petroleum taxes held only an indirect interest for Copeyanos in Lara.

Dr. Zapata and I made a four-hour trip through several *barrios* in the vicinity of Barquisimeto. We visited the following *barrios*: San Jacinto, San Benito, San Lorenzo, La Pastora, El Carmen, Los Ruices, and Barrio Unión. My general impression was that concrete evidence of *El Cambio* was visible. There were some new roads, houses, and outside recreation areas. Several children were cleaning up garbage because they saw others doing it and they wanted to help. The people were constructing houses under a system of sweat equity: i.e., through contracts with the city and state governments, people of the *barrios* were hired to build their own houses. The people also paid a small amount of money to purchase the finished houses. The Banco Obrero (Workers' Bank) was also involved in financing road improvement and the construction of small apartments. According to an engineer supervising work in one of the *barrios*, the purpose of housing construction was twofold: 1) to build houses at the lowest cost with the least possible inconvenience to residents of the area; 2) to train people to become carpenters, electricians, etc., as they build their own houses. Several Copeyanos, including the governor, believed that COPEI and the municipal council could build several *liceos* (schools) for the same price that the AD administration paid for one.

We visited the Mercado de San Juan, a large supermarket owned by the municipal council. People rented spaces there and brought their products to sell. Estrella de Rios, the administrator of the market, said one purpose of the market was to teach the people discipline and organization in the handling and sale of their products.

At the conclusion of our trip through the *barrios* one phrase stayed in my mind, perhaps because I had heard it many times—*poco a poco* (little by little). From their perspective, the supervisors, administrators, and councilmen saw *El Cambio* as a process that must progress slowly to have the most impact. But was this process proceeding rapidly enough for the many *barrio* residents who, to borrow a literary phrase, led "lives of quiet desperation"? According to a local priest, the answer was no.[23] The government had made many promises, but very little had changed. The few additional jobs did not alleviate the chronic unemployment and underemployment problems to any appreciable degree, and those people who did find work were very inefficient and ill prepared. The *padre* believed that several things were desperately needed: major emphases on education, technical schools, and new sources of work; a development corporation involving all elements of the population; and foreign technicians. He concluded his remarks by observing that no government could realize *El Cambio* in five years; at best, it might improve the situation a little.

El Cambio—Foreign Policy

The consensus among members of the political opposition—the Adecos, Communists, Mepistas, and the Urredistas—was that the Caldera government's foreign policy was nationalistic, independent, and successful. They applauded what they considered to be sincere efforts to pursue primarily Venezuelan interests, even though these might run counter to the wishes of the United States government and the business community. Along with the pacification program, the Copeyanos pointed to foreign policy as an outstanding example of *El Cambio*.[24]

The purpose of the ensuing foreign policy discussion is twofold: to analyze the relationship between ideology, economic power, and regional imperialism in determining Venezuela's foreign policy under the Christian Democratic government of Rafael Caldera, and to investigate which of these factors (if any), or what combination thereof, were the major influences on the outcomes of specific foreign policy issues.

Since the founding of their student organization in the 1930s, the Venezuelan Christian Democrats have supported the principle of social justice. Shortly after forming a political party in 1946, they supported the idea of International Social Justice, which maintained that wealthy countries were obliged to share their wealth with poorer countries. International Social Justice, along with other ideological considerations, became the overriding foreign policy themes of the Caldera administration. But the government had to seek an accommodation of ideological assumptions with social reality. Substantial pressures to increase Venezuela's economic power, together with security interests, resulted in an increase in regional imperialism.

International Social Justice

Arístides Calvani, a long-time Christian Democratic leader, contributed to the movement's ideological formulations through the early student organization and Christian Democratic labor groups. As foreign minister under Caldera, he had the opportunity to serve as a principal architect of the government's foreign policy and as a spokesman for the ideological assumptions implicit in that policy. In 1970, in a speech before the twenty-fifth session of the UN General Assembly, he explained the need for International Social Justice.[25]

Calvani pointed to the gulf between the great principles proclaimed as the basis of international relations and their concrete application.

Profound socioeconomic differences divided the people of the earth, and the differences between industrialized and developing countries —in capital, educational level, and technology—were growing each day. A fraction of the world population possessed too much wealth, leading to increased tension and disturbances resulting from the exploitation of nation by nation. Foreign aid was not the answer; it merely resulted in economic and political domination of the strong countries over the weak. Furthermore, Calvani continued, the assistance offered by the great powers was tainted, because one system practiced economic domination leading necessarily to political and cultural penetration, while another system practiced political and ideological domination leading necessarily to control and economic exploitation. These injustices existed in an environment of "war in peace"—permanent subversion; a cult of violence in the form of kidnapping, assassination, air piracy, and assault. While it was true that the major powers were not fighting among themselves, the United Nations confused avoidance of war with the search for peace. Destiny would condemn the world leaders if they failed to act. They must identify with the anticolonial forces of the Third World who were struggling for political, social, and economic development.

Calvani believed that the wealthy industrialized countries had attained their positions at the expense of the poorer ones: "the riches of the developed countries submerged their roots in the poverty of the nations in development." Not only was the situation unjust, but it jeopardized an already tenuous peace. Permanent peace required an active solidarity of all the world's people. It must be oriented toward a Universal Common Good, and be inspired in International Social Justice. Calvani recognized the two obstacles to a Universal Common Good: 1) proliferation of nationalism, and 2) ideological hatreds, resulting in the formation of opposing blocs and worldwide violence. He called for a movement away from blocs and toward "a supranational society, the period of pluralistic integration."

In one sense, the proponents of International Social Justice might be considered the modern disciples of Woodrow Wilson, supporting the idealist position in the old idealist-realist debate of the interwar years. The idealists believed that people were basically good; if they were allowed to follow their own interests, unhindered by evil governments, there would be a harmony of interests and world peace. Wilson argued that this would be achieved if all governments were democracies. Thus we observe similar means (worldwide democracy; International Social Justice) and ends (harmony of interests; Universal Common Good). But, as Calvani implied in his article and as we shall observe shortly, the Copeyanos accepted the concept of ideological pluralism and different political systems.

The belief in International Social Justice predated the Caldera government, although the latter did develop and refine the concept. During the League of Nations era, some statesmen were concerned about helping poor countries, and certainly the United Nations Charter exemplified an awareness that something must be done to lessen the gap between the wealthier industrialized countries north of the equator and the poorer rural countries to the south. Several writers have referred to the ensuing tension as a new type of Cold War, north vs. south, rather than the east vs. west of the early post–World War II years.

Within Venezuela, the Betancourt administration (1959-64) championed the anticolonial struggle, particularly under Foreign Minister Ignacio Luis Arcaya,[26] who called for the liberation of Latin America from economic dependence and from right-wing dictatorships serving as instruments of that dependence. In the United Nations, Venezuela joined Cuba in supporting the anticolonial struggle of the Third World countries, and in 1959 the two were the only Latin American countries to vote for the independence of Algeria. Venezuelan delegates to the United Nations condemned racial segregation in the Union of South Africa, and commented likewise on Portugal's policies in Angola, Mozambique, and Guinea-Bissau. Following the AD-URD break, Arcaya left the cabinet. During the last few years of the Betancourt administration Marcos Falcón Briceño, the new foreign minister, deemphasized Venezuela's support for the worldwide anticolonial struggle, instead concentrating on Latin American affairs. Venezuela's own serious guerrilla conflict during that period certainly influenced this decision.

Ignacio Iribarren was foreign minister during the Leoni administration (1964-69). The government assumed a much more vigorous anticolonial position than any heretofore. In addition to voting with the Afro-Asian bloc, Venezuela actively participated in the UN Committee of Twenty-four, whose goal was to facilitate the process of political independence for colonial areas. (The African countries, in turn, did not jointly oppose Venezuela in its territorial dispute with Guyana.)

Under Caldera, Foreign Minister Calvani continued the policy of supporting the resolutions of the anticolonial countries in the United Nations, and Venezuela participated actively in the Committee of Twenty-four's efforts and attended the conferences of the nonaligned countries. According to Calvani, these actions were manifestations of International Social Justice; they also were consistent with certain elements of the country's foreign policy as established by the AD administrations of Betancourt and Leoni. For that matter, International Social Justice predated the Caldera government as part of Christian Democratic thinking. COPEI had subscribed to International Social Justice in its 1948 program: "international political economy based on the principles of cooperation, of free access to the sources of wealth for all people, of liberty of the seas, and of the application of the principles of social justice involving the defense of the weakest in the field of international economic relations."[27] On 16 July 1959,

Caldera made the following remarks to the Chamber of Deputies of Argentina:

> Facing the United States we have to adopt an attitude that cannot only be one of friendship and of understanding, but of friendship among equals, making our efforts with a single voice. . . . We have sustained that social justice imposes on relations among individuals, that he who has more is obliged [to give] more. We only have to project this concept to the field of international relations.[28]

Speaking to the Chamber of Deputies of Peru on 26 October 1959, Caldera stated:

> We cannot continue playing the game of brothers who look, before the powerful neighbor, for the best way to receive a few more cents. We have to make [ourselves] felt as a single outcry, that if we have defended social justice between people, so that the richest have to concede more and recognize the rights of the most humble, thus in the international order the people who for one reason or another are economically powerful have to recognize, through justice and not through magnanimity, the right that the economically weak nations of Latin America are demanding with a single outcry.[29]

A world conference of Christian Democratic parties approved the following resolution:

> 15. Christian Democracy . . . proclaims the obligation of the developed people of facing the demands that create in them the new world conscience on the plane of respect and generosity. The new conscience of a universal common good imposes on those advanced nations the obligation of contributing, to a degree proportionate to their wealth, to the overcoming of misery and underdevelopment, providing human capital and stimulation that international planning can transform into the greatest work of justice and prosperity.[30]

In 1964 Godofredo González, a longtime Copeyano leader, wrote an article in which he discussed the problem of the adverse terms of trade for Latin America.[31] Economists had long recognized that the price of raw materials exported by Latin America was declining, while the price of manufactured goods imported was rising. González pointed out that, during 1958-63, the difference between Venezuelan exports and imports was 47 percent in favor of higher-priced imports. His solution was old: he argued that the price of raw materials must be raised significantly, in order to lessen the difference between exports and imports. But the novelty of his approach was that he expressed it in terms of International Social Justice. A few years later President Caldera stated that his government would "struggle for a just and stable price for primary products through cooperation with strict adherence to the international common good." [32]

Foreign Minister Calvani stated that the concept of International Social Justice, leading to a Universal Common Good, affected every aspect of the administration's foreign policy and was therefore a major change from that of the Betancourt-Leoni administrations.[33] The Adecos protested this, stressing that their own concern with the plight of the Third World was philosophically similar to the Copeyano expression of International Social Justice. Be that as it may, the Caldera government frequently stated that its foreign policy recommendations and specific actions were consistent with the tenets of International Social Justice. Venezuela must struggle for fair prices for its primary products, for technical and economic cooperation through international organisms, for a sharing of scientific and technical progress, and for an enjoyment of the benefits of exploring its own natural resources.[34]

Calvani was very specific, observing that when the OPEC countries and Venezuela raised petroleum prices, the action was consistent with International Social Justice because it helped redistribute the world's wealth. When the Caldera government favored multilateral relations through international agencies and organizations, it intended to prevent domination by one country over another and to assure that the collectivity would support the legitimate demands of the developing countries.[35] President Caldera supported the idea of a Latin American bloc because he believed it was necessary for the realization of International Social Justice.[36] He also believed that the various UN organs could be instruments toward the same end:

> The declarations of Punta del Este contain implicit recognition of international social justice when they point out the duties of the industrial states to contribute to the development of the underdeveloped countries. And the positions of UNCTAD (Conference of the United Nations for Commerce and Development) are inspired clearly in the same position. Therefore, Venezuela proposed the addition of international social justice in the document elaborated by the Labor Group on the Charter of Economic Rights and Duties of States.[37]

Ideological Pluralism

The Copeyanos demonstrated their own brand of realism in their willingness to live with many different political systems. Dictatorships govern most Latin American countries, and hemispheric leaders have experimented with a variety of political models. The Peruvian military junta nationalized the International Petroleum Corporation and instituted a land reform program. A Marxist-socialist

President, Salvador Allende of Chile, nationalized that country's copper industry, expropriated agricultural holdings and redistributed them to peasants, and set food and rent prices to favor the poorer elements of society. Fidel Castro's Soviet-supported government claimed to be redistributing the wealth in Cuba. Could these and other developments be reconciled with the concept of International Social Justice?

On 5 February 1973, President Caldera began a trip to Colombia, Ecuador, Chile, Argentina, Bolivia and Peru. Shortly after his return, he met with the Brazilian president in the Venezuelan town of Santa Elena de Uairen. In his speeches and press conferences Caldera emphasized the theme of unity within diversity.[38] The president looked for new forms of political and economic systems, based on ideological differences, that would realize internal and International Social Justice. He was neither the first nor the last to try to fit social reality into an ideological framework; in his 1956 speech, Nikita Khrushchev had faced a similar problem when he accepted the legitimacy of different roads to socialism. In a sense, Caldera allowed for different roads to International Social Justice. The form alone could not make a system legitimate, however, and individual governments would have to make conscious efforts to raise human dignity and worth on the domestic and international levels.

In accepting diversity ("ideological pluralism," to use President Caldera's words), he recognized the importance of such needs as self-determination, national sovereignty, and the necessity for different governmental forms. He also called upon Latin American political leaders to honor the principle of nonintervention. They should not feel threatened by different ideological concepts and political systems, but should welcome diversity as a necessary part of a solid foundation for a broader Latin American unity.

Caldera maintained that unity was fortified when it was constructed on ideological differences. This was not the Leninist idea of democratic centralism, which allowed full discussion among members of the same political party, who then accepted the final decision without further question. Caldera's idea of unity within diversity, "pluralistic solidarity," called for a coincidence of interests among decision-makers who resided on the same continent and who recognized that unity could be strengthened and maintained only so long as their interests did indeed coincide.

President Caldera gave specific examples of what he considered to be unity, or solidarity, within a pluralistic reality. During a press conference in Buenos Aires, Argentina, he pointed out that Venezuela was a member of OPEC, which included countries of different political systems, origins, languages, histories, and cultures. But these diverse nations shared common interests, such as a desire to avoid ruinous competition and a determination to reverse the adverse terms of trade. Caldera raised a rhetorical question: If a structure like

OPEC, with such variegated components, could achieve success, what were the possibilities of a unified effort for Latin America?

In Lima, Peru, a journalist asked President Caldera to describe his administration's position toward the governments of Peru (a military dictatorship) and Chile (a Marxist-socialist president and Communist party representation in the cabinet). Caldera pointed out that his administration supported the Chilean government's nationalization of the copper industry. He was not concerned with judging the internal political line followed by the government; instead, he was interested in the Allende government's position in defense of its natural resources. Regarding these resources, Chile had the complete support of Venezuela. The same held true for Peru. When its government nationalized the International Petroleum Corporation and was threatened by a cutoff of United States aid under the Hickenlooper amendment, President Caldera expressed his unqualified support of the Peruvian government and his opposition to the amendment.

Dictatorships

Ideological pluralism obviously required the acceptance of various forms of government, including dictatorships. This policy necessitated a change in Copeyano thinking. Throughout most of its history, COPEI had opposed dictatorships whether of the left or the right, believing that a strong commitment to democracy required equally strong opposition to dictatorial forms of government. The point was frequently made in Copeyano literature: "The United States should give more help to Latin America as equal allies in a policy that should abandon all help to dictatorships and animate, on the other hand, the democratic evolution of the hemisphere." [39]

As members of a coalition government with AD, the Copeyanos supported the Betancourt Doctrine, whereby Venezuela refused to recognize hemispheric regimes that acquired power by nonconstitutional means, and urged the expulsion of such administrations from the Organization of American States. Betancourt hoped that wide acceptance of the doctrine would discourage possible coups within Venezuela. As a result, Venezuela did not maintain diplomatic relations with Argentina, Haiti, Cuba, Panama, Peru, Bolivia, and Ecuador.

In his inaugural address, President Caldera promised that Venezuela would renew relations with *de facto* regimes in Latin America. The Betancourt Doctrine had led to moral judgments inappropriate to international politics, had impeded economic integration, and had isolated Venezuela from many Latin American neighbors. "Venezuela cannot continue exiled," he said, "without relations with peoples that are tied to us by strong fraternal bonds." [40] He was obviously not as concerned about the possibility of a coup as Presidents Betancourt and Leoni had been. The Caldera government early established diplomatic relations with all Latin American countries except Haiti and Cuba. (In September 1973, the administration recognized the military government of Chile that had overthrown Salvador Allende.)

Did the Copeyanos turn their backs on democracy in Latin America? There were valid arguments on each side of the question. The administration's *Programa de Gobierno* made a somewhat feeble effort to encourage democratic development: "We will maintain diplomatic and commercial relations with all countries, independent of the political orientation of their internal regime, always [insisting] that the States be governed in accordance with the norms of International Law. We will try to realize collective agreements within the Inter-American system for the defense of the democratic system."[41] Also in the hope of strengthening democracy, the Copeyanos supported Christian Democratic parties in several countries, including Colombia and some Central American nations. And at a Washington meeting of foreign ministers, Calvani stated that rebellion against despotism was justified.[42]

Supporters of the rejected Betancourt Doctrine argued that, Copeyano protestations to the contrary, the establishment of diplomatic relations with dictatorships had to set back democratic forces within those countries. A dictatorship, now considered to be legitimate, could continue to violate human rights without being vulnerable to outside pressures. The Copeyanos retorted that they had no choice—most Latin American governments were dictatorships, and Venezuela could not isolate itself. Brazil, for example, had a dictatorial government, but the country was a very good customer for Venezuelan products.[43] (The Leoni government had reestablished diplomatic relations with Brazil in 1966.) The administration stated that it would not establish diplomatic relations with Haiti or Cuba, for reasons peculiar to those countries. I am not certain why Haiti was singled out, unless it was because of the government's persecution of the Catholic church and the emphasis upon voodoo. Haitian-Venezuelan missions were finally exchanged late in Caldera's term.

Hoping to increase Venezuela's economic power, the COPEI administration concluded that it was important to have trade relationships with as many Latin American countries as possible. Certainly Venezuela would not be able to join the Andean Common Market if it continued to distinguish between acceptable democratic governments and unacceptable dictatorial ones. The Copeyanos answered their critics with these very practical arguments, and supported their case on the ideological grounds that political and economic relations with dictatorships were justified in the name of ideological pluralism.

Socialist Countries

In his inaugural speech, President Caldera made no direct mention of the Soviet Union or other socialist countries. Nevertheless, he did indicate the existence of a "mature public opinion concerning the establishment of relations with states having political organizations or ideologies different from ours, but whose presence in the world and whose influence in economic relations we cannot ignore." The *Programa de Gobierno* stated:

> . . . we should promote commercial interchange and offer a favorable field to investments of foreign capital within the concept of diversification and the full guarantee of that capital. For these proposals to succeed it is necessary to cultivate relations with those countries with whom we maintain them and to reinstate relations with those countries it might be convenient for us to deal with, relations which will be realized within our internal political affairs.[44]

In suggesting that Venezuela reestablish diplomatic relations with the Soviet Union and the communist governments of Eastern Europe, Caldera realized his administration would be subject to criticism. (The Leoni government had already begun to explore the possibility of trade with the Soviet Union.) He emphatically denied that the move would indicate an endorsement of communism, declaring that his administration desired broader relations on the purely pragmatic grounds of economic and political self-interest.

In a sense, normal political and economic relations with socialist countries manifested a broader application of the concept of ideological pluralism. But, in applying the concept on a worldwide basis, the administration could not use the same rationale it had applied for Latin America. Within the hemisphere, the Copeyanos had argued that ideological pluralism would lead to a broader unity and would enhance the possibilities for realizing International Social Justice. No such claims were made when seeking justification for reestablishment of diplomatic relations with Soviet-oriented countries. Instead, there was one compelling practical argument: just as the economic development of Venezuela required an end to the Betancourt Doctrine within Latin America, so it necessitated an end to a worldwide application of the doctrine. The commitment to International Social Justice could not be an obstacle to pursuit of broader diplomatic relations.

In its first year, the Caldera government established diplomatic relations with Hungary, signed an agreement for collaboration in matters of commerce and petroleum with Rumania, and began negotiations to reestablish relations with the Soviet Union. After a hiatus of approximately twenty years, the two countries finally reestablished diplomatic relations. Absence of diplomatic relations with the People's Republic of China did not stop the Caldera government from welcoming a Chinese trade mission and making a sale of 80,000 tons of urea, a petrochemical produced at El Tablazo complex. Other deals

were announced, including a new shipment of 80,000 tons of urea—
for fertilizers, animal feed, and synthetics—scheduled for 1974.[45]

Thus the desire to increase Venezuela's economic power by broadening trade and economic interchange was the primary factor determining policies toward the Soviet-oriented countries and China. Not
only would Venezuela have additional markets for exports, but the
socialist countries might also provide alternative sources of capital
investments.

The Andean Pact

The Copeyanos perceived the economic integration of the Andean
countries as an outstanding example of International Social Justice
and ideological pluralism. As they saw it, the purpose of the Andean
Common Market (ANCOM) was to increase trade among the member
states, provide mutual assistance for internal development, and thereby raise the standard of living within the Andean community. As one
of the wealthier states, Venezuela would benefit itself and the entire
community by providing capital investments. Certainly the economic
community exemplified ideological pluralism in the types of political
systems then existent: political democracy (Venezuela and Colombia), right-wing dictatorship (Bolivia), Marxist government overthrown by a right-wing dictatorship (Chile), and left-wing dictatorship (Peru). It was believed that solidarity would result from
cooperation between these diverse political systems, and that such
solidarity would lead to greater interdependence and a realization of
the common good, however individual countries might define the
term.

President Caldera, supported by Acción Democrática, made a major
effort to bring Venezuela into ANCOM. The growing economic and
political influence of Brazil, in the Caribbean as well as the Andean
area, was a major concern; one COPEI leader likened the relationship
to "sleeping with an elephant."[46] President Caldera linked Venezuela's
destiny with that of other Spanish-speaking countries, and, in the face
of growing Brazilian power, he was anxious that these countries draw
closer together—and perhaps coax Argentina into their ranks—to
provide greater economic growth and political stability. However, he
made every effort to remain friendly with Brazil.[47] The president also
wanted to hasten diversification of Venezuela's economy. It was estimated that, at the prevailing rate of extraction, proven petroleum
reserves would be exhausted in a decade. Although it might be possible to tap additional reserves in the so-called Orinoco tar belt, these
reserves would be exceedingly costly to develop, and when and if they
were available at commercially attractive prices, major industrialized
nations might already have converted to alternative energy sources.
In the long run, Caldera viewed entry into the Andean group as cru-

cial to securing a broader market for manufactured goods which, he hoped, would earn at least part of the foreign exchange lost when the country could no longer depend upon petroleum exports. For example, to operate on a low-cost basis, Venezuela's petrochemical complex required a high volume. Exports to the larger Andean community would make this volume feasible.

In order to develop support for the country's entrance into the Andean community, the Caldera government had to negotiate with the Venezuelan business sector, particularly FEDECÁMARAS (Federation of Chambers of Commerce and Production), and with the other Andean Pact countries. The president's inaugural speech indicated that he understood the fears of the private business community.[48] Venezuela's monetary stability and strong economy differed sharply from those of other Andean countries, and a flood of allegedly more cheaply produced goods from neighboring countries might "compromise gains and endanger the social conquests of the Venezuelan workers." But Caldera expressed optimism that these problems could be worked out.

Although Venezuela did not join the organization at its founding meeting in 1969, it did participate in the Andean investment corporation (Corporación de Fomento). Haydeé Castillo, the minister of development, was a major influence in keeping Venezuela from joining because of her close ties to the private business sector; political analysts concluded that she would have to be replaced to smooth the way for eventual membership. When the president made several cabinet changes later in his administration, Héctor Hernández Carabaño became the new minister of development.

The opposition of the FEDECÁMARAS industrial group, in which Eugenio Mendoza was a major influence, was one reason why the country had been no more than an observer in the Pact until 1971.[49] The industrialists argued that Venezuela would be unable to compete on equal terms with the Andean Pact countries, citing Venezuela's higher labor costs and prices. They also feared that Decision Twenty-four, the Andean statute on foreign investment, would discourage such investment because of its stricter rules.

Negotiations with the other Pact countries involved Venezuela's special treaty arrangement with the United States, and insistence on tariff exemption for some 700 items. Colombia, the group's strongest trading partner, pointed out that only 170 of its own items were exempted, but the two countries found that they had similar reservations about the investment statute.[50] After one session of the Andean Pact talks broke down, businessmen from both countries met in Bogotá and issued a communiqué stating that "the existence of different economic systems in the process of Latin American integration constitutes an obstacle to the normal development of this process."

But President Caldera was not to be denied. In 1971 he decided that Venezuela should apply for membership on special terms (thus satisfying FEDECÁMARAS), and the negotiations intensified. He also took certain steps which were interpreted by Pact members as indicating that he sought a compromise acceptable to all.[51] One objection to Venezuela's membership concerned its special trade treaty with the United States. It was felt that the treaty would make it possible for U.S. products to enter the ANCOM "through the back door," on the same terms as those of community members. At the end of 1971 Caldera denounced the treaty and stated that it would not be renewed on the same terms when it expired in June 1972. He subsequently announced a reciprocal trade agreement to replace the old treaty; in it, United States exports to Venezuela continued about the same as before. The president took two other steps: 1) by summer 1972, Venezuela's external tariffs were brought into line with those of the Andean Pact; 2) a presidential commission was appointed to draft a new foreign investment law. The commission's working paper proposed a considerable measure of alignment with the more nationalistic Andean regulations.

The president also used a United Nations report, prepared under the direction of the Israeli economist Meir Marhav, to strengthen his case for Venezuela's entry into ANCOM. Marhav pointed out that the industrial sector's share in the gross domestic product had decreased, and that, despite massive investments in agriculture, Venezuela had to import over $100 million worth of basic foodstuffs in 1972. Thus Venezuela was more dependent on petroleum exports than ever before. Membership in the Andean Common Market appeared more attractive as a means to diversify the industrial sector, increase agricultural production, and lessen the continuing overdependence upon petroleum exports.

On 13 February 1973, President Caldera signed the so-called Lima Consensus, and Venezuela formally acceded to the ANCOM, pending ratification by Congress. The ratification was published in the *Official Gazette* in 1 November 1973. Venezuela and the Pact members reached several compromises: 1) approximately 450 tariff items remained exempt from the regulations; 2) petroleum companies operating in Venezuela were exempt from the strictures placed on foreign investors; 3) there would be a time lag of 120 days after ratification by Congress before capital restrictions would take effect. This last point proved significant:

> One fear commonly expressed in Venezuela before entry was
> that several countries in the Group had comparatively cheap
> labor costs. However, the converse of this is that Venezuela holds
> the advantage in capital, and cheap labor costs may be offset by
> exporting capital by establishing capital-intensive industries and
> by investing directly in the other member countries. . . . Reports
> from Venezuela indicate that interests there are taking advantage

of the time-lag before capital restrictions take effect, and are making concerted efforts to invest in the Group as quickly as possible.[52]

Since Venezuela carried on only about 3 percent of its foreign trade with its new economic partners, little concern was expressed over the requirement to eliminate intragroup tariffs. But many businessmen believed that the stricter requirements on ANCOM's foreign investments would discourage such investment in Venezuela and dry up vital sources of capital. Their fears proved ill founded: because of the dramatic rise in petroleum prices, the country earned $10 billion in 1974 and again in 1975, compared to a maximum of $3 billion for any one year during the Caldera administration. The timing of entry into the ANCOM and the worldwide increased demand for petroleum were very fortunate indeed for Venezuela.

Another concern among those who opposed entry into ANCOM was that Venezuela faced the very real possibility of a sharp rise in prices:

The annual import bill is around $2 billion, of which by far the largest part comes from the United States. Since the objective of the Group is to promote subregional trade, it follows that a large proportion of U.S. exports will be subject to increased tariffs. The long-term aim is to alter the trading pattern of Venezuela in favor of the Group, but this process will take time; one observer has calculated that the value of Venezuelan trade with the Group may increase by only 3 percent by 1980.

Until the trading pattern alters significantly, Venezuela will continue to suffer from the tariff burden, and it seems likely that a considerable price may be paid in the short run for signing the Lima Consensus. Though the cost-of-living index for Caracas registered an increase of only 3.2 percent last year, international inflationary pressures have been building up for some time; despite the reduction in prices of imports from the United States resulting from the reevaluation of the bolívar, it appears inevitable that the tariff structure will promote an increase in the level of inflation within a short time.[53]

Inflation did become a more serious problem, but not primarily for the reasons cited here. Although prices rose during the Caldera administration, and some considered this to be an issue in the 1973 election, ANCOM membership was too recent to be considered a significant cause. Inflation became a much more serious problem when Acción Democrática assumed power under President Carlos Andrés Pérez in March 1974. The enormous increase in income from the rise in petroleum prices proved to be a major cause of inflation. Thus the petroleum bonanza provided both a blessing and a problem: needed capital, and unwanted inflation.

Ideological considerations played a minor part in Venezuela's entry into the Andean Common Market. Policy formation was determined primarily by the desire to increase the country's economic power. For some government officials, formal membership in the Andean community held the key to a greater economic diversification and a wider export market. A less important, albeit significant, factor was regional imperialism. Membership in the Andean Common Market did not connote regional imperialism per se, although in one sense it did manifest the country's desire for increased economic power. But entrance into the Andean Common Market was more than that. In part, the policy was directed toward counteracting Brazilian imperialism in Latin America. This concern provided a link between regional imperialism and the desire for increased economic power: dealing effectively with Brazilian influence in the Andean region would require an economically strong Venezuela.

Relations with the United States

Like many Latin American political parties, the Christian Democrats were often highly critical of United States actions. COPEI literature accused the United States of many imperialist offenses, including exploitation of Latin America to serve the world political interests of the U.S.; such exploitation was viewed as a major cause of the misery of the Latin American masses.[54] But, also like many political parties which possessed a measure of power, the Copeyanos concluded that the Caldera government required a successful working relationship with the United States if it was to reach many of its own goals.

President Caldera believed that a successful relationship with the United States must be based on International Social Justice. The United States should recognize its obligations not only to Venezuela, but to the rest of Latin America. He reiterated this theme during his visit to the United States: "I am convinced that the future of the hemisphere depends on the measure in which that great people [of the United States] makes its decision to be converted into the pioneer of International Social Justice."[55]

Specifically citing petroleum policy, the Copeyanos stated that Venezuela had defended its right of access to the U.S. petroleum market for reasons of International Social Justice and of continental strategic policy.[56] For this reason they had struggled to strengthen OPEC. They also insisted that any advantage Venezuela received for exporting its prime material should be extended to the rest of Latin America, and that any other Latin American country should likewise extend its particular commercial advantage to the entire continent. Furthermore, the Copeyanos pointed out that a United States–Latin American relationship based on International Social Justice might not succeed if the U.S. were able to dominate other individual countries. During his trip to the United States, President Caldera discussed these matters with various officials and political leaders.

184 Christian Democracy in Venezuela

COPEI's leaders emphatically stated that they wanted Venezuela to be treated as an equal by the United States. (Several officials at the U.S. Embassy were particularly sensitive to this point.) And although Venezuela was in the same camp with the United States in terms of a commitment to liberty and liberal democracy, COPEI leaders insisted that their country should have an independent foreign policy.[57] By "independent," they meant pursuing policies which they considered to be in the interests of Venezuela, although such might be frowned upon by the United States. These included higher petroleum prices, diplomatic relations with communist countries, and membership in the Andean Common Market. When President Nixon sent Governor Nelson Rockefeller on a mission to Latin America, the Caldera government asked Rockefeller not to include Venezuela in his trip, claiming that there was nothing to be gained by the visit, and that it might engender an undesirable (and unnecessary) incident. The Copeyanos referred to their action as "independent and autonomous."

Did an independent foreign policy vis-à-vis the United States also signify the seeking of other alternatives to the traditional Venezuelan–United States relationship? We have indicated that the long-range effect of membership in the Andean Common Market might alter traditional trading patterns; however, if this does become a reality, it probably will not occur for many years. The question was raised again when President Gustav Heinemann of West Germany visited Venezuela in the spring of 1971. He visited all the Andean Common Market countries except Chile, whose Allende government had recognized East Germany. At the time, several Caracas commentators believed that Western Europe and Venezuela had a mutual interest in developing stronger trade relations which would, in turn, weaken their commercial ties with the United States.[58] According to their view, Europe had rebuilt itself after World War II; in light of the low Latin American profile of the Nixon administration, European interests could be particularly important in filling the vacuum of technology and credit facilities created by official American reluctance. The West Germans were particularly interested in purchasing petroleum and gas and investing in Venezuelan private industry.

But if United States officials were concerned, their fears proved ill founded. The resultant increase in Venezuelan–West German trade did not appreciably affect the traditional trading pattern with the United States. In addition, when petroleum prices dramatically increased toward the end of the Caldera administration, the country's need for European capital was not as great as it otherwise might have been.

Other points of possible friction arose which might have weakened Venezuelan–United States relations. For example, the Caldera and the Castro administrations began to work toward an accommodation. However, as one Latin American analyst observed, relations with the United States continued to be very good:

Despite greater independence and rising economic nationalism, the Caldera administration has maintained its country's traditionally friendly relations with the United States. Unlike the one-sided relationship between the United States and many Latin American nations, ties between the United States and Venezuela derive from mutuality: the United States emphatically needs Venezuelan oil and Venezuela genuinely needs United States technology, capital, and exports. Evidence of this interdependence abounds. In his April 18, 1973, energy message, President Nixon referred to Venezuela as a secure source of oil within the Western Hemisphere. And during a May 14, 1973 visit to Caracas, then-United States Secretary of State William P. Rogers referred to the close ties between his country and Venezuela, stating that the United States was prepared to sign an accord to provide capital and technology to develop the Orinoco tar belt.[59]

A primary concern of the Caldera government was to accommodate the Venezuelan-United States relationship to the development of Venezuelan economic power. If Venezuela was to increase its economic power, and thereby assume greater independence in foreign policy, that relationship would have to be modified. The ideological underpinning of the modification was, again, International Social Justice. The concept not only explained the obligations of the United States toward Venezuela and the rest of Latin America, but also provided a rationale for steps taken to increase Venezuela's economic power, particularly assuming greater control over the petroleum industry and increasing the export price of petroleum.

Greater independence from the United States would also be necessary for Venezuela to effectively challenge Brazil's increasing influence in Latin America. Not only would Venezuela need greater freedom in foreign policy decision-making, but U.S. imperialism in Latin America would have to be limited. Because the growing Venezuelan–United States interdependence would necessarily place outer limits on an independent foreign policy for either nation, not only Venezuela, but also the United States also would have to deal with this reality.

The Caribbean and Central America

Foreign Minister Calvani believed that the government's actions in the Caribbean provided another example of its desire to realize International Social Justice. Venezuela's efforts, unlike those of Argentina and Brazil, were not a manifestation of imperialism. Instead, Calvani maintained that his country was obliged to help the poorer areas develop and provide a better life for their people. It would not do for the government's policy to be regarded as "aid," which would reflect an imperialistic mentality. Quite the contrary, the emphasis was on cooperation for the benefit of all concerned.[60]

186 Christian Democracy in Venezuela

In our discussion during the summer of 1971, Calvani said that Venezuelan penetration of the Caribbean had three goals: to blunt the imperialistic designs of Brazil, to further the cause of International Social Justice, and to prevent future Cubas. The latter two reasons might be considered cause and effect, since the realization of International Social Justice would lessen the attractiveness of the Cuban model. (The Caldera government subsequently shifted in its attitude toward the Cuban regime.) The first factor mentioned, growing power and influence of Brazil, continued to be a prime concern. It affected the government's actions with respect to the Caribbean and Central America, its membership in the Andean Common Market, and efforts to develop the southern part of Venezuela, along the Brazilian frontier.

Upon assuming office, the Caldera administration addressed itself to the Caribbean and Central America. Government technicians exchanged visits with their counterparts in Trinidad and Tobago; officials of the two countries subsequently signed an agreement, creating mixed industries to develop the fishing industry.[61] Venezuela voted to accept Jamaica into the Organization of American States, and the two countries developed joint cultural and economic projects. Calvani visited several countries (the Dominican Republic, Guatemala, El Salvador, Nicaragua, Honduras, Costa Rica, and Panama), leading to cooperation in economic, technical, and cultural areas. Calvani also contributed to bringing about a settlement that ended the war between Honduras and El Salvador. Venezuela joined and contributed several million dollars to the Caribbean Development Bank.[62] (Besides referring to the opportunity to increase trade and investment, Calvani told doubting Venezuelan businessmen that the country must join in the name of International Social Justice.)

Efforts to increase Venezuelan influence in the Caribbean and Central America continued throughout the Caldera administration. Calvani's report to the Congress indicated the pervasiveness of these efforts:

> ... the Fourth Meeting of the Mixed Dominican–Venezuelan Commission, during which questions relative to technical cooperation, financial, industrial, transport, and communications [matters] were analyzed; the resumption of our diplomatic relations with the Republic of Haiti; the Joint Declaration subscribed to by the minister of agriculture of Venezuela with the [agricultural ministers] of Dominica and Barbados; the visit to Barbados of a Venezuelan delegation to negotiate an agreement of technical cooperation in matters of housing and urbanization and, finally, the visit to Venezuela of a group of advisors and professionals of Trinidad and Tobago to exchange ideas about investments, tourism, education, and communication.[63]

In addition, several Venezuelan banks were established throughout the area, and private investors set up a number of joint ventures with local businessmen.

Relations with Guyana, the former British colony, were more complicated because of a territorial dispute. Nevertheless, Calvani's visit to London resulted in an end to the Venezuelan policy of excluding Guyana from Caribbean affairs. He reversed the administration's previous decision and agreed to invite Guyana to the Caribbean conference on the sea, held 5 June 1973 in Santo Domingo.[64] Once again, the catalyst for this reversal proved to be concern over Brazilian influence. According to the account in *Latin America*,

> The conciliatory Venezuelan attitude to Guyana is based more on enlightened self-interest than on general goodwill. For some time now Venezuela has been concerned about growing pressures from its neighbour, Brazil. The recent forays by Brazil's foreign minister, Mario Gibson Barbosa, into the Caribbean and Central America have carried Brazilian influence directly into Venezuela's front garden. But Caracas has been even more concerned by the growth of Brazilian pressure in its own backyard—Guyana. The Venezuelan government has evidently realized that it cannot afford to continue an old quarrel which only pushes Guyana into the arms of its more powerful rival, Brazil. Venezuela has therefore now agreed to recognize Guyana's traditional links with the Caribbean, and has welcomed it into the family that Caracas aspires to lead.

President Caldera continued to develop and strengthen relations with Caribbean and Central American countries through the final weeks of his administration:

> A basic agreement on technical cooperation between Haiti and Venezuela has been signed in Caracas providing for the implementation of joint technological and scientific cooperation programs, research projects, establishment of centers for the training and specialization of researchers, holding of workshops and seminars, information and document-exchange. Under the pact, a joint Haitian–Venezuelan Commission will be set up for the purpose of assigning priorities to the various areas of endeavor and for initiating specific projects.[65]

Venezuela would also supply half of the financing for a $300 million oil refinery in Puerto Limon, on Costa Rica's Atlantic coast; the other half would come from the Central American Bank for Economic Integration. "The plant will process Venezuelan crude and the surplus production will go to other Central American countries."[66]

Foreign Minister Calvani might have expressed the government's motivation in terms of International Social Justice; nevertheless, the results manifested two-power competition on a regional scale. As the Caldera government knew, and as traditional Argentinian–Brazilian competition exemplified, the effectiveness of Venezuela's efforts would be directly proportional to the increase in the country's economic power. Since the dramatic increase in petroleum prices did not occur until the end of Caldera's term, one would expect Venezuela's efforts at blunting Brazilian imperialism to be more effective in the subsequent administration.

Cuba

In analyzing the question of possible diplomatic relations with Cuba, President Caldera had to consider Venezuela's experience with the Castro regime since the Betancourt administration. President Betancourt had looked favorably upon the Cuban Revolution, and the newly installed Cuban and Venezuelan regimes had cooperated at first. But relations between the two countries soon began to deteriorate. Cuba did not pay for a year's oil supply which it received from Venezuela in 1959, and when Castro took the Cuban Revolution in a communist direction, in late 1959 and early 1960, he chose Venezuela for his largest effort to export his version of communism to other Latin American countries. Cuba trained Venezuelan guerrillas, gave them arms, and even sent in some Cuban "technical advisors." When the Betancourt government obtained concrete evidence of these acts, it broke diplomatic relations with Cuba and led the move within the OAS to have sanctions applied by other Latin American states. COPEI, represented in the Betancourt coalition government, threatened to break with the government if diplomatic relations were restored with Cuba. Thus President Betancourt's Cuban policy was consistent with COPEI's anti-communism, and with the Copeyano view that Fidel Castro had betrayed the Cuban Revolution.

In the early years of the Caldera government, the Copeyanos deplored what they called Cuban Castro-communism. Although they would not sanction outside interference in Cuban affairs, they expressed "support for the Cuban people in their struggle for freedom." President Caldera stated that, rather than being a problem of economic exchange, the problem of Cuban-Venezuelan relations was one of fundamental political orientation. Venezuela would maintain a multilateral policy: the policy toward Cuba must be established within the OAS; Venezuela would not act unilaterally; and diplomatic relations required the Cuban government's commitment to the principle of noninterference in the internal affairs of Latin America.[67]

The shift in policy toward Cuba occurred late in Caldera's term. Professional, cultural, and athletic contacts increased between the two countries. In May 1973, Castro publicly praised Venezuela's decision to abrogate its thirty-year-old bilateral trade agreement with the United States, and he offered to support the Venezuelan government's petroleum policies. That summer Cuba and Venezuela announced their first negotiations in a decade, to draft a bilateral anti-hijacking pact.[68] Foreign Minister Calvani led the fight within the OAS General Assembly to remove the sanctions and to allow individual countries to conduct relations with Cuba according to their own interests. (Venezuela had abstained the previous year, when Peru had presented a similar proposal.) Calvani pointed out that international organizations such as the United Nations recognized Marxism-Leninism as a political and economic model for particular states, even though the OAS did not.

Why did the Caldera government make such a significant shift, considering COPEI's long-standing anticommunism and its position during the coalition government of President Betancourt? There were several possible reasons.[69] In view of the upcoming December 1973 election, the Copeyanos believed that closer relations and ultimately renewed ties with Cuba would be an important gain for the party's presidential candidate, attracting leftist voters while not offending anyone not already on the extreme right. The step might also be seen as standing up to the United States. The government argued that better relations with Cuba were a counterpart to a pacification policy which emphasized establishing a *modus vivendi* with communism at home and abroad.

On the economic side, the foreign and state-owned petroleum corporations wanted to be the primary source of Cuba's petroleum purchases of over 100,000 barrels a day. The Caldera government also experimented with a long-considered plan to use Soviet tankers, which were supplying Cuba with Russian oil, to carry Venezuelan crude to European markets. At least two "special dispensations" allowed private companies to use Soviet tankers, despite an OAS recommendation that vessels trading with Cuba not be permitted to touch OAS member ports. For its part, the Venezuelan private sector, seeing opportunities for new export markets in Cuba, objected to the fact that businessmen in countries then recognizing the Cuban regime— Argentina, Barbados, Chile, Jamaica, Mexico, Peru, and Trinidad and Tobago—were making important inroads into the Cuban market while they were excluded.

The Copeyanos did not have difficulty rationalizing their policy shift. Ideological pluralism made a rapprochement possible, particularly since the Copeyanos were convinced that the Castro regime had discarded its earlier efforts to export the revolution, and thereby to interfere in the internal affairs of Latin America. Still, while Rafael Caldera was president, Venezuela and Cuba did not formally establish diplomatic relations. During the 1973 campaign the Copeyanos realized (perhaps too late) that their advocacy of closer relations with Cuba hurt their presidential candidate more than it helped him. The two countries finally established diplomatic relations under the AD administration of President Carlos Andrés Pérez. In the summer of

1975, at an OAS meeting in San José, Costa Rica, both Venezuela and the United States voted with the majority to lift sanctions against Cuba.

Although not expressed explicitly by the Copeyanos, I believe a major factor influencing the government's efforts to improve relations with Cuba was the Venezuelan fear of Brazil. Because the competition for influence extended into the Caribbean and Central America, it was only logical that the Caldera government approach the Cuban regime. The Venezuelan government had an advantage over its Brazilian counterpart, in that the Brazilian dictatorship would not support the idea of normal diplomatic relations with communist-oriented Cuba; nor did the Castro regime desire diplomatic relations with such a government.

While the idea of closer Cuban-Venezuelan relations was consistent with the concept of ideological pluralism, I believe ideological considerations were a rationalization, rather than a cause, of policy. Ideologically, it was difficult to overcome COPEI's long-standing anticommunism. But diplomatic relations with Cuba would be good business. Although such relations would not significantly affect Venezuela's economic power, Cuba could provide another market for petroleum (albeit a small one, compared to the United States), and could thereby lessen the amount of oil that had to be shipped all the way to Western Europe.

Colombia

For several years Colombian-Venezuelan relations have been affected by two areas of controversy: the status of illegal Colombian immigrants (*indocumentados*) on Venezuelan soil, and a territorial dispute concerning the demarcation of each country's sovereignty in the Gulf of Venezuela. The former became a "problem" after it was intertwined with the latter; i.e., concern over the *indocumentados* increased as geological surveys indicated sizeable petroleum deposits in the Gulf of Venezuela.

According to the most common estimate by Venezuelan officials, around 500,000 Colombians entered Venezuela illegally during the 1960s, and "Colombians and their children might amount to nearly 10 percent of Venezuela's total population. . . . Until the conflict over the Gulf of Venezuela disturbed relations between the two countries in 1970, Colombians had been entering Venezuela in large numbers on tourist cards and frontier passes to stay illegally as residents."[70] The *indocumentados* were welcome in Venezuela, a country more heavily urbanized than its neighbor, and with much vacant land. Norman Gall has written of this situation:

> But the Colombian peasants were allowed to remain, since the Venezuelan countryside has been so depopulated that no Vene-

zuelan peasants are available to send in their place. The Venezuelan government has begun a crash program to build an economic infrastructure along its frontiers, but it faces an apparently impossible task in finding Venezuelans to occupy these remote areas. Meanwhile, most of the coffee, cattle, and banana *haciendas* of Western Venezuela have become utterly dependent on Colombian *indocumentados* as the basic source of manpower for their farming operations. This is especially true of the cattle and banana plantations to the south and west of Lake Maracaibo; most of this land was cleared by Colombian *indocumentados* in the late 1950s after the opening of the Pan-American Highway in the area.[71]

The *indocumentados* were also welcome in the cities, supplying a cheap source of labor as housemaids, masons, carpenters, gardeners, and chauffeurs. In Maracaibo, the first dwellers in most *barrios* were Colombians. Many would sell their house lots at a profit and either return to Colombia or move on to found new *barrios*.

Because of the enormous differences in income levels and employment opportunities, more and more *indocumentados* continued to cross the unguarded 1,500 mile frontier into Venezuela. Colombian and Venezuelan government officials began discussions about this matter shortly after Rómulo Betancourt assumed the presidency;[72] these meetings were concerned primarily with the social and economic consequences of several hundred thousand *indocumentados* living in Venezuela. After 1970 the Venezuelan army began to patrol the frontier, and Venezuelan governmental officials expressed concern over their country's sovereignty in areas with large numbers of *indocumentados* adjacent to the Gulf of Venezuela. They were worried because the expulsion of the hundreds of thousands of *indocumentados* would provoke serious internal convulsions, as well as a confrontation with Colombia. The press in both countries reported troop mobilizations.

Although Venezuela and Colombia share the Guajira peninsula that borders the gulf, a zone that contains petroleum deposits calculated to be worth billions of dollars, on several occasions President Caldera reiterated that the problem lay not in whether or not petroleum was to be found, but in the matter of sovereignty.[73] He stated that the Gulf of Venezuela was vital to Venezuelan interests, being the gateway to the country's second-largest city and to its oil riches in the Lake of Maracaibo. The *indocumentados* were a major obstacle to Venezuela's efforts to exercise that sovereignty. The president listed several problems caused by the presence of the *indocumentados*, including the fact that many public hospitals in western Venezuela, particularly in Maracaibo, were almost totally occupied by Colombians, when in fact there was a shortage of hospitals in the country. Answering the Colombian news media's charge that his gov-

MAP 7.1. Gulf of Venezuela and Continental Shelf. Closeup of area in dispute shown between the boundaries proposed by Venezuela and Colombia.

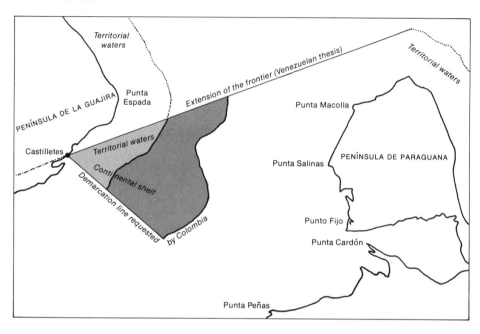

SOURCE: Mauro Barrenechea, "Delimitaciones Disputadas en el Golfo de Venezuela," in *SIC*, Caracas, March 1971, p. 111; cited by Gall, "Los Indocumentados Colombianos."

MAP 7.2. Lake Maracaibo and the Gulf of Venezuela, embracing the Gulf basin in dispute between Venezuela and Colombia.

SOURCE: Hernando Holquín Pelaez, *Controversia de Límites: Colombia y Venezuela* (Bogotá, 1971); cited by Gall, "Los Indocumentados Colombianos."

ernment had adopted a hard line by deporting *indocumentados*, the president stated that his government would not continue to ignore the situation. At one press conference Caldera asserted that the number of *indocumentados* had become excessive, and that his government was "only attempting to put an end to a problem that was becoming grave." The Copeyanos did not consider International Social Justice in the border dispute with Colombia. Foreign Minister Calvani stated that the demarcation line must be decided upon before one could talk about International Social Justice.[74]

The following account succinctly places the territorial dispute in its historical perspective:

The Colombian territorial access to the Gulf of Venezuela through the semidesert and sparsely populated Guajira region (See map) was first established in a somewhat ambiguous arbitration decree in 1891 by the Princess Regent María Cristina of Spain, and then confirmed in a 1941 treaty between the two countries that more specifically defined their land frontier. During most of the 1960s the relations between the two countries were excellent, since many leaders of the ruling Acción Democrática party had lived in Colombia as exiles in the 1920s and 1930s from the long dictatorship (1908-35) of Juan Vicente Gómez. When Carlos Lleras Restrepo visited Caracas in 1966 as Colombia's President-elect (1966-70), he was greeted by Venezuelan President Raúl Leoni (1964-69), who as a young political exile had earned his living by running a fruit stand in Barranquilla, with these words: "My friendship with the man who today is President-elect of Colombia began many years ago, when I arrived in Bogotá in flight from the persecutions of Gómez, and on the platform of the railroad station of La Sabana was a group of student leaders, among them Carlos Lleras." However, the trouble over the Gulf began during Llera's presidential term as Colombia began negotiating contracts with foreign companies for exploratory offshore drilling along the Guajira coast, which prompted the Venezuelan Minister of Mines and Petroleum, Manuel Pérez Guerrero, to make a hasty trip to Bogotá to protest that Colombia may be issuing concessions on a continental shelf that it does not own. Although the Venezuelan Foreign Ministry insisted that the Gulf consists of "waters that are traditionally and historically Venezuelan contained within Venezuelan coasts," it has never denied Colombian claims to a share of the continental shelf. The two governments exchanged visits of Cabinet Ministers to quietly explore ways of reaching an agreement until 1970, when Lleras, in his last presidential message to the Colombian Congress, touched off renewed controversy in the press and parliaments of both countries when he declared that Venezuela could not claim complete possession of the Gulf. In the flurry that followed, both nations ostentatiously negotiated for arms purchases in Europe, while formal negotiations between themselves proceeded in Caracas [and] in Rome. Meanwhile, both nations have tacitly agreed to suspend exploratory drilling in the Gulf until an agreement is reached.[75]

The negotiations focused on a demarcation line which would divide the adjacent offshore shelf. To determine ownership of continental shelves, the generally accepted practice is to establish a line midpoint from the continental mainland of each country. However, Venezuela claims possession of the sandspit islands of Los Monjes, which are much closer to the Colombian portion of the Guajiran peninsula than to Venezuelan territory. (That claim was recognized by Colombia in 1953.) The Caldera government proposed that a line be drawn between the Colombian coast of the Guajiran peninsula and Los Monjes islands. Throughout the talks the Colombians insisted that an imaginary line, equidistant from both countries, should instead form the division; they argued that this was justified because 10 percent of the surrounding territory was Colombian (see maps).

President Caldera successfully aroused public opinion, the news media, and opposition political parties to support his position. He made a trip to Los Monjes islands, which was carefully reported in the media. He "proposed the creation of a great front of national opinion, without political or class distinctions, to support the Venezuelan State in defense of our sovereignty in the dispute over delimitation of marine and submarine areas that we maintain with the Republic of Colombia."[76]

Caldera did not want press reports and emotional speeches in Congress to lead to an uncontrollable situation, however, and throughout his administration he made efforts to maintain friendly relations with Colombia. In the summer of 1969 he traveled to Bogotá and signed the Declaración de Sochagota, under which the two countries listed various cooperative projects. Other steps were also taken: studies were made to develop economic and technical cooperation; a mixed commission was established to study economic, social, cultural, and juridical relations; a declaration to establish the basis of an agreement for the commercialization of agriculture and to adopt measures to eliminate illegal traffic of agricultural products was also given.[77] Although such steps might have led to an easing of tension, they did not end the impasse over the territorial dispute.

In the spring of 1973, the two countries broke off the fifth and final round of talks to take place during the Caldera administration.[78] The respective negotiators had not made significant progress on the question of how to divide the Gulf of Venezuela, and the two sides were unable to decide on the course their future talks should take. The Colombians wanted the issue to be taken to arbitration, preferably at the International Court in The Hague, rather than to a third country;

the Venezuelans believed that the matter could and should be settled by the two countries themselves, at the foreign minister level. The Caldera government was politically unable to negotiate the Colombian claims because the next presidential election was fast approaching. Other alternatives, such as formal economic integration or joint exploitation of the Guajiran peninsula and the Gulf (suggested by the Colombian geologist Diego Llinas Mimienta), would also have to face domestic political considerations in both countries.

The Colombian-Venezuelan territorial dispute must be considered in terms of economic power and conflicting national interests, rather than in terms of ideological questions or regional imperialism. Each country was concerned with its declining proven petroleum reserves, and with the dramatic increase in economic power that would follow the development of large new deposits. The question of economic power included the domestic implications and effects upon development, as well as any change in either nation's relative power position which would result from a sudden increase in its neighbor's wealth. Given the stakes involved, an impasse was probably inevitable.

Guyana

In the east (*Oriente*) the Caldera government had to deal with a long-standing Venezuelan territorial claim concerning Guyana. As in the case of the Colombian-Venezuelan dispute, the Copeyanos did not apply the concept of International Social Justice. Rather than involving the question of a wealthier country sharing its riches with a poorer one, the dispute involved opposing territorial claims as perceived through different national interests.

At the close of the nineteenth century, the British considered a large slice of territory west of the Essequibo River to be part of their colony of British Guiana. Said territory was awarded to British Guiana in an arbitration treaty of 1897. Although the Venezuelans protested, claiming that the treaty was forced upon them by the United States and Great Britain, two years later a tribunal confirmed its validity. As Leslie B. Rout has pointed out,[79] Venezuela received a sympathetic hearing from many countries concerning its dispute with Great Britain. But when the state of Guyana became independent in 1967, Venezuela was vulnerable to accusations of aggression against its weaker neighbor.

In anticipation of the colony's independence, the Betancourt government opened the territorial question in 1962, contending that the arbitration award was null and void. President Leoni pressed the issue, and his efforts were rewarded when representatives of Great Britain, Venezuela, and British Guiana signed the Geneva Agreement of 1966. As two important points of the agreement, Great Britain publicly recognized that Venezuela was making a territorial claim, and a mixed commission was formed which had to reach an agree-

MAP 7.3. Territorial Claims in the Disputed Area between the Orinoco and Essequibo Rivers.

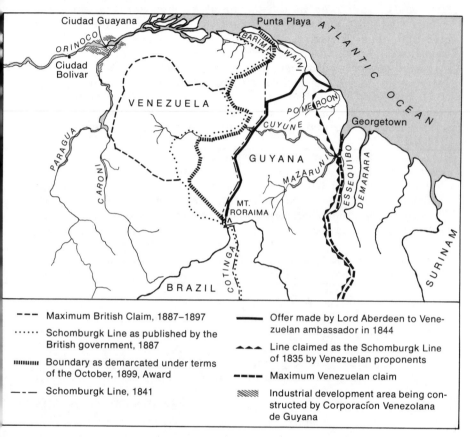

- - - Maximum British Claim, 1887–1897

...... Schomburgk Line as published by the British government, 1887

ıııııııı Boundary as demarcated under terms of the October, 1899, Award

— · — Schomburgk Line, 1841

——— Offer made by Lord Aberdeen to Venezuelan ambassador in 1844

▲▲▲ Line claimed as the Schomburgk Line of 1835 by Venezuelan proponents

- - - - Maximum Venezuelan claim

▧ Industrial development area being constructed by Corporacíon Venezolana de Guyana

SOURCE: Leslie B. Rout, Jr., *Which Way Out?*

ment by 17 February 1970. (If it failed to do so, the matter would go before an international tribunal, according to Article 33 of the United Nations Charter.) As in the territorial dispute with Colombia, the Venezuelans did not want the matter to go before an international tribunal; thus the Caldera government had to take some action. In contrast to Acción Democrática, COPEI had never seriously considered the question fundamental to its party position, so President Caldera could deal more flexibly with the problem because he did not have to be concerned about serious party opposition. Furthermore, the Copeyanos knew that the potential of the disputed area was great, with strong indications of petroleum, bauxite, and other mineral wealth.

At the outset of their administration, the Copeyanos assumed a rigid position. The *Programa de Gobierno* stated, "The Guyana Essequibo was, is, and will be Venezuelan. Our just demand should be carried through to a good end, within the limits of friendship and American comprehension, but without denigrating the legitimate and sovereign territorial rights of the country." [80] Negotiations through 1969 and early 1970 proved fruitless; the deadline specified by the Geneva Agreement passed, and still the impasse could not be broken. The Copeyanos ignored the deadline, however, and in mid-June 1970 they announced that an agreement had been reached.

Under the Protocol of Port-of-Spain (Protocolo de Puerto España), the two countries agreed to make no claim on each other's territory for twelve years. Other points stated that the protocol was renewable for successive twelve-year periods, and that previous claims were still valid. Thus, although the protocol froze the dispute in place, the two countries committed themselves to exploring "all possibilities of better understanding between them."

Anticipating domestic opposition, President Caldera stated that the protocol was in the spirit of the Geneva Agreement, in that "The rights of Venezuela with respect to the demand of the Guyana Essequibo are plainly safeguarded. . . ." [81] But many congressional leaders were not appeased, and the protocol was tied up for more than a year in the Senate foreign relations committee under the chairmanship of the URD Senator Jesús Soto Amesty. Acción Democrática was divided over approving the protocol, and COPEI took the leadership in bringing about final congressional approval.

President Caldera and Foreign Minister Calvani dealt with the political opposition very effectively [82]—no mean feat, considering the extent of opposition to the protocol. Pedro José Lara Peña—former colleague of Caldera and Calvani in their student days, congressman, former minister of agriculture, and vice-president of the Committee for the Defense of Our Guyana Essequibo—accused the Caldera government of taking no measures to safeguard the rights of Venezuela. He further pointed out that, according to the Leoni Decree of 1968, petroleum companies with concessions in Venezuela could not exploit alleged resources in the disputed areas; however, nothing in the protocol prevented Guyana from making such arrangements. Reinaldo Leandro Mora, former minister of the interior under Leoni, stated on television that he was pessimistic over Venezuelan rights in the protocol. Although President Caldera met with congressional leaders from most opposition parties and tried to persuade them that the protocol was in the country's interests, their support was not forthcoming. When Calvani presented the protocol to the Congress, several of the smaller parties (URD, FDP, FND) came out in strong opposition.

In a press conference in summer 1970, Caldera reminded the Congress that their leaders had been informed about negotiations over the protocol from the very beginning, and that he had sent them a general outline of the protocol's contents before agreement was announced. Caldera then declared that the armed forces had pledged their support for the protocol. The matter now rested with AD, the largest bloc in Congress.

The Adecos were in a quandary. Former President Leoni stated that the protocol was a disaster; he and Rómulo Betancourt had been the prime movers behind the campaign to incorporate the disputed territory, and approval of the protocol would indicate a renunciation of their policies. But disapproval might hamper the party's 1973 presidential candidate, who might also have to deal with the matter (and possibly ask for COPEI support) if elected. As Rout observed, there were two alternative resolutions to the dispute: military action, or diplomacy to obtain the most favorable terms possible. Caldera and Calvani asked the Adecos to choose diplomacy, and the Adecos eventually provided the necessary congressional support to approve the protocol.

Calvani stated that joint development projects could be initiated between the two countries once the protocol had been approved, and that this could make cooperation easier.[83] There was not enough time to judge whether this approach (economic cooperation leading to political accommodation) was effective during the Caldera administration. The Copeyanos might express joint development and aid in terms of International Social Justice; but, as was stated earlier, that concept did not affect the government's policies in this particular territorial dispute. In fact, the signing of the protocol did not open the doors of the Organization of American States and the Inter-American Development Bank to Guyana. "To join the IDB, a country must be a member of the OAS. To join the OAS, an applicant cannot have a border dispute with a member state."[84] A change in the IDB charter would have had to be ratified by a sufficient number of member states to authorize Guyana's entry. Nevertheless, the Caldera government did succeed, against formidable domestic political opposition, in easing tension in an area adjacent to a vast and developing

Venezuelan industrial complex. By accomplishing this feat, the Copeyanos left their successors with the foundation for a permanent political settlement.

Venezuela has been developing an iron and steel industry in the Orinoco River Valley. An industrial city, Ciudad Guayana is growing; also being built are an aluminum plant, a paper and pulp processing plant, and the Guri Dam, which promises to be one of the world's largest producers of hydroelectricity. The government hoped that the continued development of this industrial complex would increase Venezuelan economic power and provide a much-needed diversification of the economy.

Consideration of economic power was linked to the question of regional imperialism in three ways. Two concerns, Guyana's view of Venezuelan imperialism and Venezuela's desire to increase its influence in the disputed area, were solved, in part, by the Port-of-Spain Protocol. If Guyana and Venezuela could indeed cooperate to their mutual advantage during the life or extension of the protocol, Guyana's fear of Venezuelan imperialism could be transformed into a welcoming of technical assistance and capital investments from its wealthier neighbor. The frontier then might be more easily defined. Although a third consideration, the reality of Brazilian imperialism, will perhaps not fade away, the effectiveness of that imperialism might decline in direct proportion to the increase in significant Venezuelan-Guyanese cooperation.

Conclusions

Although International Social Justice and, to a lesser extent, ideological pluralism were major foreign policy themes of the Caldera government, their impact on particular foreign policy issues was minimal. Rather than serving as determinants, they merely helped to rationalize decisions that had already been made. It was true that the Copeyanos did (and do) believe in International Social Justice, but other factors were much more important in determining the outcome of foreign policy decision-making.

The desire to increase Venezuela's economic power had the major impact on the foreign policy issues we have considered, with efforts to engage in regional imperialism to compete with Brazil coming second in importance. Several foreign policy issues were concerned primarily, if not exclusively, with questions of economic power. Such were the Venezuelan–Colombian dispute, and the question of reestablishment of diplomatic relations with Latin American dictatorships and socialist countries, with the additional hope that the Soviet Union and its allies might expand Venezuela's sources of capital investment. Questions of economic power and regional imperialism were primary (and by no means separate) determinants in decisions concerning membership in the Andean Common Market, Venezuelan–United

States relations, policies toward the Central American and Caribbean countries (including Cuba), and an immediate and long-term policy toward Guyana.

In his famous *Politics among Nations*, Hans J. Morgenthau defined imperialism "as a policy that aims at the overthrow of the status quo, at a reversal of the power relations between two or more countries. A policy seeking only adjustment, leaving the essence of these power relations intact, still operates within the general framework of a policy of the status-quo."[85] Thus, the administration's policy toward the United States was not one of imperialism. The Copeyanos wanted more flexibility in dealing with the United States, but they accepted U.S. paramountcy in Latin America and in fact accepted the goal of stronger United States–Venezuelan relations.

Venezuela and Brazil did, however, compete for sub-paramountcy in Central America, the Caribbean, and to a lesser degree in the Andean community. The Caldera government engaged in regional imperialism to alter the Venezuelan–Brazilian relationship, hoping to make Venezuela, rather than Brazil, the major Latin American power in those areas. But since the effectiveness of regional imperialism was dependent upon a significant increase in Venezuela's economic power, that power was more important than any imperialistic motives in determining the Caldera government's foreign policy.

Post-Electoral Governmental Actions

After COPEI's candidate was defeated, President Caldera served three more months (from December 1973 to March 1974) before relinquishing office to his successor. Since COPEI had presented the results of *El Cambio* to the voters for approval or rejection, their post-electoral activities cannot be considered part of The Change. But because they were part of the history of the Caldera administration, the government's final months should be considered here.

In his New Year's speech, President Caldera recommended that the petroleum industry be nationalized immediately; that the *bolívar* be reevaluated as an anti-inflationary measure; that the electric companies, television and radio stations, and milk companies be nationalized; and that the provisions of the labor law, which at that time applied only to urban workers, be extended to agricultural workers.[86] According to the constitution, Caldera could and did use presidential decrees to enforce all of his recommendations except the nationalization of petroleum. For example, foreign interests in the radio and television stations were liquidated within thirty days.

The president's speech and actions produced storms of protest and bitter confrontations. Alfredo Paul Delfino, the president of FEDECÁMARAS, called the extension of the labor law "isolated and precipitous; of dubious effect and legally questionable." He added that "the President of the Republic has exposed rural employers to public hate and disdain." The Cattle Raisers Association approved Delfino's declaration, accusing the government of having no agricultural policies for five years, and then answering their legitimate economic complaints with measures exacerbating them. Caldera's most visible support came from COPEI's youth group, the JRC, which organized demonstrations in front of the FEDECÁMARAS headquarters and demanded Delfino's arrest.

President Caldera had a decree on his desk which he would have signed to nationalize the petroleum industry if COPEI had won the election. The party's defeated presidential candidate, Lorenzo Fernández, sent Caldera a telegram urging him to take action immediately; however, the president concluded that a step of such importance required full discussion and congressional approval through legislation, and should not be made a presidential decree. The nationalization of the petroleum industry would await the new administration. COPEI did announce that it would introduce a bill proposing immediate nationalization soon after the newly elected Congress convened in March.

President Caldera took two other actions pertaining to the petroleum industry. For one thing, the government ordered Creole Petroleum Company, the Exxon subsidiary and the nation's largest producer, to hand over two oil fields which, according to the authorities, were not being exploited. (The petroleum reversion law provided for earlier reversion without compensation for uneconomic concessions.) Creole appealed that decision to the courts. The government also ordered foreign petroleum companies to hand over to the state petroleum corporation (CVP) 100,000 barrels a day, in lieu of royalty payments, for sale to other Latin American countries. This petroleum was shipped to Brazil, Honduras, Costa Rica, Guatemala, and Puerto Rico, all of them having asked for increased supplies.[87]

Most political analysts agreed that these last-moment measures by President Caldera were more of a guide to COPEI's strategy in opposition than signs of genuine reformist zeal. The Copeyanos wanted to place their party to the left of AD as the major political opposition. The Adecos were particularly critical, asking why the administration had not advocated the nationalization measures earlier, during the five years of Copeyano leadership. COPEI answered that it was trying to avoid an "acute regression" of social policies under the new administration. But the weight of the argument was with the critics, and COPEI was judged by its performance during the five years of Caldera, rather than during the three months of lame-duck government.

The Caldera Government: Conclusions

Whereas the former Christian Democratic government of Eduardo Frei in Chile (1964–70) promised to realize a "revolution in liberty," the Copeyanos under Caldera made no such commitment. In their own words, they offered the people a "democratic progressive" government which would prepare Venezuela for more revolutionary changes under the next Christian Democratic administration. Given the political reality, they maintained that this was all they could hope for in their first term.[88]

Although change did take place under Caldera, several factors determined that *El Cambio* was to be limited. The Generation of 1936 was not psychologically prepared to engineer structural changes in the society, and conservative interest groups reinforced their inclination. Added to this was the AD's insistence that any significant changes must have that party's stamp of approval, as exemplified by the politics of the agricultural reform program (PRIDA). Nevertheless, AD-COPEI cooperation through the *coincidencia* did result in change, particularly in the first part of the Caldera administration.

In spite of these factors, some younger Copeyanos believed the government could have done much more. A JRC leader in Táchira wanted it to break with the *desarrollistas* in order to fulfill electoral promises identified with various programs, such as *Promoción Popular*, which, he maintained, was not accomplishing anything in his state. He spoke to Rodolfo José Cárdenas, himself a former leader of the more progressive wing of the JRC, but was told that electoral agreements must be honored.[89] A nationally recognized leader of the JRC pointed to needed reforms in the political system which would bring about a better distribution of wealth, accelerate and extend the agrarian reform program, and extend Popular Promotion (designed to increase participation of the popular sector). But he admitted that these measures could not be realized because of the makeup of the Caldera government's leadership.[90]

Another COPEI *técnico* believed that, although the government could not fulfill its electoral promises of *El Cambio* as understood by the masses, it still might have done certain things. It should have let the country know, for instance, that it could not make certain changes because the political opposition would not allow them. But because the government did not convince the public that this was so, AD appeared to be much more aggressive. (The first Ali-Frazier fight was televised live in Caracas during that time. The young Copeyano technocrat compared the defensive posture of Ali and COPEI to the aggressive style of Frazier and AD.) This observer went on to say that although COPEI had an opportunity to change its attitude and style through Caldera's press conferences and television appearances, the president held those events as if they were university classes, rather than putting AD on the defensive. Thus *El Cambio* might have been more effective, had the government and COPEI taken the offensive in executive-congressional and AD-COPEI relations.[91]

As we have indicated, the government's performance in the legislative area was determined largely by the AD-COPEI relationship. Not only did AD initiate and mold most of the major legislation, but the respective party leaders' perception of political reality also affected the legislative outcome. In Congress, for example, COPEI knew that AD would have to support the nationalization of the gas industry, and AD knew that COPEI would have to modify the agrarian reform bill (PRIDA) into a less partisan measure. COPEI was also aware that AD would not touch the Port-of-Spain Protocol, and that AD was not going to embarrass the Copeyanos over the Colombian–Venezuelan dispute.

When President Caldera turned the presidency over to his successor, the magazines *Semana* and *Resumen* published analyses of the outgoing administration.[92] The latter was much more critical than the former. Consider, for example, their comments on the presidential dialogues. *Semana*: "There had not been a President in Venezuela, in all its history, who maintained a policy of dialogue with the people, so lively and dynamic. . . . He informed the nation about . . . progress of the government and problems of the administration." *Resumen*: "Another of the causes of confusion is to have interpreted the silence with which the country received his 'dialogues' (in reality autocratically televised 'monologues') as faithful reverence for everything he said." Both magazines agreed, however, with the general consensus that Caldera's image was one of the most positive results of the five-year COPEI administration. His civility, his sensitivity to acting within the Constitution, and his intelligence and dignity raised the international prestige of Venezuela to new heights. In a sense, the government and COPEI were overwhelmed by the *personage* of Caldera. Since the Venezuelan Constitution stipulates that an outgoing president may not run for that office again for a full two terms, COPEI's 1973 presidential candidate had to follow in Caldera's footsteps and was quite naturally compared to him.

Commenting on his government's performance approximately halfway through his term of office, President Caldera said there were several things he would have liked to accomplish but found very difficult, given political and social realities: i.e., Popular Promotion, adequate housing, raising the level of the *marginados* (those living on the margin of the society), and holding down the increasing wealth of the rich.[93] We have already discussed the problems of Popular Promotion, partly political and partly a question of priorities. The question of adequate housing became the subject of continuous AD-COPEI debate, intensifying as the 1973 election approached.[94] The thousands of slum dwellings covering the hillsides around Caracas illustrated only too well how inadequately successive governments had dealt with this problem since 1958. The president acknowledged that the gap between the rich and poor was widening, rather than narrowing—a phenomenon which we witness in many developing countries as they try to modernize. One can ask whether Caldera's successor, with a surplus of billions of dollars at his disposal due to the dramatic rise in petroleum prices, was able to narrow the gap.

President Caldera mentioned two other goals of his government: to further develop popular consciousness, and to further strengthen democracy.[95] He was pleased with the government's efforts to have the people participate in improvements in their own areas, and he singled out the *barrios* in Caracas, including the area of Paraíso, and those in Barquisimeto. As we commented earlier, this effort was successful, although not as extensively as desired by some younger Copeyanos and by the political opposition.

The Caldera government's performance helped strengthen political democracy in three areas: by encouraging various organizations, and private citizens, to speak up and participate; and through the dialogue engendered by weekly television talks and press conferences. Caldera believed that one way to strengthen democracy was to give full play to all views.[96]

In terms of economic performance, the statistics and summaries were mixed. Earlier we referred to the United Nations study conducted under the Israeli economist Meir Marhav, issued in spring 1972.[97] The report, which resulted from an examination of the Caldera administration's five-year plan, criticized both the government and industry for their failure to diversify and so reduce the country's dependence on petroleum, and on the totally inadequate number of new jobs that would be created over the next few years. The report pointed out that diversification of the Venezuelan economy had not succeeded—if anything, participation of new industry in the economy was decreasing. In the past few years the industrial sector's share in the gross domestic product had decreased from 9 to 6 percent annually. The targets set by the private sector reflected no genuine change in the future industrial development, because even the estimated level of exports of manufactured goods was insignificant. The domestic market was no more promising: great inequality in the distribution of incomes, together with the then relatively small population of eleven million, made expansion plans unrealistic. (We recall that one of President Caldera's arguments for Venezuela's entrance into the Andean Common Market was the existence of a much larger Andean community for the country's exports.)

The UN economists also pointed out that unemployment was a continuing problem. Agriculture, whose contribution to total output was very small, controlled an important part of the work force—7 percent of GDP and 22 percent of the employed population in 1973. The petroleum sector, generating more than 20 percent of the internal production, employed less than 2 percent of the work force. According to *Latin America*,

Projections to 1978 show that unemployment will be at the level of 8 percent of the working population—that is, 247,000 people will be out of work. New industry has failed to absorb many of the unemployed in the past, and it seems that this would not change during the life of the present economic plan. During its five years the plan only projected the creation of 100,000 more jobs—although the number of those seeking employment is increasing by 100,000 annually. Of those projected, 30,000 were in the artisan sector, which offers irregular employment for a very small return.

The report concluded that the Venezuelan economy was even more vulnerable to the vicissitudes of the petroleum sector than before. The only way the UN team could envisage an improved situation was to have Venezuela alter its economic philosophy to concentrate on a massive development of its exports; that, the report said, should ease the grave unemployment problem and could reduce the country's high industrial costs. We have mentioned two developments occurring since the report was written: Venezuela's entry into the Andean Common Market, and the fourfold increase in world petroleum prices. It remains to be seen whether these developments will alleviate the problems raised in the UN report.

A subsequent study by the Inter-American Development Bank (IDB) painted a brighter picture, and some of its conclusions did not coincide with observations made in the UN report.[98] Apparently the intervening two-year period resulted in a better performance in some areas of the economy, although the serious and related problems of unemployment and diversification of industry remained. According to the IDB, in 1973 the real gross domestic product (GDP) increased 6 percent, compared to an average of 5 percent during 1970–72. This was the result of a general recovery of the economy, especially the resurgence of the petroleum sector after two successive years of declining production. As in previous years, the non-petroleum sectors expanded more rapidly than the overall gross product, led by agriculture and mining, and not by diversification of industry.

National income posted a 20 percent increase in 1973, compared with 11 percent for 1970–72. In 1973, petroleum prices rose from $3 a barrel in January to $8 a barrel in December, while salaries and wages declined from 51 percent to 46 percent of the total during the same period. As these statistics indicate, economic development and unequal distribution of income were in inverse ratio.

The UN and IDB reports differed concerning the seriousness of unemployment. According to the IDB, unemployment declined from 13 percent to 5 percent between 1961 and 1973. However, in Venezuela as well as in other Latin American countries, an important indicator —and one very difficult to measure—is underemployment. We do not know whether that rate increased or decreased under Caldera. The IDB report also pointed out that illiteracy declined significantly between 1971–73, and that improvements in sanitation and nutrition brought about a decline in the death rate. Government per capita outlays for education increased by nearly 70 percent between 1969 and 1973. The IDB report stated that the performance of the non-petroleum sector was better than had been indicated by the UN economists. In 1973, the manufacturing sector continued to grow at a rate approaching 8 percent; the items posting the most dynamic growth rates were paper and its products, beverages, furniture, textiles, and metal products. However, in 1973, the growth rate of the construction sector fell to 11 percent, compared to the 25 percent recorded in 1972.

In 1973, total business sales increased by 5 percent in real terms, up from 3 percent in 1970–72. Retail sales volume accounted for more than 65 percent of the total value added, whereas the wholesale volume was only 20 percent. On the other hand, services increased by 6 percent, accounting for 30 percent of GDP.

In concluding our discussion of some economic indicators during the Caldera administration, we refer to the IDB report's observation that price rises on the international market had a direct bearing on the country's balance of payments. But, as we have noted elsewhere in this study, the changes came too late in the Caldera administration (coupled with AD's resistance to the administration's investment plans) for the Copeyanos to benefit from the new international situation. The IDB statistics corroborated the UN report's contention that the country became progressively more dependent upon the petroleum industry:

> In 1973 the value of exports was $5,573 million, a 69 percent
> increase compared to the average growth of the previous three
> years—12.6 percent. This favorable development resulted from
> the higher price of hydrocarbons stemming from the resolution
> adopted by the Organization of Petroleum Exporting Countries
> (OPEC). It was especially favorable for Venezuela, which in-
> creased her revenue from sales of crude oil and its by-products
> by 74 percent, compared to the three previous years, in spite of a
> 2 percent reduction in the actual volume exported. As a share of
> the total value of shipments, this item rose to 95 percent.
>
> Exports of iron ore, which are much less important, amounted
> to $167 million, exceeding the average level during 1970–72 by
> 19 percent. This was due mainly to a 14 percent increase in the
> volume exported as a result of stronger world demand by the
> steel industry.
>
> Cacao was the most dynamic farm commodity and the value
> of its exports rose 77 percent over 1970–72, owing mainly to a
> 68 percent increase in international prices. The upsurge in inter-
> national coffee prices more than offset the 18 percent decline in
> the volume of exports. Revenue from non-traditional exports fell
> 17 percent from the average level in 1970–72, owing to a 15 per-

cent decline in the production of sugar, which made it necessary to import this item for domestic consumption.

In summary, we might say that the Caldera government had the elements of both failure and success. It failed (as had its post–1958 predecessors) to realize far-reaching structural changes in Venezuelan society. Inequality continued to be a tragic reality for too many Venezuelans. As one study puts it, "We thus witness a curious and frequently violent mixture of the culture of petroleum and the culture of poverty."[99] If we consider the less ambitious goal of reform rather than revolution, *El Cambio* was a reality; but it was uneven, noticeable in some areas and merely a hope in others. In foreign policy, however, the government was innovative, and Venezuela asserted itself more noticeably in Latin America than it had heretofore. Thus, the Caldera government succeeded in acting as the catalyst, and sometimes the initiator, of reforms and new directions which served as guides for successive governments.

PART III

COPEI: An Evaluation

CHAPTER 8

Conclusions

THIS STUDY WILL conclude with an evaluation of three important elements in recent COPEI history. First, was the Caldera government true to COPEI policies and programs that had been hammered out with no little difficulty? Second, what was COPEI's role as the loyal opposition after the 1973 election? Finally, an analysis of the 1978 election will be presented (with special attention given to the COPEI campaign), and we shall consider what these recent political events suggest for the future of the Venezuelan political system.

COPEI and the Caldera Government

When considering the performance of the Caldera government in light of COPEI's established principles, it is crucial to bear in mind that one cannot simply compare the day-to-day actions of the Caldera regime with the eighteen principles of COPEI established in 1946, even though these eighteen principles remain in the background as standards that are mentioned, if not worshipped, from time to time.

The 1946 document emphasized the need for revolutionary change to elevate the human condition; at the same time, party leaders called for strong support of Catholicism and the church, and emphasized an anticommunist position. However, as political events transpired, important elements in the party gave more attention to the urgency of solving social problems and less to the theme of anticommunism per se. In fact, a sort of *détente* with the Communist party was reached. Later, as the JRC and FTC elements became more vocal, elements within COPEI put greater pressure on the government to change the basic structure of society and to implement a more equitable distribution of wealth. Thus, the Caldera government faced a situation not uncommon in revolutionary or fast-changing political systems: different factions rise to the surface from time to time, confronting the government with alternative and even radical interpretations of basic political documents.

We have seen that the idea of social justice has remained a consistent theme in Copeyano literature and pronouncements. The eighteen principles of COPEI stated that social justice was to be the desired goal of mankind; the means to this goal would be "profound reform," which in itself was "revolutionary." The eighteen principles also identified social justice with nationalism and called for state intervention "when needed in the social interest."

The Caldera government was a reform government. By definition, a revolutionary government would have taken steps leading to profound changes in the society and its institutions, and Caldera was not prepared or able to go that far. Nevertheless, the government's interpretation of *El Cambio* included an effort to extend agricultural reform through PRIDA, which, among other benefits, would increase production and thereby raise the standard of living of many rural people. Also included was Popular Promotion, an effort to improve the conditions of residents in urban slum areas. The commitment to build 100,000 houses per year was another part of *El Cambio*. One might argue that the government never intended to realize such programs, and that the conservative pressure groups which obtained political payoffs by government appointments were proof of this contention. Nevertheless, our study has shown evidence of the aforementioned elements of *El Cambio*. By emphasizing the importance of efforts to alleviate, if not solve, social and economic problems, the government reflected COPEI as it became more progressive.

In addition to calling for a more active role for the state, the eighteen principles demanded the "economic liberation of Venezuela." Although the political opposition, particularly AD, initiated almost all major legislation, the Caldera government supported the laws that were expressed in terms of nationalism and resulted in a greater role for the state. The government's actions in the post–1973 electoral period, although motivated by the effort to place COPEI to the left of AD as the main political opposition, were also within this context.

Theoretically, one might say that the government's actions were consistent with the eighteen principles and, therefore, in accord with COPEI as it had been. But regardless of the eighteen principles, the political opposition forced the government to the left. In fact, the government tried to weaken the petroleum legislation. Important elements within the party agreed with the purpose behind that legislation: to accelerate the process of transferring economic control from foreign to state and local interests. The Caldera government, reluctantly or otherwise, was thus placed in the forefront of Venezuelan nationalism and thereby reflected the increasingly progressive nature of COPEI.

It was no longer necessary for the government to defend Catholicism and the church, as the Copeyanos had felt compelled to do during the party's early years. The situation had grown very different because of the evolution of the church, COPEI, and the AD-COPEI relationship. Nevertheless, there was evidence that the government made public funds available to Catholic schools. This was not a question of the government reflecting a particular period in the evolution of COPEI; instead, certain individuals within the administration probably decided to take such action.

By virtue of representing the Christian Democratic movement, the Copeyanos always believed (as stated in the eighteen principles) that democracy was the best system of government to guarantee human rights. It might be said that the party's commitment to democracy was stronger following the 1945–48 period and the Pérez Jiménez dictatorship. Be that as it may, Venezuelan democracy was strengthened during the Caldera administration, largely due to the attitude and actions of President Caldera himself.

If the government's performance was consistent with the party's long-standing position toward democracy, the same cannot be said with regard to communism. The pacification program, which sought an accommodation with the Marxists and communists, rejected the 1946 document, which had explicitly stated that the party was anticommunist and would combat communism. But the party had evolved from this position prior to Caldera's term, and his government's policy reflected the changes within COPEI.

In the domestic sphere, the Caldera government's performance was consistent with evolving COPEI policies and ideology. Under the Generation of 1936, the administration translated the more progressive Christian Democratic (and church) positions into specific policies. In some instances the government might have been pushed into more progressive positions, as exemplified by the congressional debates over petroleum legislation and budget proposals (Tinoco Plan). Perhaps, in the final analysis, the realities of a minority position in the Congress and the rising tide of Venezuelan nationalism were more significant determinants of governmental policies.

Regarding foreign policy, it is more difficult to identify examples of the government's performance and relate them to past, present, and future policies and ideology of COPEI. Nevertheless, we can point to specific examples. For one thing, the Caldera government chose to make the concept of International Social Justice its major foreign policy theme. (We have discussed elsewhere whether or not the idea actually determined governmental policies.) By frequently referring to the idea and expressing specific foreign policy issues in terms of it, President Caldera and Foreign Minister Calvani projected the Copeyano adherence to social justice into the international sphere.

But another foreign policy theme, ideological pluralism, rejected those of the eighteen principles which "repudiated totalitarianism and autocracy." For reasons we have discussed, the government concluded that it was in Venezuela's interests to establish relations with all Latin American governments, including dictatorships, thereby rejecting the Betancourt Doctrine. The same conclusion can be made about establishing relations with the Soviet Union, Soviet-supported socialist governments, and Cuba. Although the Caldera government did not establish diplomatic relations with Cuba, its more cordial relations with the Castro regime, however consistent with the pacification policy of accommodation with local Marxists and communists, were contrary to a long-standing Copeyano position.

Was the Caldera government different from other Venezuelan governments because it was Christian Democratic? Or did it basically follow the same programs as the other post–1958 governments? In the domestic sphere, the Betancourt, Leoni, and Caldera administrations did not differ significantly in certain fundamentals. All sought to give the state a greater role in economic life. All addressed themselves to the problems of the poor and supported various programs to alleviate human misery. All worked toward strengthening and stabilizing the democratic political system. Caldera's government might have differed in its approach to certain problems—Popular Promotion, agricultural reform under PRIDA, pacification—but, with the possible exception of the pacification program, these differences were merely in emphasis, rather than in fundamentals. True, AD had the largest voting bloc in Congress; but I doubt whether the Caldera government's policies would have been much different had there been a Christian Democratic majority. In foreign policy, the Caldera regime asserted itself more boldly in certain areas, discarded old dogmas (anticommunism, the Betancourt Doctrine), demonstrated increasing anxiety over the power and influence of Brazil, and placed its actions into the framework of the International Social Justice and ideological pluralism. Its performance was consistent with the dynamics of Venezuela's nationalism (and internationalism) as exemplified by the Betancourt and Leoni administrations.

In summary, the Caldera and AD administrations differed in certain ideological and programmatic emphases. The former was innovative on specific foreign policy issues. Although an in-depth study of comparative governmental output might prove otherwise, differences between the governmental performances of Venezuelan Social Democracy and Christian Democracy, from 1959 to 1974, seem not very significant.

The 1973 Election

The election of President Rafael Caldera was a turning point in the history of COPEI. In the past, he had been both the party's secretary-general and its presidential candidate; but when he assumed the presidency, Arístides Beaujon became secretary-general. As the 1973 election approached, the party had to choose a new secretary-general (or reelect Beaujon) and designate a presidential candidate. The two issues were politically intertwined, and different groups supported different people. Party officials publicly denied that President Caldera was involved in the political maneuvering, but it was evident that the new secretary-general and presidential candidate had his support. The leadership of the labor group (FTC) supported Herrera Campins for president.[1] Most of the youth group (JRC) supported Vivas Terán for secretary-general and Herrera Campins for president.[2] They believed that Vivas Terán had assumed a position of criticism, and that he would bring the JRC's ideas more forcefully into the party. Because of President Caldera's known opposition, support for Beaujon's reelection as secretary-general, or his nomination for the presidency, had weakened considerably.

At COPEI's Twelfth National Convention (August 1971), four candidates were nominated for secretary-general: Beaujon, Pedro Aguilar, Vivas Terán, and Edecio La Riva. Aguilar won on the first ballot by 135 votes; Beaujon ran second, and Vivas Terán a poor third.[3]

Two ballots were necessary to nominate the presidential candidate at the Second Extraordinary Convention held in March 1972.[4] The results were as follows. First ballot: Fernández, 433; Herrera Campins, 297; Beaujon, 193; Edecio La Riva, 33; abstentions, 14. Second ballot: Fernández, 506; Herrera Campins, 443; abstentions, 21. Many political observers and Copeyanos believed the nomination of Lorenzo Fernández was imposed by Caldera. The Herrera Campins supporters accused the Fernández forces of buying delegates' votes; some of them also signed a document denouncing several acts by governmental officials allegedly supporting Lorenzo's candidacy.[5] Whether or not the accusations were true, the nominating convention generated a great deal of bitterness which had to be dealt with before an effective electoral campaign could be mounted.

During the campaign, the Popular Front (URD, MEP, and the Communist party) continued to have political difficulties and, for all practical purposes, broke up.[6] The URD formally repudiated the selection of Paz Galarraga (MEP) as the coalition's presidential candidate and withdrew from the Popular Front early in December 1972. The MEP and the Communist party continued to support Paz Galarraga, while URD nominated its founder, Jóvito Villalba. All efforts to persuade the Movimiento al Socialismo (MAS) and the Frente Democrático Popular (FDP) of former junta president Wolfgang Larrazábal to join the coalition were of no avail. Thus, with disunity both of the right (over the failure of the candidacy of Pérez Jiménez) and of the left, an AD or COPEI victory was assured.[7]

In 1973 the Supreme Electoral Council legalized the MAS (split from the Communist party a few years earlier) and the Movimiento de la Izquierda Revolucionaria (MIR) as parties eligible to participate in the election.[8] Through a presidential decree of his own, President Caldera cancelled President Leoni's executive order declaring the MIR illegal, returning to that party its legal political status after eleven years of clandestine action.

The assassination of Chilean President Salvador Allende and the overthrow of his government three months before the Venezuelan election proved to be a serious problem for COPEI and its candidate.[9] The sympathies of the COPEI leadership, including Lorenzo Fernández, were with the more conservative Chilean Christian Democratic leaders, such as Eduardo Frei and Patricio Aylwin, who had given the new military regime conditional support and had attempted to place the prime responsibility for the coup on Allende and his ousted government. Pedro Pablo Aguilar said that the Chilean coup was due to "the hate and cannibalism, characterizing political strife, and to Dr. Allende's failure to communicate." The party's secretary for international affairs, Bernardo Level, said COPEI sympathized with the analysis of the coup given by Frei and Aylwin. Shortly thereafter, the Caldera government recognized the military junta. But many Venezuelans were shocked by the Chilean events, and elements of the party's youth wing joined other students in protest demonstrations. Allende's fall was a devastating blow to the candidacy of Paz Galarraga, whose coalition was admittedly patterned after Chile's Unidad Popular. Jorge Dáger, secretary-general of the Democratic Popular Force (FDP), supporting Lorenzo Fernández, expressed concern for the "vacillating position of the Venezuelan Christian Democrats" with regard to the coup. Both AD and URD openly condemned the military takeover.

COPEI thus found itself caught in political crossfire of its own making. The government tried to appeal to the Venezuelan left by seeking a rapprochement with Cuba, but that policy antagonized significant conservative elements of the electorate. (The Chilean coup also ruled out any unilateral Venezuelan action to renew relations with Cuba.) But COPEI's attitude toward events in Chile antagonized groups on the left, and provided additional fodder for AD in its criticism of the Copeyanos. Perhaps the Generation of 1936—which was the major element in the government, the party, and was represented by the presidential candidate—could not have reacted otherwise. Nevertheless, the spectre of communism through the Allende government arose to haunt the Copeyanos during a crucial election campaign.

Table 8.1 contains the national vote totals for the major presidential candidates.[10]

T A B L E 8.1. Results of the 1973 Presidential Election

	Votes	%
Carlos Andrés Pérez (AD)	2,130,743	48.70
Lorenzo Fernández (COPEI)	1,605,628	36.70
Jesús Angel Paz Galarraga (PF)	221,827	5.07
José Vicente Rangel (MAS)	186,255	4.26
Jóvito Villalba (URD)	134,478	3.07

(Other candidates received less than one percent each.) We can make several observations based on these figures. First, the total vote for AD and COPEI candidates was approximately 85 percent, compared with only 57 percent in 1968. Lorenzo Fernández did considerably better on a percentage basis than Rafael Caldera had done (36 percent of the total, compared to 29 percent). In 1968 Burelli, the independent candidate, had received 22 percent of the vote, and Prieto Figueroa, the MEP candidate, had claimed 19 percent. In 1973, however, no independent candidate reached even 1 percent, and the MEP candidate made a comparatively poorer showing. The candidates to the left—Popular Front (Communist party and MEP), MAS, URD—totaled only 12 percent, whereas early polls had indicated that the MAS candidate might win 10 percent by himself.

Carlos Andrés Pérez won in every state and territory except Zulia. In fact, as Table 8.2 indicates, he ran very well in the traditional Andean stronghold of COPEI.

The makeup of the Congress was as follows: in the Chamber of Deputies, AD and allies (PRN) claimed 102 seats, while COPEI and allies (IP, MJP, FDP) won 64. Senate figures were 28 and 13 for the two groups. The total membership in the Chamber of Deputies was 200, while that in the Senate was 47. Thus AD won a majority in both houses.

Why did COPEI lose the election? Of the many factors that probably affected the outcome, we can identify four major ones: the candidates, inflation, the anticommunist issue, and political polarization. Political analysts concluded that the differences between the two major candidates was the principal factor.[11] Lorenzo Fernández proved a weak candidate, compared to his Adeco opponent; he might have been more effective had he been allowed to be himself—a sympathetic, nonaggressive type of person—rather than attempting to be a *caudillo* with the image of the *mano duro* (hard hand). The electorate did in fact desire the *caudillo* type, but Carlos Andrés Pérez projected this image more effectively than Lorenzo did.

Food prices rose appreciably in 1973. Many food items were imported, and while the government could not control the prices of those (e.g., peanut butter and canned corned beef), the prices of basic staples produced within the country also rose markedly. It was a difficult situation for the government to deal with. For example,

TABLE 8.2. 1973 Presidential Results in Andean States

	Carlos Andrés Pérez	*Lorenzo Fernández*
Mérida	49.10%	43.30%
Táchira	53.99	41.06
Trujillo	54.19	38.38
Zulia	40.39	43.50

President Caldera put pressure on the milk producers, who allegedly were limiting the availability of milk in order to obtain higher prices. Liquid milk disappeared from the market for a time, and Caldera threatened to put the milk producers in prison. Not only were the lower and middle classes upset by higher prices and scarcities, but the businessmen were also concerned; consequently, most of them supported Acción Democrática, because they perceived the Caldera government as unpredictable.

The anticommunist sentiment of the electorate, particularly in the traditional COPEI stronghold of the Andean states, was a major factor in COPEI's defeat. Considering the party's historical anticommunist orientation, it was strange that this factor should weaken Lorenzo's electoral efforts. But many believed that COPEI had moved too far to the left, and that the government was encouraging the development of communism in Venezuela, as shown in the rapprochement with the Castro regime. Again, not only were the lower classes concerned, but businessmen and members of the middle class also felt threatened; the latter believed they would lose everything under communism.

Partly because Pérez Jiménez was barred from candidacy, the 1973 election exemplified a so-called Venezuelan polarization. (Betancourt convinced Caldera to support the constitutional amendment barring Pérez Jiménez from seeking public office again. Lorenzo was opposed, because he feared he would lose the Pérez Jiménez vote.[12]) In 1968, most of the votes were divided among four candidates: Caldera (COPEI), 29 percent; Barrios (AD), 28 percent; Burelli (URD), 22 percent; and Prieto (MEP), 19 percent. In 1973, the strongly polarized vote between AD and COPEI was seen as a rejection of both the far right and the far left. Venezuelan society is basically conservative. Denied a viable candidate on the right, the half of the population thirty and younger still did not vote for the left in any great numbers. The left was too badly divided to unify behind a popular candidate. Nevertheless, in its first election the MAS candidates were particularly strong in Caracas, outpolling MEP six to one and sending five of nine deputies from the capital to Congress. Furthermore, no strong independent stepped forward, as had occurred in previous elections.

The Copeyanos ran a very good campaign, well financed, well organized, and professional. Many Adecos even admitted that COPEI helped modernize Venezuelan politics. But the Copeyanos suffered from internal crises in some states, and from the "multiplicity of organs directing the campaign."[13] Some young COPEI *técnicos* believed that internal disputes in Lara and Táchira discredited the party in those regions. They also complained that the National Committee was often ill informed about the actions and decisions of the various organs directing the campaign. After Lorenzo was nominated, the people who had supported other candidates worked for him, in varying degrees. Different groups organized but refused to help others. There was no effective coordination, and, compared to 1968, the COPEI campaign was not a unified effort.[14] Apparently AD did not suffer from such problems. The Adecos were relatively well organized and unified, and COPEI underestimated their effort. The efficiency of AD's electoral machine was also formidable.

The final factor to be mentioned (one which U.S. politicians can appreciate) was that the last few weeks of the campaign proved crucial. The AD effort peaked during this period, and most of the undecided vote turned to Carlos Andrés Pérez.

Return to the Loyal Opposition

After the 1973 election, the COPEI leaders concluded that there was no future toward the right of the Venezuelan political spectrum; they also decided to move the party just slightly to the left of AD. Any move further to the left was out of the question, because the leaders wanted to maintain their broad general appeal to the center. They also knew that they could not woo votes away from MAS and the Communist party. In short, the COPEI leaders sought to keep the rural peasants and the urban middle class as the backbone of their support. They felt that these groups wanted progress and order but would reject a party closely identified with either the confession or radical change.[15] If the COPEI leadership is successful in bringing about this perception in the public mind, ideological conflicts and generational differences should be less serious than in the past.

The actions of the AD government would determine, in large part, whether COPEI would succeed in placing itself to the left of AD. Shortly after he assumed office President Pérez made strong reformist pronouncements, promising to return to the populist and nationalist principles on which AD was originally launched. The country was at peace, money was flowing in from petroleum exports, and the president promised that he would carry out far-reaching policies. He said he wanted to put the economy in the hands of Venezuelans, and his government early addressed itself to such questions as foreign investments, the petroleum industry, and iron mining interests.

In office only two months, the government announced to foreign investors that they must reduce their ownership of plants, service industries, and other activities to 20 percent of the facilities within three years.[16] President Pérez strictly interpreted Decision Twenty-four of the Andean Pact, which governed foreign investments in the Andean Common Market. The provisions established formulas for foreign investment percentages in many industries, including raw material exploitation and certain service and product industries. (By early 1977, however, the government relaxed its controversial regu-

lations on foreign investments, and many companies which had expected to have to sell off 80 percent of their capital did not have to do
so.[17])

In April 1974, President Pérez promised nationalization of U.S.
iron mining interests. (The government also said that it would take
over a chain of supermarkets, partially owned by the Rockefeller family, and the Sears Roebuck chain of department stores.) In 1960 fifty-
year iron ore concessions had been granted to U.S. Steel and Beth-
lehem Steel. On 1 January 1975 they were nationalized. The
Corporación Venezolana de Guayana administered the industry after
the takeover; U.S. Steel received $83 million and Bethlehem Steel
$17 million, to be paid over a ten-year period in government bonds at
7 percent interest.

The political process leading to the nationalization of the petroleum industry was much more complex. COPEI called for immediate
nationalization, but the government announced that it would not be
rushed into so momentous a decision; it would nationalize all foreign-
owned industries, and the owners would receive compensation. It also
announced its intention of creating a special thirty-member commission composed of representatives of all political parties, labor, business, and the military to make recommendations for the takeover.

COPEI, MEP, and AD introduced their own nationalization bills in
Congress.[18] The principal difference in the three versions was that
Article Five of the AD bill allowed the government to form mixed
companies, with private foreign companies involved in different
phases of marketing, refining, and technological development. Such
arrangements would be made under contracts guaranteeing state control. The contracts would require the prior authorization of Congress
meeting in joint session.[19] The government argued that Venezuela
lacked a great deal of technical expertise, particularly in oil transport,
refining, and marketing. For the country eventually to develop the
heavy crude oil of the Orinoco tar belt, with its estimated extractable
reserves of 70 billion barrels, such expertise would be crucial.

Article Five was attacked by COPEI, MAS, the Popular Front, the
petroleum federation (FEDEPETROL), and an important group of
independent technologists and petroleum experts. The opposition
argued that the article opened the way to foreign participation in refining and marketing—the very areas of the oil industry's operation
that added the greatest value to the product, and so gave the highest
profits. They also feared renewed dependence on the foreign companies and increased foreign pressures on the government. Former
President Caldera eloquently expressed COPEI's opposition in an address to the Senate.[20]

The government reluctantly concluded that it must use its majority
in both houses to insure congressional approval of Article Five. This
occurred in the summer of 1975, with only AD and the CCN of Pérez
Jiménez voting yes and the other opposition parties voting no. After

approximately six months of debate, Congress approved a nationalization law effective 1 January 1976.

The actions of the government in restricting foreign investors and the nationalization of the mining interests and petroleum industry prevented COPEI from placing itself to the left of AD. In fact, the Adeco government and AD appeared to be to the left of COPEI.

As the major opposition party, COPEI referred to its position as flexible and not sectarian; facing the Pérez government, COPEI would be firm but constructive.[21] During the first part of the AD administration, COPEI took positions on the issues of foreign policy and economic matters. Arístides Calvani, who had served as Caldera's foreign minister, periodically criticized the government's policies. For example, he denounced the administration for not being more aggressive on the first OAS vote to lift sanctions on Cuba. (Because that vote did not receive the necessary approval of two-thirds of the membership, sanctions were not lifted until a subsequent meeting.) Herrera Campins took President Pérez to task for concentrating on foreign policy and not making a sufficient effort to solve domestic problems.[22] Alfredo Tarre Murzi, formerly President Caldera's minister of labor and a former ambassador to international organizations in Geneva, strongly criticized the government's policy toward Bolivia.[23] He felt that President Pérez's trip there and a $60 million loan served to "endorse and praise Bolivia's autocratic regime."

COPEI was even more aggressive in denouncing the government on the economic front. At the beginning of his administration President Pérez announced a broad range of economic measures which, he hoped, would transform Venezuela's economic, social, and financial system.[24] He asked Congress for special powers to impose the economic measures by executive decree. (The constitution establishes that special powers can be granted to the president to dictate "extraordinary measures in financial and economic matters when they are required in the public interest and have been authorized by a special law.") The request was approved by all parties in the Chamber of Deputies, with COPEI abstaining. MAS approved the measures and offered the collaboration of its intellectuals in state cultural organizations and the foreign service. COPEI opposed the measures as "anti-democratic."

COPEI economist Leonardo Ferrer, a member of the Chamber of Deputies, claimed that the government was squandering the COPEI-induced increase in petroleum prices: "The exaggerated increase in imports, taking place beyond government control, is creating the habit of consuming superfluous foreign-made goods. There are no incentives to substitute local production for these imports."[25] According to COPEI leader Godofredo González, Venezuela's imports in 1973 amounted to $2.5 billion, while in 1975 they totaled more than $10 billion. If the trend continued, he believed the country would experience its worst trade deficit since 1920.[26]

222 Christian Democracy in Venezuela

The Copeyanos continually criticized the government for the increased rate of inflation,[27] perhaps feeling that, if the issue had worked against them in 1973, it might work against AD in 1978. At the end of 1975 a party document referred to the "alarming rate of inflation," which had moved up from a 7-11 percent range before 1973 to a 13-20 percent average more recently. (According to Central Bank statistics, the 1975 inflation rate was 8 percent.) It referred to recent growth as "modest and distorted, within a framework of inflation that each day reduces the real income of the average Venezuelan." In the spring of 1976 the trade unions denounced several government measures: higher prices for most agricultural products, the end of the wheat subsidy, and strict limits on bank loans. Rafael Caldera, speaking as a COPEI senator, claimed that the government had given a "residence visa" to inflation.

After a meeting of its National Committee in April 1976, COPEI's attacks on a whole range of government policies increased perceptibly. The party demanded a vote of censure against the five ministers who constituted the president's economic team; it organized a large women's demonstration in Caracas (dispersed by the police) to protest price rises; it accused the government of trying to suppress the constitutional right of free speech and assembly; and it held a massive protest demonstration in the capital, during which Eduardo Fernández protested the arrest of several Copeyanos and referred to the AD government's performance as "two wasted years." At the beginning of 1977 Senator Godofredo González, the acting president of COPEI, accused the government of waste, inefficiency, and corruption.[28] (The comptroller general had resigned because of corruption charges.) The secretary-general of AD, Luis Piñerúa Ordaz, attacked COPEI's extra-parliamentary activities by saying that not even the parties of the extreme left, self-proclaimed enemies of the state, had resorted to such methods.

In the post-dictatorial era, COPEI was in political opposition to an AD government during the administrations of Leoni (1964-1969) and Pérez (1974-79). Due to the Leoni government's weakened position following the 1963 election, and to the subsequent AD-MEP split, COPEI was then in a fairly strong position. Although COPEI's electoral strength increased considerably after the 1973 election, the party remained in a weaker position than it had been in during the Leoni period. One obvious reason for this situation was that the Pérez government was much stronger than Leoni's. The 1973 election gave AD a majority in both houses of Congress; it was also the dominant party in the labor and peasant movements. In addition, the government had effectively taken over COPEI programs, expanded them, and introduced new programs of its own. A salient example was the nationalization of the petroleum industry, advocated by COPEI after the 1973 election but designed according to the AD stamp of approval, as exemplified by the inclusion of Article Five. The government also continued and expanded most of the Caldera administration's foreign policy initiatives, as demonstrated by Venezuelan investments in certain Latin American countries. These investments were made possible, in large part, by additional petroleum income.

The AD-COPEI relationship was not visibly weakened during the Pérez administration.[29] Regardless of the clattering of pots and pans in the streets by COPEI followers protesting the rise of food prices, AD and COPEI leaders understood the limits of dissent and the need for accommodation.[30] We can expect the protests, charges and countercharges, and perhaps street demonstrations to increase each time presidential elections approach. It has been so with all elections since 1958.

The 1978 Election

The 1978 campaign officially began on April 2. The new president was elected on 3 December, to take office in March 1979.[31]

Prior to the respective party nominating conventions a Copeyano, Rodolfo José Cárdenas, noted that the situations within AD and COPEI had changed since 1973.[32] In 1973, AD had been unified behind Carlos Andrés Pérez, while COPEI experienced a struggle between Lorenzo Fernández and Luis Herrera Campins. In 1978 COPEI was united behind Herrera Campins, while AD experienced a struggle between Luis Piñerúa Ordaz (the party's secretary-general) and congressional leader Jaime Lusinchi.

In July 1977, AD nominated Piñerúa. In AD's first internal presidential primary he defeated Lusinchi, 440,000 to 260,000 votes.[33] Former President Betancourt supported Piñerúa, and President Pérez supported Lusinchi. In August, COPEI nominated Luis Herrera Campins by acclamation. Arístides Beaujon dropped out of contention a few days before the convention because he could only count on the support of 300 of the 4,200 delegates.[34]

The parties of the left in this campaign were MAS, MEP, MIR, the Communist party, and the Communist Vanguard (Vanguardia Unitaria Comunista-VUC). They made several efforts to unite behind a single candidate, but to no avail; each principal party then nominated its own candidate, and VUC supported the MAS candidate.

Before the presidential campaign officially opened, Renny Ottolina was an announced candidate. A popular radio and television personality, he had been expected to make serious inroads into the voting strengths of AD and COPEI. The political scene changed when Ottolina died in an airplane crash late in March.

The day after Ottolina's death, Diego Arria resigned as minister of information and tourism, and he announced his presidential candidacy shortly thereafter. Arria, governor of the Federal District of Caracas early in the Pérez administration, is also an economist who formerly worked for the Inter-American Development Bank in Washington. Arria adopted an essentially anti-party program,[35] contending that the traditional parties had failed to resolve the most pressing national problems and therefore should be rejected by the voters. In denouncing political machines (because they threaten or intimidate public functionaries), he stated that he had no ties to any political machine or interest. Furthermore, Arria claimed to have made no promises or deals with any political party. Ideologically, he was "a man of the center."

The AD candidate, Piñerúa Ordaz, stated that he would concentrate less on foreign affairs and more on domestic policy.[36] He pledged to continue the AD government's plans, with particular emphasis on resolving domestic problems such as crime, shortages of water and housing, agricultural insufficiencies, and administrative corruption. (The principal theme of Herrera's speech at his party's nominating convention was the need for a crackdown on administrative corruption.)

AD attacked COPEI for the alleged tactic of electoral radicalization, and for actions "prejudicial to the democratic system." The Adecos also accused some Copeyanos in Congress of carrying on verbal attacks against Gonzalo Barrios, the president of the Senate and the Congress. Piñerúa answered criticism of the Pérez administration by asking them to compare the Caldera and Pérez governments.[37]

However, the AD campaign was hurt by infighting between Rómulo Betancourt and Carlos Andrés Pérez.[38] In the weekly *Resumen* Betancourt attacked two important Pérez supporters, Gumersindo Rodríguez, the former planning minister, and Carmelo Lauría, the secretary to the presidency. This put Piñerúa in a most difficult position during an election year.

COPEI organized its campaign around two parallel groups: the National Committee of the party, and the Comando Nacional Electoral (National Electoral Command). Some National Committee members also served on the electoral committee.[39] As the campaign intensified, the party formed other groups, such as a strategy commission, which included former President Caldera. The four principal coordinators of the campaign were Rafael Montes de Oca (campaign director), José Curiel (functional organizations), Enrique Pérez Olivares (finances, public opinion and propaganda), and Hilarión Cardozo (political analysis and national strategy). Admitting that poor coordination between the party and the electoral committee had been a serious problem during the 1973 campaign,[40] the party leaders created an apparatus for the 1978 election in which the National Committee and the electoral committee functioned as one unit. Together they analyzed the reports from members of the electoral committee and the monthly polls commissioned by the party. Also as a result of the 1973 experience, COPEI leaders made efforts to project a more positive image of the candidate—as someone who was strong, firm, and in control. A media consultant from the United States, David Garth, was very helpful in this regard; he worked with Pérez Olivares in developing *cuñas* (television film strips) and other media items. The party also decided to make a greater effort to direct the campaign toward the *marginados*.

There were three phases to the COPEI campaign.[41] In the first, denunciation, various party leaders including the presidential candidate attacked Acción Democrática, the Pérez administration, and Piñerúa. This proved so effective that it carried over into the next two phases. The second, affirmation, began around the middle of October, presenting the positive alternative to what the first phase had been criticizing. The third and final phase, exaltation, began fifteen or twenty days before the election; it emphasized the personal attributes of Herrera Campins.

The Copeyanos denounced administrative corruption throughout the campaign. In part, this corruption involved the use of funds by some public institutes.[42] There had been some cases of corruption under Caldera, but they were not as extensive as had been the case in the Pérez administration. The country then went through a period when the allegations of corruption became both real and specific, as in the Carmona case.

Ramón Carmona Vásquez, a Caracas attorney who had been investigating corruption and the use of public funds, was assassinated on 28 July 1978. The director of the police force was implicated, and he was removed for obstructing the course of justice. Subsequently, an examining magistrate ordered the arrest of five police officers, all members of an antiterrorist squad, in connection with the murder. *Resumen* linked the murder with land deals on the Venezuelan island of Margarita. The case received considerable media coverage, and the investigation continues at the time of this writing (January 1979).

A very effective Copeyano slogan was *¿Dónde están los reales?* (Where are the funds?) This meant that, although the Pérez government had additional billions of dollars at its disposal due to the rise in petroleum prices, the problems of human misery and an inadequate standard of living continued to plague many Venezuelans. As one prominent magazine pointed out, the slogan pressed the government to justify its expenditure of the additional petroleum income. Piñerúa had to include a defense of government works during the campaign, because COPEI's slogan had created doubts about AD's capacity to administer the country. President Pérez reluctantly took a more active role in defending his administration and in supporting Piñerúa.[43]

Former President Caldera played an important part in the campaign, particularly in the first phase, of denunciation. He was often abroad during the early part of the campaign, but he returned to

Venezuela and became active during the last three months, and particularly during the last six weeks. This was part of an overall plan: Herrera wanted to create his own image as a presidential candidate before Caldera took an active part in the campaign. In contrast to Piñerúa, who many believed was Betancourt's chosen candidate, Herrera wanted the voters to know that he was his own man.[44] Once this was established, Caldera traveled throughout the country visiting particular states, giving television and press conferences, and attending rallies with Herrera and other COPEI leaders. In all of these activities, his major theme was to denounce the Pérez administration.[45]

Ideas and alternatives for the second phase, of affirmation, were developed before the 1978 campaign got underway. A 1972 article referred to the party's initiation of studies of major problems by specialists.[46] In 1975, COPEI began to develop a program of government under the directionship of Enrique Oberto.[47] Discussions were held in various regions over a two- or three-year period. However, once Herrera was nominated, he was allowed to modify the program.

Herrera's ideas can be found in a variety of sources.[48] The *Programa de Gobierno*, reflecting his campaign promises, concentrated on domestic concerns. His first priority was education, and during the campaign Herrera stated that he would be the "President of Education." In addition to concentrating on the training of skilled manpower, he wants to develop greater social consciousness and social responsibility. Herrera wants to perfect democracy by increasing participation through popular organizations. During the campaign he stated that the people were not worth much, because of the concentration of state power. Herrera called for the state to transform its power in a creative way, and to stimulate social initiative in the civil sphere. His *Programa de Gobierno* also addressed itself to the "marginal" parts of the population and explained his plans to bring the poorer people into the mainstream of economic and social life.

Historically, Acción Democrática had been identified with democracy and with the poor. One could always meet an Adeco political leader in the *barrios*, where it was very difficult to find a Copeyano leader.[49] COPEI and Herrera attacked both assumptions. Democracy under AD was questioned: there existed presidentialism and a weak Congress, the concentration of economic and political power in the state, paternalism, the overwhelming power of the Adeco party and government. In addition, COPEI, gearing its campaign to the poor, asked whether the people were indeed living better.

Finally, Herrera called for the overhauling of the public service to make it more efficient and less corrupt. While the sixty-seven-page *Programa de Gobierno* dealt with many other matters, education, the role of the state and democracy, the *marginados*, and administrative corruption were high on the list of priorities.

The phase of exaltation lasted literally until the last hour. Herrera's attacks on Piñerúa continued to erode his credibility and to place his capacity in doubt. The exaltation of Herrera as a person contrasted with the denigration of Piñerúa, and was accompanied by increased numbers of marches, fiestas, and songs.

Within the overall three-phase plan, the Copeyanos utilized several strategies and tactics. They concentrated on the heavily populated industrial corridor on the north-central coast and the northwest, running from Caracas to Zulia and south to Mérida,[50] where approximately 55 percent of the voters live. Particular party leaders concentrated on certain cities and states—Eduardo Fernández on Caracas, Hilarión Cardozo on Zulia. Within this defined area they made a major effort to influence the *marginados*, youth, and undecided voters. Party functional organizations were given specific responsibilities; for example, the JRC was in charge of winning the youth vote for COPEI.[51]

In the summer, the party formed a commission under Pedro Pablo Aguilar to choose candidates for Congress and for the state assemblies.[52] Its members included Montes de Oca, Eduardo Fernández, Rodríguez Sáez, Vivas Terán, Alvarez Paz, Pérez Díaz, Godofredo González, and Juan Rachadell. The commission received two lists, one for Congress, and another for the state assemblies. The lists originated in the districts, were passed up through the regions, and eventually reached the commission. The latter was allowed to make changes on no more than 30 percent of the names, and to specify the order in which they would appear on the lists (*planchas*). It also decided that one-third of the slots would be reserved for independents, party directors, and members of other political groups.

According to one observer, Caldera and Herrera presented their own lists.[53] The selection process was very tense, and the COPEI campaign stopped for a few weeks until it was settled. Although the party ultimately united behind Herrera's candidacy, the selection process as it now stands could lead to serious problems in future elections, thereby weakening internal support for the party's presidential candidate.

Shortly before the election President Pérez called a highly respected Copeyano, Luis Alberto Machado, and asked him to appear at Miraflores on election day to advise the president.[54] This was the first time in Venezuela (and perhaps in Latin America), that a member of the principal opposition party had been called to the presidential palace under such circumstances. Machado accepted the invitation, but he also spoke to Caldera and Herrera before going to Miraflores. He believed that his presence was requested for something more than simply advice. President Pérez thought that AD and Piñerúa would win a close election, and he probably wanted a witness to prove that the government had not manipulated the results. Machado arrived at Miraflores at dawn on election day and remained until 3:00 A.M.

He was given an office with a government official who had direct contact with the various ministers. Machado had direct telephone contact with President Pérez, Caldera, and Herrera.

The Copeyanos had planned a victory demonstration. A month earlier Godofredo González had stated, "When we know the results, we have given instructions to Copeyanos throughout the country to go into the streets and defend the victory."[55] Before the final results were known, word reached Miraflores that a COPEI victory celebration was about to begin in the interior. Machado communicated with the minister of defense and then called Herrera Campins, who sent instructions not to hold the demonstration. Then someone in the government wanted to send word to the Adeco state governors that Piñerúa had won. According to Machado, this could have led to "war"; he spoke to the minister of defense and President Pérez, and no message was sent to the governors.

By 11:00 P.M. it was clear that Herrera had won. Machado believed that his presence was a major reason for the government's acceptance of the results. Within twenty-four hours President Pérez acknowledged Herrera's victory, whereas in 1968 it had taken a week for AD to acknowledge Caldera's victory.

The following day Machado visited Betancourt and Piñerúa to congratulate them on a well-fought campaign, and he suggested that Piñerúa likewise congratulate Herrera. Within two days Piñerúa sent Herrera a telegram of congratulations.

With regard to some of the major themes of this study, Machado's role at Miraflores leads to two conclusions. First, the evolution of the AD-COPEI relationship reached its culmination. Regardless of President Pérez's reasons for inviting Machado, the relationship between the two parties and their mutual trust overcame unforeseen developments. The parties' relationship provided a linkage between electoral politics and the democratic process. Second, depending upon the exigencies of future elections, the incident at Miraflores might lead to a further institutionalization of Venezuelan democracy.

Table 8.3 gives the national vote totals for the presidential candidates.[56]

TABLE 8.3. Results of the 1978 Presidential Election

	Votes	%
Luis Herrera Campins (COPEI)	2,469,042	46.63
Luis Piñerúa Ordaz (AD)	2,295,052	43.34
José Vicente Rangel (MAS)	272,595	5.14
Diego Arria (Causa Común)	90,379	1.70
Luis Beltrán Prieto Figueroa (MEP)	58,723	1.10
Américo Martín (MIR)	51,972	0.98
Héctor Mujica (PCV)	28,835	0.54

(Other candidates received far less than 1 percent each.) Although Piñerúa won in eleven of the country's twenty-three states, districts, and territories, Herrera won in twelve states where the votes counted most—in the heavily populated corridor running between Caracas and Valencia to the state of Zulia. He also won the Federal District, as well as the states of Miranda, Zulia, Lara, Carabobo, and Mérida. The party's concerted efforts in this area were very successful. Although most traditionally Adeco states remained Adeco, the entire country shifted toward COPEI. AD's vote increased in some states and decreased in others; the total AD vote was 6 percent greater than in 1973. In the eleven states Piñerúa carried, his margin of victory was smaller than that of President Pérez in every state but Bolívar. Herrera increased the COPEI vote in all states, districts, and territories—more than 50 percent over 1973. Piñerúa repeated AD's 1973 victory in Táchira, the home state of President Pérez and the recipient of important public works. Herrera won the other two Andean states of Mérida and Trujillo, and he received broad support from all sectors of the country.

Herrera's margin of victory was 174,000 votes, approximately 3.3 percent. The number who did not vote—out of either ignorance, protest, or confusion in the voting process—was 800,000, or approximately 13 percent.

The Venezuelan voter stamps a large card for the presidential candidate and a small card for the legislative candidates (for Congress and the state assemblies). A vote for different political parties on the large and small cards is the equivalent of ticket-splitting in United States elections. URD, FDP, and Opina Nacional (a small group which supported Burelli in 1973) supported Herrera Campins on the large card; however, they ran their own candidates on the legislative *planchas* with COPEI. Thus, one could vote for Jóvito Villalba as the URD-COPEI senator from Nueva Esparta, and for Herrera Campins for president. Usually a presidential candidate on the large card runs ahead of his party on the small card. Table 8.4 shows the national vote totals for the legislative candidates. (Other parties and political groups received from 0 to 1.5 percent.) For the first time in the party's history, the difference between COPEI's vote on the large and small cards was very narrow, and the Copeyano vote on the small card matched that of AD. This factor indicated broad COPEI support throughout the country, prompting one party leader to remark that for the first time COPEI was indeed a national party. People voted for Herrera on the large card and for other parties on the small card for a variety of reasons. Many supporters of the small left-wing parties voted this way, although most MAS supporters seemed to vote for their own presidential candidate. Some young Copeyanos supported Herrera but also voted for MAS or MIR, perhaps wanting to see a better balance in Congress; others wanted to keep the president and the two major parties on their toes. Because of COPEI's impressive

T A B L E 8.4. Results of 1978 Legislative Elections
(for Congress and State Assemblies)

	Votes	%
COPEI	2,086,579	39.72
AD	2,085,409	39.70
MAS	319,730	6.08
MIR	122,679	2.33
MEP	115,944	2.20
Causa Común	89,232	1.69
URD	88,802	1.69
PCV	55,068	1.04
FDP	13,537	0.25
Opina Nacional	7,905	0.15

showing on the small card, the AD-COPEI congressional strength will be equally divided, with each party having eighty-two members in the Chamber of Deputies and twenty-two in the Senate. The COPEI total included four URD deputies and two URD senators.

The municipal elections were held in June 1979. (This was the first time that they were held separately from the presidential and congressional elections.) A compromise was reached between those who wanted individual candidates and those who wanted party control through *planchas*. Although the elections were separate and the voters supposedly able to know their candidates better, municipal office-seekers also ran on *planchas* under party control. The results were a sweeping victory for COPEI, a serious defeat for AD, and an impressive showing for the parties of the left (including MAS) that had combined for the elections: COPEI, 50 percent; AD, 30 percent; the left, 18.5 percent.

We can identify four principal reasons for COPEI's victory in 1978: increasing polarization, the candidates themselves, the antigovernment vote, and the *marginados*.[57] Increasing polarization, particularly Herrera's use of it, was probably the main factor in the Copeyano victory. In 1973, approximately 85 percent of the voters supported the COPEI and AD presidential candidates; that figure increased to 90 percent in 1978. The two parties dominated the media, creating a certain inclination among the people to choose one of the major parties.[58] Herrera used the polarization by presenting himself as the only real alternative to AD, and most undecided voters responded. A significant percentage of the leftist voters also supported Herrera on the large card, and although the Adecos maintained that there was a leftist-Copeyano agreement, this was not the case.[59] Herrera's leftist support gave further evidence that he was indeed the only viable candidate opposing AD; it also constituted a protest vote against the Adeco party, candidate, and government.

Increasing polarization meant that URD and Jóvito Villalba proved very important. Although the URD national vote total declined from that of 1973, the party's 1.69 percent of the 1978 vote (mostly from the east) was of no small consequence, given the closeness of the Herrera-Piñerúa totals. Villalba's role in working for votes, most notably in the *Oriente*, was a significant element in Herrera's campaign plan. Villalba used his own appeal to change the mentality of many *Orientales* and to convince them that Herrera was a true national candidate, the only one worthy of their support.

The difference between the candidates was another major factor. Herrera was *sencillo* (unassuming) and at the same time a more charismatic and forceful candidate; he displayed a sense of humor and made a good impression in television interviews. He also better represented the changing Venezuelan society than did his Adeco opponent, in the eyes of a more sophisticated and growing middle class with approximately 1,200,000 new voters. On the other hand, Piñerúa was a dull speaker, and he almost never appeared on the AD television filmstrips until late in the campaign. It was a tactical mistake for him to reject Herrera's challenge to a television debate.

In a developing country there is a great deal of social dissatisfaction and a tendency to blame the government for most ills. This phenomenon favors the opposition in elections. The anti-government vote —compounded by the high incidence of crime, inflation, inadequate public services, and particularly extensive administrative corruption —turned a significant number of voters toward Herrera and COPEI. Since the Mycon surveys (conducted by a U.S. political consulting firm that worked with Acción Democrática) indicated that President Pérez was Venezuela's most popular politician, it appears that the strategy of denunciation was effective to the extent that the target was the government or the Adecos, and not President Pérez.

Finally, the support of the *marginados* proved crucial for the Copeyanos. For the first time in the party's history, a high percentage of the darker-skinned, poorer people voted in large numbers for COPEI and its presidential candidate.

A Two-Party System

Venezuela has evolved into a two-party system with Acción Democrática and COPEI as the major components. This two-party system is different from that found in the United States, or even in Great Britain. The Venezuelan model will be dominated by AD and COPEI for the foreseeable future, even though their combined percentage might drop in future elections. The domination of the major parties might be tempered by two developments: the emergence of a popular nonparty candidate, who could win from 10 to 20 percent of the vote; and the strength of the smaller parties on the left, which might or might not unify behind a single candidate.

According to a Copeyano estimate, in 1973 AD had approximately 1,000,000 votes from non-Adecos, and COPEI had approximately 600,000 from non-Copeyanos.[60] Thus, AD and COPEI must also relate policies and programs to their supporters outside the party. "The urban vote has tended to be nonparty (and often, antiparty) fluctuating wildly from election to election and leader to leader. In the long run, if the dominant parties cannot extend their organizations into Caracas, which now holds about one-fifth of the nation's population, then the future capacity of the system must be in doubt, as the strength of its institutions will continue to depend on control of a declining element in the population."[61] In addition to receiving a combined national total of 85 percent in 1973, AD and COPEI received 82 percent of the Caracas vote. In 1978, when the AD-COPEI national total was 90 percent, their combined Caracas vote was again 82 percent, indicating not only that the democratic system was strengthened, but also that the combined strength of the two major parties in the Federal District provided a most important underpinning for the two-party system.

The smaller parties have been in disarray, troubled (until recently) by the left's continuing disunity and by splits within some parties. The Movement of the Revolutionary Left (MIR) has occasionally admonished the Movement to Socialism (MAS) for not supporting leftist unity. The MIR position has been welcomed by the Communist party and MEP. Although MAS had steadfastly refused to join any leftist coalition, it did combine with the left-wing parties in the 1979 municipal elections. Rather than form a serious threat to AD-COPEI dominance, however, the municipal elections will probably lead to greater AD-COPEI cooperation in the municipal councils of various cities. AD was weakened in the municipal elections, but the combined AD-COPEI vote was still 80 percent. It remains to be seen whether leftist unity will be a major factor in the 1983 presidential election.

Three parties have split. Vice-Admiral Wolfgang Larrazábal led a group out of the FDP and formed a new political group; in addition, the Vanguardia Unitaria Comunista broke away from the Communist party, and the Movimiento de Renovación Nacional split from the URD.

If there is no serious threat to AD-COPEI dominance from the left, is there such a threat from the right? Although extreme poverty can provide sympathetic listeners for a right-wing *caudillo*, I agree with the assessment of former President Caldera.[62] When AD and COPEI cooperate, the influence of Pérez Jiménez or a prospective leader of his type declines. We also recall the constitutional amendment prohibiting Pérez Jiménez from running for president, thereby weakening the right even further.

In addition to adequate income from petroleum exports, the continued health of Venezuelan political democracy will require that a political and economic elite make attacking the maldistribution of wealth one of its highest priorities. This will be a difficult task for a basically conservative middle-class elite. In fact, while the authors of a recent study are "guardedly optimistic about the viability of the present system for the immediate future," they are more pessimistic about the continuing effectiveness of the democratic system in the long run.[63]

The pessimists may simply be realists when assessing the nation's future. Nevertheless, it may well be that twenty-two years of effective cooperation between the leaders of AD and COPEI have provided a sufficient basis for stable democracy in Venezuela.

Appendix

Eighteen Principles of COPEI

In his analysis of the eighteen principles, Caldera explained that they were divided into two parts: the principles themselves, which inspired the movement, and the general slogans translated by the party into immediate objectives of struggle.

The eighteen principles had three major themes: 1) nationalism, 2) social justice (requiring a profound reform in favor of the dispossessed classes; to be based on justice with harmony, unity, peace, and equilibrium), and 3) Christian Democracy (requiring a popular and democratic government, respect for the individual, elevation of the people). According to Caldera, these were the three basic pillars of the program of COPEI.

The theme of nationalism was incorporated into Principles Fourteen, Fifteen, Seventeen, and Eighteen. Principle Fourteen stated in general terms the usual concept of nationalism, utilizing such phrases as "unity of Venezuela," "civic responsibility," and "national interests." The latter three principles referred more specifically to "Copeyano Nationalism" as a force directed toward international considerations. It was "pacific, constructive, and unifying in its international conception," implying certain fundamental ideas: 1) pacific collaboration with other countries; 2) the strongest collaboration with the countries of *Gran Colombia* and with the Bolivarian countries in general (countries liberated by the armies of Simón Bolívar); 3) broad and spiritual identification with the countries of Ibero-America; 4) rejection of imperialism in any form; 5) rejection of interference in other countries, contrary to self-determination; and 6) economic liberation of Venezuela.

In discussing the second theme of social justice, Caldera announced that the principal slogan of the newly formed party was "For Social Justice in a Better Venezuela." The movement must struggle for human dignity and well-being through better conditions of life and work: "We are Christians, but for that very reason we fight for the defense of the worker and the improvement of the humble classes."

Caldera then addressed himself to the question of revolution. Since reform was so urgent, COPEI was sincerely revolutionary. However, he rejected violence. Instead, COPEI was to be a revolutionary movement, providing the necessary harmony and peace for justice to come to fruition: "COPEI aspires to a profound reform in order to give the dispossessed classes a human degree of well-being and social security.

Social justice, inspired in the Christian idea of dignity of work and tending to realize a healthy equilibrium, offering a solid base to social peace, will be the basis of COPEI revolutionary action."

The remainder of Caldera's discussion of social justice, incorporated into Principles Ten, Eleven, Twelve, and Thirteen, dealt with the general ideas of the concept analyzed in Chapter 1. The major emphasis seemed to be on striving for social harmony and peace by providing the opportunity to work, and elevating the conditions of the worker and his family. Caldera took this a step further by identifying social justice with nationalism. In accord with the theoretical base of the movement, the economic life of man should be subject to moral norms. Economic development must serve the public well-being; state intervention was defended when it was in society's best interest. Caldera explained that, while COPEI supported the conciliation of state intervention with private initiative, the state's role in enhancing human development was important in its own right in such areas as ensuring the social function of private property, enacting fiscal and administrative reforms, implementing agrarian reform based on justice, and safeguarding national interests.

The third theme, Christian Democracy, can be found in Principles Six, Seven, Eight, and Nine. Caldera stated that democracy, as a system of government, was inspired in the Christian sense of life:

> 6. COPEI repudiates totalitarianism and autocracy; it considers democracy as the best system of government and understands it, not only as the expression of the principle that sovereignty resides in the people, but also as the guarantee of the rights of the human person, whose denial is not admissible by any power.

Another aspect of Christian Democracy, according to Caldera, was that COPEI did not mix religion and politics. The Christian idea was basic in social life, and therefore in the organization of the people. But COPEI was a political party, not an arm of the church.

Comprehending the Christian ideal in its fundamental value, Caldera pointed out that COPEI struggled for education and for the family, "because it is in the school and in the home where the moral life is forged and where the future life of a country is defined." He also emphasized that defense of the family and school was not abstract, but appeared in concrete proposals. For this reason COPEI supported a minimum salary for the family as outlined in the constitution of 1947.

In his closing remarks, Caldera once again pointed out that COPEI was unequivocally anticommunist. The organization could not be indifferent:

> 16. COPEI combats communism as a system contrary to social peace and justice, contrary to national sovereignty and national security, and the enemy of democracy and of Christian civilization.

During its formative years, in the 1940s, Caldera and his colleagues viewed COPEI as an electoral committee to present candidates in the forthcoming elections—in this case, for the Constituent Assembly, the presidency, Congress, legislative assemblies, and municipal councils. But, like Acción Nacional, the leaders of COPEI soon realized that it would be necessary to form a national party whose interests would reflect national needs and extend beyond immediate electoral struggles.

Although its leaders considered COPEI to be anticommunist, they still saw themselves as ideological revolutionaries. But, as Chapter 1 has indicated, and as Caldera made clear in explaining the eighteen principles, the Christian Democratic revolution emphasized improving the condition of workers and peasants in nonviolent ways. In this revolutionary effort, COPEI leadership looked for the state to play an active role, in concert with the private sector.

These principles of COPEI placed the Venezuelan movement, as well as other hemispheric Christian Democratic movements, apart from most Latin American political organizations. And, as indicated by Caldera's analysis, there were some clear guidelines for implementing these principles.

1. COPEI Party Organization and Structure

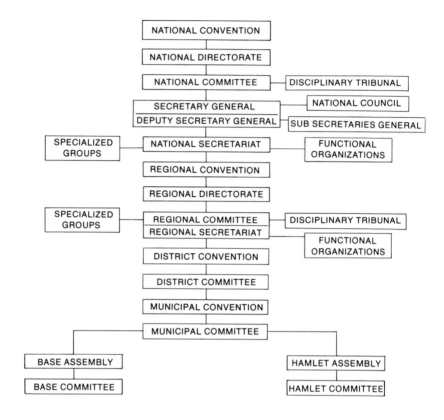

Source: José Elías Rivera Oviedo, *Los Social Cristianos en Venezuela.*

Partido Social Cristiano COPEI

ESTATUTOS (Outline)

DE LA X CONVENCION NACIONAL
CARACAS, 9 DE ABRIL DE 1967

General
  A. Statutes of organization first presented and approved at Third
     National Convention, 22 March 1948
  B. Modifications by subsequent conventions—most recently Tenth
     National Convention, 9 April 1967
  C. Also a series of additional rules, some with a national character
     and others regional

Title 1. General Dispositions

  A. Article 1
     1. Name: COPEI, Social Christian Party of Venezuela
     2. Keeps the original designation of Comité de Organización
        Política Electoral Independiente
  B. Article 4. Party can also be identified by other names: Social
     Christian Party, Christian Democratic Party, Christian De-
     mocracy

Title 2. Of the Militancy

  A. Article 6. Primary position of the National Committee
  B. Article 7. Duties of the militant. To participate in the courses,
     seminars . . . that the Party may organize to improve the ideo-
     logical and political formation of the militancy
  C. Article 8. Rights of the Militant
     1. Can be heard and present his point of view to the various
        organs
     2. Presents his position only within the organs of the party,
        and not outside—his criticisms and observations
     3. Once a decision is made by the majority, he must abide by
        the decision

Title 3. Of the Organization

  Chapter 1. General Dispositions
  A. Article 11. National authorities of COPEI:
     1. The National Convention
     2. The National Directory
     3. The National Committee

        a. Permanent executive organ of national direction of the Party

        b. And the National Council, its consultative organ

    4. The National Disciplinary Tribunal

B. Article 12. National Committee coordinates and controls partisan work in determined areas, working through a Secretariat.

C. Also regional organizations of the above

Chapter 2. Of the National Convention

A. Article 13. The National Convention is the supreme authority of the party

B. Article 14. The National Convention will ordinarily meet every two years. An Extraordinary National Convention can also be called by the decision of the National Committee or the National Directory, or by petition of the majority of the regional organisms or a resolution of the Convention

C. Article 15. Date, place, and purpose of the National Convention are fixed by the National Directory or, if it is not able, the National Committee

    1. Two-thirds vote of members present can add matters to be discussed

D. Article 18. Delegates to the National Convention

    1. Principal and supplementary members of the National Committee

    2. Principal and supplementary members of the National Disciplinary Tribunal

    3. Senators and Deputies to the National Congress, members of COPEI

    4. Presidents and Secretaries-General of the Regional Committees

    5. Delegates of the regional organs, elected in the respective conventions

    6. Delegates of the functional organs, elected in conformity with the respective Regulations

    7. The members of the National Council

E. Duties of the National Convention

    2. Elect principal and supplementary members of the National Committee

    3. Elect principal and supplementary members of the National Disciplinary Tribunal

    5. Decide about the postulation of the candidate for the Presidency of the Republic

    6. Approve, reject, or modify the lists of candidates for the National Congress, and for the remaining popular elections of a national character

    8. Dictate measures relative to the organization or reorganiza-

tion of Sectionals and the platforms, *planchas* or lists of candidates, and remaining questions concerning elections of a regional character when the interests of the party make it indispensable

11. Analyze and judge the activities of the members of the Party who exercise public functions, and order measures to be taken according to the interests of COPEI

Chapter 3. Of the National Directory

A. Article 26. Membership. Members of the National Committee, the National Secretaries, members of the National Disciplinary Tribunal, National Directors of the specialized fractions or groups, regional Presidents and Secretaries-General, three Delegates by each Regional Organism which are designated by the Regional Directorate or by the Regional Committee in cases of urgency and previous authorization of the National Committee, the delegates of the Functional Organisms, the Representatives of the Parliamentary Group
B. Article 27. Ordinarily meets every two years unless it is the year in which the National Convention meets
C. Article 30. Duties of the National Directory
   1. Carries out the duties of the National Convention when the latter cannot meet
      a. But cannot modify the statutes or the program of COPEI
   2. Carries out directions of the National Convention
   3. Analyzes problems to fix the political line of the Party
   4. Other duties indicated by the Statutes and Regulations. This is the second authority of COPEI

Chapter 4. The National Committee

A. Article 31
   1. Highest executive authority of the Party
   2. Membership: the National President, two Vice-Presidents, the Secretary-General, and eleven members elected by the National Convention; also the National Secretaries-General of the Front of Copeyano Workers, of the Copeyano Feminine Front, of the Social Christian Agrarian Movement, of the Social Christian Teachers Movement, and of the Movement of Social Christian Professionals and Technicians
   3. National Convention also elects alternates who attend all the meetings with a voice but not a vote
B. Article 32. Duties of the National Committee
   1. Carry out the decisions of the National Convention and the National Directory
   2. Determine its own Regulation, to realize specific work of each member under the national direction of the Party

5. Convoke the National Convention, the National Directory, and the National Council
7. Name and remove the National Secretaries, the National Directors or Coordinators of Units, services, or specialized groups, and the remaining functionaries designated by the Statutes and Regulations of the Party, as well as those of a national character whose designation may not be attributed to any other authority
8. Present before the National Disciplinary Tribunal or before the Regional Disciplinary Tribunals the disciplinary proceedings which may take place, without prejudice relative to what any member of the party may have done
10. Put forth candidates for the exercise of important public charges such as Ministers, Directors of Autonomous Institutes, State Governors, Secretaries-General of Government, Chief of Diplomatic Missions, etc.
11. Declare in a state of reorganization, with a favorable two-thirds vote, any of the regional and functional organizations of the party or units and specialized groups, on a national scale, assuming direct and indirect direction of same
12. Authorize the Regional Committees to declare the district or municipal sectionals in a state of reorganization
   a. On petition of the Regional Committee
C. Article 33. The decisions of the National Committee will be adopted by the absolute majority of its members present
D. Article 34. The National President of the Party will preside over meetings of the National Committee, of the National Council and of the National Directory, and he will exercise the representation of the Party in all acts of public, administrative, civil, and economic character
E. Article 36. Secretary-General. Will have as his charge the immediate direction of the work of the National Committee, the National Secretaries, and the units, services, or specialized groups
F. Article 37
   1. Secretary-General suggests to the National Committee a Deputy Secretary-General
   2. Sub-Secretaries-General are designated in the same manner
G. Article 38. The National President of the Party, the National Secretary-General, the Deputy Secretary-General can speak collectively or individually for the Party

Chapter 5. The National Council

A. Article 39. Consultative organ of the National Committee—helps the National Committee carry out its functions
B. Article 40. Members

1. Members of the National Committee
2. The National Secretaries
3. The National Advisers, designated by the National Committee but numbering no more than eleven
4. Regional Secretary-General of the Federal District
5. The Directors or National Coordinators of units, services, or specialized groups may attend certain meetings of the Council on the advice of the National Committee
6. National Directors of the professional and technical units
7. Director of the Parliamentary Group

C. Article 41. Its meetings called by the National Committee

Chapter 6. The National Secretariat

A. Article 43. Includes the National Secretary-General, the Deputy Secretary-General, the General Sub-Secretaries, and the National Secretaries
B. J. E. Rivera Oviedo, *Los Social Cristianos en Venezuela*, pp. 199–200
    1. Coordinates the daily activities of the party
    2. National Secretaries
        a. Have a specific task within the organization
        b. Idea of decentralizing administrative work
        c. Various ones
            (1) University Secretary
            (2) Feminine Secretary
            (3) Trade Union Secretary
            (4) Youth Secretary
            (5) Agrarian Secretary
            (6) Teachers' Secretary
            (7) Finance Secretary
            (8) Political Formation Secretary
            (9) Political Relations Secretary
            (10) Technical Matters Secretary
            (11) Operative Organs Secretary
            (12) Regional Organs Secretary
            (13) Economic Organs Secretary
            (14) Cultural Organs Secretary
            (15) Electoral Matters Secretary
            (16) Professional Organs Secretary
            (17) Municipal Action Secretary
            (18) International Relations Secretary
            (19) Organization Secretary
            (20) Parliamentary Matters Secretary
            (21) Popular Action Secretary
            Thus the party is organized functionally in the form of fractions and specialized groups

Title 4. The Regional Organizations

Chapter 1. General Dispositions

A. Article 45. Each regional organ is autonomous in respect to its functions
B. Article 48. National Committee authorizes the inscription of a regional organ
C. Article 49. Each regional organ can ask the National Committee to convoke the National Convention or the National Directory— must be done if five or more of the regional organs petition

Chapter 2. Regional Authorities of the Party

A. Article 50
   1. Regional Convention
   2. Regional Directory
   3. Regional Committee
   4. Regional Disciplinary Tribunal

Chapter 3. Regional Conventions (Articles 51-60)

National Convention
Regional Convention
District Convention
Municipal Convention
Base

Chapter 4. The Regional Directories (Articles 61-65)

Chapter 5. The Regional Committees (Articles 66-70)

Chapter 6. Special Dispositions (Articles 71-72)

Chapter 7. Regional Organization in the Federal District (Articles 73-80)

A. Under the National Committee which sets it up
   1. Appoints and removes the Secretaries
B. Has a Regional Convention, Regional Secretary, etc.

Title 5. Districts, Municipal, and Base Organs

Chapter 1. District and Municipal Conventions (Articles 81-84)

Chapter 2. District and Municipal Committees (Articles 85-88)

Chapter 3. Base Organs (Articles 89-91)

A. Village or *barrio* organizations under a committee

Title 6. Functional Organs (Articles 92-96)

A. Organized functionally in the form of groups, nationally or regionally

B. National parliamentary groups. State legislative groups follow the general line of the National and Regional Committees
C. Article 96. Various functional organizations
  1. Frente de Trabajadores Copeyanos
  2. Juventud Revolucionaria Copeyana
  3. Frente Femenino Copeyano
  4. Movimiento Agrario Socialcristiano
  5. Movimiento Magisterial Socialcristiano
  6. Movimiento de Profesionales y Técnicos Socialcristianos
D. Regulations determined by the National Committee

Title 7. Financial Regulation (Articles 97-102)

A. Article 99
  1. Contributions—national congressmen, others on national bodies
    a. percentage fixed by resolution or by the National Convention
  2. Contributions of members of municipal and district bodies, state legislators
    a. Percentage fixed by National or Regional Conventions
  3. Contributions of Regional Committees
  4. Special contributions for electoral campaigns
  5. Contributions of the militants
B. Article 101
  1. Disciplinary action against those who procrastinate, particularly public functionaries
    a. Disciplinary Tribunal

Title 8. Disciplinary Regime

Chapter 1. General Dispositions
A. Article 103
  1. Regarding infractions against the Statutes, Regulations, directed orders, political lines, fixed action of certain organs
  2. Punishment: warning, relieved of duties for two years, suspended for two years, definitive expulsion
B. Article 104
  1. National Committee can suspend a member until the disciplinary organs decide what to do
    a. Two-thirds vote
    b. A member can appeal to the most immediate National Directory of the Party
C. Article 105
  1. Regional Committees can do same
  2. A member can appeal to the National Committee
D. Article 106
  1. National and Regional Committees must submit their find-

ings to the disciplinary organs within two months following
the suspension
E. Article 107
    1. Disciplinary organs
        a. National Disciplinary Tribunal
        b. Regional Disciplinary Tribunals

Chapter 2. The National Disciplinary Tribunal

A. Article 110
    1. Five members elected by the National Convention
    2. National Convention elects five *suplentes*
        a. To fill in, in case of illness, etc.
B. Article 111
    1. The Tribunal writes a National Disciplinary Regulation
    2. It elects a president and secretary from its members
C. Article 113
    1. Tribunal can act regarding all members—Congress, public
       functionaries, functional organizations, Governors, etc.
        a. Can call a meeting of the National Directory to discuss
           the matter

Chapter 3. Regional Disciplinary Tribunals (Articles 116-20)

Title 9. The Exercise of Public Functions (Articles 121-25)

A. Article 124
    1. National Committee can cause the retirement, temporary or
       definitive, of any party militant who exercises public func-
       tions—representatives, administrators, political positions
    2. Anyone who attacks the National Committee in its action
       will be suspended as a militant of the party

Title 10. Final Dispositions (Article 126)

The present Statutes are the same approved 22 March 1948 by the
Third National Convention, modified 5 October 1958 by the Seventh National Convention, reformed 12 April 1960 by the Eighth
National Convention, modified 29 February 1964 by the First Extraordinary National Convention, and reformed partially 9 April
1967 by the Tenth National Convention of the Party

Notes

Chapter 1

1. The discussion of the nineteenth century is based on the study by Eric R. Wolf and Edward C. Hansen, *The Human Condition in Latin America*, pp. 216–25.
2. E.g., see Edwin Liewen, *Venezuela*, pp. 48–49.
3. See Samuel P. Huntington, *Political Order in Changing Societies*, pp. 39–59.
4. See María de Lourdes Acedo de Sucre and Carmen Margarita Nones Mendoza, *La Generación Venezolana de 1928*.
5. Clemy Machado de Acedo, *La Política en Venezuela*, p. 12.
6. Robert J. Alexander, *The Communist Party of Venezuela*, pp. 163–64.
7. José Elías Rivera Oviedo, *Los Social Cristianos en Venezuela*, pp. 18–19.
8. See John D. Martz, *Acción Democrática*, pp. 120–25.
9. Estados Unidos de Venezuela, Servicio Secreto de Investigación, *La Verdad de las Actividades Comunistas en Venezuela*, pp. 140–42.
10. Ibid., p. 225.
11. See Lourdes Acedo de Sucre and Nones Mendoza, *Generación Venezolana*, pp. 100–114.
12. Interview with Miguel Angel Landáez, 28 October 1970. Among his many activities and official positions, Landáez was a student leader during the period under discussion and was one of the founders of the Christian Democratic party. At the time of our conversation, he was a member of the Supreme Court of Venezuela.
13. Interview with Pedro José Lara Peña, 21 October 1970. Lara Peña, a member of the student group that split from the FEV, was one of the founders of two small political parties that were precursors of the Christian Democratic party.
14. Included in the Bloque de Abril were the Movimiento de Organización Venezolano (ORVE), founded by Rómulo Betancourt and the Generation of 1928, the Progressive Republican Party (PRP), and the National Republican Union (UNR).
15. See *La Esfera* and *El Universal*, May 1936.
16. Gonzalo Barrios, *Bloque de Abril*, pp. 7–8.
17. Interview with Jesús María Pérez Machado, 15 February 1971. Very active in the early student movement, Pérez Machado was a founder of the student organization that split from the FEV and of one of the parties that preceded the Christian Democratic party. In 1968 he led the "Independientes para COPEI." At the time of the interview, he was the chief of the legal department of the Consultaría Jurídica. Also see the article by Rafael Caldera in *El Universal*, 3 May 1936.
18. The meeting is described in *El Universal*, 8 May 1936.
19. Interview with Pérez Machado. The meeting also included Víctor Giménez Landínez, Ezequiel Monsalve Casado, Carlos Rodríguez Uzconga, and a few others.

20. Pérez Machado described and interpreted the Congress during our conversation.

21. "Manifiesto de la Unión Nacional Estudiantil a la Opinión Pública Venezolana," *La Esfera*, 11 May 1936. Various newspapers carried arguments by the FEV and UNE explaining their positions; see *El Universal* and *La Esfera*, 7–8 May 1936.

22. Interview with Hilarión Cardozo, 10 December 1970. Active for many years in student and party affairs, Sr. Cardozo was deputy secretary-general of the Social Christian-COPEI at the time of the interview. He was appointed governor of the state of Zulia on 22 April 1971, a position he relinquished after the 1973 election.

23. Interview with Víctor Giménez Landínez, 2 July 1971. Giménez Landínez has been very active within the Christian Democratic movement. A founder of the UNE and the Social Christian-COPEI party, he was minister of agriculture during part of the Betancourt administration and direc· tor of the National Agrarian Institute early in the Caldera government.

24. Interview with former President Raúl Leoni (1964–69), 11 June 1971. Sr. Leoni died in July 1972.

25. See the discussion by Ambrosio Romero Carranza, *Qué es la Democracia Cristiana*, pp. 131–34.

26. Various UNE publications developed those ideas. See *Consignas aprobadas por el Primer Congreso Nacional Uneísta* and *Por los Legítimos Ideales del Estudiante Venezolano*. The official newspaper of the UNE con· tinued publication into the early 1940s.

27. *Consignas aprobadas por el Primer Congreso Nacional Uneísta*, p. 45.

28. Ibid., p. 54.

29. *UNE*, vol. 3, no. 131, 22 April 1939.

30. Ibid.

31. E.g., see *Por los Legítimos Ideales del Estudiante Venezolano*, p. 54.

32. *UNE*, vol. 4, no. 165, 16 December 1939.

33. *Por los Legítimos Ideales del Estudiante Venezolano*, p. 11.

34. *UNE*, vol. 3, no. 112, 3 December 1938.

35. Interview with Miguel Angel Landáez.

36. The Caracas dailies of 17 December 1938 listed the party's organizers, who included Carlos Navas Spinola, Eduardo López de Ceballos, Miguel Rivas Berrizbeitia, Carlos Rojas Guardia, Manual B. Pocaterra, Alberto J. Plaza, Francisco Carrillo Batalla, and Juan José Mendoza, Jr.

37. *El Universal*, 3 February 1942.

38. This information is based on interviews with political leaders in the respective states: Miguel Angel Parada, a founder of the Christian Democratic party in Táchira, 28 June 1971; Bernardo Aranguren Marquina, the deputy secretary-general of Acción Democrática in Mérida, 30 June 1971.

39. Published in the magazine *SIC* (*Seminario Interdiocesano Caracas*), vol. 5, no. 45, May 1942.

40. *El Universal*, 22 April 1942.

41. *Acción Nacional*, vol. 1, no. 3, June 1944.

42. Interview with Miguel Angel Landáez.

43. See *El Universal*, 25 January 1943.

44. *Acción Nacional*, vol. 1, no. 1, March 1944.

45. Rivera Oviedo, *Los Social Cristianos*, p. 65.

46. Interviews with Pedro José Lara Peña and Martín Pérez Matos. Lara Peña felt that Medina Angarita was pro-fascist but not pro-Nazi. The president appeared as a liberal during World War II when he saw that developments were moving to the "left." He had a strong hand and was anticommunist. López Contreras was a liberal but also anticommunist; he wanted to work with the left, but this group was too strongly under com-

munist influence as exemplified by Rómulo Betancourt and Luis Beltrán Prieto. Thus López was forced to take harsh measures against the left. However, Lara Peña's analysis can be questioned. Medina worked with the communists to a considerable degree during his presidency. Was López Contreras a liberal? Did he want to work with the left, and had he been prevented from doing so by the "communism" of Betancourt and Prieto? Actually, Betancourt had ceased being a communist, and Prieto had never been one.

47. *El Universal*, 14 October 1945.
48. *SIC*, vol. 32, no. 314, April 1969.
49. Interview with Padre Genaro Aguirre, S.J., 25 November 1970.
50. *SIC*, vol. 32, no. 314, April 1969.
51. Miguel Angel Landáez told me that the students considered *Esquema de la Doctrina Social Católica* as their bible.
52. Manuel Aguirre Elorriaga, S.J., *Esquema de la Doctrina Social Católica (Temas y custionarios para los Círculos de Estudios)*, p. 24.
53. *SIC*, vol. 2, no. 14, April 1939, pp. 120–22.
54. Ibid., no. 15, May 1939, p. 155.
55. Ibid.
56. Ibid., no. 16, June 1939, p. 187.
57. Ibid., no. 17, July 1939, p. 220.
58. Ibid., vol. 7, no. 62, February 1944, pp. 68–69.
59. Ibid., vol. 8, no. 75, May 1945, p. 221.
60. Ibid., no. 71, January 1945, p. 12.

Chapter 2

1. For a discussion of the Revolution of 1945, see John D. Martz, *Acción Democrática*, pp. 56–62.
2. *El Nacional*, 15 April 1946. See the party newspaper *COPEI*, no. 6, 27 April 1946.
3. Rodolfo José Cárdenas, *El Combate Político Solo Para Líderes Nuevos*, pp. 15–16.
4. Rafael Caldera, *Ganar la Patria una Responsibilidad Mancomunada*, p. 15.
5. Interview with Miguel Angel Landáez, 28 October 1970. It should also be noted that the Christian Democratic party is officially known as the Social Christian–COPEI. The party leaders decided to maintain the original abbreviation of the 1946 electoral committee, and the party's literature refers to the organization as COPEI.
6. Presidencia de la República, *Documentos que Hicieron Historia*, vol. 2, "Manifiesto de COPEI," pp. 385–402.
7. COPEI, Secretaría de Propaganda, "Qué Es El COPEI?"
8. "Manifiesto de COPEI."
9. Ibid.
10. The eighteen principles appeared in a pamphlet published by the Partido Socialcristiano, Secretaría Nacional de Propaganda, "Programa del Movimiento Político COPEI," 3a edición. Caldera's analysis of the eighteen principles appeared in the party newspaper *COPEI*, 9 September 1959. The newspaper article summarized one of his speeches delivered on 8 September 1949. See the Appendix for the full analysis.
11. Interview with Francisco Peña Blanco, *hijo*, 6 July 1971. An active Copeyano in the early years, Peña left COPEI in 1950 to support Pérez Jiménez. At the time of our discussion, he and others were trying to unite various groups and individuals who supported the former dictator into one political organization, the Frente Unido Nacionalista (FUN).

12. Interview with José Luis Zapata, 8 March 1971. Zapata was a member of the UNE in Lara and a founder of COPEI in that state. At the time of the interview, he was a federal deputy in Congress from Lara. He subsequently became the leader of the COPEI parliamentary group.

13. Interviews with Padre José Ignacio Arneto and Padre Martínez Galdeano of Centro Gumilla, 22 June 1971.

14. Interview with Monsignor Pedro T. Pérez Viros, Iglesia La Catedral of San Cristóbal, Táchira, 29 June 1971.

15. Interview with Miguel Angel Parada, 28 June 1971. Parada, a founder of COPEI in Táchira, was the attorney general of the state at the time of our conversation.

16. These facts were related by an Adeco and a Copeyano. Interview with Bernardo Aranguren Marquina, 30 June 1971; Aranguren Marquina was deputy secretary-general and political secretary of AD in Mérida at the time. Interview with Carlos A. Gainxa M. and others, 1 July 1971; Gainxa was then a Copeyano member of the legislative assembly.

17. Boris Bunimov Parra, *Introducción a la Sociología Electoral Venezolana*. All the cited statistics of the 1946 election were taken from this work.

18. See the article by Martín Fierro in *El Nacional*, 1 November 1946.

19. El Comité Regional de COPEI, *Manifiesto del Comité Regional de COPEI al Pueblo de Táchira*, 1 November 1946.

20. "Plataforma Electoral de COPEI," *La Esfera*, 29 September 1946.

21. In the party newspaper (*COPEI*, no. 32, 2 November 1946) the following were listed: Rafael Caldera, Lorenzo Fernández, F. Romero Lobo, Pbro. Carlos Sánchez E., Ines de Lara, Patrocino Peñuela Ruiz, Antonio Sánchez Pacheco, Pbro. José R. Pulido Méndez, Elio Súarez Romero, Luis Roberto Riera, José Ramón Barrios Mora, Pbro. J. Humberto Contreras, José Desiderio Gómez, Atilio Araujo, Carlos Quintero Delgado, Pbro. José León Rojas, Lorenzo Lara Labrador, Elfraim Rodrigo, Edecio La Riva Araujo.

22. Estado Unidos de Venezuela, *Diario de Debates*, vol. 1, no. 2, 31 December 1947, p. 11.

23. Ibid., vol. 3, no. 33, 4 March 1947, pp. 28–29, 60.

24. Ibid., no. 36, 9 March 1947, pp. 27–28.

25. *El Gráfico*, 24 July 1947.

26. *Diario de Debates*, vol. 2, no. 26, 13 February 1947, p. 36.

27. *El Popular*, 7 May 1947.

28. The discussion of the 1947 election is based on the analysis by Bunimov Parra, *Introducción a la Sociología*, pp. 67–80, 309–10.

29. The figures are cited by Rómulo Betancourt, *Venezuela: política y petróleo*, p. 221.

30. Samuel P. Huntington, *Political Order in Changing Societies*, pp. 9–10.

31. *COPEI*, no. 1, 16 March 1946.

32. *El País*, 14 April 1946.

33. *COPEI*, no. 13, 14 June 1946.

34. *COPEI de Táchira*, no. 1, 4 May 1946.

35. The meeting is described by *El Nacional*, 20 June 1946, and *COPEI*, no. 14, 22 June 1946.

36. "Manifiesto de las Mujeres Venezolanas del Sector Feminino Independiente," 1946.

37. *COPEI de Lara*, no. 1, 3 August 1946.

38. *COPEI de Táchira*, no. 36, 1 February 1947.

39. *El Gráfico*, 13 September 1947.

40. See *El Gráfico*, 20–22 November 1947.

41. Ibid., 3 June 1948, 25 June 1948.

42. For an analysis of the factors leading up to the coup and the coup itself, see Winfield J. Burggraaff, *The Venezuelan Armed Forces in Politics*, pp. 79–111.

43. *El Gráfico*, "Comunicado de COPEI Ante de la Situación Actual," 3 December 1948.

44. Interview with Luis Beltrán Prieto Figueroa, 14 June 1971. Prieto, a former member of AD, was a member of the revolutionary junta of 1945–48, the second and then the first vice-president of the party, secretary-general of AD, and president of the Venezuelan Senate. In 1968, he and a group of supporters left AD to form the Movimiento del Pueblo (MEP). Prieto was the president of MEP, and in 1968 was that party's unsuccessful presidential candidate.

45. Edwin Lieuwen, *Venezuela*, p. 87.

46. Interview with Aristídes Calvani, 7 July 1971. Long active in COPEI, Calvani was foreign minister under President Caldera.

47. Interview, 18 June 1971.

48. Interview with Gonzalo Barrios, 16 November 1970. Although he was studying abroad in 1928, Barrios is considered to be a member of the Generation of 1928 and is a founder of AD. He was the party's unsuccessful presidential candidate in 1968; he then became the president of Acción Democrática.

49. Interview with Jesús Angel Paz Galarraga, 5 March 1971. Paz was a member of AD for some time, serving as its secretary-general for seven years. He left with the group that formed MEP in 1968 and then became that party's secretary-general.

50. Interview with Miguel Angel Landáez, 4 November 1970.

51. Rafael Caldera, "Venezuela on Election Eve," *Commonweal*, vol. 44, 4 October 1946, pp. 590–92.

52. Burggraaff, *Venezuelan Armed Forces*, pp. 86–89.

53. Cárdenas, *Combate Político*, pp. 23–24.

54. *El Gráfico*, 9 March 1949.

55. "Comunicación del Comité Nacional de COPEI a la Junta Militar de Gobierno," 17 March 1949.

56. *El Gráfico*, 2 November 1949.

57. "Informe Que el Comité Regional de COPEI de Táchira Presenta a la Consideración de la 8a Convención Regional del Partido," 25 November 1949.

58. *El Gráfico*, 28 March 1950.

59. Letter from Gustavo Ramírez Corredor, secretaría de propaganda de COPEI en Mérida, to Valmore Acevedo. The letter, written in Mérida, is dated 2 August 1950.

60. "COPEI Dice," *El Nacional*, 25 February 1967.

61. For the provisions of the political party act, see Burggraaff, *Venezuelan Armed Forces*, pp. 125–26.

62. *COPEI Frente al Estatuto Electoral y la Actual Situación Política*, 1951.

63. José Augustín Catala, ed., *Documentos para la Historia de la Resistencia*, vol. 1, 1948–52, "Pérez Jiménez y su Regimen de Terror," p. 264.

64. *COPEI Ante las Elecciones: La 6a Convención de COPEI a la Nación Venezolana*, 14 September 1952.

65. The source for the cited figures is the party newspaper, *COPEI*, "Historia del Socialcristianismo en Venezuela," 13 January 1961. Other sources vary slightly. See Leo B. Lott, "The 1952 Venezuelan Elections," *Western Political Quarterly*, 10 September 1957, p. 549.

66. *Informe* del Secretariado Regional de COPEI en el Distrito Federal ante la 8a Convención del Partido, 25 April 1953.

67. *Por Qué COPEI no asiste a la Constituyente*, 9 January 1953.

68. *COPEI*, 24 June 1959.
69. Interview with·Francisco Peña Blanco, *hijo*, 6 July 1971.
70. *Discurso Pronunciado Por El Dr. Rafael Caldera*, n.d. [but probably April 1953].
71. *Clarificación* del Comité Nacional de COPEI, September 1953.
72. Edward J. Williams, *Latin American Christian Democratic Parties*, pp. 163–64.
73. John J. Johnson, *The Military and Society in Latin America*, p. 107.
74. Interview, 27 July 1971. He preferred to remain anonymous.
75. Interview with Miguel Angel Landáez, 28 October 1970.
76. Ibid.
77. Interview with Jesús Angel Paz Galarraga, 5 March 1971.
78. Interview with Víctor Giménez Landínez, 7 July 1971.

Chapter 3

1. The founding of *TIELA* is described by Herrera Campins in the party newspaper *Seminario COPEI*, 12 March 1971. One of *TIELA*'s founders, José Luis Zapata, corroborated the facts of the newspaper's foundation in an interview on 8 March 1971.
2. *TIELA*, Bulletin no. 6, October 1957.
3. Luis Herrera Campins, "La Victoria de Eduardo Frei," *Publicaciones de la Fracción Parlamentaria de COPEI*, vol. 2, no. 24, p. 677.
4. The discussion of COPEI organizational activities during the dictatorship is based on an interview with Enrique Pérez Olivares, 24 November 1970. At the time of our conversation, Pérez Olivares was dean of the law school of the Central University of Venezuela. He is the author of *Introducción a la Democrácia Cristiana*. President Caldera appointed him to the cabinet as minister of education in 1971.
5. Interview with Hilarión Cardozo, 10 December 1970.
6. Interviews with Valmore Acevedo Amaya, 10 February 1971, and Luis Guillermo Pilonieta, 1 April 1971. At the time of the interview, Pilonieta, of a more recent generation of Copeyanos, was the deputy director-general of the party's parliamentary group and secretary-general of COPEI in the state of Bolívar.
7. Interviews with Jesús Angel Paz Galarraga, 5 March 1971, and Raúl Leoni, 11 June 1971.
8. Interview with Miguel Angel Parada, 28 June 1971.
9. Interview with Carlos A. Gainxa M., 1 July 1971.
10. Interview with Rafael Montes de Oca, 18 March 1971. Montes de Oca was governor of Lara at the time.
11. Interview with Manuel Guanipa Matos, 26 May 1971. Besides holding the position of secretary-general, Guanipa Matos was a member of the state legislature.
12. Interview with Hilarión Cardozo, 10 December 1970.
13. *Christian Democratic Review*, vol. 4, no. 1, March 1954.
14. Interview with Pedro Grases, 6 March 1971.
15. Interview with Rodolfo José Cárdenas, 1 April 1971.
16. Interview with Valmore Acevedo Amaya, 19 February 1971.
17. Interview with Raúl Leoni, 11 June 1971.
18. Interview with Luis Beltrán Prieto Figueroa, 14 June 1971.
19. Interview with Enrique Pérez Olivares, 24 November 1970.
20. Samuel P. Huntington, *Political Order in Changing Societies*, p. 10.
21. See Winfield J. Burggraaff, *The Venezuelan Armed Forces*, pp. 141–51.
22. For a discussion of urban slum dwellers, see David Eugene Blank, *Politics in Venezuela*, pp. 68–70.

23. See Presidencia de la República, *Documentos que Hicieron Historia,* pp. 420–29.

24. See *Así se Fraguó la insurrección.*

25. Luis Herrera Campins, *Frente a 1958.*

26. Interview with Gonzalo Barrios, 16 November 1970.

27. *Gaceta Oficial de la República de Venezuela,* nos. 25 and 541, 20 December 1957.

28. *El Heraldo,* 10 December 1957.

29. See Burggraaff, *Venezuelan Armed Forces,* pp. 139–68, and Philip B. Taylor, Jr., *The Venezuelan Coup d'Etat of 1958.*

30. Robert J. Alexander, *Latin American Political Parties,* p. 344.

31. "Pacto suscrito por los Partidos Acción Democrática, Partido Social Cristiano COPEI y Unión Republicana Democrática," 31 October 1958.

32. "Declaración de Principios y Programa Mínimo de Gobierno," 6 December 1958.

33. Based on the analysis by Boris Bunimov Parra.

34. Daniel H. Levine, *Conflict and Political Change in Venezuela,* pp. 36–60.

35. For an analysis of the actions and fate of the Communist party of Venezuela in the unsuccessful guerrilla movement, see Robert J. Alexander, "The Impact of the Sino-Soviet Split on Latin American Communism," in Donald L. Herman, ed., *The Communist Tide in Latin America.*

36. Levine, *Conflict and Political Change,* p. 56.

37. *COPEI,* 8 January 1960. The party newspaper began publication shortly after the fall of Pérez Jiménez.

38. Interviews with Valmore Acevedo Amaya, 10 February 1971, and Jesús Angel Paz Galarraga, 5 March 1971.

39. Interview with Raúl Leoni, 11 June 1971.

40. Interview with Luis Beltrán Prieto Figueroa, 14 June 1971.

41. *COPEI,* 30 September 1960.

42. Ibid., 2 October 1959.

43. Ibid., 18 August 1961.

44. Interview with Bernardo Aranguren Marquina, 30 June 1971.

45. *COPEI,* 25 September 1959.

46. Interview with Manuel Guanipa Matos, 26 May 1971.

47. Publicly, URD left the coalition because of the government's attitude toward the Castro regime. Several years later, however, Jóvito Villalba of URD stated that his party had joined the coalition to break up what he considered to be the AD–COPEI alliance. See *El Universal,* 4 February 1971.

48. *COPEI,* 1 February 1963.

49. See Martz, *Acción Democrática,* pp. 108–9.

50. Interview with Gonzalo Barrios, 16 November 1970.

51. Interview with Miguel Angel Landáez, 28 October 1970.

52. Interview with José Luis Zapata, 8 March 1971.

53. Interview with Jesús Angel Paz Galarraga, 5 March 1971.

54. Interview with Abdón Vivas Terán, 24 May 1971. Vivas Terán has been a recognized leader of the JRC's left wing. At the time of our discussion, he was the director of the Corporación de Fomento (development). He was elected to the Chamber of Deputies in 1973.

55. Interview with Miguel Angel Parada, 28 June 1971.

56. Interview with Miguel Angel Gómez Bonilla, 28 May 1971. At the time of our discussion, Gómez Bonilla was the regional secretary of Acción Democrática in Zulia; he was also the former president of the legislative assembly and a deputy of that body.

57. Interview with Rafael Montes de Oca, 18 March 1971.

58. See Alexander, *Political Parties,* pp. 345–46.

59. *COPEI*, 30 August 1963.
60. Interview with Francisco Urquía Lugo, 5 May 1971. At the time of our conversation, Urquía Lugo was a member of the COPEI labor organization, the FTC. He was also secretary of organization of the main labor organization in the country, the CTV. Within COPEI, Urquía Lugo was deputy secretary-general for regional matters and represented the party as a deputy in the national Congress.
61. Interview with José Asunción Cárdenas, 28 June 1971. At the time of our conversation, Cárdenas was secretary of organization of the FTC in Táchira.
62. *COPEI*, 27 April 1962.
63. Ibid., 5 July 1963.
64. Alexander, *Political Parties*, p. 346.
65. For statistics of the 1963 election, see Institute for the Comparative Study of Political Systems, *The Venezuelan Elections of 1 December 1963*.
66. *COPEI*, 29 February 1964.
67. Interview with Raúl Leoni, 11 June 1971.
68. Interview with Jesús Angel Paz Galarraga, 5 March 1971.
69. Interview with Miguel Angel Landáez, 28 October 1970, and Valmore Acevedo Amaya, 10 February 1971.
70. See Alexander, *Political Parties*, p. 347.
71. *COPEI*, 29 February 1964, and Luis Herrera Campins, "La Campañas Doblan por la 'Ancha Base.'"
72. *El Nacional*, 12 and 23 November 1966.
73. Interview with Raúl Leoni, 11 June 1971.
74. Interview with Gonzalo Barrios, 16 November 1970.
75. Interview with Valmore Acevedo Amaya, 10 February 1971.
76. Alexander, *Political Parties*, pp. 347–48. I have respected the request of several Copeyanos to withhold their names.
77. Blank, *Politics in Venezuela*, pp. 159–61.
78. See *El Nacional*, "COPEI dice," 23 November 1966; *Documentos*, no. 27, October-December 1966.
79. *Documentos*, no. 34, July-September 1968.
80. Several interviews with Adecos and Copeyanos, 1970–71.
81. The Copeyanos requested that their names not be used.
82. Interview with Ramón Tenorio Sifontes, 22 April 1971. He was a major spokesman for URD and a member of the Chamber of Deputies at the time of our discussion.
83. David J. Myers, *Democratic Campaigning in Venezuela*, pp. 105–8.
84. Interview with José Luis Zapata, 8 March 1971.
85. Interview with Jesús Angel Paz Galarraga, 5 March 1971.
86. For data on the election, see República de Venezuela, Consejo Supremo Electoral, *Datos Estadísticos de las Votaciones de 1968*.
87. Alexander, *Political Parties*, pp. 349–51.

Chapter 4

1. The discussion of IFIDEC in Zulia is based on an interview with Lesbia Hernández Márquez, administrative secretary of IFIDEC in Zulia, 29 May 1971.
2. For the rules and regulations of a national convention—calling the convention, the sessions, elections and votes, resolutions, motions—see Partido Social Cristiano de Venezuela COPEI, "Reglamento Interno de las Convenciones Nacionales."

3. See the discussion by José Elías Rivera Oviedo, *Los Social Cristianos en Venezuela*, pp. 201–2. Also see the Appendix for a chart of the party's structure and organization.

4. Franklin Tugwell, "The Christian Democrats of Venezuela," *Journal of Inter-American Studies*, vol. 7, no. 2, p. 256.

5. Partido Socialcristiano COPEI, *Manual del Activista*, p. 44.

6. Among the various documents and reports, see "Reglamento Provisional del Comité Femenino Copeyano" (Seccional Táchira), 12 January 1949; "Carta Fundamental del Magisterio Social Cristiano de Venezuela," 4 October 1958; "Movimiento de Profesionales y Técnicos Copeyanos," *Seminario COPEI*, vol. 1, 3-10 February 1970; "El MEP Obtuvo 4 Cargos y COPEI 3 en Elecciones del Colegio Médico de Zulia," *El Nacional*, 2 March 1971; Publicación de la Secretaría Nacional de Organismos Profesionales del Partido Socialcristiano COPEI, "I Congreso Nacional de Profesionales y Técnicos de COPEI e Independientes Socialcristianos," 1963; "Triunfo de Ingenieros e Independientes de COPEI en Elecciones Universitarias," "COPEI dice," *El Nacional*, 18 May 1966.

7. *COPEI*, 16 February 1962.

8. See John Duncan Powell, *Political Mobilization of the Venezuelan Peasant*, pp. 184–90, 200–205.

9. "Entrevista con Teófilo Borregales, Secretario Nacional Agrario del MASC," *Seminario COPEI*, vol. 1, 21-27 August 1970.

10. Interview with Henry Mora Carrero, 16 June 1971. At the time of our discussion, Mora was a member of the state legislative assembly of Mérida and of the national directorate of MASC.

11. Interview with Manuel Alfredo Duplat Pulido, 8 July 1971. At the time of our discussion, Duplat was a deputy in Congress and a national director of MASC.

12. Interview with Henry Mora Carrero, 16 June 1971.

13. Interview with Nelson Marquez Pulido, 28 June 1971. At the time of the interview, Marquez was secretary-general of MASC in Táchira and a deputy in Congress.

14. Interview with Manuel Alfredo Duplat Pulido, 8 July 1971.

15. Ibid.

16. Interview with Pedro J. Linares, 16 June 1971. Linares, owner of a large farm in the state of Miranda, was working with FUNDECA. The discussion of ISER and FUNDECA is based on the interview.

17. FUNDECA, *Fundación para el Desarrollo Rural y la Educación Campesina*.

18. Interview with Manuel Alfredo Duplat Pulido, 8 July 1971.

19. Much of the following discussion is based on the excellent study by Ramón H. Silva T., *Introducción al Estudio del Sindicalismo Venezolano*.

20. Interview with Ramón Silva, 23 April 1971. Silva is a Copeyano, author, and professor at the Catholic University. He has held executive positions in various Christian labor organizations.

21. See *Frente*, January 1971. Some early FTC leaders included Elio Aponte, Antonio Barreto, José Camacho, Dagoberto González, Nelson Pinto Espinoza, and Francisco Urquía Lugo.

22. *El Gráfico*, 30 March 1950.

23. Interview with Ramón Silva, 23 April 1971.

24. *Semana*, 24-30 September 1970.

25. *Elite*, 30 October 1970.

26. Interview with Rubén Darío González, deputy secretary-general of the FTC, 6 May 1971.

27. Interview with Francisco Urquía Lugo, 5 May 1971.

28. Interview with Dagoberto González Ascanio, 18 June 1971.

29. The information on the Seventh CTV Congress was based on a letter I received from an anonymous source, dated 24 May 1976.

30. Interview with Dagoberto González Ascanio, 18 June 1971.

31. Following their successful efforts at the Sixth CTV Congress, the national AD-COPEI labor leadership proposed a pact to weaken MEP at the forthcoming convention of the Zulia CTV affiliate, Fetrazulia. The COPEI labor leader in the state, Alí Moncayo, opposed the suggested pact because he wanted to be assured of the presidency of Fetrazulia; furthermore, he believed that COPEI representation on the executive council of Fetrazulia should be greater than that which was proposed. In the end, Moncayo and his followers accepted the formula of the AD-COPEI CTV leadership. Interview with Guillermo Montiel, secretary of organization of the FTC of Zulia, 27 May 1971.

32. CODESA, *Estatutos de la Confederación de Sindicatos Autónomos de Venezuela.*

33. Interview with Dagoberto González Ascanio, 18 June 1971.

34. Interview with Rubén Darío González, 6 May 1971.

35. Luis Herrera Campins and Dagoberto González, "El 'Informe Confidencial.' "

36. Instituto Nacional de Estudios Sociales, *La Organización Sindical*; also *La Formación de Dirigentes Sindicales Cristianos de Venezuela.*

37. *Frente* (FTC newspaper), 1 May 1971.

38. Dagoberto González and José Rodríguez S., "La Situación Sindical," p. 24.

39. Ibid. Also see the interview with Dagoberto González, *El Nacional*, 10 January 1971.

40. Although the FTC was answerable to COPEI, the labor group periodically had its own fund-raising drives. One such effort asked the workers to donate a day's salary to the FTC: Frente de Trabajadores Copeyanos, Secretaría Nacional de Organización, "Il Campaña Sindical Financiera 1971," 10 June 1971.

41. See two mimeographed documents: Asamblea Nacional del Frente de Trabajadores Copeyanos, FTC, "Tesis de Formación Sindical"; 4a Asamblea Nacional del Frente de Trabajadores Copeyanos, "Tesis Política."

42. Interview with Francisco Urquía Lugo, 5 May 1971.

43. Interview with Rubén Darío González, 6 May 1971.

44. Dagoberto González expressed this view in *Seminario COPEI*, 3-10 February 1970.

45. Comisión Organizadora de la 5a Asamblea Nacional del FTC, "5a Asamblea Nacional del Frente de Trabajadores Copeyanos."

46. Interview with Rubén Darío González, 6 May 1971.

47. Interview with Guillermo Montiel, secretary of organization of the FTC of Zulia, 27 May 1971.

48. Interview with José Asunción Cárdenas, secretary of organization of the FTC of Táchira, 28 June 1971.

49. Comité Nacional de COPEI, "Reglamento Orgánico de la Juventud Revolucionaria Copeyana."

50. *COPEI*, 27 February 1948.

51. El Comité Juvenil de COPEI del Táchira, "El Comité Juvenil de COPEI protesta públicamente contra las calumniosas aseveraciones de 'Fronteras,' " 1947. Also see Juventud Revolucionaria Copeyana, "Comunicado de la Fracción Universitaria de COPEI al Estudiantado," 1949.

52. *El Gráfico*, 2 February 1949.

53. Letter from Rafael Caldera to Sr. Br., Francisco Sánchez Carrillo, Caracas, 15 May 1950.

54. Based on interviews with two former student leaders who were

secretaries-general of the JRC: Julio César Moreno, 15 May 1971, and Abdón Vivas Terán, 24 May 1971.

55. Leo B. Lott, *Venezuela and Paraguay: Political Modernity and Tradition in Conflict*, p. 268.

56. Regardless of JRC-COPEI friction, support of the strike and other JRC tactics resulted in greater Christian Democratic influence in the universities. COPEI claimed 34 percent of the total vote in the 1964 student election, compared with PCV's 25 percent, MIR's 21 percent, and AD's 11 percent. Among secondary school students, AD claimed second place: PCV/MIR, 41 percent; AD, 33 percent; COPEI, 11 percent. COPEI was not yet as strongly organized in the secondary schools as in the universities. See Claudio Veliz, ed., *The Politics of Conformity in Latin America*, p. 148.

57. Interview with Delfín Sánchez, 11 May 1971. At the time of our discussion he was a functionary in the ministry of public works.

58. Delfín Sánchez F., "Un Programa para la Juventud," Macarao, 4 April 1970.

59. Interview with Julio César Moreno, 15 May 1971.

60. Much of this information is based on an interview with Abdón Vivas Terán, 24 May 1971.

61. These have been compiled by Tarsicio Ocampo V., *Venezuela 'Astronautas' de COPEI 1965–1967*.

62. Rafael Caldera discussed the subject in his *Ideario—La Democracia Cristiana en América Latina*, pp. 142–56.

63. *Documentos*, no. 29, April-June 1967, "Documento de Sectores 'Astronautas' y 'Avanzados' del COPEI." It appeared as a confidential document and was circulated at the Tenth National Convention of COPEI.

64. E.g., see JRC, "Una Mística para el Cambio."

65. Interview with Delfín Sánchez, 11 May 1971.

66. Interview with Julio César Moreno, 15 May 1971.

67. Interview with Abdón Vivas Terán, 24 May 1971. Also see Vivas Terán's "La Alternativa Ideológica," which originally appeared in *Summa*, May 1971.

68. See *Momento*, 19 June 1966.

69. Information on the television program was based on the interview with Abdón Vivas Terán, 24 May 1971. Also see the compilation by Tarsicio Ocampo V.

70. *El Nacional*, 26 November and 3 December 1966.

71. According to *Documentos*, April-June 1967, January-March 1968, April-June 1968, the expulsions and suspensions continued unabated. In June 1967, for example, three university directors—Rafael Iribarren, Oliver Belisario, and Saúl Rivas Rivas—were accused of factionalism and lack of discipline. They refused to appear before the National Directory because they considered it dominated by the rightist forces of the party. Other disciplinary action was taken in Táchira, Zulia, Carabobo, and Falcón.

72. *El Nacional*, 14 and 19 May 1970.

73. Interview with Delfín Sánchez, 11 May 1971.

74. Interview with Julio César Moreno, 15 May 1971.

75. *Semana*, 26 November and 2 December 1970.

76. Ibid. See also *Daily Journal*, 2 September 1970; *El Nacional*, 2 December 1970; *Bohemia*, 30 November-6 December 1970.

77. Although not as much as in 1965-70, the party continued to take disciplinary action against certain JRC members. For example, the party expelled two Astronautas, Carlos Eduardo Febres and Gustavo Cegarra Mesa, and cautioned seven others. The expelled men classified Lorenzo Fernández, COPEI's presidential candidate, as right wing and said they

intended to work toward socialism within one of the existing left-wing parties. *Latin America*, 1 December 1972.

78. *El Nacional*, 23 March 1970.

79. Interview with Jesús Indalicio Guerrero, secretary-general of the JRC of Mérida, 30 June 1971.

80. Interview with eight JRC members, from the *liceos* to the high schools, Zulia, 26 May 1971.

81. Vivas Terán received a great deal of media exposure during that period; e.g., Abdón Vivas Terán, "El Grito Juvenil Copeyano," *Summa*, May 1971.

82. The information on the Seventh Convention of the JRC was in a letter I received from a JRC member, Beltrán Navarro, dated 18 March 1976. Sr. Navarro is a student at Indiana University in Bloomington, Indiana.

83. See the account in *El Nacional*, 8 April 1967.

84. Interview with an anonymous Copeyano, 27 October 1970.

85. *Panorama Democrática Cristiana*, no. 15, August-October 1969.

86. The discussion of the national secretary of organization is based on interviews with several Copeyanos and an article in the magazine *Semana*, 22-29 October 1970. The Copeyanos said that the article was accurate.

87. Much of this information is based on correspondence with Copeyanos and discussions with colleagues.

88. See *Latin America*, 9 January and 20 February 1976.

89. An anonymous source provided the following political makeup of the National Committee. The name of each Herrera Campins supporter has an asterisk (*). The names of the Caldera supporters are unchecked, and Beaujon (X) is considered to be apart from both camps. Some members of the Generation of 1936 now support Herrera. The breakdown (February 1977) shows Herrera, eleven; Caldera, eight; Beaujon, one (himself). Officers: president, Pedro Del Corral; first vice-president, * Godofredo González; second vice-president, * José Antonio Pérez Díaz; third vice-president, Arístides Calvani; fourth vice-president, * Rafael León León; secretary-general, * Pedro Pablo Aguilar. Committee members: * Luis Herrera Campins, Eduardo Fernández, Oswaldo Alvarez Paz, * Abdón Vivas Terán, * José Rodríguez Saez, * Juan José Rachadell, Hilarión Cardozo, * Luis Enrique Oberto, * Rafael Montes de Oca, * Julio César Moreno. Permanent members: Rafael Caldera, Lorenzo Fernández, Edecio La Riva Araujo, X Arístides Beaujon.

90. Interview with Johnny Díaz Apitz, national secretary of organization of the FTC, 21 March 1974.

91. Interview with William Franco, president of CODESA, 20 March 1974.

92. William Franco, "Poder Social," document presented to the National Committee of COPEI on 19 March 1974.

93. Interview with Ramón Guillermo Aveledo, secretary of the parliamentary group of COPEI, 22 March 1974.

94. *Latin America*, 12 December 1975.

95. Based on the letter from Beltrán Navarro, 18 March 1976.

Chapter 5

1. In 1960, Jorge Dager, Domingo Alberto Rangel, and others left AD to form the MIR (Revolutionary Movement of the Left). In 1962, Dager left the MIR and formed the FDP (Popular Democratic Forces).

2. Luis Herrera Campins, *Un Año de Esfuerzos para el Cambio*, p. 6.

3. Mobil Oil Company of Venezuela, *Special Report to Management*.

4. *Seminario COPEI*, vol. 1, no. 12, 18 March 1970.
5. Interview with Jesús Angel Paz Galarraga, 5 March 1971.
6. Publicaciones de Acción Democrática, *Democracia y Extremismo: 2 Entrevistas con Carlos Andrés Pérez*, p. 15.
7. *El Nacional*, 21 February 1974.
8. Ibid., 8 March 1971.
9. Herrera Campins, *Un Año de Esfuerzos*, p. 10.
10. While he was associated with the *Daily Journal* of Caracas, Clem Cohen wrote a series of short articles entitled "Afterthoughts." Some of the information in this chapter, such as that concerning the AD meeting, appeared in those articles.
11. The administrative reforms of Governor Guillermo Alvarez Bajares, tending toward streamlining the administration and the bureaucracy, were defeated in the state legislature by the combined vote of AD, MEP, and URD.
12. Interview with Rafael Guerra Ramos, 20 March 1974. Guerra Ramos is a member of the Movimiento al Socialismo (MAS), a relatively new political party that split from the Communist party of Venezuela (PCV). At the time of our discussion, he was a member of the Chamber of Deputies and director of the MAS parliamentary group.
13. Interview with Armando Sánchez Bueno, 29 June 1971. Sánchez Bueno has been active in Acción Democrática for many years. During the Caldera administration he was a member of the Chamber of Deputies, president of the Comisión de Contraloría (comptroller), and political secretary of AD. In 1974 President Carlos Andrés Pérez appointed him to the cabinet as minister of communications. In 1975 he became minister of justice.
14. Interview with Eduardo Fernández, 26 March 1974. Fernández became active in COPEI in 1958. Rising through the ranks, he was deputy secretary-general of the presidency under President Caldera. After the 1973 election he became deputy secretary-general of COPEI and director of the parliamentary group.
15. Interview with Padre José Ignacio Arneta and Padre Martínez Galdeano, "Centro Gumilla," 22 June 1971.
16. Interview with Padre Martínez Galdeano, Centro Gumilla, 22 October 1970. A priest from Spain, Padre Martínez had been in Venezuela for seven years.
17. Interview with Miguel Angel Parada, 28 June 1971.
18. Interview with Carlos A. Gainxa M., 1 July 1971.
19. Interview with Padre Mauro Barrenechea, S.J., Centro Gumilla, 9 June 1971. In the state budgets of Mérida and Táchira, funds for private Catholic schools appeared in the same list with funds for public schools. E.g., the Táchira budget included the following under Distrito Cárdenas: Seminario Diocensano "Santo Tomás de Aquino" Palmira, Colegio "Padre Frias," Escuela Privada Mons. Arias Blance La Florida. See *Gaceta Oficial del Estado Táchira*, "Ley de Presupuesto para el Ejercicio Fiscal 1971" (Número Extraordinario), and *Gaceta Oficial del Estado Mérida*, "Ley de Presupuesto de Ingresos y Gastos Públicos del Estado, Año Fiscal 1971."
20. A collection of newspaper reports, letters, and various documents concerning the incident can be found in William Ford, *Wuytack: El Cura que Faltó a la Ley*.
21. The discussion of Opus Dei is based on several interviews. The Copeyanos asked to remain anonymous. Also see the article in *Momento*, 3 January 1971.
22. Interview with Armando Sánchez Bueno, 29 June 1971.
23. For an exposition of his ideas concerning church-state relations, see José Rodríguez Iturbe, *Iglesia y Estado en Venezuela (1824–64)*.

24. Interview with Anly Luis Chong León, 28 May 1971. At the time of our conversation, Chong León was a member of the Comando Juvenil of MEP in Zulia. He stated that he was also a member of Peace and Justice, which he described as the left-wing equivalent of Opus Dei.

25. Interview with Luis Beltrán Prieto Figueroa, 14 June 1971. Many of his numerous publications deal directly with educational questions; others treat various topics, but even there we see the incorporation of his views concerning educational matters; e.g., see Louis Beltrán Prieto Figueroa, ¡*Joven, Empinate*! and *La Política y los Hombres*.

26. Frank Bonilla, *The Failure of Elites*, pp. 27, 50–51, 78–79.

27. Interviews with Ramón Tenorio Sifontes (URD), 22 April 1971, and Luis Beltrán Prieto Figueroa (MEP), 14 June 1971. Also see the article by former Senator Miguel A. Capriles, who broke with the Caldera government, in *Crítica*, 28 May 1971.

28. Myers, *Democratic Campaigning*, pp. 109, 118.

29. See the article in *Elite*, 14 May 1971.

30. Based on interviews with various military officers, priests, bureaucrats, and politicians.

31. Interview with Luis Beltrán Prieto Figueroa, 14 June 1971.

32. See David Eugene Blank, *Politics in Venezuela*, pp. 170–71.

33. Ibid.

34. Interview with President Rafael Caldera, Miraflores, 13 June 1971.

35. This information is based on my discussion with a bureaucrat who served in various administrations from Pérez Jiménez to Caldera.

36. Interview with Armando Acosta, secretario agrario (agrarian secretary) of COPEI in Lara, 20 March 1971.

37. Interview with Pablo Pérez González, 20 March 1971. He was responsible for political education.

38. Interview, 20 March 1971. He is a long-time resident of Lara.

39. *El Nacional*, 22 March 1969.

40. See Kenneth F. Johnson and María Mercedes Fuentes, *Política de Poder y Participación Política en América Latina*, pp. 87–89.

41. See the detailed account in *Semana*, 5-11 November 1970.

42. Johnson and Mercedes Fuentes, *Política de Poder*, p. 89. Italics in original.

43. *El Nacional*, 1 March 1969.

44. *Times of the Americas*, 3 May 1972.

45. See *El Nacional* and *El Universal*, 30 December 1970.

46. Daniel H. Levine, *Conflict and Political Change in Venezuela*, p. 198.

47. From approximately 21 October 1970 to the end of the year, various newspapers and magazines covered the events. See *El Nacional, El Universal, Daily Journal, Times of the Americas, Momento*.

48. See *Times of the Americas*, 3 May 1972, and *Latin America*, 23 May 1973.

49. Actually President Leoni had legalized the Communist party under the name Unión Para Avanzar. President Caldera allowed it to use its real name, Partido Comunista de Venezuela.

50. For information on the pacification program, see *Latin American Digest*, September 1969; *Ultimas Noticias*, 12 August 1969; *Times of the Americas*, 24 June 1970; *Latin American Digest*, March 1970; *El Nacional*, 20 January 1970; *Current History*, January 1974.

51. Interview with Governor Rafael Montes de Oca, 18 March 1971.

52. Interview, 20 March 1971.

53. Interview with Ramón Echegaray, 27 March 1974. At the time of our conversation, Echegaray represented the Popular Democratic Force (Fuerza Democrática Popular or FDP) in the Chamber of Deputies.

54. See *El Nacional*, 30 March 1973.

55. Interview, 30 March 1974.
56. Interview with Eduardo Fernández, 26 March 1974.
57. See Leo B. Lott, *Venezuela and Paraguay*, pp. 306–10.

Chapter 6

1. Interview, 12 March 1971. He asked to remain anonymous.
2. See the article by the FND deputy Pedro Segnini La Cruz, "Quién Gobierna Aquí?", *El Nacional*, 27 November 1970.
3. Interview with Armando Sánchez Bueno, 29 June 1971.
4. Interview with Luis Herrera Campins, 16 March 1971.
5. See Clem Cohen "Afterthoughts," *Daily Journal*, 19 February, 2, 3 and 10 March 1971.
6. *New York Times*, 25 January 1971.
7. See *Daily Journal*, 6 January and 2 May 1971.
8. Also see José Antonio Mayobre, *Las Inversiones Extranjeras en Venezuela*.
9. Based on a discussion in Mobil Oil Company of Venezuela, *Special Report to Management*.
10. Clem Cohen, "Afterthoughts," *Daily Journal*, 13 February 1971.
11. Interview with Radamés Larrazábal, 16 April 1971.
12. Interview with Ramón Tenorio Sifontes, 22 April 1971.
13. Interviews with various Copeyanos including José Luis Zapata, 8 March 1971, and Valmore Acevedo Amaya, 10 February 1971.
14. Franklin Tugwell, "Petroleum Policy," paper delivered to the Latin American Studies Association annual meeting, San Francisco, November 1974.
15. Interview with Pedro Pablo Aguilar, 27 October 1970. An active militant for many years, Pedro Aguilar was a member of the National Committee and leader of the COPEI parliamentary group in the Chamber of Deputies. He was subsequently elected secretary-general of the party.
16. See *New York Times*, 26 January 1970.
17. See Leo B. Lott, *Venezuela and Paraguay*, pp. 309–10.
18. *Daily Journal*, 4 October 1970.
19. See *New York Times*, 21 February 1970.
20. Mobil Oil Company, *Special Report*.
21. *New York Times*, 2 June 1970.
22. Quoted in *Times of the Americas*, 10 June 1970.
23. *New York Times*, 18 June 1970.
24. Mobil Oil Company, *Special Report*.
25. *Seminario COPEI*, 9 December 1970.
26. Interview with Ramón Echegaray, 27 March 1974.
27. Various newspapers covered the debates extensively. See *El Nacional, El Universal*, and *Daily Journal*, 15-30 December 1970.
28. Tugwell, "Petroleum Policy," p. 7.
29. Quoted in Mobil Oil Company, *Special Report*.
30. Ibid.
31. Oficina Central de Información/OCI, "En la Instalación de la Federación Latinoamericana y del Caribe de Asociaciones de Exportadores," *Metas de Venezuela*, vol. 4, pp. 415–16.
32. These developments were reported by the *Daily Journal*, 29 December 1970 and 4 February 1971.
33. George W. Grayson, "Venezuela's Presidential Politics," *Current History*, January 1974, p. 26.
34. Tugwell, "Petroleum Policy," p. 8.
35. Interview with Paul T. Green, 4 July 1971. After receiving his doc-

torate in economics from Columbia University, Dr. Green accepted a position as an economist in the treasury department of Creole Petroleum Corporation.

36. Quoted in *Daily Journal*, 23 June 1971.

37. *Latin America*, 30 June 1972.

38. Tugwell, "Petroleum Policy," p. 8.

39. Interview, 21 June 1971. He asked to remain anonymous.

40. The administration's investment plans for the additional income received harsh treatment in the Chamber of Deputies. Besides accusing the administration of electioneering and demagoguery, AD's Armando Sánchez Bueno stated that "COPEI still continued thinking with the totalitarian and fascist ideology that characterized its birth in 1936." See *El Nacional*, 21 May 1971.

41. Interview with Alvaro Rodríguez R., 21 March 1974. Rodríguez was the advisor for planning and the development of personnel for Mobil Oil Company.

42. Interview, 19 March 1974. He asked to remain anonymous.

43. Published in the Official Gazette, Extraordinary Issue no. 1, 591, 22 June 1973.

44. *Latin America Economic Report*, 22 February 1974.

Chapter 7

1. Luis Herrera Campins, *Un Año de Esfuerzos para el Cambio*. For a detailed explanation of the administration's programs, see *Programa de Gobierno de Rafael Caldera, Presidente de Venezuela, 1969–1974*.

2. Partido Social Cristiano (COPEI), "COPEI 25 Años."

3. "El V Mensaje del Presidente Rafael Caldera," *Resumen*, 17 March 1974.

4. *Seminario COPEI*, 16-22 December 1969.

5. Interview with Gonzalo Barrios, 16 November 1970.

6. *Daily Journal*, 18 May 1971.

7. Interviews with Valmore Acevedo Amaya, 10 February 1971, and Eduardo Fernández, 26 March 1974.

8. Two very good books on the barrios are Lisa Redfield Peattie, *The View from the Barrio*, and Talton F. Ray, *The Politics of the Barrios of Venezuela*.

9. *Seminario COPEI*, 28 April 1971.

10. Oficina Central de Información/OCI, *Cuenta Ante El País*, 1971.

11. José Curiel, "Interconexión Fluvial en el Hinterland Sudamericano," *Pueblo Unido*, p. 16.

12. Interview with two Mepistas Jesús Sebastiani and Anly Luis Chong León, 28 May 1971. Sebastiani was a director of the Maracaibo district of MEP.

13. Interview with several Adecos, 28 May 1971. The principal spokesman was Miguel Angel Gómez Bonilla, regional secretary of AD in Zulia, a deputy of the legislative assembly, and former president of the assembly. Others included Br. Pablo Pérez Herrera, responsable de la fracción universitaria; Br. Reina Beatriz Josefina Avila F., fracción feminina; Br. Alberto Pinedo, secretario juvenil regional, and Ing. Augusto Ibarra, a visitor from the state of Lara and associated with that state's Instituto Politécnico Superior.

14. Interview with Governor Hilarión Cardozo, 27 May 1971.

15. Interview with Manuel Guanipa Matos, 26 May 1971.

16. Interview with José Asunción Cárdenas, secretary of organization of

the FTC of Táchira, and Miguel Angel Parada, a founder of COPEI in the state, 28 June 1971.

17. Interview with Governor German Briceño Ferrigni, 1 July 1971.
18. Interview with Jesús Indalicio Guerrero, secretary-general of the JRC of Mérida, 30 June 1971.
19. Interview with Bernardo Aranguren Marquina, political secretary and deputy secretary-general of AD in Mérida, 30 June 1971.
20. Interview with Reinaldo Vásquez Sebira, secretary-general of CODESA (Committee of Autonomous Trade Unions) and deputy in the Lara legislative assembly, 20 March 1971.
21. Interview with Governor Rafael Montes de Oca, 18 March 1971.
22. Interview with Dr. Carlos Zapata, a physician and long-time member of the Barquisimeto city council, 19 March 1971.
23. Interview with a local priest, 20 March 1971. He asked to remain anonymous.
24. I presented a version of this section at the International Studies Association annual meeting, Toronto, 29 February 1976.
25. Arístides Calvani, "Una Paz Compartida y Solidaria."
26. See the article by Demetrio Boersner, "Venezuela y el Colonialismo," *Summa*, March 1971.
27. Cited by Rafael Caldera, *El Bloque Latinoamericano*, p. 166.
28. Cited by Hilarión Cardozo, national youth secretary of COPEI, "Letter to President John F. Kennedy," 1961.
29. Ibid.
30. "Estructuras Económicas y Sociales Según la Democracia Cristiana," 1961.
31. Godofredo González, "Contra Los Desequilibrios Económicos," 1964.
32. Oficina Central de Información/OCI, "Ante el Cuerpo Diplomático luego de tomar posesión del cargo," *Metas de Venezuela*, 1969.
33. Interview with Foreign Minister Arístides Calvani, 7 July 1971.
34. *Programa de Gobierno*, p. 276.
35. Interview, 7 July 1971.
36. See Caldera, *El Bloque Latinoamericano*.
37. Rafael Caldera, *Justicia Social Internacional y Nacionalismo Latinoamericano*, p. 140.
38. Rafael Caldera, *La Solidaridad Pluralista de América Latina*, pp. 6, 81, 169, 191, 194–95.
39. Cardozo, "Letter to President John F. Kennedy."
40. "Discurso Inaugural del Presidente Caldera," *Documentos*, p. 264.
41. *Programa de Gobierno*, p. 276.
42. *Semana*, 4-10 February 1971.
43. Interview with Pedro Pablo Aguilar, 27 October 1970.
44. *Programa de Gobierno*, p. 277.
45. *Alliance for Progress Weekly Newsletter*, 6 August 1971.
46. Interview with Eduardo Fernández, 26 March 1974. Also see George W. Grayson, "Venezuela's Presidential Politics," *Current History*, January 1974, p. 27.
47. "Caldera . . . was especially apprehensive about Brazil's growing presence on the southern border. Believing that Venezuela must either begin developing its frontier lands along the Brazilian border or run the risk of incrementally losing control over them, President Caldera created the Southern Development Commission (CONDESUR). Reporting directly to the President's trusted minister of public works, CONDESUR focused on developing an infrastructure that would tie the frontier with Brazil into Venezuela's heartland. . . . Colonization of the South was a second important CONDESUR priority. . . ." See David J. Myers, "Frontier Settlement

264 *Notes to Pages 179–91*

Policy in Brazil," paper presented to the International Studies Association annual meeting, Toronto, 25 February 1976.

48. "Discurso Inaugural del Presidente Caldera," pp. 264–65.

49. See *Latin America*, 22 September 1972.

50. The foreign investment code (Decision 24) required that all foreign companies wishing to invest in the common market agree to a majority local ownership, to take effect within fifteen years in the case of Chile, Colombia, and Peru, and within twenty years in the case of Bolivia and Ecuador. The code also placed a general limit of 14 percent (raised to 20 percent in 1976) of investment on repatriation of profits. What caused resentment, especially among Colombian and Venezuelan businessmen, was the rule barring any new direct foreign investment in certain sectors, notably commercial banking, insurance, domestic transport, telecommunications, newspapers, and broadcasting. The Colombian and Venezuelan private business sectors argued that the resultant loss of foreign investments could not be replaced by internal resources, and that a high overall investment level was vital to national development. In the case of Venezuela, however, the banking law and other recently passed legislation weakened this argument.

51. See *Latin America*, 5 May 1972.

52. Article in the monthly *Bolsa Review* quoted in the *Alliance for Progress Weekly Newsletter*, 2 July 1973.

53. Ibid.

54. Such statements appear in Cardozo, "Letter to President John F. Kennedy."

55. Oficina Central de Información/OCI, "En el Congreso de los Estados Unidos de América," *Metas de Venezuela*, 1971, p. 247.

56. Herrera Campins, *Un Año de Esfuerzos*, pp. 18–20.

57. Interview with Pedro Pablo Aguilar, 27 October 1970.

58. See Clem Cohen, "Afterthoughts," *Daily Journal*, 23 March 1971, and *Summa*, April 1971.

59. Grayson, "Venezuela's Presidential Politics," pp. 39–40.

60. Interview with Foreign Minister Arístides Calvani, 7 July 1971.

61. For the text of the agreement, see *El Nacional*, 8 January 1971.

62. Oficina Central de Información/OCI, *Venezuela en 1969*, pp. 233–35; *Venezuela en 1971*, pp. 64–65.

63. Oficina Central de Información/OCI, *Cuenta Ante El País*, 1973, p. 71.

64. See the analysis in *Latin America*, 12 May 1972.

65. *OAS Weekly Newsletter*, 25 February 1974.

66. *Latin America*, 1 March 1974.

67. See *Programa de Gobierno*, p. 276; *Metas de Venezuela*, Primer Año de Gobierno, p. 607, and Segundo Año de Gobierno, pp. 236–37; *Habla El Presidente*, 1972, p. 156.

68. *Vision Letter*, 12 July 1973.

69. Ibid.

70. Norman Gall, "Los Indocumentados Colombianos," p. 6. I have relied on Mr. Gall's excellent study for much of the factual material on the *indocumentados*.

71. Ibid., p. 7.

72. Valmore Acevedo, "Frente a una Política de Mutuo Recelo," *El Nacional*, 22 February 1971. Venezuelans who participated in the discussions were Valmore Acevedo (then a COPEI federal deputy from the state of Táchira), Carlos Andrés Pérez of AD, and General Martín García Villasmil.

73. The president's remarks were summarized in *Daily Journal*, 29 December 1970 and 29 January 1971.

74. Interview with Foreign Minister Arístides Calvani, 7 July 1971.
75. Gall, "Indocumentados," pp. 15–16. For an in-depth study, see Rubén Carpio Castillo, *El Golfo de Venezuela*.
76. *Elite*, 29 January 1971.
77. "Declaración de Sochagota," *Documentos*, 1969, pp. 87–90; *Venezuela en 1969*, p. 235; *Cuenta ante el País*, 1973, p. 72.
78. See *Latin America*, 27 April 1973.
79. See the excellent study by Leslie B. Rout, Jr., *Which Way Out?*
80. *Programa de Gobierno*, p. 277.
81. Oficina Central de Información/OCI, *Venezuela en 1970*, p. 275.
82. See Rout, *Which Way Out?*, pp. 102–10.
83. Interview with Foreign Minister Arístides Calvani, 7 July 1971.
84. *Times of the Americas*, 28 May 1975.
85. Hans J. Morgenthau, *Politics among Nations*, p. 46.
86. See *Latin America*, 11 January 1974, and *Latin American Report*, January 1974.
87. *Latin America Economic Report*, 25 January 1974.
88. Interview with Rodolfo José Cárdenas, 1 April 1971. A party activist of many years' standing, Rodolfo Cárdenas was the head of the Oficina Central de Información/OCI at the time of our discussion.
89. Interview with Flavio Granados Pomento, 28 June 1971. At the time of our discussion he was a lawyer, secretary of the Democracia Cristiana Universitaria, and an assessor of the party's labor organization, the FTC.
90. Interview with Abdón Vivas Terán, 24 May 1971.
91. Interview, 12 March 1971. He asked to remain anonymous.
92. *Semana*, 14-20 March 1974, and *Resumen*, 17 March 1974.
93. Interview with President Rafael Caldera, 13 July 1971.
94. *Latin America*, 27 July 1973.
95. Interview.
96. President Caldera said, "It might have seemed like anarchy but actually it was good for democracy."
97. *Latin America*, 19 May 1972, and *Times of the Americas*, 4 October 1972.
98. Inter-American Development Bank, *Economic and Social Progress in Latin America*, pp. 427–33.
99. Kenneth F. Johnson and María Mercedes Fuentes, *Política de Poder y Participación Política en América Latina*, p. 98.

Chapter 8

1. Interview with Dagoberto González Ascanio, 18 June 1971.
2. Interview with Julio César Moreno, 15 May 1971.
3. *Semana*, 12/18 August 1971.
4. Ibid., 16/22 and 23/29 March 1972.
5. Interview with a Copeyano militant, 21 March 1974. He asked to remain anonymous. Also see *El Nacional*, 22 April 1972.
6. See Robert J. Alexander, "Venezuela's 'New Force' Broken," *Hemispherica*, December 1972.
7. *Daily Journal*, 8 June 1973.
8. See *Ultimas Noticias*, 19 April 1973, and *Daily Journal*, 22 June 1973.
9. See *Latin American Report*, September 1973; *Latin America*, 28 September 1973; *Times of the Americas*, 17 October 1973.
10. Consejo Supremo Electoral, *Memoria y Cuenta 1974*.
11. *Latin American Report*, December 1973; interview with an anonymous Adeco, very active in the campaign, 20 March 1974; interview with

the late José Elías Rivera Oviedo, a young COPEI militant, 25 March 1974; interview with Hilarión Cardozo, 27 March 1974; José A. Lazcano, "Reflexiones Post-Electorales," *SIC*, January 1974.

12. Interview with Jesús Angel Paz Galarraga, 26 March 1974.

13. "Exposición que sobre la situación post-electoral presentan Pedro Paúl Bello y Pedro Raúl Villasmil Soules a la consideración del Comité Nacional y del Directorio Nacional de COPEI," *Revista Elite*, 22 March 1974.

14. Interview with Miguel Toro, assistant to the deputy secretary-general of COPEI, 26 March 1974. Conflicts also arose between the *oficialistas*, *herreristas*, and *beaujonistas* during the process of constituting the party's legislative and municipal *planchas* or lists. John D. Martz and Enrique A. Baloyra, *Electoral Mobilization and Public Opinion: The Venezuelan Campaign of 1973*, pp. 86–87.

15. Interview with Hilarión Cardozo, 27 March 1974.

16. *Christian Science Monitor*, 16 May 1974.

17. See *Latin America Economic Report*, 25 February 1977.

18. For the text of the COPEI bill, see *Daily Journal*, 23 March 1974.

19. See *Latin America*, 21 March 1975.

20. See John D. Martz, "Policy-Making and the Quest for Consensus: Nationalizing Venezuelan Petroleum," *Journal of Interamerican Studies and World Affairs*, November 1977.

21. Interview with Eduardo Fernández, 26 March 1974.

22. Radio program from the University of Texas, "Latin American Review," 21 May 1975.

23. Paris, AFP in Spanish, 8 August 1975.

24. See *Latin American Report*, May 1974.

25. *Vision Letter*, 30 June 1975.

26. *Times of the Americas*, 28 April 1976.

27. See *Latin America*, 30 August 1974, 14 and 28 May 1976; *Times of the Americas*, 29 October and 10 December 1975.

28. *Daily Journal*, 19 January 1977.

29. In the 1975 Congress, Gonzalo Barrios of AD was elected president of the Senate and Oswaldo Alvarez Paz of COPEI was elected president of the Chamber of Deputies. AD and COPEI refused to give MAS any vice-presidencies. The AD-COPEI congressional presidents and vice-presidents were reelected in 1976, 1977, and 1978. See *El Nacional*, 25 February 1977, and *El Universal*, 3 March 1978.

30. According to a report in *Latin America*, 15 October 1976, Betancourt and Caldera had a meeting in September. They were said to have discussed six points: when to start the 1978 election; whether the government's plan to raise the current level of public debt, about $3,250 million, to above $10,000 million was excessive; the Niehous kidnapping and its ramifications; the agricultural crisis; corruption in government; and municipal reform. Both parties were expected to support bills dealing with the electoral law, corruption in government, and municipal reform.

31. For a more complete analysis of the 1978 election and the role of COPEI, see my chapter on the party in Howard R. Penniman, ed., *Venezuela at the Polls*.

32. Rodolfo José Cárdenas, "La difícil elección de Acción Democrática," *Resumen*, 24 October 1976.

33. *Keesing's Contemporary Archives*, 6 January 1978.

34. *ZETA*, 28 August 1977.

35. See *El Nacional*, 19 April 1978; "Focus on Venezuela—1978," *International Herald Tribune*, June 1978.

36. *Venezuela Special Report*, a supplement to *LAER*, January 1978. Also see *International Herald Tribune*, June 1978.

37. See *El Nacional,* 5 July 1977; *El Universal,* 7 March 1977, 19 February 1978.
38. *Latin American Political Report,* 27 January 1978.
39. Interview with Hilarión Cardozo, 15 December 1978. During the 1978 campaign, Cardozo represented COPEI on the Supreme Electoral Council and was also the party coordinator of political analysis and national strategy. As a result of the election, he won a seat for the Senate from the state of Zulia.
40. Interview with Pedro Pablo Aguilar, 15 December 1978.
41. Interview with Asdrubal Aguiar Aranguren, 13 December 1978. Aguiar Aranguren is a lawyer and a professor of international law at the Catholic University. During the campaign, he worked with COPEI's electoral committee as the deputy director of the office of the presidential candidate.
42. Interview with Alejandro Alfonzo, 16 December 1978. He is the director of Conciencia 21, a private institute of social research.
43. *Resumen,* 28 May 1978.
44. Interview with Jesús Angel Paz Galarraga, 11 December 1978.
45. See *El Nacional,* 20 October 1978.
46. Ramón Adolfo Illarramendy, "Hacia la Democracia de Participación," *Nueva Política,* January-March 1972.
47. Interview with Pedro Méndez Mora, 14 December 1978. Méndez works with COPEI's national secretary of formation, teaching party militants to understand better the ideological components of Christian Democracy.
48. See Partido Socialcristiano COPEI, "Mi Compromiso con Venezuela," *Programa de Gobierno . . . 1979–83*; Alfredo Peña, *Conversaciones con Luis Herrera Campins.*
49. Interviews with Arturo Fremont and Freddy Valera, 14 December 1978. Both are political directors of MAS. Fremont is a metallurgical trade union director and a member of the MAS National Directory; Valera is the former director of the Student Federation of University Centers and a regional director of MAS in Carabobo.
50. Interview with Pedro Pablo Aguilar, 15 December 1978.
51. Interview with Abelardo Vásquez, 18 December 1978. Vásquez is an economist, a professor in the School of Economy at the central university (UCV), and a member of the JRC National Directory.
52. *El Universal,* 1 July 1978.
53. Interview, 12 December 1978. He asked to remain anonymous.
54. Interview with Luis Alberto Machado, 15 December 1978. He was in charge of the office of the president under the Caldera administration. A well-known author, he traveled to many countries before returning to Venezuela and becoming active in the campaign in May 1978. During the campaign Machado was responsible for providing information to Caldera and Herrera for use in the media.
55. *El Nacional,* 14 November 1978.
56. Consejo Supremo Electoral, *Elecciones 1978,* Boletín Información no. 13.
57. Based on December 1978 interviews with a variety of people: Adecos, Copeyanos, Mepistas, Masistas, and neutral political observers.
58. See Conciencia 21, "Analisis de Medios de Comunicación Social," 4 September-1 October 1978.
59. Interview with Jorge Véliz P., 12 December 1978. Véliz is the assistant deputy secretary-general of AD.
60. Interview with Eduardo Fernández, 26 March 1974.
61. Daniel H. Levine, *Conflict and Political Change in Venezuela,* p. 256.

62. Interview with President Rafael Caldera, 13 July 1971.

63. "Venezuelan Democracy and the Future," in John D. Martz and David J. Myers, ed., *Venezuela: The Democratic Experience.*

Bibliography

I. Magazines and Periodicals

Acción Nacional, Caracas, 1942–44
Alliance for Progress Weekly Newsletter, Washington, D.C., 1971–73.
Auténtico, Caracas, 1976–78
Bohemia, Caracas, 1970–78
El Carabobeño, Valencia, 1973–76
Christian Democratic Review, New York, 1948–58
Christian Science Monitor, Boston, 1974–78
COPEI, Caracas, 1946–64
COPEI de Lara, Lara, 1946–47
COPEI de Táchira, Táchira, 1946–47
Crítica, Maracaibo, 1973–76
Current History, Philadelphia, 1974
Daily Journal, Caracas, 1970–78
Elite, Caracas, 1970–78
La Esfera, Caracas, 1936–41, 1958–73
Frente (FTC), Caracas, 1971–78
El Globo, Caracas, 1973–76
El Gráfico (COPEI), Caracas, 1947–50
Hemispherica, New York, 1972–78
El Heraldo, Caracas, 1935–48, 1953–58
International Herald Tribune, Paris, 1978
Keesing's Contemporary Archives, London, 1978
Latin America, Washington, D.C., 1972–76
Latin American Digest, Tempe, 1970–78
Latin America Economic Report, London, 1970–78
Latin America Political Report, London, 1970–78
Latin American Report, New York, 1973–78
Latin America Venezuela Special Report, a supplement to LAER, London, 1978
Momento, Caracas, 1966–78
El Mundo, Caracas, 1970–78
El Nacional, Caracas, 1943–78
New York Times, New York, 1970–78
Nueva Política, Caracas, 1972–78
OAS Weekly Newsletter, Washington, D.C., 1974–76
El País (pro-AD), Caracas, 1944–48
Panorama, Maracaibo, 1973–78
Panorama Democrática Cristiana, Caracas, 1969
El Popular (Communist party newspaper), Caracas, 1936–47
PRELA, Madrid, 1976–78
Pueblo Unido (COPEI), Caracas, 1974–78
Punto (MAS), Caracas, 1970–78
La Religión, Caracas, 1968–78
Resumen, Caracas, 1974–78

Reventon, Caracas, 1974–78
Semana, Caracas, 1970–78
Seminario COPEI, Caracas, 1969–71
SIC (Seminario Interdiocesano Caracas), Caracas, 1939–78
Summa, Caracas, 1971–78
TIELA (COPEI), Rome, 1953–57
Times of the Americas, Washington, D.C., 1970–78
Ultimas Noticias, Caracas, 1970–78
UNE, Caracas, 1936–42
El Universal, Caracas, 1936–78
La Verdad, Caracas, 1970–78
The Vision Letter, New York, 1973
ZETA, Caracas, 1977–78

II. Books, Articles, Documents, and Pamphlets

Aguirre Elorriaga, S.J., Manuel. *Esquema de la Doctrina Social Católica (Temas y custionarios para los Círculos de Estudios)*. Caracas: "Ediciones Sic," 1940.
Alexander, Robert J. *Latin American Political Parties*. New York: Praeger, 1973.
———. *The Communist Party of Venezuela*. Stanford: Hoover Institution Press, 1969.
———. "Venezuela's 'New Force' Broken." *Hemispherica*, December 1972.
Asamblea Nacional del Frente de Trabajadores Copeyanos, FTC. "Tesis de Formación Sindical." Caracas, 28–30 October 1966.
Asamblea Nacional del Frente de Trabajadores Copeyanos, 4a, "Tesis Política." Caracas, 3 October 1966.
Así se Fraguó la insurrección: documentos clandestinos, 1956–1958. Caracas: Ediciones de la Revista Cruz del Sur, 1958.
Baloyra, Enrique. "Regime Maintenance and Public Opinion in Venezuela." Paper delivered to the Latin American Studies Association annual meeting, San Francisco, November 1974.
Barrios, Gonzalo. *Bloque de Abril*. Caracas: Litografía y Tipografía Vargas, 1946.
Betancourt, Romulo. *Venezuela: Política y Petróleo*. México: Fondo de Cultura Económica, 1956.
Blank, David Eugene. *Politics in Venezuela*. Boston: Little, Brown, 1973.
Boersner, Demetrio. "Venezuela y el Colonialismo." *Summa*, March 1971.
Bonilla, Frank. *The Failure of Elites*, Volume 2 of *The Politics of Change in Venezuela*. Cambridge: MIT Press, 1970.
Bunimov Parra, Boris. *Introducción a la Sociología Electoral Venezolana*. Caracas: Editorial Arte, 1968.
Burggraaff, Winfield J. *The Venezuelan Armed Forces in Politics, 1935–1959*. Columbia: University of Missouri Press, 1972.
Caldera, Rafael. *El Bloque Latinoamericano*. Caracas: Oficina Central de Información, 1970.
———. *Ganar la Patria una Responsabilidad Mancomunada*, Discurso de clausura del acto de instalación de COPEI. Caracas: Versión taquigráfica de Juan V. Rodríguez, Tipografía La Nación, 13 January 1946.
———. *Habla El Presidente*. Caracas: Ediciones de la Presidencia de la República, 13 November 1969.
———. *Ideario—La Democracia Cristiana en América Latina*. Barcelona: Ediciones Ariel, 1970.

————. *Justicia Social Internacional y Nacionalismo Latinoamericano.* España: Seminarios y Ediciones, S.A., 1973.

————. *La Solidaridad Pluralista de América Latina.* Caracas: Oficina Central de Información/OCI, 1973.

————. "Venezuela on Election Eve—The Land of Bolívar the Liberator Struggles to Liberate Herself." *Commonweal,* vol. 44, 4 October 1946.

Calvani, Arístides. "Una Paz Compartida y Solidaria." Caracas: Oficina Central de Información, September 1970.

Cárdenas, Rodolfo José. *El Combate Político Solo Para Líderes Nuevos.* Caracas: Editorial Arte, 1965.

Cardozo, Hilarión, National Youth Secretary of COPEI. "Letter to President John F. Kennedy." For Second National Plenum of JRC, January 1961.

Carpio Castillo, Rubén. *El Golfo de Venezuela—Mar del Territorial y Plataforma Continental.* Caracas: Ediciones del Congreso de la República, 1971.

"Carta Fundamental del Magisterio Social Cristiano de Venezuela." Caracas, 4 October 1958.

Catala, José Augustín, ed. *Documentos para la Historia de la Resistencia,* vol. 1, 1948–52, "Pérez Jiménez y su Régimen de Terror." Caracas, 1969.

Chen, Chi-Yi, and Brücker, Enrique. *Economía Social del Trabajo—Caso de Venezuela.* Caracas: Librería Editorial Salesiana, 1969.

Clarificación del Comité Nacional de COPEI. Caracas: Edit. Mercurio, September 1953.

CODESA. *Estatutos de la Confederación de Sindicatos Autónomos de Venezuela.* Mimeo, n.d.

Comisión Organizadora de la 5a Asamblea Nacional del FTC. "5a Asamblea Nacional del Frente de Trabajadores Copeyanos." Caracas, 21-24 January 1971.

Comité Nacional de COPEI. "Reglamento Orgánico de la Juventud Revolucionaria Copeyana," Caracas: Tipografía Garrido, 1948.

El Comité Juvenil de COPEI del Táchira. "El Comité Juvenil de COPEI protesta públicamente contra las calumniosas aseveraciones de 'Fronteras,' diario marxista y anticlerical del Dr. Ruiz Pineda." 1947.

El Comité Regional de COPEI. *Manifiesto del Comité Regional de COPEI al Pueblo del Táchira.* San Cristóbal, 1 November 1946.

"Comunicación del Comité Nacional de COPEI a la Junta Militar de Gobierno." Caracas, 17 March 1949.

"Comunicado de COPEI Ante de la Situación Actual." 3 December 1948.

Conciencia 21 "Analisis de Medios de Comunicación Social," 4 September– 1 October 1978.

Consejo Supremo Electoral. *Elecciones 1978,* Boletín Información no. 13.

————. *Memoria y Cuenta 1974.*

Consignas aprobadas por el Primer Congreso Nacional Uneista. Caracas: Tipografía La Nación, 20 January 1939.

COPEI Ante las Elecciones: La 6a Convención de COPEI a la Nación Venezolana. Caracas: Tipografía Santander, 14 September 1952.

"COPEI Firme en su Puesto de Lucha." Manifiesto del Comité Nacional al Pueblo Venezolano—Analisis del Proceso Electoral—El cómputo final de las votaciones reafirma el arraigo popular de COPEI. Caracas, 1 November 1946.

COPEI Frente al Estatuto Electoral y la Actual Situación Política. Caracas: Avila Gráfica, S.A., 1951.

COPEI, Secretaría de Propaganda. "Qué Es El COPEI?" Caracas, 1946.

Curiel, José. "Interconexión Fluvial en el Hinterland Sudamericano." *Pueblo Unido,* Cuaderno de Lectura Quincenal, 1974.

"Declaración de Principios y Programa Mínimo de Gobierno" suscritos por el Sr. Rómulo Betancourt, el Contralmirante Wolfgang Larrazábal y el Dr. Rafael Caldera, candidatos a la Presidencia de la República, en la Sede del Consejo Supremo Electoral, 6 December 1958.

"Declaración de Sochagota." *Documentos*, July–September 1969.

"Discurso Inaugural del Presidente Caldera." *Documentos*, January–March 1969.

Discurso Pronunciado Por El Dr. Rafael Caldera, Secretario Nacional General, en La Casa Central de COPEI, Con Motivo del Acto de Instalación de la 8a Convención Regional del Partido en el Distrito Federal. N.d. [but probably April 1953].

"Documento de Sectores 'Astronautas' y 'Avanzados' del COPEI." *Documentos*, no. 29, April–June 1967.

Documentos, Revista de Información Política, Instituto de Estudios Políticos, Facultad de Derecho, Universidad Central de Venezuela, Caracas.

Estados Unidos de Venezuela, Servicio Secreto de Investigación. *La Verdad de las Actividades Comunistas en Venezuela; Relación y Parte de la Numerosa Documentación que Posee el Servicio Secreto de Investigación Acerca de la Realidad de la Propaganda Comunista dentro del País*. Caracas, 1936.

Estados Unidos de Venezuela. *Diario de Debates* de la Comisión Permanente de la Asamblea Nacional Constituyente.

"Estructuras Económicas y Sociales Según la Democracia Cristiana." (Definición aprobada por la 3a Conferencia Mundial Democrática Cristiana), Santiago de Chile, 27-30 July 1961, Cortesía de la Fracción Parlamentaria del Partido Socialcristiano COPEI.

"Exposición que sobre la situación post-electoral presentan Pedro Paúl Bello y Pedro Raúl Villasmil Soules a la consideración del Comité Nacional y del Directorio Nacional de COPEI." Revista *Elite*. Caracas, 22 March 1974.

Fernández, Lorenzo. *MIRANDO HACIA EL FUTURO: Un programa de gobierno nacionalista para la conquista del futuro ya*. Caracas, 1973.

Ford, William. *Wuytack: El Cura que Faltó a la Ley*. Caracas: Gráfica Moderna, 1970.

La Formación de Dirigentes Sindicales Cristianos de Venezuela. Mimeo, n.d.

Franco, William. "Poder Social." Caracas, March 1974.

Frente de Trabajadores Copeyanos, Secretaría Nacional de Organización. "2a Campaña Sindical Financiera 1971." 10 June 1971.

FUNDECA. *Fundación para el Desarrollo Rural y la Educación Campesina*—Educación para el Desarrollo-Desarrollo por la Educación—. Caracas: Editorial Arte, n.d.

Gaceta Oficial de la República de Venezuela. Official publication of the Venezuelan government.

Gaceta Oficial del Estado Mérida. "Ley de Presupuesto De Ingresos Y Gastos Públicos Del Estado—Año Fiscal 1971." Año LXXI, Mérida. Edición Extraordinaria, 1 January 1971.

Gaceta Oficial del Estado Táchira. "Ley de Presupuesto para el Ejercicio Fiscal 1971." Año LXX, San Cristóbal, Número Extraordinario, 1 January 1971.

Gall, Norman. "Los Indocumentados Colombianos." American Universities Field Staff *Reports*, 1972.

González, Dagoberto, and Herrera Campins, Luis. "El 'Informe Confidencial.'" Publicaciones de la Fracción Parlamentaria de COPEI, no. 11. Caracas, 1963.

González, Dagoberto, and Rodríguez, José S. "La Situación Sindical," Colección Diálogo, Publicaciones del Programa Extraordinario. Caracas: Editorial Arte, 1968.
González, Godofredo. "Contra Los Desequilibrios Económicos." Fracción Parlamentaria de COPEI, Caracas, Segunda Etapa, no. 25, 1964.
Grayson, George W. "Venezuela's Presidential Politics." Current History, January 1974.
Habla El Presidente: Diálogo Semanal con el Pueblo Venezolano, IV, 16 March 1972–8 March 1973. Caracas: Ediciones de la Presidencia de la República, 1973.
Herman, Donald L., ed. The Communist Tide in Latin America: A Selected Treatment. Austin: University of Texas, 1973.
Herrera Campins, Luis. Un Año de Esfuerzos para el Cambio. Caracas: T. G. Ilustraciones, S.A., 1970.
————. "Las Campañas Doblan por la 'Ancha Base.'" Publicaciones de la Fracción Parlamentaria Partido Socialcristiano COPEI, no. 37 (Tercera Etapa). Caracas, 1966.
————. Frente a 1958: Material de Discusión política electoral Venezolana. Caracas-Roma, Ediciones Hercamdi, 1957.
————. "La Victoria de Eduardo Frei." Publicaciones de la Fracción Parlamentaria de COPEI, no. 24 (Segunda Etapa). Caracas, 1964.
Huntington, Samuel P. Political Order in Changing Societies. New Haven: Yale University Press, 1968.
Illarramendy, Ramón Adolfo. "Hacia la Democracia de Participación," Nueva Política, January–March 1972.
Informe del Secretariado Regional de COPEI en el Distrito Federal ante la 8a Convención Regional del Partido. Caracas, 25 April 1953.
"Informe Que el Comité Regional de COPEI de Táchira Presenta a la consideración de la 8a Convención Regional del Partido." San Cristóbal, 26 November 1949.
Institute for the Comparative Study of Political Systems, The Venezuelan Elections of December 1, 1963, Part III, Final Provisional Election Returns, Presidential and Legislative, Broken Down by Region and State. Washington, D.C., 1964.
Instituto Nacional de Estudios Sociales. La Organización Sindical. Mimeo, n.d.
Inter-American Development Bank. Economic and Social Progress in Latin America—Annual Report 1974. Washington, D.C., 1975.
Johnson, John J. The Military and Society in Latin America. Stanford: Stanford University Press, 1964.
Johnson, Kenneth F., and Fuentes, María Mercedes. Política de Poder y Participación Política en América Latina. Caracas: Ediciones IDELA, 1973.
JRC. "Una Mística para el Cambio." Caracas, 1970.
Juventud Revolucionaria Copeyana. "Comunicado de la Fracción Universitaria de COPEI al Estudiantado." 1949.
Lazcano, José A. "Reflexiones Post-Electorales: País Político y País Electoral." SIC, January 1974.
Levine, Daniel H. Conflict and Political Change in Venezuela. Princeton: Princeton University Press, 1973.
Lieuwen, Edwin. Venezuela. London: Oxford University Press, 1969.
Lott, Leo B. "The 1952 Venezuelan Elections: A Lesson for 1957." Western Political Quarterly, 10 September 1957.
————. Venezuela and Paraguay: Political Modernity and Tradition in Conflict. New York: Holt, Rinehart and Winston, 1972.
Lourdes Acedo de Sucre, María, and Nones Mendoza, Carmen Margarita.

La Generación Venezolana de 1928: Estudio de una Elite Política.
Caracas: Ediciones Ariel, 1967.
Machado de Acedo, Clemy. *La Política en Venezuela.* Caracas: Centro Gumilla, 1969.
Machado, Luis Alberto. "COPEI contra la Reforma Tributaria." Publicación de la Socialcristiano COPEI no. 42, (Cuarto Etapa). Caracas, 1967.
"Manifiesto de las Mujeres Venezolanas del Sector Feminino Independiente." Edit. "Crisol" C.A., 1946.
Martz, John D. *Acción Democrática: Evolution of a Modern Political Party in Venezuela.* Princeton: Princeton University Press, 1966.
————. "Policy-Making and the Quest for Consensus: Nationalizing Venezuelan Petroleum." *Journal of Interamerican Studies and World Affairs,* November 1977.
————, and Baloyra, Enrique A. *Electoral Mobilization and Public Opinion: The Venezuelan Campaign of 1973.* Chapel Hill: University of North Carolina Press, 1976.
————, and Myers, David J. *Venezuela: The Democratic Experience.* New York: Praeger, 1977.
Mayobre, José Antonio. *Las Inversiones Extranjeras en Venezuela.* Caracas: Monte Avila Editores, C.A., 1970.
Metas de Venezuela, Primer Año de Gobierno I, II; Segundo Año de Gobierno II, III, IV; Tercer Año de Gobierno V.
Mobil Oil Company of Venezuela. *Special Report to Management.* Caracas, 1971.
Morgenthau, Hans J. *Politics among Nations: The Struggle for Power and Peace.* 5th ed. New York: Alfred A. Knopf, 1973.
"Movimiento de Profesionales y Técnicos Copeyanos." *Seminario COPEI,* 3-10 February 1970.
Myers, David J. "Frontier Settlement Policy in Brazil: International Provocation or National Development." Paper presented to the International Studies Association annual meeting, Toronto, 25 February 1976.
————. *Democratic Campaigning in Venezuela: Caldera's Victory.* Caracas: Fundación La Salle de Ciencias Naturales; Instituto Caribe de Antropología y Sociología, 1973.
Ocampo V., Tarsicio. *Venezuela 'Astronautas' de COPEI 1965-67, Documentos y Reacciones de Prensa.* Cuernavaca, México: CIDOC, (Centro Intercultural de Documentación) Dossier no. 17, 1968.
Oficina Central de Información/OCI. "Ante el Cuerpo Diplomático luego de tomar posesión del cargo." Caracas, 12 March 1969. *Metas de Venezuela: Selección de Discursos del Presidente de la República,* Dr. Rafael Caldera, Primer Año de Gobierno, 11 March 1970.
————. *Cuenta Ante El País*—Mensaje del Presidente de la República y Exposiciones de los Ministros del Gabinete ante El Congreso Nacional en El Segundo Año de Gobierno, 1971; El Cuarto Año de Gobierno, 1973.
————. "En el Congreso de los Estados Unidos de América." *Metas de Venezuela: Selección de Discursos del Presidente de la República,* Dr. Rafael Caldera, Segundo Año de Gobierno, 11 March 1971.
————. "En la Instalación de la Federación Latinoamericana y del Caribe de Asociaciones de Exportadores." *Metas de Venezuela: Selección de Discursos del Presidente de la República,* Dr. Rafael Caldera, Segundo Año de Gobierno, 11 March 1971.
————. *Venezuela en 1969.* Primer Mensaje del Presidente de la República, Dr. Rafael Caldera al Congreso Nacional, 11 March 1970.
————. *Venezuela en 1971,* 9 March 1972.

————. "Pacto suscrito por los Partidos Acción Democrática, Partido Social Cristiano COPEI y Unión Republicana Democrática." 31 October 1958.

PALABRAS—Pronunciadas por el Dr. Rafael Caldera en el Mítin de antier de la Plaza Bolívar por el Partido Unión Federal Republicana. Mérida, 2 October 1946.

Partido Socialcristiano COPEI—"25 Años—La Patria in Marcha." Caracas, 1971.

————. "Mi Compromiso con Venezuela." *Programa de Gobierno para el Periodo 1979–1983.*

————. "Reglamento Interno de las Convenciones Nacionales." Caracas, 1971.

————. Secretaría Nacional de Propaganda, "Programa del Movimiento Político COPEI." 3a edición. Caracas, 1958.

————. Sub-Secretaría General Nacional-organización electoral, Secretaría Nacional de Organización, Secretaría Nacional de Formación Política. *Manual del Activista.* Caracas, n.d. (but before 1968 election).

Peattie, Lisa Redfield. *The View from the Barrio.* Ann Arbor: University of Michigan Press, 1968.

Peña, Alfredo. *Conversaciones con Luis Herrera Campins.* Caracas: Editorial Ateneo, 1978.

Penniman, Howard R. (ed.) *Venezuela at the Polls.* Washington, D.C.: American Enterprise Institute for Public Policy Research, forthcoming.

Pérez Olivares, Enrique. *Introducción a la Democracia Cristiana.* Caracas: Partido Socialcristiano COPEI, Secretaría de Formación Política, Departamento de Formación, 1965.

Por los Legítimos Ideales del Estudiante Venezolano. Caracas: Publicaciones "UNE," 1937.

Por Qué COPEI no asiste a la Constituyente. Caracas: Poligráfica Nacional, 9 January 1953.

Powell, John Duncan. *Political Mobilization of the Venezuelan Peasant.* Cambridge: Harvard University Press, 1971.

Presidencia de la República. *Documentos que Hicieron Historia.* Vol. 2, De La Revolución Azul a Nuestros Días (1868–1961), "Manifiesto de COPEI," 1946. Caracas: Ediciones Conmemorativas del Seisquicentenario de la Independencia, 1962.

————. *Documentos que Hicieron Historia.* Siglo y Medio de Vida Republicana, 1810–1961, II. "Pastoral del Arzobispo Arias Blanco," 1 May 1957.

Prieto Figueroa, Luis Beltrán. ¡*Joven, Empinate!* Caracas, 1968.

————. *La Política y los Hombres.* Caracas, 1968.

Programa de Gobierno de Rafael Caldera, Presidente de Venezuela, 1969–1974. Caracas, 1971.

Publicación de la Secretaría Nacional de Organismos Profesionales del Partido Socialcristiano COPEI. "I Congreso Nacional de Profesionales y Técnicos de COPEI e Independientes Socialcristianos—Acta Final." Caracas, 1963.

Publicaciones de Acción Democrática. *Democracia y Extremismo: 2 Entrevistas con Carlos Andrés Pérez.* Caracas, 1970.

Ray, Talton F. *The Politics of the Barrios of Venezuela.* Berkeley and Los Angeles: University of California Press, 1969.

"Reglamiento Provisional del Comité Femenino Copeyano." (Seccional Táchira) 12 January 1949.

República de Venezuela, Consejo Supremo Electoral. *Datos Estadísticos de las Votaciones de 1968.* Caracas, 1970.

Rivera Oviedo, José Elías. *Los Social Cristianos en Venezuela*. Caracas: Impresos "*Hermar*," 1970.

Rodríguez Iturbe, José. *Iglesia y Estado en Venezuela (1824–1964)*. Caracas: Universidad Central de Venezuela, 1968.

Romero Carranza, Ambrosio. *Qué es la Democracia Cristiana*. Buenos Aires: Ediciones del Atlántico, 1959.

Rout, Leslie B., Jr. *Which Way Out? An Analysis of the Venezuela-Guyana Boundary Dispute*. East Lansing: Latin American Studies Center, Michigan State University, 1971.

Sánchez F., Delfín. "Un Programa para la Juventud." *Macarao*, 4 April 1970.

Silva Michelena, José A. *The Illusion of Democracy in Dependent Nations*: vol. 3 of *The Politics of Change in Venezuela*. Cambridge: M.I.T. Press, 1971.

Silva T., Ramón H. *Introducción al Estudio del Sindicalismo Venezolano*. Estudio Sociográfico de Venezuela realizado por El Centro de Investigación y Acción Social (CIAS). Caracas: Centro Gumilla, 1968.

Taylor, Philip B., Jr. *The Venezuelan Coup d'Etat of 1958: The Fall of Marcos Pérez Jiménez*. Washington, D.C.: Institute for the Comparative Study of Political Systems, 1968.

Tugwell, Franklin. "The Christian Democrats of Venezuela." *Journal of Inter-American Studies*, vol. 7, no. 2, 1965.

————. "Petroleum Policy." Paper delivered to Latin American Studies Association annual meeting, San Francisco, November 1974.

————. *The Politics of Oil in Venezuela*. Stanford: Stanford University Press, 1975.

Veliz, Claudio, ed. *The Politics of Conformity in Latin America*. London: Oxford University Press, 1967.

Vivas Terán, Abdón. "El Grito Juvenil Copeyano." *Summa*, May 1971.

————. "La Alternativa Ideológica." *Summa*, May 1971.

Williams, Edward J. *Latin American Christian Democratic Parties*. Knoxville: University of Tennessee Press, 1967.

Wolf, Eric R., and Hansen, Edward C. *The Human Condition in Latin America*. London: Oxford University Press, 1972.

Index

Acción Democrática. *See* AD
Acción Electoral, 14, 15, 16, 17, 23
Acción Nacional, 14, 15, 16, 17, 22, 23
Acevedo Amaya, Valmore, 19, 46, 59, 64, 77, 89, 140
Acosta, Armando, 127
Acosta Hermoso, Eduardo, 121
AD (Acción Democrática), 4, 6, 15–17, 23, 55, 66, 68, 78, 83, 103, 106, 108, 112, 119, 121, 122, 127, 133, 135, 137, 138, 165, 168, 179, 182, 189, 198, 199, 202, 214, 220, 221; and students, 8, 44–45, 54, 58, 130; and early years of COPEI, 25–31; relationship with COPEI, 31–36, 48, 51–52, 80, 81, 82, 83, 90, 112, 131, 134, 136, 203, 212, 223, 228, 232, 233; during dictatorship 1948–52, 36–38; 1952 election, 39–41; opposition to dictatorship 1953–58, 44–47, 48–50; exiled leadership of, 47–50, 194; 1958 election, 52–53; and labor, 54, 58, 77, 78, 82, 113; militants in, 55; tension with COPEI, 55–56; *guanábana*, 56–59; COPEI coalition, 56, 57, 79, 176; Leoni administration, 61–64; schism within, 64, 67, 79; 1968 election, 64–67, 111; split with MEP, 67, 74, 79, 83, 113, 222; and peasants, 75–76; *trienio*, 77; *arsista* faction, 79, 83; youth groups, 90; *coincidencia*, 113–17, 140, 145, 163–64, 203; big business, 123–24; petroleum policy, 141, 149, 150, 154, 157, 158; break with URD, 172; 1973 election, 215–19; 1978 election, 223–31
Adecos (members of AD), 25, 29, 37, 108, 158, 218, 219, 231; and 1948 coup d'état, 34, 35; and Copeyanos, 35–36, 46–47, 48, 52, 56, 62, 64, 68, 79–80, 111–12, 126–29, 134–36, 144, 174, 224, 230; and students, 44, 108; resistance to dictatorship, 45, 47; and dispute of CTV, 81–83; in *coincidencia*, 112–16, 140; during *El Cambio*, 162–67, 170, 199, 202

Aggrupación Cívica Boliviarana, 14, 15
Aggrupaciones Pro-Candidatura Presidencial, 17
Aggrupación Revolucionaria de la Izquierda. *See* ARDI
Agrarian Reform Law, 73, 204
Agricultural and Livestock Bank. *See* BAP
Agriculture, 3, 117, 205; products of, 4, 5, 207; reform of, 15, 29, 51, 57, 76; Reform Law, 73, 204; development, 136; reform program, 162, 166, 167, 181, 202, 203, 212, 214. *See also* PRIDA
Aguilar, Andrés, 54
Aguilar, Eduardo, 97, 102
Aguilar, Pedro Pablo, 40, 44, 90, 95–108 passim, 116, 149, 150, 215, 216, 227
Aguirre, Padre Manuel Elorriaga, 18, 19, 25, 44, 60, 77, 78, 86, 120; ideas of, 20, 21, 22
Ahrensburg, Germán, 92
Alexander, Robert J., 6, 62, 67
Alfonzo, Rafael Jacobo, 89
Alfonzo Ravard, Francisco, 10
Algeria, 144, 152, 172
Allende, Salvador, 97, 113, 139, 175; government, 177, 184; assassination of, 216
Alliance for Progress, 167
Alvarez Paz, Oswaldo, 90, 94, 95, 96, 97, 100, 102, 227
Alvarez Paz, Pumar, 90, 94, 97
Amazonas, 53
American Chamber of Commerce of Venezuela, 159
Ancha Base (Wide Base), 63
ANCOM (Andean Common Market), 177, 179, 181, 182, 183, 184, 186, 200, 205, 206, 219
Andean Pact, 117, 180, 181, 219
Andean states, 4, 14, 38, 41, 61, 73, 117, 120, 218
Andes, 27, 28, 53, 167
Anticommunism, 21, 22, 24, 89, 90, 91, 92, 94, 96, 98, 188, 189, 190, 211, 214, 218
Anti-imperialism, 6, 14. *See also* Imperialism; Nationalism
Anti-proyecto de Ley Orgánica de Educación Nacional, 9